COMPANY LAW
FUNDAMENTAL PRINC⌐

We work with leading authors to develop the strongest
educational materials in Law, bringing cutting-edge thinking
and best learning practice to a global market.

Under a range of well-known imprints, including Longman,
we craft high quality print and electronic publications
which help readers to understand and apply their content,
whether studying or at work.

To find out more about the complete range of our
publishing please visit us on the World Wide Web at:
www.pearsoneduc.com

COMPANY LAW
FUNDAMENTAL PRINCIPLES

Third Edition

===

Stephen Griffin LLB, M.PHIL

Reader in Law,
University of Wolverhampton

Chapter 13 on Insider Dealing
contributed by Michael Hirst LLB LLM,
Professor of Law,
De Montfort University

PEARSON

Longman

Harlow, England • London • New York • Boston • San Francisco • Toronto
Sydney • Tokyo • Singapore • Hong Kong • Seoul • Taipei • New Delhi
Cape Town • Madrid • Mexico City • Amsterdam • Munich • Paris • Milan

Pearson Education Limited
Edinburgh Gate
Harlow
Essex CM20 2JE
England

and Associated Companies throughout the world

Visit us on the World Wide Web at
http://www.pearsoneduc.com

———————————

First published in Great Britain in 1994
Second edition published 1996
Third edition published 2000

© Pearson Professional Limited 1994, 1996
© Pearson Education Limited 2000

ISBN 0 273 64221 9

British Library Cataloguing in Publication Data
A CIP catalogue record for this book can be obtained
from the British Library.

10 9 8 7 6 5 4
07 06 05 04 03

Typeset by 7 in 10/12pt Sabon
Printed in Great Britain by Henry Ling Limited, at the Dorset Press, Dorchester, DT1 1HD

CONTENTS

PREFACE

UK company law, which is predominantly a creature of statute, is presently governed by the Companies Act 1985, albeit that a number of the Act's provisions have been amended or added to by the Companies Act 1989. In addition to domestic legislation, UK company law has also been affected by European Community (E.C.) legislation. Yet, although company law is principally regulated by statute, it would be very misleading to suppose that it is devoid of common law and equitable influences. It is also to be noted that recent times have witnessed a substantial expansion in the number of Law Commission and DTI reports which aim to promote ideas and suggestions for the reform of company law. Indeed, during the process of publishing this work, three such reports were released. Unfortunately, it has been impossible to include the recommendations of the said reports within the main text; however, they are included in an appendix, at the end of the book.

As with the first two editions of this work, the third edition is designed to encourage and assist a student's understanding and perception of the fundamental principles of company law, however as company law represents a vast subject area, it has not been possible to include all corporate law topics within the book. Instead, I have concentrated on those areas of corporate law which represent the common constituents of the UK undergraduate/postgraduate company law courses.

I have made every effort to write this book in a style which is clear and unambiguous. I have also sought to maintain a substantive degree of academic analysis in its presentation. In the hope that students may have sufficient time to explore some of the issues developed in the individual chapters of this book, I have expanded the suggested reading lists which were found in the previous editions of the work. Company law is at times a controversial subject and it is therefore not surprising to discover that diverse opinions are abundant in the representation of its academic debate.

While at times technical, I firmly believe that company law is a subject which will interest the majority of law students, a subject which begs analysis, argument and debate. I hope that this book aptly conveys such qualities and that it will be of benefit to students in their study of company law.

I have endeavored to state the law as of the 1 January 2000.

Stephen Griffin.

ACKNOWLEDGEMENTS

I would, as ever, like to express my sincere thanks to my wife Donna for her understanding nature and patience. Donna's assistance in the completion of the case and statute tables was also invaluable. Michael Hirst is to be thanked for revising Chapter 13, as are my publishers for their general help and assistance; special thanks go to Pat Bond and Emily Pillars. I would also like to thank the many company law students and academics who have written to me to commend the previous two editions of this work – the encouragement has been most welcomed.

We are grateful to The Butterworths Division of Reed Elsevier (UK) Ltd for permission to reproduce and extract from *12–13 Butterworth Company Law Cases – BCLC 739*.

DEDICATION

This work is dedicated to my Mum and Dad, Peggy and Barrie Griffin who, in the year of the publication of this edition, celebrate their ruby wedding anniversary. Well done, Mum and Dad!

TABLE OF CASES

TABLE OF STATUTES AND STATUTORY MATERIALS

ABBREVIATIONS

SPECIALIST COMPANY LAW REPORTS

BCC	British Company Cases (published by CCH).
BCLC	Butterworth's Company Law Cases
PCC	Palmer's Company Cases

LEGISLATION

CA 1948	Companies Act 1948
CA 1980	Companies Act 1980
CA 1985	Companies Act 1985
CA 1989	Companies Act 1989
CDDA 1986	Company Directors Disqualification Act 1996
CJA 1987	Criminal Justice Act 1987
CJA 1993	Criminal Justice Act 1993
FSA 1986	Financial Services Act 1986
IA 1986	Insolvency Act 1986
IDA 1985	Companies Securities (Insider Dealing) Act 1985
s	Section
SI	Statutory Instrument
Reg	Regulation

LAW JOURNALS

CLR	Criminal Law Review
CLJ	Cambridge Law Journal
Co Law	The Company Lawyer
JBL	Journal of Business Law
LMCLQ	Lloyds Maritime & Commercial Law Quarterely
LQR	Law Quarterely Review
LS	Legal Studies
MLR	Modern Law Review
NILQ	Northern Ireland Legal Quarterely
NLJ	New Law Journal
OJLS	Oxford Journal of Legal Studies
SLPQ	Scottish Law & Practice Quarterly

1

THE LEGAL CHARACTERISTICS
OF A REGISTERED COMPANY

INTRODUCTION

This chapter seeks to explain the fundamental legal characteristics of a company which is registered with a limited liability status. The Chapter also examines the historical roots of the modern registered company.

THE LEGAL CONSEQUENCES OF INCORPORATION

A company may be perceived as an artificial entity in the sense that it is but a vehicle, occupied and controlled by its management and membership for the purpose of pursuing business goals. The human constituents of the company will ultimately determine the route which is to be taken by the corporate enterprise. Nevertheless, in law the artificial nature of a company is ignored to the extent that a company registered in accordance with the provisions of the companies legislation (currently the Companies Act 1985) is, as from the date of its incorporation, a body corporate (s 13(3), CA 1985). As such, the registered company is a separate legal entity, it possesses rights and is subject to duties in much the same way as a natural person. For example, a company may sue and be sued in its own name and will be liable to pay its own form of tax, i.e. corporation tax.

In addition to a registered company's separate legal identity, the vast majority of registered companies are incorporated with limited liability. (Note that a company may be registered as an unlimited company, see Chapter 4.) A company may be limited by shares or by guarantee. (Unless otherwise stated, this book will concentrate on the former; for a discussion of companies limited by guarantee, see Chapter 4.) Limited liability means that a member of a company ceases to incur liability to contribute to the debts of the company once the shares held by that member have been fully paid for, i.e. the nominal value of the share has been paid to the company (price of share when first issued). A registered company with a limited-liability status is therefore responsible for its own actions and will be predominately liable for its own debts, i.e. where its debts exceed its membership's limited liability.

The immediate result of a company's incorporation is the creation of two independent bodies: the company and its membership. The membership of a limited company take shares in the company. The shares held represent a member's interest in the company. The nature and extent of this interest will determine the member's right to participate in dividend payments as well as a member's right to participate in determining the managerial and decision-making policy of the company (discussed further in Chapter 19). Subject to any prohibition contained in a company's constitution, a shareholder may freely sell or dispose of his shareholding interest. In respect of the company's existence, it is quite irrelevant that the identity of its shareholders may change. A company's legal existence is not dependent upon the survival of individual shareholders. Accordingly, a company is said to have perpetual succession.

The legal rights and duties of shareholders, in respect of their relationship with the company and fellow shareholders, are determined by the company's constitution (see Chapters 7 and 10). Despite the fact that a person may have exclusively owned the property and assets of a business prior to its incorporation as a registered company, the property vested in the company will belong to the company, a shareholder has no right of ownership in respect of the company's property or assets. For example, in *Macaura v Northern Assurance Co* [1925] AC 619 a timber merchant converted his business into an incorporated company; the timber merchant held the majority shareholding. The property of the newly incorporated company was destroyed by fire as a result of which the merchant sought to recoup his loss by making a claim against his insurance company. Although the property was insured, the insurance policy was held in the merchant's name. As the merchant no longer owned the property to which the claim related, the property having been transferred to the company, the insurance company was held not to be liable to meet the claim. On the incorporation of the business, the insurance policy should have been transferred into the name of the new owner of the property, i.e. the company (see also *Re Lewis Wills Trust* [1985] 1 WLR 102).

Although one person may in effect control and execute the affairs of a company by occupying several positions in the company, for example, an individual may be the majority shareholder, the company's managing director and at the same time the company's sole employee, such a person is not to be regarded as the company, the company is a separate legal entity; see e.g. *Lee v Lee's Air Farming* [1961] AC 12 and *Barakot v Epiette Ltd* [1998] 1 BCLC 283. Whilst a company holds its property and assets for the ultimate benefit of the associated rights of its membership, a member of a company may still be convicted of theft from the company, notwithstanding that the member in question holds all or substantially all the shares in the company; see e.g. *A–G's Ref (No 2 of 1982)* [1984] 2 WLR 447 and *DPP v Gomez* [1993] AC 442.

The principal advantage of incorporating a business is undoubtedly the limited liability of a company's membership coupled with the commercial status which the public often affords to a limited liability concern. The principal disadvantage of incorporation is a loss of privacy for the business. Unlike partnerships (discussed in Chapter 4), registered companies are subject to many disclosure requirements. For example, an annual return (report of company's affairs) must be filed with the Registrar of Companies in accordance with s 364 of the Companies Act 1985, together with an annual report of the company's accounts. Particulars of a company's directors and secretary must also be filed, as must copies of the company's constitutional documents and copies of all the special or extraordinary resolutions passed by the general meeting of a company (company resolutions are discussed in Chapter 18).

THE HISTORY OF THE REGISTERED COMPANY

The concept of the registered company was born of the mid-nineteenth century and as such company law is a comparatively modern legal phenomenon. Nevertheless, prior to the mid-nineteenth century, business associations existed in such a form as to warrant them being properly described as ancestors of and necessary catalysts to our present system of company law.

The chartered company

Chartered joint stock companies were developed in the seventeenth century, largely as a result of the expansion in the world shipping trade, examples of which included the Massachusetts Bay Company formed in 1629 and the Hudson's Bay Company formed in 1670. A joint stock company was an association of members, each member contributed capital towards specific trade ventures. The joint stock company was a sophisticated form of partnership concern, created by royal charter. The charter often provided the association with monopolistic rights in specific trades. In addition, the company was deemed to have a separate legal identity, although unless specifically provided for in the charter, the membership of such companies were devoid of any form of limited liability. A member of a company would take shares in the company in proportion to his initial contribution towards the company's stock.

The growth in joint stock companies mirrored an expansion in the number of share dealings. By the early part of the eighteenth century speculation in share values had become another means by which the gentry could amuse their gambling instincts. One such company in which the speculative fervour thrived was the South Sea Company. This company was founded in 1711 with the objective of obtaining a monopoly of trade with the colonies in South America. The company prospered and in an ambitious attempt to expand its wealth entered into a venture whereby it proposed to purchase the national debt. The company proposed to buy out government creditors or to persuade them to take shares in the South Sea Company in exchange for their claims on the national debt. In an attempt to secure this transaction members of the government and other high ranking officials were rewarded with shares in the company. The rationale behind this venture was that the national debt was a profitable high interest bearing loan. Confidence in the South Sea Company's proposals escalated. In 1719, the year in which the company had offered to purchase the national debt, a £100 share in the company was quoted at £136 whereas by mid-1720, prior to a crash in the markets, the share price had reached £1000. The surge of confidence in the South Sea shares resulted in a general increase in share dealings and a speculative boom in the general value of share prices of other companies. Unfortunately, many companies with dubious corporate objectives, many of which had been formed by purchasing charters of long extinct companies, thrived as a result of the general acceptance by naive investors that a company share could do nothing but escalate in value.

A collapse in the markets was inevitable, fraudulently conceived companies were prosecuted, members of the government who had been involved in the share dealings fell from grace and Parliament, in an attempt to curb the improper use of the corporate form, passed the so-called Bubble Act of 1720. The purpose of this Act was to prevent share transactions other than those involving the shares of companies granted powers by individual Acts of Parliament or those with legitimate charters. The new Act imposed a stricter regime on the ability of businesses to trade as companies. The South Sea bubble episode was the first speculative boom and crash in British history, although it was certainly not to be the last.

Unincorporated associations

The decline in the popularity of the corporate form as a business medium continued until the start of the nineteenth century. The nineteenth century witnessed an increase in the number of companies created by individual Acts of Parliament, such companies were basically large trading concerns; the expense of incorporating by this method was extremely prohibitive of smaller business ventures. However, despite the growth in statutory companies, which included concerns such as banks, canal companies, railway companies, etc., by far the most popular form of business organisation of this time was the unincorporated association, formed under a trust deed (the deed of settlement), whereby members of the association would, in a similar way to joint stock companies, invest capital in an association and in return take shares in the association. Yet, unlike joint stock companies, the property and assets of the association were not held by the business as a separate legal entity. The property and assets were held by trustees who could sue and be sued on behalf of the association. The principal disadvantage of the unincorporated association was that the members of these businesses did not have limited liability. In addition, the legality of the right of members to freely transfer shares in the associations remained undoubtedly questionable under the provisions of the Bubble Act, an Act which was not repealed until 1825.

The Joint Stock Companies Act 1844

The Joint Stock Companies Act 1844 gave birth to the first form of registered company. As a result of the 1844 Act, a company could be incorporated by a registration procedure as opposed to incorporation by royal charter or by an individual Act of Parliament. Under the Act, companies could be incorporated by registration provided the company had more than 25 members. The 1844 Act also created the Registrar of Companies with whom particulars of registered companies had to be lodged. Despite the creation of the registered company, the 1844 Act did not confer limited liability on the membership of these companies. Limited liability was, at that time, seen as a means by which undercapitalised concerns might exploit the corporate form to the detriment of creditors and the investing public.

Limited liability

Despite severe reservations about granting limited liability to small business concerns (see, for example, the report of the Royal Commission on Mercantile Law and the Law of Partnership in 1854), the Limited Liability Act of 1855 allowed companies with at least 25 members, each holding shares to the minimum value of £10 with at least one-fifth fully paid up on the share, to incorporate with a limited-liability status. A company was required to have not less than three-quarters of its nominal capital subscribed and the word 'limited' added to its name. Liability was (as it still is today) limited to the nominal value of the share. The 1855 Act was incorporated into the Joint Stock Companies Act 1856 which required an obligation on the part of a company to have and register constitutional documents, namely the memorandum and articles of association (these in effect replaced the deed of settlement). In addition, and to encourage smaller business enterprises to register as companies, the 1856 Act removed the restrictions relating to the minimum amount of capital to be contributed by members of a company and also reduced the minimum number of members required for the purposes of incorporation from 25 to seven members. The companies legislation was consolidated into the Companies Act of 1862.

Whilst many statutory changes have occurred in the field of company law since the creation of the registered company, for example a private limited company can now be incorporated with just one member, and a public company with two members, the skeleton of the Victorian legislation remains a definite characteristic of modern company law. Indeed, incorporation by the process of registration, the recognition of a company as a separate legal identity and the ability to incorporate with a limited-liability status are characteristics at the very heart of modern company law. The birth of the registered limited liability company was and remains a means by which businessmen can limit the risk of investing funds into a business enterprise. Encouraging the growth and expansion of companies is of the utmost importance to the national economy; successful companies generate wealth and employment.

THE JUDICIAL ACCEPTANCE OF THE COMPANY AS A SEPARATE LEGAL ENTITY

In relation to the incorporation of large established business concerns, the judicial interpretation of the Victorian legislation in its recognition of the registered company as a separate legal entity was generally accepted without much dissent. As long as a large business concern was registered in accordance with the companies legislation, it was taken that it could benefit from the advantages of incorporation; see e.g. the House of Lords' decision in *The Princess of Reuss* (1871) 5 LR 176, a case in which the existence of an enterprise properly incorporated as a limited-liability company under the Companies Act 1862 was unsuccessfully challenged on the basis that its membership was comprised of 'foreigners'!

Nevertheless, despite the general judicial recognition of the separate legal existence of the larger registered company, the judicial acceptance of smaller registered companies, often incorporated with only one substantial shareholder, was a matter of some uncertainty. The incorporation of small 'one-man type' businesses had, at the start of the 1860s been rare, but towards the end of the nineteenth century the incorporation of small businesses dramatically increased to the extent that by the start of the twentieth century the small incorporated concern represented an overwhelming majority of all registered companies.

The case heralded as the one which finally established the applicability of the registered company as an acceptable and valid form of business medium for small businesses was *Salomon v A Salomon Ltd* [1897] AC 22 (however, it should be noted that earlier examples of the judicial acceptance of the ability to incorporate small businesses do exist; see e.g. *Re George Newman & Co* [1895] 1 Ch 674).

The facts of the *Salomon* case were as follows. The proprietor of a small but successful leather business, a Mr Salomon, incorporated his business as a limited company in accordance with the registration provisions contained within the Companies Act 1862. Section 6 of the 1862 Act provided that seven or more persons together could incorporate a business, provided that it was associated for a lawful purpose. The seven subscribers to A Salomon Ltd were Mr Salomon, his wife and their five children. The company, A Salomon Ltd, purchased Mr Salomon's business in a solvent state for a consideration to a value of approximately £39 000. Mr Salomon received 20 000 fully paid-up £1 shares, an issue of debentures to the value of £10 000 (a debenture acknowledges a loan or other credit agreement between the company and its creditor and is normally secured against the assets of the company; in Salomon's case the debenture was secured by means of a floating charge: see Chapter 14) and the remainder of the sale price in cash. The remaining members of the family were each allotted one £1 share in the company.

Unfortunately, A Salomon Ltd did not prosper. Mr Salomon's debentures were transferred to a Mr Broderip in return for £5000; this amount was then pumped back into the company by Mr Salomon. Despite further efforts on the part of Mr Salomon to keep the company afloat, less than a year after its incorporation, the company had fallen into an insolvent state. The company could not meet Broderip's debenture interest payments and fearful that his investment would be lost, Broderip sought to realise his security by appointing a receiver. The company, which had other creditors, was subsequently put into liquidation. The liquidation (sale) of the company's assets realised sufficient funds to meet the company's debt to Broderip but not the debts owed to the company's other creditors; unlike Broderip the other creditors had no secured interest (debentures). In the High Court (heard as *Broderip v Salomon* [1895] 2 Ch 323), the liquidator admitted the validity of Broderip's prior claim to be repaid from the company's assets, i.e. as holder of a secured loan. Nevertheless, the liquidator counter-claimed that the company (and therefore the company's unsecured creditors) were entitled to be reimbursed by Salomon personally. The trial judge, Vaughan Williams J, agreed with this contention. Whilst admitting that upon its registration a company had a legal entity distinct from its corporators, the learned judge opined that A Salomon Ltd (the company) was no more than an agent of its principal, i.e. Mr Salomon. As such, the principal was responsible for the debts of its agent. The basis for the agency argument was that the company was a mere alias of its founder and had not been formed in accordance with the true spirit of the 1862 Companies Act. Vaughan Williams J believed that the 1862 Act, in its requirement for 'seven persons associated for a lawful purpose' meant seven persons with a bona fide intention of participating in a trading venture, and not, as in the present case, a company which was in reality akin to a one-man business.

On appeal, the decision of Vaughan Williams J was upheld, although in the Court of Appeal's opinion the correct analogy between the company and Mr Salomon was that of a trust relationship, i.e. the company held its property on trust for its beneficiary, Mr Salomon. As such, the creditors of A Salomon Ltd were entitled to a claim against Mr Salomon through the company. As at first instance, the Court of Appeal recognised that A Salomon Ltd, in complying with the registration provisions of the 1862 Act, had been validly incorporated as a separate legal entity. However, the court would not recognise that the liability of A Salomon Ltd should be divorced from that of its founder, Mr Salomon, in so far as they agreed that in relation to the requirements of incorporation, the correct interpretation of the Companies Act 1862 was that the seven persons who became members of the company should participate in the venture rather than have a superficial interest in the company.

Notwithstanding that the business had been profitable prior to its incorporation, Lindley LJ was of the opinion that the manner in which it had been formed indicated that it had been created for an illegitimate purpose, that it was 'a device to defraud creditors' (at p 339). Indeed, in the Court of Appeal's opinion the company's illegitimacy stemmed from the fact that it was in reality a one-man company. Lopes LJ stated:

'If we were to permit it to succeed, we should be authorising a perversion of the Joint Stock Companies Act. We should give vitality to that which is a myth and a fiction ... To legalise such a transaction would be a scandal.' (at p 341)

The House of Lords, in reversing the decision of the Court of Appeal, rigorously denied the belief held by the lower courts that a company could not be formed by one dominant character together with six other persons divorced of a substantial interest in the business venture. According to the House, the statutory language of the Companies Act 1862 (s 6) was clear. A company could be incorporated providing it had at least seven members irrespective of whether or not all seven members made a substantial contribution to the company's affairs.

Although both the High Court and the Court of Appeal recognised that A Salomon Ltd, having complied with the registration provisions of the 1862 Act, was a corporate entity, they had not contemplated the fact that once incorporated, the company could not be considered as anything other than an independent entity, totally separate and distinct from its founder, Mr Salomon. The House of Lords' interpretation of the separate legal identity of a company was, in respect of A Salomon Ltd, absolute. Lord Macnaughten stated thus:

'It may be that a company constituted like that under consideration was not in the contemplation of the legislature at the time when the Act authorising limited liability was passed; that if what is possible under the enactments as they stand had been foreseen a minimum sum would have been fixed as the least denomination of share possible; and that it would have been made a condition that each of the seven persons should have a substantial interest in the company. But we have to interpret the law, not to make it; and it must be remembered that no one need trust a limited company unless he so please, and that before he does so he can ascertain, if he so pleases what is the capital of the company and how it is held.' (at p 46)

His lordship then went on to state:

'The company is at law a different person altogether from the subscribers to the memorandum; and though it may be that after incorporation the business is precisely the same as it was before, and the same persons are managers, and the same hands receive the profits, the company is not in law the agent of the subscribers or trustee for them. Nor are the subscribers as members liable, in any shape or form, except to the extent and in the manner provided by the Act.' (at p 51)

The House of Lords in considering the agency and trust arguments of the lower courts concluded that both were contradictory to the view that the company was a separate legal entity. The finding of an agency or trust relationship would have rendered as illusory the limited liability of the company's majority shareholder, Mr Salomon, i.e. the finding of an agency or trust relationship would have meant that Mr Salomon would have been personally liable for the company's debts. Lord Herschell said of the decisions of the lower courts:

'It is to be observed that both courts treated the company as a legal entity distinct from Salomon and the members who composed it, and therefore as a validly constituted corporation ... Under the circumstances I am at a loss to understand what is meant by saying that A Salomon & Co Ltd is but an alias for A Salomon.' (at p 42)

Lord Halsbury remarked:

'Once the company is legally incorporated it must be treated like any other independent person with rights and liabilities appropriate to itself, and that the motives of those who took part in the promotion of the company are absolutely irrelevant in discussing what those rights and liabilities are.' (at p 30)

A problem for unsecured creditors?

One of the most worrying implications of the *Salomon* decision is that a trader in incorporating a business will not only be able to take the advantage of limited liability but, could also ensure, by taking debentures in the company, that he would have first call on the assets of the company should the company be put into liquidation, i.e. by having a secured charge over the company's assets. In theory, this problem should be diminished because if a founding member of a company was to take debentures in the company his secured interest would be registrable and as such any future creditor of a company would have the opportunity to check the register of company charges to discover the existence of the charge; should a creditor fail to check the register he would nevertheless be deemed to have constructive notice of a registrable charge (company charges and priority interests are discussed in Chapter 15). Yet, commercial expediency dictates that small trade creditors are unlikely to expend time and money on making such checks and therefore the decision in *Salomon* may be said to place unsecured trade creditors in a perilous position should a company be put into liquidation without sufficient assets to discharge all of its debts (however, note that in such circumstances specific statutory provisions may remove the shield of limited liability, see Chapter 20).

Suggested further reading
Historical development of company law from 1825
Gower's Principles of Modern Company Law (1992) 6th edn. London: Sweet & Maxwell, Chapters 2 and 3.

2

THE COURTS' ABILITY TO DISLODGE THE CORPORATE VEIL AT COMMON LAW OR IN EQUITY

INTRODUCTION

A company is regarded as a distinct legal entity with a separate existence from its membership and management team (see Chapter 1). The independent legal status of the corporate entity is said to cast a veil between the company and its human constituents, 'the corporate veil'. Although, as the following chapter will illustrate, case law and statutory exceptions (discussed further in Chapter 20) exist to dislodge the corporate veil, it must be stressed from the outset, that a company's separate legal existence represents a fundamental and essential characteristic of company law, a characteristic which is crucial to the understanding of the study of corporate law.

In the majority of situations in which the veil is dislodged under common law or equity, it is merely pierced (as opposed to being totally removed) for the purpose of imposing some form of liability on a company's shareholders and/or directors. Where the veil is not completely removed, the separate legal existence of the company will subsist. In other instances, for example, those concerned with groups of companies, the corporate veil may be removed, to the extent that individual corporate entities (subsidiary companies) are treated as but a division of another corporate entity (the holding company); in such cases the holding company will be merged with its subsidiaries, and the group of companies will, for practical purposes, be treated as one economic entity as opposed to a collection of different corporate entities.

DISLODGING THE CORPORATE VEIL

Although the judiciary has universally accepted the principle of a company as a separate legal entity, an entity which is divorced from the interests of its membership and management, the courts have in exceptional instances dislodged the corporate veil. Notwithstanding the general reluctance of the courts to depart from the principles enunciated in *Salomon v A Salomon Ltd*, the effect of the case law exceptions have been more acute than the statutory exceptions (see Chapter 20). While the majority of the statutory provisions impose some form of penalty on a company's human constituents, they normally do so without denying the separate legal responsibilities of the company. In contrast, the case law examples generally penetrate deeper and in some instances may have the effect of lifting the corporate veil in its entirety, thereby abandoning the recognition of a company as a separate legal entity.

Dislodging the corporate veil in times of national emergency

When the nation is at war or finds itself in some other serious form of political or economic conflict, it may be expedient for the court to dislodge the corporate veil to prevent, for example, the payment of moneys from companies registered in the UK to the 'enemy' state or citizens of that state. For example, in *Daimler v Continental Tyre & Rubber Co* [1916] 2 AC 307 the Continental Tyre Co sought to enforce a debt owed to it by Daimler. The membership of the Continental Tyre Co was comprised of German nationals. As the UK was at war with Germany, the House of Lords (reversing the decision of the Court of Appeal) refused to sanction the enforcement of the debt. In doing so, and despite the fact that Continental was registered in the UK, the House refused to recognise that Continental was an entity which was independent from its membership.

This example of the judicial piercing of the corporate veil is obviously limited in terms of its potential application, i.e. it is dependent upon a state of hostility between the UK and some other nation. The justification for interfering with the corporate veil is primarily concerned with invoking a substantial penalty against individuals who, in this specific instance, have a significant connection with an enemy state (see also *The Polzeath* [1916] 32 TLR 674, *Bank voor Handel en Scheepvaart NV v Slatford* [1953] 1 QB 248).

Fraud or façade cases

The ability to disturb the corporate veil may be justified where the formation and subsequent existence of a company can properly be regarded as fraud or façade. The fraud or façade exception will occur where the underlying motive for the incorporation of a company is to enable its membership to impugn an existing binding obligation with a third party or instigate some other form of fraud. In such a case the court may recognise the existence of the corporate entity but may nevertheless pierce the corporate veil to prevent those involved in the façade or fraudulent act from escaping a liability which would have otherwise been enforceable had the company not been incorporated. Indeed, in *Salomon v A Salomon Ltd* had the motive for the company's incorporation been a fraudulent one, the case would have had a different outcome. The evidence in that case suggested that although Mr Salomon had overvalued the price of his pre-incorporated business, the overvaluation had not been of a fraudulent character. As Lord Macnaughten remarked:

'If, however, the declaration of the Court of Appeal means that Mr Salomon acted fraudulently or dishonestly, I must say I can find nothing in the evidence to support such an imputation.' (at p 52)

Mr Salomon had done everything possible to keep A Salomon Ltd afloat, including disposing of his debentures and using his own personal funds to inject capital into the company.

Therefore, it may be observed from the *Salomon* decision that the motive behind a company's incorporation is highly relevant to the determination of whether or not the corporate veil may be dislodged to impose a liability on the members of a company. For example, in *Gilford Motor Co v Horne* [1933] Ch 935, Mr Horne (H) entered into a contract with Gilford Motor Co by which he agreed to abide by a restrictive covenant which provided that should he leave Gilford's employment he would not solicit their customers. On leaving Gilford's employment H, through nominees, formed a company through which he sought to escape the terms of the restrictive covenant. The court held that the company was a 'sham', an alias of H and as such an injunction was granted to enforce the covenant. The restrictive covenant was enforced against both H and the company, i.e. the company's corporate existence was not denied although the company's corporate veil was pierced to recognise H's personal culpability for the breach of the restrictive covenant.

A further illustration of a fraud or façade is provided by *Jones v Lipman* [1962] 1 WLR 832, in which a Mr Lipman (L) sought to escape specific performance of a contract entered into for the sale of land, by transferring the said land to a company which he had recently incorporated. It was held that the incorporation of the company was a façade, a device to evade L's contractual responsibility and as such specific performance of the sale of land was granted against both L and the company. Once again, the company's corporate existence was judicially recognised (in so far as the order was granted against the company), although its corporate veil was pierced to the extent that the court recognised L's personal culpability.

In respect of a holding company–subsidiary relationship, it should be noted that in *Adams v Cape Industries* [1990] Ch 433, (see below at p 16) the Court of Appeal could find no legal objection where the corporate structure of a group of companies had been used to ensure that any **future** legal liability, which might be attached to the group enterprise, would fall on a subsidiary of the holding company, rather than on the holding company itself. In other words, it would appear quite legitimate for a company to eliminate the risk of being held potentially liable for pursuing future business activities, activities which could carry a high risk of failure, by transferring such interests to an existing subsidiary company over which it, the holding company, maintained a significant degree of control. Although the Court of Appeal considered that the manipulation of a group structure was a legitimate means for a holding company to evade liability, it must be said that it is difficult to substantiate the acceptance of such manipulation as anything other than a blatant abuse of the incorporation process. Accordingly, it is regrettable that it has been afforded a legitimacy which would appear to be both unwarranted and unjust.

Economic entity

Although the following discussion of the concept of an economic entity will concentrate itself upon a holding company–subsidiary relationship, it should be noted that companies under the control of a dominant person or persons (as opposed to a dominant holding company) may also be viewed as constituting a single economic entity; see e.g. *Creasey* v *Breachwood Motors* [1992] BCC 639 (discussed below at p 21).

Where two or more companies operate together in a group relationship and do so under the dominant control of one of their number (the holding company), the corporate veils of the other company/companies or the subsidiary company/companies may in specific circumstances be lifted, with the result that the group of companies is viewed as a single economic entity. However, it must be stressed that a group relationship does not in itself imply that the group can be regarded as one economic entity. Further, it does not necessarily follow that a company, which is a wholly owned subsidiary of its holding company, is to be classed as but a division of the holding company and therefore part of one economic entity. Indeed, in order to establish that a group of companies is in reality one economic entity, it must be shown, at the very least, that the holding company exerts a substantial, if not absolute degree of control over the affairs of the subsidiary company, to the extent that the holding company must be in a position whereby it controls the subsidiary. The holding company's degree of control must extend beyond control based upon its control of a majority of the subsidiary's shares.

The case law which is pertinent to the determination of the existence of an economic entity is far from uniform in nature. While at one time an economic entity could be established without any necessity to prove that the holding company had absolute control over its subsidiary, in more recent times, the need to establish absolute control has become a clear prerequisite of establishing the existence of an economic entity.

Establishing the necessary degree of control

In *Holdsworth & Co* v *Caddies* [1955] 1 WLR 352, a dispute arose over a managing director's service contract, a contract which he alleged had been breached as a result of the holding company's decision to exclusively restrict his managerial duties to a subsidiary company. The managing director contended that he could not, as a result of his employment contract with the holding company, be employed by its subsidiary, in so far as in accordance with an application of the *Salomon* principle, the subsidiary was a distinct and quite separate legal entity from the holding company. The House of Lords (Lord Keith dissenting) ruled against the managing director on the premise that in terms of the economic realities of the case the subsidiary was

13

but a division of the holding company in so far as the subsidiary was wholly owned by its holding company, the holding company appointed all of the subsidiary's directors and further, it was in a position whereby it was able to dictate the subsidiary's corporate policy. Accordingly, the House of Lords in lifting the corporate veil of the subsidiary company merged the legal entities of the holding company and its subsidiary to constitute one economic entity.

Similarly, in *Scottish Co-op Wholesale Society v Meyer* [1959] AC 324 the House of Lords found that the economic reality of a group relationship was such that the corporate veil of the holding company's subsidiary should be lifted to create one economic entity. Although in this case the subsidiary company was not wholly owned by its holding company, the holding company did control the corporate policy of the subsidiary. The corporate veil of the subsidiary was lifted in this case so as to enable Dr Meyer, a minority shareholder in the subsidiary, to obtain relief under s 210, CA 1948 (this section of the Companies Act has since been replaced by s 459, CA 1985, see Chapter 22).

In order to obtain relief under s 210 of the CA 1948, Dr Meyer had to establish that the company of which he was a member (the subsidiary) had conducted its affairs in a manner which was oppressive to his shareholding interest. The oppression complained of was the holding company's positive policy of running down the subsidiary company; the subsidiary company had, in the eyes of the holding company, become surplus to requirements. The holding company controlled a majority of the voting shares in the subsidiary and appointed a majority of the subsidiary's directors. The said directors had failed, due to their inactivity, to prevent the subsidiary's decline. For Dr Meyer's claim to succeed, he sought an order for the holding company to purchase his shares in the subsidiary company at a fair value. The corporate veil of the subsidiary had to be lifted so that the oppressive conduct of the holding company could be interpreted as being the oppressive conduct of one single economic entity of which the subsidiary was a part.

The House allowed Dr Meyer's claim, although it must be observed that Lord Morton (and to a lesser extent Lord Denning) expressed reservations on the ability of the court to lift the veil. Lord Morton preferred to rest his decision on the fact that the directors of the subsidiary had 'conducted' the subsidiary's affairs. (However, note the decision in *Nicholas v Soundcraft Electronics Ltd* [1993] BCLC 360, here the Court of Appeal confirmed that in appropriate circumstances a holding company could be held responsible for conducting the affairs of its subsidiary.)

Another leading case, often quoted to support the argument that a single economic entity can be established in circumstances where a holding company dominates the corporate policy of its subsidiary company, is the decision of the Court of Appeal in *DHN Food Distributors Ltd v Tower Hamlets LBC* [1976] 1 WLR 852. The case involved a group of three companies. The holding company, DHN, traded from premises owned by its subsidiary company, Bronze Ltd. The third company in the group operated a transport business for the sole benefit of DHN. The litigation in this case occurred when Tower Hamlets Borough Council ordered that the land upon which the business premises of the group were located (land registered to Bronze Ltd) be made the subject of a compulsory purchase order. In accordance with the terms of the order, compensation was payable to the owner of the land, i.e. Bronze Ltd and for any disturbance to the landowners' business. As Bronze Ltd did not carry on an independent business, the Council claimed that this latter form of compensation should not be payable. The Court of Appeal unanimously disagreed. Lord Denning opined that the three companies should for all practical purposes be treated as one entity and that a technical rule of company law, i.e. the separate legal identity of each company in the group could be disregarded where, as in this case, the ownership and control of the two subsidiary companies were completely in the hands of the holding company, the two subsidiary companies having no independent existence. Shaw LJ was of the same opinion. However, it should be noted that Goff LJ was more reluctant to justify his decision in favour of DHN on the basis of the existence of an economic entity. Instead, Goff LJ rationalised his decision in favour of the DHN group by concluding that Bronze Ltd held the property in question on trust for DHN, with the effect that DHN held an equitable interest in the property, a beneficial interest which was sufficient enough to entitle it to compensation for the disturbance of the group's business interests.

However, as previously mentioned, a company's or an individual's ability to control the overall policy structure of another company may now of itself be insufficient to justify the lifting of the corporate veil, based upon the concept of the economic entity. Indeed, in more recent times, the courts have generally been most reluctant to depart from the principles enunciated in *Salomon v A Salomon Ltd*, based on the premise that a holding company controlled the corporate policy of its subsidiary. In order to dislodge the corporate veil of the subsidiary, the courts have demanded something more, namely, they have required, in addition to a holding company's control over the policy structure of its subsidiary, the finding of a façade or fraud in relation to the incorporation of the subsidiary company. For example, in *Woolfson v Strathclyde Regional Council* (1978) SLT 159 the House of Lords, in upholding a decision of the Scottish courts, refused to dislodge the corporate veil even though the *Woolfson* case bore many similarities to the facts encountered in *DHN Food Distributors Ltd v Tower Hamlets LBC*. Indeed, the House of Lords doubted whether the Court of Appeal's decision to dislodge the corporate veil in the *DHN* case could be properly justified.

Although the respective cases of *Woolfson* and *DHN* were in many respects similar, it should be pointed out that in *Woolfson* there was never any holding company–subsidiary relationship, rather this case was concerned with an individual's control over a group of companies. The individual in question, Mr Woolfson (W), held 99.9 per cent of the shares in Campbell Ltd (C Ltd). C Ltd carried on a retail business in a chain of shops, three of which were owned by W and the other two by Solfred Ltd (S Ltd), a company in which W held two-thirds of the shares; his wife held the remaining shares in S Ltd and the remaining 0.1 per cent of shares in C Ltd.

The dispute in this case arose when the local council acquired the shop premises in accordance with a compulsory purchase order, the terms of which provided that compensation was payable for disturbance to an occupier or to an owner-occupier but not to an owner who was not an occupier. C Ltd occupied the premises and W and S Ltd sought further compensation for disturbance on the grounds that they formed one economic entity with C Ltd, i.e. they sought compensation as owner-occupiers. However, although the three businesses were associated under the dominant influence of W, unlike the *DHN* case, the three businesses were not completely controlled by one entity; indeed the House of Lords distinguished the *DHN* case on that basis. In reaching its decision to refuse to merge the three business enterprises into one economic entity, the House of Lords concluded that the corporate veil should not be dislodged, save in cases where the relationship between a group of enterprises was that of a façade. Yet, unfortunately, the House of Lords did not elaborate upon the meaning to be attributed to the term 'façade'.

Further, in *Bank of Tokyo Ltd v Karoon* [1987] AC 45 the Court of Appeal denied that a strong economic link between a group of companies could justify a finding of an economic entity for the purpose of merging the group of companies into one legal entity. Goff LJ denied the existence of an economic entity:

> '**Counsel suggested beguilingly that it would be technical for us to distinguish between parent and subsidiary company in this context; economically he said, they were one. But we are concerned not with economics but with law. The distinction between the two is in law fundamental and cannot be bridged.**' (at p 64)

In *Adams v Cape Industries* [1990] Ch 433, the Court of Appeal, in following the lead taken by the House of Lords in *Woolfson*, concluded that a holding company's apparent control over its subsidiary company's corporate policy would not in itself justify the court in finding the existence of a single economic entity for the purpose of dislodging the corporate veil of the subsidiary. In reaching its decision, the Court of Appeal undertook an extensive review of the authorities related to the circumstances in which the corporate veil had previously been dislodged in a group relationship.

The facts of the case were as follows. The holding company, Cape Industries plc (Cape), was involved in the asbestos industry. Cape was an English company with a mining subsidiary in South Africa and a wholly owned marketing subsidiary (NAAC) in the USA. The employees of NAAC successfully brought an action (Tyler 1 action) against NAAC in which NAAC was obliged to pay $5.2 million in compensation to employees pursuant to an action for damages, following illnesses contracted by the employees whilst working with asbestos at the NAAC factory. Although NAAC was obliged to pay this compensation, in effect the cost of the action fell on the Cape group. To prevent the incursion of any further liability against the Cape group in the USA, NAAC was put into liquidation.

The American marketing base of the Cape group was nevertheless continued by another company, CPC, which whilst not a subsidiary of Cape, was nevertheless set up with substantial financial support from the Cape group. CPC operated from the premises previously occupied by NAAC, and CPC's managing director, who was also the company's majority shareholder, had previously been the managing director of NACC. A Liechtenstein-registered company, AMC, controlled by the Cape group, acted as Cape's agents in the American market; AMC, in effect, were middle men in the relationship between Cape and CPC.

Shortly after NAAC's liquidation, a second series of actions were successfully commenced in the American courts by the former employees of NAAC (Tyler 2 action). The Court of Appeal was called upon to determine whether the judgments in favour of the American employees were enforceable against Cape. Cape argued that any liability which may have fallen on NAAC should not now fall on its shoulders because NAAC was no longer in existence. Cape argued that it should not be made party to proceedings in the USA because it was no longer present in the USA. In addition, Cape argued that notwithstanding its removal from the USA, any responsibility attached to NAAC or CPC should rest with those companies as distinct and separate legal entities. The plaintiffs contended that NAAC and CPC were part of one economic entity, i.e. the Cape group and that Cape was still present in the USA through CPC.

In finding in favour of Cape, the Court of Appeal denied the validity of the distinct entities being part of one economic entity. This denial was understandable in respect of the relationship between Cape and CPC, in so far as CPC was not even a Cape subsidiary. However, the court's finding that NAAC had not been part of one economic entity was a much more debatable proposition. The court conceded that Cape had controlled the general corporate policy of NAAC, i.e. the holding company determined the subsidiary's expenditure and financial policy. Nevertheless, the court was of the opinion that the subsidiary was an independent entity in so far as NAAC was not totally dependent on Cape. NAAC managed the day-to-day running of its own business, for example, it was allowed to enter into business contracts and employ its own staff. In denying the existence of an economic entity, the Court of Appeal took the view that control, in the sense of satisfying the requirement for the recognition of an economic entity, meant absolute control in a manner which would have justified a finding that the subsidiary was an alias of the holding company, a mere façade.

The Court of Appeal gave two examples of what it considered would warrant a finding of façade. The first example was the relationship between Cape and AMC, which was basically one of agency, in which AMC had been created exclusively for the purpose of carrying out its master's instructions. However, the finding of a façade in this relationship did not assist the plaintiffs because AMC had not been involved in the running of the asbestos factory, nor had it been present in the USA. The second example was the case of *Jones* v *Lipman* [1962] 1 All ER 442 (see Chapter 2). The court's guidance would therefore seem to indicate that the creation of a company within a group of companies may be regarded as a façade where it was either created on the pretext that it would be without any corporate independence of its own, i.e. it was a mere alias for its master or, alternatively where, it was a device created for the purpose of exploiting the corporate form in order to satisfy an improper or illegitimate purpose.

The Court of Appeal in reaching its decision in the *Adams* case distinguished cases such as *Holdsworth v Caddies, Scottish Wholesale Co-op Society v Meyer* and *DHN Food Distributors Ltd v London Borough of Tower Hamlets*, cases which had merged a group of companies into one economic entity, on the premise that the wording of a particular statute or contract had, in such cases, been of a type which would justify the treatment of a parent and subsidiary as one unit. The Court of Appeal's distinction is, however, suspect because the aforementioned cases indicate that justifications independent from the particular statutory and contractual provisions had first to be established before the corporate veil could be dislodged. Once the corporate veil had been pierced then, and only then could the particular statutory or contractual provision be applied. Accordingly, it may be said in respect of such cases that the removal of the corporate veil allowed the application of the statutory or contractual provision. As such, the wording of the statutory or contractual provision did not in itself provide an automatic right to pierce the corporate veil so as to instigate a merger of the enterprises into one economic entity.

Agency

An ability to establish an agency relationship between a holding company and its subsidiary will facilitate a finding that the holding company (the principal) is responsible for the actions of its subsidiary (the agent), although it must be observed that there will be no disturbance of the subsidiary's corporate veil, in so far as the principal and agent will be regarded as distinct legal entities. In the context of an agency relationship between corporate entities, agency may be tentatively defined as a relationship which is based upon the express or implied consent of both the subsidiary company and its holding company, that the former will act on the latter's behalf, and by the subsidiary so acting, it will be made subject to the holding company's control (see, for example, the judgment of Lord Pearson in *Garnac Grain Co Inc v HMF Faure and Fairclough Ltd* [1968] AC 1130 at p 1137).

Following the Court of Appeal's decision in *Adams v Cape Industries*, the circumstances which may give rise to the removal of the corporate veil in a group relationship are, in instances of a façade based upon a company acting as an alias for another, in effect, similar to or indeed the same considerations which will substantiate a finding of an agency relationship. Indeed, in *Adams v Cape Industries*, in addition to the issue relating to whether the relationship between Cape and its subsidiaries constituted an economic entity, the plaintiffs also contended that the relationship between the group of companies had been one of agency. With regard to Cape's relationship with NAAC, the court denied the existence of an agency relationship because Cape did not completely control its subsidiary. NAAC, the subsidiary, employed its own staff, rented its own warehouses, occasionally purchased asbestos on its own behalf, earned its own profits and paid USA tax. The control argument also defeated the claim that CPC could be regarded as Cape's agent.

For the purpose of establishing an agency relationship it is therefore crucial to establish that one dominant company had absolute control over the affairs and actions of another company. For example, in *Smith Stone & Knight Ltd v Birmingham Corp* [1939] 4 All ER 116 (the facts of which are almost identical to *DHN Food Distributors Ltd* v *London Borough of Tower Hamlets*, discussed above), an agency relationship was established in a group relationship on the basis that the subsidiary company was a mere tool working for the ultimate benefit of its holding company. By contrast, in *Kodak* v *Clarke* [1902] 2 KB 450 the court denied the existence of an agency relationship between an English holding company and its overseas subsidiary because, the English company, which held 98 per cent of the subsidiary's shares, had never attempted to interfere with the management of the subsidiary.

In determining an agency relationship, it must be stressed that it does not necessarily follow that a wholly owned subsidiary will be regarded as the holding company's agent; see e.g. *Gramophone & Typewriter Ltd* v *Stanley* [1908] 2 KB 89. Conversely, it does not follow that an agency relationship will not be present in a situation where the subsidiary is not wholly owned, albeit that it must clearly be under the absolute control of the holding company. For example, in *Re FG (Films) Ltd* [1953] 1 All ER 615 the court was called upon to determine whether a film made by an English registered company was a British film as defined by the Cinematograph Films Act 1938, s 25(1). The English company (FG Films) which claimed to have made the film had a share capital of 100, £1 shares, 90 of which were held on behalf of an American company which financed the film in question. Vaisey J held that the participation of the English company in making the film was so small as to be negligible, it had acted as a nominee of and agent for the American company. The film was therefore deemed not to be a British film, but one which had been made exclusively under the control of the American company.

Finally, it is to be noted that the discussion of agency has concentrated its attention on the group relationship without any mention of whether an individual shareholder/director of a company may be considered to be in a position to control the activities of the company, to the extent that the company would in effect be the agent of the shareholder/director. This proposition was rejected in *Salomon* v *A Salomon Ltd* (discussed above) and although in *IRC* v *Sanson* [1921] 2 KB 492, Lord Sterndale (at p 503) observed that in an appropriate case it might be possible to establish an agency relationship between a majority shareholder and the 'one-man company' under his control, the validity of such a contention must be seriously doubted. Notwithstanding, that a company may be dominated and controlled by an individual shareholder in a manner akin to a holding company's dominance over its subsidiary, to permit a finding of agency as between a single company and its controlling shareholder would be to challenge the very heart of corporate law, which allows and encourages an individual to pursue his/her business objectives through the medium of a corporate entity.

Removing the corporate veil for justice's sake?

The ability of a court to lift the corporate veil has thus far been considered in the light of circumstances (the accepted headings) which may be indicative of the existence of a state of national emergency: a façade, an economic entity or an agency relationship. The aforementioned circumstances may be viewed as giving rise to specific exceptions to the judicial acceptance of a company's separate legal identity; alternatively they may be seen as masking the fundamental justification for denying the preservation of the corporate veil, namely to prevent injustice, a perversion of the corporate form.

In order to substantiate a claim that principles of justice determine the judicial disturbance of the corporate veil, it is necessary to decide whether or not the case examples hitherto examined may, in those cases where the corporate veil has been disturbed, be explained in terms of the application of equitable principles. Do the circumstances which invoke the disturbance of the corporate veil point to one primary justification for the disobedience of the principles enunciated in *Salomon* v *A Salomon Ltd*, a justification based upon the interests of justice, or are the specific accepted instances in which the corporate veil has been disturbed based upon rigid and self-contained rules?

In attempting to answer the above question it is important to note that prior to the Court of Appeal's judgment in *Adams* v *Cape Industries* the courts had shown a general reluctance to define a specific set of accepted instances by which the corporate veil could be dislodged. Indeed, Lord Denning advocated that a court's power to lift the corporate veil should be viewed as a discretionary power as opposed to a tool which could only be employed in specific and defined circumstances; see, for example, Lord Denning's judgments in *Littlewoods Mail Order Stores Ltd* v *IRC* [1969] 1 WLR 1241 and *Wallensteiner* v *Moir* [1974] 1 WLR 991. For instance, in the *Littlewoods* case Lord Denning stated:

> 'The doctrine laid down in *Salomon*'s case has to be watched very carefully. It has often been supposed to cast a veil over the personality of a limited company through which the courts cannot see. But that is not true. The courts can and often do draw aside the veil. They can and often do pull off the mask and look to see what really lies behind.' (at p 1254)

If the courts do possess a general discretion to draw aside the corporate veil, then such a discretion gives validity to the view that the individual merits – the justice of a case – may ultimately justify a court in disturbing the corporate veil. Indeed, in *Re a Company* [1985] 1 BCC 99, 421 Cumming-Bruce LJ was adamant that:

'... the cases before and after *Wallensteiner* v *Moir* [1974] 1 WLR 991 show that the court will use its powers to pierce the corporate veil if it is necessary to achieve justice irrespective of the legal efficacy of the corporate structure under consideration.' (at pp 99, 425)

However, in *Adams* v *Cape Industries* the Court of Appeal forcefully denied that the corporate veil could be disturbed by considering issues relevant to the justice of a case. For example, Slade LJ opined that:

'If a company chooses to arrange the affairs of its group in such a way that the business carried on in a particular foreign country is the business of its subsidiary and not its own, it is, in our judgement, entitled to do so. *Neither in this class of case nor in any other class of case is it open to this court to disregard the principle of Salomon* v *Salomon & Co Ltd* [1897] AC 22, *merely because it considers it just to do so.*' (at p 513) (emphasis added)

Notwithstanding that in *Adams* v *Cape Industries*, the Court of Appeal unequivocally denied that issues of justice could form the basis of a decision to dislodge the corporate veil, the first instance judgment of Richard Southwell QC, sitting as a deputy High Court judge in *Creasey* v *Breachwood Motors Ltd* [1992] BCC 639, attempted to reassert the belief that the underlying justification for lifting the corporate veil could, if necessary, be couched in terms of equitable considerations.

The facts of the *Creasey* case were as follows. The plaintiff, a Mr Creasey (C), was dismissed from a company, Welwyn Motors Ltd (W) where he had worked as the company's general manager. W carried on its business at premises owned by Breachwood Motors Ltd (B). The two directors of B were its only shareholders, the same two persons were also the only directors and shareholders of W. Therefore, although there was no holding company–subsidiary relationship between W and B, the two companies were related, in so far as the control of both were in the hands of the same persons (by analogy see *Woolfson* v *Strathclyde Regional Council*, discussed above).

As a result of his employment being discontinued, C commenced an action against W for wrongful dismissal. However, before proceedings could be brought against W, the company ceased trading (after about one year's business activity). B took over all of W's assets and paid off W's trade creditors, with the exception of C's claim for compensation. B carried on the business (sale of Saab motor cars) as previously undertaken by W and indeed traded under the name of Welwyn Saab, from W's former premises. C's solicitors continued to communicate with solicitors acting on behalf of W, who were in effect acting on B's instructions. B's solicitors claimed that the existence of W as a separate legal entity could, as a result of its informal takeover by B Ltd, no longer be substantiated and as such they considered it pointless to offer any particulars of defence to C's claim for unfair dismissal. Nevertheless, at the initial hearing of the unfair dismissal claim, an order was made in favour of C. Shortly after the hearing, W was struck off the Companies Register pursuant to s 652 of the Companies Act 1985, i.e. for not carrying on any business. As the effect of the order was to end the legal existence of W, C's solicitors successfully applied to have W substituted by B as the defendant to the order made in favour of C. B appealed to the High Court; the grounds for the appeal included the contention that as both W and B were separate legal entities, it therefore followed that B, in accordance with its distinct legal identity, could not be made responsible for the compensation payable to C.

B failed in its appeal. The court in removing the corporate veil of W, considered W to be but part of B. Therefore, B was prima facie deemed to be responsible for the payment of the compensation order in favour of C. However, in a quest for justice between the parties the court decided that B should be given the opportunity to defend the action for wrongful dismissal. In reaching his decision to remove the corporate veil of W so as to merge that company with B, thereby creating a single economic entity, Richard Southwell QC first considered whether W could properly be regarded as a façade so as to meet the requirement expounded in *Adams* v *Cape Industries*. However, the evidence of the case was not conclusive of the finding of a façade. In *Creasey*, the corporate veil was lifted for justice's sake. Richard Southwell QC, opined that:

> 'The power of the court to lift the corporate veil exists. The problem for a judge of first instance is to decide whether the particular case before the court is one in which that power should be exercised recognising that this is a very strong power which can be exercised to achieve justice where its exercise is necessary for that purpose, but which, misused would be likely to cause not considerable injustice.' (at pp 646–7)

The decision of Richard Southwell QC was subsequently followed in *The Tjaskemolen* [1997] CLC 521. Here Clarke J, in referring to *Creasey*, stated as follows:

> 'That case is thus an example of piercing the veil where assets are deliberately transferred from A to B in the knowledge that to do so will defeat a creditor's claim or potential claim, even if that has not proved to be the purpose of doing so. The judge in that case would have regarded the case as even stronger if the purpose of the transaction was to defeat the creditor's claim. I agree with the reasoning in *Creasey*.' (at p 529G)

Nevertheless, despite the equitable and common-sense approach in *Creasey*, subsequent decisions of the English courts have, in reaffirming the lengthy and powerful comments of the Court of Appeal in *Adams* v *Cape Industries*, sought to deny that individual issues of justice may in appropriate cases facilitate the removal of the corporate veil. Indeed, in *Ord* v *Belhaven Pubs Ltd* [1998] 2 BCLC 447 the Court of Appeal condemned the reasoning applied in *Creasey* in no uncertain terms, stating that the case should no longer be treated as authoritative. This case followed the earlier judgment of Robert Walker J in *Re Polly Peck International plc (No 3)* [1996] 1 BCLC 428, where the learned judge opined that lower courts should not seek to expound the concept of justice as a means by which the corporate veil could be disturbed.

Returning to *Ord* v *Belhaven Pubs Ltd*, the principles involved in this case were very similar to those which had arisen in *Creasey*. In *Ord*, the plaintiffs took a 20-year lease of a public house from the defendant (B) based on the B's representation of the pub's turnover and profitability. B was a subsidiary within a group of companies controlled by Ascot Holdings plc (A). The plaintiffs alleged serious misrepresentations and breach of warranty and claimed damages in tort and contract. The action progressed slowly. Prior to the trial of the proceedings the group of companies restructured with the result that B no longer retained any substantial assets. Given that B was left with no assets, the plaintiffs applied for leave to substitute A for B.

At first instance, the deputy High Court judge (Judge Alton) allowed the application for substitution. Judge Alton based her decision on the economic unity of the group and the control that A exerted over the group. The learned judge concluded that it was unjust to permit B to take advantage of the reconstruction to avoid a contingent liability. The Court of Appeal, in reversing the first instance decision, applied the principles of law enunciated in *Adams* v *Cape Industries* and concluded that the defendant company could not be construed as a mere façade in so far as the transfer of B's assets was undertaken without any intention to prejudice the plaintiffs. The court held that the motive for the reconstruction had been based upon an understandable business decision which had been undertaken as a consequence of a decline in the property market. The court found that the decision of Judge Alton, in removing the corporate veil, had been one based upon a misconception that the veil could, in just circumstances, be removed in a situation where there was a strong economic unity between a group of companies. Hobhouse LJ, in giving the judgment of the Court of Appeal, stated:

'The approach of the judge in the present case was simply to look to the economic unit, to disregard the distinction between the legal entities that were involved and then to say: since the company cannot pay, the shareholders [the holding company (A)] who are the people financially interested should be made to pay instead. That of course is radically at odds with the whole concept of corporate personality and limited liability and the decision of the House of Lords in *Salomon* v *A. Salomon & Co Ltd*.' (at p 457)

In rejecting the decision in *Creasey*, the Court of Appeal has thus sought to remove the judiciary's discretion to remove the corporate veil in circumstances where the economic realities of a given situation are, when coupled with issues of justice, indicative of a finding that the corporate veil should be removed for the purpose of protecting the interests of an innocent third party. In *Creasey*, it is submitted that the removal of the corporate veil was a just and reasonable exercise of the court's discretion and as such it is submitted that the case should have been distinguished by the Court of Appeal rather than overruled. Although the factual circumstances of *Creasey* were similar to *Ord* v *Belhaven Pubs Ltd*, there was, nevertheless, a significant difference between the two cases. In *Ord* there were strong economic reasons to explain why the assets were transferred away from B; indeed, the Ascot group may have been prejudiced if that transfer had not been undertaken, whereas, in *Creasey*, the justification for the transfer of assets appeared far less significant, in so far as a failure to transfer the assets would have been unlikely to cause any prejudice to the shareholders of Breachwood Motors Ltd, i.e. the motive for the transfer of funds in *Ord* may have been justifiable and indeed, understandable, whereas, the motive for the transfer of the assets in *Creasey* appears to have been far more suspect.

However, in accordance with the decision of Toulson J in *Yukong Lines Ltd of Korea* v *Rendsburg Investments* [1998] BCC 870, it would appear that where in a group relationship a transfer of funds takes place from one company to another, for the purpose of avoiding the incursion of a contingent liability by the transferor, then any ill-perceived motive in relation to the transfer of such funds should be ignored, in respect of considering whether at common law the corporate veil of the transferor may be lifted. Briefly, the facts of this case concerned the repudiation of a charterparty agreement. The issue in the case was whether the agreement had been entered into on behalf of the defendant (D) by its brokers M, or whether Y, an individual who held a majority shareholding in both D and M should, together with L (another company which was controlled by Y) be held liable as undisclosed principals. D had transferred the vast majority of its funds to L, funds which may have been used to meet any liability resulting from the breach of the charterparty. The funds had been transferred from D to L on the actual day of the charterparty's repudiation. Alternatively, it was contended by the plaintiff that the corporate veil of D could be removed on the basis of a fraud/sham or in accordance with the decision of Richard Southwell QC in *Creasey* v *Breachwood Motors Ltd*.

In respect of the fraud argument, this was defeated on the premise that the charterparty was not (unlike, for example, *Gilford Motor Co* v *Horne*, discussed above) entered into with a view to defeating any pre-existing contractual obligation. In relation to the agency argument, the learned judge, in purportedly following *Adams* v *Cape Industries* and in distinguishing *Smith Stone & Knight Ltd* v *Birmingham Corporation*, concluded that an agency agreement could only be established where the relevant parties consented to the agreement; in this case, Toulson J found no such consent, in so far as Y had signed the charterparty agreement in his capacity as the managing director of M, on behalf of R. In effect, Y had signed the agreement as an agent of M and not as its principal or as the principal of R. Clearly, there was no express consent in respect of the alleged agency agreement, but what of implied consent based upon control? Indeed, it is interesting that the learned judge appeared to rule out the significance of such implied consent, despite the fact that in *Adams* v *Cape Industries*, the absolute control of one company by another, or by an individual (Cape's control of AMC), was cited as an example of a façade/agency relationship. Finally, *Creasey* v *Breachwood Motors Ltd* was distinguished, albeit that the grounds given by Toulson J for distinguishing the case were somewhat vague, relating primarily to the fact that, in *Creasey*, unlike the present case, there had been a total transfer of the undertaking.

Summary

Following the Court of Appeal's decision in *Adams* v *Cape Industries*, the courts' ability to pierce or remove the corporate veil is now limited to cases where a company was formed to defeat a pre-existing statutory/contractual obligation or to cases involving an 'enemy corporation'. In addition, the practical effect of removing the corporate veil may be achieved by establishing an agency relationship. The survival of a flexible approach to allow for the removal of the corporate veil, based on the justice of a particular case, would now appear to be very much in the shadow. While the disadvantage of the justice approach is its dependence on the judicially perceived merits of an individual case, a dependence which may lead to uncertainty in the law, the rigidity of the rules expounded in *Adams* v *Cape Industries* may in future lead to an unreasonable and unjust conclusion in situations where the corporate form is used as a shield to protect a holding company (or individual) in a situation where that protection unfairly prejudices the rights of an innocent party.

LIABILITY IN TORT

Where a director of a limited liability company causes the company to be involved in a tortious act, the normal presumption of liability will, in accordance with a company's separate legal identity, be against the company and not the individual officer; see, for example, *Rainham Chemical Works Ltd* v *Belvedere Fish Guano Ltd* [1921] 2 AC 465. Nevertheless, in exceptional circumstances a director may be deemed to be personally responsible for the commission of the tortious act. The ability to impose personal liability against a director will be dependent upon establishing that he exhibited a personal as opposed to a corporate competence for directing or procuring the wrongful act. For instance, in *Fairline Shipping Corp* v *Adamson* [1975] 2 QB 180, although the plaintiff's contract was with a company, a director of that company was held to be personally liable in tort for the performance of a negligent act in so far as the director conducted the negotiations with the plaintiff on a personal as opposed to corporate footing, by for example, personally writing to the plaintiff, as opposed to writing *qua* director on company note paper. The court held that the director had created a clear impression that he was to be personally responsible for carrying out the performance of the contract with the plaintiff.

By contrast, in *Trevor Ivory Ltd* v *Anderson* [1992] 2 NZLR 517, although the director of a company negligently advised the plaintiffs in relation to the manner by which a product, supplied by the company, should be used, the director was held not to be personally liable for the negligent advice, in so far as in his dealings with the plaintiff, the director had always acted *qua* director, that is, he had never sought to deal with the plaintiff other than as an agent of the company.

The evidence to substantiate a claim that a company director should be made personally responsible for the company's commission of a tortious act must be little short of overwhelming, a fact recently illustrated by the decision of the House of Lords in *Williams* v *Natural Life Health Ltd* [1998] 1 BCLC 689. In *Williams*, the plaintiffs entered into a franchise scheme operated by Natural Life Health Ltd (N). The plaintiffs were in part induced into entering into the scheme by the company's marketing brochure which contained misleading statements falsely alluding to the company's expertise in, for example, product knowledge, finance, management techniques and marketing. However, and of more relevance to the claim, the plaintiffs relied upon projected figures which had been drawn up by the company and which had misleadingly projected a profit of £30 000 for the first 18 months of trading. In reality, the plaintiffs made a loss of £38 600 for that period. Following the commencement of proceedings N, originally the sole defendant to the action, was put into liquidation. Thereafter, the plaintiffs' claim was pursued against M, the company's managing director and majority shareholder. M's role in the franchise agreement, albeit of an indirect nature, had nevertheless been a considerable one. Indeed, the company's own purported expertise in franchising was exclusively based upon M's own personal experience of the franchise business. The plaintiffs had relied upon the projected figures for their franchise as a result of M's personal proficiency in the franchise business. M was clearly the principal driving force behind the company.

In accordance with the first instance judgment of Langley J [1996] 1 BCLC 288, the Court of Appeal concluded that a director would only incur personal liability in special and exceptional circumstances. However, the circumstances of this case were such that M was held to be personally liable to the plaintiffs. Hirst LJ, in delivering the leading judgment of the Court of Appeal, analysed the legal principles derived from the decisions of the House of Lords in *Hedley Byrne* v *Heller & Partners Ltd* [1964] AC 465 and *Henderson* v *Merrett Syndicates Ltd* [1995] 2 AC 145. His lordship found that as a prerequisite to establishing M's liability, it was necessary to establish a special relationship between the plaintiff and tortfeasor. Having established that relationship, it was then necessary, in accordance with the facts of the present case, to ascertain whether M had assumed a personal responsibility for the negligent acts and whether the respondents had relied upon that assumption of responsibility. In harmony with the views expressed by Langley J, Hirst LJ asserted that the ability to establish the assumption of responsibility was devoid of any necessity to ascertain any form of personal dealings between the parties. Accordingly, Hirst LJ observed that personal liability could be imposed against a director for an act of negligence where it was evident that he had acted as an instrumental figure in the ordinance of the wrongful act, albeit that his involvement and relationship with the plaintiff was of an implied, as opposed to, an express nature. M's role in the franchise agreement had been a considerable one and as such it was held that there had been, on M's part, an implied assumption of personal responsibility, a responsibility which extended beyond his capacity as a director of the company.

On appeal to the House of Lords, the decision of the Court of Appeal was reversed, notwithstanding that the House accepted that it was patently evident that the respondents relied upon negligent advice. The House found that the responsibility for the negligent act resided in the company and not in M and resolved that the Court of Appeal had misapplied the principles enunciated in *Hedley Byrne & Co v Heller & Partners Ltd* and *Henderson v Merrett Syndicates Ltd*. Lord Steyn, in giving the judgment of the House, stressed that the internal arrangements between a director and his company could never be the foundation of a director's personal liability in tort. Lord Steyn considered that the evidence of the case before him was akin to that represented in *Trevor Ivory Ltd v Anderson*. Although, the company had relied almost exclusively on M's personal expertise, such expertise was never marketed or advanced otherwise than under the company's corporate umbrella. While M viewed and impliedly approved the financial projections for P's franchise business, M never sought to play an active role in their preparation, nor had he ever expressly held himself out as having done so. Further, in dealings with the company, the respondents had not identified M, other than as a part of the company. Lord Steyn remarked (at p 435) that Hirst LJ had been wrong to surmise that:

> the relevant knowledge and experience was entirely his *qua* Mr Mistin (M), and not his *qua* director.'([1997] BCLC 131 at p 153)

Lord Steyn concluded that in so far as M had held himself out at all times as the managing director of a limited company, it followed, that on his part there had never been an assumption of personal responsibility.

In accordance with the common law's strict desire to uphold the independent legal status of a corporate entity, the decision of the House of Lords in *Williams v Natural Life Health Ltd* is, to say the least, of a conforming nature. The decision confirms that a company director's personal liability in tort may never be presumed on the premise that the director held a dominant position in, or was an integral part of the company's directing mind. Further, the decision of the House of Lords expounds the principle that notwithstanding that a director was portrayed by his company as the instrumental figure in respect of any given business venture, the director will not be presumed to have assumed any personal responsibility for that venture other than where he himself expressly or impliedly affirms an assumption of personal responsibility. Accordingly, the assumption of personal responsibility must be evidenced by an act which transgresses the director's corporate authority, to the extent that the accountability for the tortious act will, in reality, become the director's and his alone.

Notwithstanding the House of Lords' decision in *Williams v Natural Life Health Ltd*, the importance of the courts' ability to impose tortious liability, other than as against a company in whose name the tortious act was committed, may be of great significance, especially in respect of a group relationship where, for example, a holding company directs and controls the corporate policy of its subsidiary. In such a relationship, if the subsidiary undertakes the performance of a tortious act at the direct bequest of its holding company, could not the holding company be deemed to be responsible for the said act in a situation where an injured third party expressly or impliedly relied upon the skill and expertise of the holding company?

Indeed, following the recent decision of the Court of Appeal in *Lubbe* v *Cape plc* (unreported, 30 July 1998), it may appear possible to answer the aforementioned question in the affirmative. The primary issue in the said case involved a dispute over the jurisdiction in which a claim in negligence should be made, namely South Africa or England. The action was commenced by a number of ex-employees of a South African company engaged in the asbestos industry. The said company was a subsidiary of Cape plc (C). The plaintiffs sought to advance their claim in the English courts on the ground that C (an English registered company) was itself to be regarded as responsible for the acts of negligence, notwithstanding that the effect of the tortious acts had been perpetrated in South Africa. The plaintiffs alleged that C should be deemed responsible in so far as it exercised *de facto* control over its subsidiary, decisions relating to the policy and management of the subsidiary having been taken in England and not South Africa.

The Court of Appeal concluded that plaintiffs had established that there was a case to answer in the English courts and that C itself could, if the allegations were substantiated, be liable to the plaintiffs. Establishing liability would be dependent on the plaintiffs' ability to prove that C controlled the operation of the South African operation. Interestingly, the Court of Appeal defined control in much broader terms than in *Adams* v *Cape Industries*, by providing that control equated to proving that C's directors and senior personnel were responsible for the decisions which led to the business being carried on in the way that it was, in terms of policy and instructions to the local workforce. Control did not have to be substantiated on the basis that Cape controlled the day-to-day implementation of those policies and instructions (compare the judgments in *Adams* v *Cape Industries*).

DISLODGING THE CORPORATE VEIL BY STATUTE

The Companies Act 1985, permits a company to be incorporated with a separate legal identity and limited liability. However, specific statutory provisions may, in instances where the statutory provision is clear and unambiguous in its intention to disturb the corporate veil, interfere with the privileges normally associated with incorporation (see the general comments of Lord Diplock in *Dimbleby & Sons Ltd* v *NUJ* [1984] 1 All ER 751 at 758). Further, it is to be observed that legislation specifically concerned with the taxation of companies is usually interpreted in a manner so as to prevent the use of the corporate form as an instrument for tax avoidance; see e.g. *Firestone Tyre & Rubber Co* v *Lewellin* [1957] 1 WLR 464.

Examples of statutes which disturb the corporate veil

Section 157(1) of the Environmental Protection Act 1990 (EPA)

This provision disturbs the corporate veil in so far as it provides that any director, manager, secretary or other similar office holder of a company, or a person who was purporting to act in any such capacity, who consented or knew of, or was negligent of the fact that an offence had been committed under any provision of the EPA by the company, will (together with the company) be guilty of that offence. The EPA was implemented to regulate and control, amongst other matters, pollution, waste disposal, genetically modified organisms and hazardous substances on, over or under land.

The Employment Rights Act 1996 (ERA)

Although the case of *Lee* v *Lee's Air Farming Ltd* [1961] AC 12 establishes that a majority shareholder/director of a company can, for the purposes of an insurance contract, be regarded as an employee of the company, UK employment legislation may, in some respects, appear to contradict such reasoning. For example, in *Buchan* v *Secretary of State for Employment* [1997] BCC 145 a shareholder (B) with a 50 per cent holding in a private company was, following the company's liquidation, denied what he perceived to be his right as a full-time employee of the company, i.e. to a claim for a redundancy payment and arrears of wages. Notwithstanding that B had been paid an annual salary, had paid tax and national insurance contributions, he was denied the status of an employee in so far as the ERA was construed in a manner whereby a person in control of a company and who was able to prevent the passing of a motion to dismiss him, was not to be regarded as an employee.

However, it is to be noted that in *Secretary of State* v *Botrill* [1999] BCC 177 the Court of Appeal, in dismissing an appeal from the Secretary of State, upheld a decision of the Employment Appeal Tribunal (EAT) to the effect that a sole shareholder, who was also a director of a company, could be regarded as an employee for the purposes of recovering redundancy payments under the ERA. The Court of Appeal dismissed the Secretary of State's appeal on the premise that there was no one simple test to determine the status of an employee and that the ERA did not itself specify any such test. The court held that the determining factor in the *Buchan* case, namely, a director's influence over voting rights so as to prevent his own dismissal, was one factor to consider amongst a number of other factors in each individual case. Accordingly, no one factor could be taken to be conclusive. The court found that the employment tribunal had been correct in its conclusion that there was a genuine contractual relationship between Mr Botrill and the company.

Although, as stated by the Court of Appeal, each case must be decided on its own merits, it may be possible to distinguish the cases of *Buchan* and *Botrill* on the basis that in the former case, the shareholder/director worked for the company without the benefit of a service contract, whereas in *Botrill*, the director/shareholder worked under the terms of a service contract.

Disturbing the veil to impose liability

Where a statutory provision purports to disturb the corporate veil, its effect will normally be to pierce the corporate veil for the purpose of imposing a liability on a human constituent of the company; the veil will not be completely removed. The overwhelming majority of statutory provisions which have a capacity to dislodge the corporate veil are aimed at curbing and penalising delinquent company directors of insolvent companies. In seeking to impose some form of liability on directors to, for example, contribute towards the debts of a company, the corporate veil is dislodged in the sense that as a separate legal entity a company would normally have an absolute responsibility to discharge its own debts and liabilities. The statutory provisions which target the delinquent activities of company directors of insolvent companies are dealt with in Chapter 21.

Although, as previously stated, the statutory examples of dislodging the corporate veil are predominantly concerned with matters relating to the delinquent activities of company directors involved in the management of insolvent companies, there is, nevertheless, one example of a statutory provision which purports to dislodge the corporate veil for the purpose of imposing a liability on a shareholder, namely, s 24 of the Companies Act 1985. This provision provides that if a company, other than a private company limited by shares or guarantee (companies which are now exempt from the provision as a result of the Companies (Single Member Private Limited Companies) Regulations 1992), carries on business for more than six months with less than two members then any person who (a) was a member of the company during that time and (b) knew it was carrying on business with less than two members, will be jointly and severally liable with the company for the company's debts during the aforementioned requisite period. This statutory provision is very rarely invoked and as a result of the now legitimised 'one-man company' the likelihood of it being applied in the future is even more remote (for an example of a case (pre-implementation of 1992 Regulations) in which the provision was applied, see *Nisbet* v *Sheperd* [1994] 1 BCLC 300). The section, in imposing liability on the company in addition to an individual shareholder, does not completely remove the corporate veil, although where applicable it does seriously disturb the corporate veil by upsetting a shareholder's claim to limited liability.

Finally, it is to be noted that whilst the wording of s 122(1)(g), Insolvency Act 1986 (the just and equitable winding up order provision, discussed in Chapter 23) does not in itself dislodge the corporate veil, the application of this section, in relation to small domestic or quasi-partnership type companies, will usually result in a disturbance to a company's corporate veil. In such cases the court will pierce the corporate veil in order to investigate the relationship between the company's membership. In investigating this relationship the court will then consider whether it is just and equitable to wind the company up. It should also be noted that under ss 459–461 of the Companies Act 1985 (see Chapter 23), the court has a very wide discretion in its power to grant an order for relief to a petitioner who substantiates an action in circumstances where the affairs of a company have been conducted in an manner unfairly prejudicial to the interests of the member. The order may have the effect of disturbing a company's corporate veil; see e.g. *Re Nuneaton Borough AFC (No 2)* (discussed further in Chapter 23).

Suggested further reading

Samuels [1964] JBL 107
Pickering (1968) 31 MLR 481
Smithoff [1976] JBL 305
Whincup (1981) 2 Co Law 158
Dee (1986) 7 Co Law 248
Rixon (1986) 102 LQR 415
Ottolengui (1990) 53 MLR 338
Griffin (1991) 12 Co Law 16

3

THE FORMATION OF A COMPANY

INTRODUCTION

The purpose of this chapter is to examine the procedures and rules relating to the formation of a limited company. For a business concern to obtain the benefits of limited liability it must comply with the registration provisions contained in the Companies Act 1985. Prior to obtaining a certificate of registration, the preparations involved in forming a limited company must be undertaken. A large part of this chapter will concern itself with an analysis of the legal principles in relation to the promotion of a company and the validity of contracts entered into by persons acting for or on behalf of a company prior to its legal incorporation. For issues relating to the reform of this topic, see the Appendix at p. 373.

THE PROMOTION OF A COMPANY

Although companies legislation has never sought to provide a definition of the legal characteristics which identify a promoter, the promoter is nevertheless essential to the creation of a new corporate entity. Although some guidance as to the type of person who would not ordinarily be regarded as a promoter was provided for by s 67(3) of the Companies Act 1985, this section of the Companies Act has since been repealed by the Financial Services Act 1986. Section 67(3) was concerned with the liability of promoters in relation to misleading statements contained within company prospectuses and provided that a person who supplied professional services in order for a business to achieve incorporation, for example, a solicitor, accountant, bank manager, etc. should not ordinarily be regarded as a promoter.

To establish that a person acted as a promoter of a company, the case law is indicative of the necessity to show that the person concerned contributed some essential element towards the incorporation of the company. The level of contribution may be substantial, for example, the negotiation of the purchase of business premises or, on the other hand, it may be less extensive, for example, a person may be deemed to be a promoter by organising the appointment of a company director. In *Whaley Bridge Calico Printing Co v Green* (1879) 5 QBD 109 Bowen J was of the opinion that in deciding the question of whether a person could be properly described as a promoter, the court should bear in mind that:

'The term promoter is not a term of law but one of business, usefully summing up in a single word a number of business operations familiar to the commercial world.' (at p 109)

The promotion of a public or large private company is likely to be undertaken by a professional agency, but where a small business is to be incorporated, the promotion will normally, although not exclusively, be carried out by the owner of the pre-incorporated business.

THE PROMOTER'S DUTIES

A promoter cannot be considered to be an agent or trustee of the company which he undertakes to promote, because prior to incorporation the company has no legal existence. Nevertheless, a promoter occupies a position which the courts have recognised as one which is liable to abuse and one which should therefore be subject to fiduciary duties. A promoter's fiduciary duties are similar to those owed to a company by its directors (for a discussion on directors' duties see Chapter 17). A promoter, in common with a director, is also subject to the common law duty to exercise reasonable care and skill in the performance of his duties.

As a consequence of the promoter's assumed fiduciary position, a promoter must make full disclosure of any personal interest in the promotion process. Accordingly, the promoter must disclose whether he obtained a profit as a result of the promotion of the company concerned. For example, in *Gluckstein* v *Barnes* [1900] AC 200 a syndicate of businessmen purchased the Olympia Exhibition Hall in west London from a company in liquidation for a sum of £140000. The syndicate promoted a company which then purchased the hall for £180000. On the public issue of the company's shares the prospectus disclosed the purchase profit of £40000. However, the prospectus failed to disclose that in addition to purchasing the Olympia Exhibition Hall, the syndicate had also purchased certain secured debts of the insolvent company, i.e. debts secured against the insolvent company's assets. The syndicate purchased the secured debts for £20000 and on the realisation of the insolvent company's assets made a £20000 profit. The House of Lords held that the syndicate, i.e. the promoters of the company, were liable to account to the company for the amount of the undisclosed profit, i.e. £20000.

Disclosure of a promoter's personal interest in the promotion of a company must be made to the company. At one time it was thought that disclosure to the company could only be satisfied by disclosure to a full and independent board of the company's directors; see e.g. *Erlanger* v *New Sombrero Phosphate Co* (1878) 3 App Cas 1218. However, the *Erlanger* case was decided before the decision of the House of Lords in *Salomon* v *A Salomon Ltd* [1897] AC 22 in which disclosure of the balance between the true value of Mr Salomon's business and the overvalued price paid by the company, which he promoted, had never been made to an independent board of directors. As a consequence of the decision of the House of Lords in *Salomon*, it is sufficient for a promoter to satisfy the disclosure duty by making disclosure to those who have invested or are about to invest in the company, i.e. the company's shareholders or potential shareholders; see e.g. *Langunas Nitrate Co* v *Langunas Syndicate* [1899] 2 Ch 392.

Where a promoter fails to disclose any benefit obtained as a result of entering into a contract which is connected to a company's promotion, the contract whilst not void, will be voidable. The company, if it is to successfully rescind the contract, must not delay in avoiding it, neither must its actions or, for that matter its inactivity, be construed as indicative of the ratification of the contract. The restitution of the subject matter of the contract must also be possible, although where it is not, the court may order financial adjustments to be made between the parties.

Much of the case law which is relevant to the extent and enforcement of a promoter's duties is rooted in the mid to late nineteenth century, a time when it was quite a common practice for newly incorporated companies to offer shares to the general public. The duties imposed on promoters were a means by which investors could be protected from any fraudulent attempt on the part of a promoter to obtain undeclared and unwarranted profits from the promotion of what was often an unknown and untested business entity. In today's world the vast majority of public issues take place as a result of established private companies electing to become public companies. As such, the likelihood of fraud is less probable. Nevertheless, the protection of the investing public is still necessary, especially to protect the public interest from offers for company securities which may contain untrue or misleading information (see Chapter 11).

PRE-INCORPORATION CONTRACTS

Prior to incorporation, the promoter(s) of a company will usually be required to enter into contractual agreements appertaining to the future needs of the pre-incorporated company. However, until a company is incorporated it will not exist as a separate legal entity and therefore cannot be bound by contracts made in its name or on its behalf; see e.g. *Natal Land & Colonisation Co* v *Pauline Colliery Syndicate* [1904] AC 120. A company, even after its incorporation, cannot expressly or by conduct retrospectively ratify or adopt a contract made in its name or on its behalf; see e.g. *Re Northumberland Avenue Hotel Co* (1886) 33 Ch D 16. Neither may a company claim to have adopted a pre-incorporation contract by including the terms of the contract within its articles; see e.g. *Browne* v *La Trinidad* (1887) 37 Ch D 1. Indeed, the only method by which a company may take the benefit of a pre-incorporation contract is by entering into a new contract with the party with whom the promoter dealt, i.e. a novation. Evidence of the existence of a novation may be found where the re-negotiation of the terms of the original pre-incorporation contract have resulted in the express or implied creation of a new set of obligations between the company and the other contracting party; see e.g. *Howard Patent Ivory Manufacturing Co* (1888) 38 Ch D 156. It should be observed that neither the company nor the party with whom the promoter originally contracted is obliged to enter into a new contract following the company's incorporation. However, following the Court of Appeal's decision in *Rover International Ltd* v *Cannon Film Sales Ltd* [1988] BCLC 710, where a contract is entered into for the benefit of a company which as of the date of the contract is not incorporated, moneys mistakenly paid by the company to a third party in the belief that the contract was valid may be recovered as against the third party. In addition, the court may grant a *quantum meruit* award to the company for services provided during the period in which the company was under the mistaken belief that the pre-incorporation contract was valid. Equally, the aforementioned remedies may be awarded against a company in circumstances where a third party mistakenly believed that the company with which it had contracted was incorporated and as a consequence of the mistaken belief paid moneys to the company or performed services for that company.

The liability of a promoter

Prior to its legal incorporation, a company does not possess the legal capacity to enter into a contractual relationship. Therefore, where a promoter enters into a contract for or on behalf of the unincorporated company, is the promoter to be regarded as having entered the contract as a principal, i.e. can the promoter sue or be sued on the contract in his own name?

Before the UK's accession to the EC in 1972, common law rules exclusively determined whether a promoter could be regarded as a principal to a pre-incorporation contract. The common law rules operated on the basis of a technical and artificial distinction related to the manner in which the promoter signed the contract. Where a promoter entered into a contract signing the contract as the company's agent, or on behalf of a company, the promoter could be held personally liable on the contract; see e.g. *Kelner* v *Baxter* (1866) LR 2 CP 174. On the other hand, where a promoter entered into a contract by signing the contract using the company's name and merely added his own name to authenticate that of the company's, then, following *Newborne* v *Sensolid* (*Great Britain*) *Ltd* [1954] 1 QB 45, the promoter would not be regarded as a principal to the contract and would hence escape any personal liability for a purported breach of the contract's terms. The contract would be classed as having been made with a non-existent entity and as such would be declared a nullity. However, it should be noted that where a contract was declared a nullity a promoter could still incur liability for breach of warranty, i.e. in a situation where the promoter in authenticating the contract did so as an officer of the company. By authenticating the contract with his own signature, which was expressed to represent the signature of a director of the unincorporated company, the promoter would misrepresent his authority, in so far as at the time of signing the contract the company had no legal existence and therefore no validly appointed officers; see e.g. *Collen* v *Wright* (1857) 8 E & B 647.

As a consequence of the UK's entry to the EC, the UK was obliged to implement Art 7 of the First Company Law Directive. As a result of the UK's implementation of Art 7 the artificial distinction in the rules of common law, as applicable to pre-incorporation contracts, were eradicated. Art 7 provided:

> 'If, before a company has acquired legal personality (i.e. before being formed) action has been carried out in its name and the company does not assume the obligations arising from such action, the persons who acted shall, without limit, be jointly and severally liable therefor, unless otherwise agreed.'

Article 7 was implemented in the form of s 9(2) of the European Communities Act 1972, which subsequently became s 36(4) of the Companies Act 1985 and which is now (as a result of s 130(4) of the CA 1989) s 36C(1) of the Companies Act 1985. Section 36C(1) is expressed in the following form:

> 'A contract which purports to be made by or on behalf of a company at a time when the company has not been formed has effect, subject to any agreement to the contrary, as one made with the person purporting to act for the company or as agent for it, and he is personally liable on the contract accordingly.'

In accordance with s 36C(2) CA 1985, s 36C(1) will apply –

(a) to the making of a deed under the law of England and Wales; and
(b) to the undertaking of an obligation under the law of Scotland as it applies to the making of a contract.

The wording of s 36C(1) is not materially different from that used in its predecessor (s 36(4), CA 1985), the statutory language of both being derived from s 9(2) of the European Communities Act 1972. The effect of s 36C(1) is to render a promoter personally liable on a pre-incorporation contract irrespective of whether the promoter signed the contract in the company's name or on behalf of the company.

One obvious difference between Art 7, and what is now s 36C(1), CA 1985, is that whilst Art 7 expressly states that a company, once formed, may 'assume the obligations' contained within a pre-incorporation contract, s 36C(1) does not. While the party with whom the pre-incorporation contract was made may agree to enter into a new contract with the company (a novation), the new contractual obligation cannot be deemed to be an assumption of the obligation contained in the pre-incorporation contract; the present position subsists despite the fact that in 1962 the Jenkins Committee (Cmnd 1749) recommended that companies should be given the statutory power to adopt pre-incorporation contracts.

Where s 36C(1) is applicable, its effect is to remove the technical distinctions found in the common law prior to the UK's implementation of the EC First Company Law Directive. Indeed, in *Phonogram* v *Lane* [1982] QB 938, Lord Denning stated that the distinction between cases such as *Kelner* v *Baxter* and *Newbourne* v *Sensolid*, had been 'obliterated'. The almost unbelievable facts of *Phonogram* v *Lane* were as follows. A company, to be named Fragile Management Ltd, was to be formed for the purpose of managing a musical band known as 'Cheap, Mean and Nasty'. The plaintiff, Phonogram Ltd, agreed to finance the group to the sum of £12 000, which was to be payable in two instalments. The first payment was sent to the defendant, the group's manager, in anticipation of a recording contract being entered into within a specified time period; the money was to be returned if the contract had not been completed within the time period. For administrative reasons, the cheque was made payable to Jelly Music Ltd – the defendant was a director of that company. The defendant, at the request of the plaintiff, signed the financial agreement 'for and on behalf of Fragile Management Ltd'.

The management company (Fragile Management) was never incorporated. The plaintiff sued the defendant for the return of the first instalment, i.e. £6000. The defendant contended that the then relevant legislation, s 9(2) of the European Communities Act 1972, only applied (in accordance with the French translation of Art 9) to a company already in the course of formation (Fragile Management had never been in the course of formation). The defendant also argued that in accordance with s 9(2) personal liability could only be imposed where a person had contracted as the company's agent, i.e. the defendant argued that as Fragile Management had never been formed, there could be no principal for which an agent could act. Notwithstanding the defendant's protestations, the Court of Appeal held that the wording of s 9(2) of the EC Act 1972, and not the French translation of Art 9, was the provision which it was obliged to construe and in accordance with the interpretation of s 9(2) the defendant was personally liable to account to the plaintiff for the sum in question.

Avoiding section 36C(1) of the Companies Act 1985

In order for a promoter to avoid the threat of being made personally liable on a pre-incorporation contract, an express statement excluding the promoter's liability must be included within the contract, so held in *Phonogram* v *Lane*. Despite the theoretical possibility of the appearance of such a clause, its practical effect would be to prevent the party with whom the promoter dealt from seeking specific performance or damages for non-performance or non-compliance with the terms of the pre-incorporation contract, i.e. neither the company, once incorporated, nor its promoter would be liable.

The judicial interpretation of section 36C(1) of the Companies Act 1985

Section 36C(1) of the CA 1985 deems that a person who purports to contract for a company which, as of the date of the contract, was not then formed may, in relevant circumstances, be made personally liable on the contract. Somewhat surprisingly the section does not provide that a person who purports to act for the company (the promoter) has a right to enforce the terms of a pre-incorporation contract. However, in the light of basic contract law principles, it is to be assumed that both parties would be able to enforce the contract's terms.

Given a wide, but none the less plausible interpretation of s 36C(1) of the CA 1985, the possible application of the section would not exclusively be confined to the standard type of mischief against which it is aimed, i.e. a promoter's ability to escape personal liability in respect of pre-incorporation contracts. Indeed, the section may be interpreted to be potentially applicable to any situation whereby a person contracted on behalf of a company which, as of the date on which the contract was made, was not, for whatever reason, legally incorporated in accordance with registration procedures, i.e. if one construes the term 'formed' to mean legally incorporated.

However, the judicial interpretation of s 36(4) of the CA 1985 and its predecessor, s 9(1) of the European Communities Act 1972 (the wording of both are akin to s 36C(1), CA 1985), adopted a restrictive stance in respect of the applicability of the legislation, a fact which is illustrated by the following three decisions of the Court of Appeal.

The first of the three cases, *Oshkosh B'Gosh Inc* v *Dan Marbel Inc Ltd* [1989] BCLC 507, involved the acquisition of an off-the-shelf company, which in 1979 was acquired under the name of Egormight Ltd. In 1980, the company passed a resolution to alter its name to Dan Marbel Inc Ltd. As a result of an administrative oversight by the company, a certificate confirming that the company's name had been changed, was not issued until 1985. Yet, from 1980 onwards, the company (the first defendants) traded as Dan Marbel Inc Ltd.

The plaintiff, a creditor of the company, commenced an action against the second defendant, who was a director of the company, for the non-payment of debts. The action was commenced against the second defendant on the premise that s 9(2) of the European Communities Act 1972 was applicable. The plaintiff contended that he entered into contracts (on which the debts arose) with the second defendant, who acted on behalf of the company (Dan Marbel Inc Ltd), at a time when that company had not been formed. Strictly speaking, the assertion was correct. Dan Marbel Inc Ltd had not been incorporated until 1985. Nevertheless, the Court of Appeal concluded that s 9(2) of the 1972 Act was not applicable, in that the company with which the plaintiff traded had been formed and was not merely in the process of formation. Whilst the Court of Appeal conceded that the company had been trading under an incorrect name, the court could not appreciate how s 9(2) of the 1972 Act could be successfully pleaded unless the company, as under its first name, was a completely different entity from the company under its second name.

The Court of Appeal reached its conclusion notwithstanding that the company traded under the name of Dan Marbel Inc Ltd at a time when that specific company was without legal existence. Although the second defendant purported to enter into a contract on behalf of a company structure that was in existence at the time the contract was made, the company structure in question could not be identified with a company named Dan Marbel Inc Ltd, i.e. the company registered under the name of Egormight Ltd would most probably have had a completely different constitutional framework to that of Dan Marbel Inc Ltd: different directors, objects, subscribers, etc. The two differently named companies were not, in terms of corporate theory, the same entities. (An action under s 108(4) of the CA 1948 – now s 349(4), discussed in Chapter 20 – was also commenced against the second defendant; this action failed on the basis that the relevant instruments had never been signed, i.e. they were outside the ambit of the section.)

The second of the three cases, *Badgerhill Properties Ltd* v *Cottrell* [1991] BCLC 805, concerned a director of Badgerhill Properties Ltd, Mr Twigg (T), who entered into two contracts with a Mrs Cottrell (C). The contracts related to building work which was to be carried out by two different businesses; both businesses were in fact controlled by Badgerhill Properties Ltd. At the bottom of both contracts the company's name had been misrepresented as Badgerhill Property Ltd, i.e. instead of Badgerhill Properties Ltd.

C alleged that the building work had been carried out in an unsatisfactory manner and claimed damages totalling a sum of £80 000. As Badgerhill Properties Ltd was in a poor financial state, C pursued an action against T under s 36(4) of the CA 1985 on the basis that T had purported to enter into contracts on behalf of a company at a time when the company, i.e. Badgerhill Property Ltd, had not been formed. The Court of Appeal refused to apply s 36(4) on the premise that the contracts were not entered into with a non-existent company Badgerhill Property Ltd, but rather by the businesses controlled by the genuine company, Badgerhill Properties Ltd, a company which had been formed. Woolf LJ stated that:

> 'The only relevance of the name **Badgerhill Property Ltd** appearing on the contractual documents was that it was an indication that the businesses were not being conducted by Mr Twigg personally but by a company and the name of that company was Badgerhill Property. It was not therefore a situation where Badgerhill Property had purported to make the contract.' (at p 813)

However, despite the Court of Appeal's findings, the non-existent company, Badgerhill Property Ltd was, by the appearance of its name on the two contracts, representing itself to be in control and responsible for the businesses operated by Mr Twigg, i.e. theoretically, Badgerhill Property Ltd and not Badgerhill Properties Ltd would have been ultimately responsible for a breach of the contracts entered into by the businesses.

The final case example is that of *Cotronic (UK) Ltd* v *Dezonie* [1991] BCLC 721. In this case the plaintiff company commenced an action for the recovery of a sum of money in respect of building work carried out in their capacity as sub-contractors to a company called Wendaland Builders Ltd (W1), a company controlled by the defendant, Mr Dezonie (D). D contended that the debt owing to the plaintiff was outstanding as a result of a failure on the part of the owner of the property (O), to make payment for the work provided. As a result of O's failure to settle the debt, D commenced third-party proceedings against O.

At first instance, D succeeded in a claim for third-party proceedings against O. As a result of which O appealed on the premise that at the time of entering into the contract with W1, that company had ceased to exist; the company, unknown to D, had at the time of the contract been struck off the Companies Register. Hence, O argued that as it was impossible to contract with an entity which had not been in existence at the time the contract was made, accordingly the contract must have been a nullity and thus void.

In defending this claim, D contended that s 36(4) was applicable, i.e. D should be allowed to sue O for a breach of the contract in much the same way as D could, given different circumstances, have been personally liable to O under the terms of s 36(4). D's contention as to the applicability of s 36(4) was based on the fact that after becoming aware that W1 had been struck off, he had formed and incorporated another company Wendaland Builders Ltd (W2). In effect, therefore, D was a person who had entered into a contract on behalf of a company that had, at the time of the contract, not been formed.

The Court of Appeal concluded that D was not entitled to rely on s 36(4), although he was entitled to a *quantum meruit* award (a monetary claim against O for the building services provided). In reaching its decision, the court stated that it was impossible to argue that D had entered into the contract for the benefit of company W2, for at the time of making the contract, D never had any intention to form company W2, i.e. the contract could not have been made on behalf of W2. As Dillon LJ stated:

> 'At the time of the ... building agreement no one had thought about forming a new company at all. Accordingly it is not possible to say that the contract purports to be made by the new company.' (at p 723)

Yet, despite the apparent logic of Dillon LJ's words, the Court of Appeal's decision in *Cotronic* may nevertheless be criticised in the sense that D actually made the contract on behalf of Wendaland Builders Ltd. As the contract could not have been made on behalf of W1, for at the time of the contract W1 had no legal existence, it must have been made for a company which at the time of the contract, had not been formed, i.e. W2. Therefore, as with the two previously discussed Court of Appeal decisions, it is at least arguable that the case facts of *Cotronic* were technically within the ambit of s 36(4), i.e. if one construes the term 'formed' so used in the section, to mean legally incorporated.

Notwithstanding the above arguments, the Court of Appeal's construction of the statutory language of the section now represented by s 36C of the CA 1985 may be defended as rational in that it is difficult to imagine the section having been designed to impose liability on individuals who enter into contracts with the genuine intention of contracting for or on behalf of a registered company which had been formed in accordance with the registration procedures, but which had mistakenly used an incorrect representation of its name. (Although by comparison, consider the stricter approach taken by the judiciary in relation to the construction of s 349(4) of the CA 1985, discussed in Chapter 20.)

The application of the common law principles

Where the court finds that s 36C(1) is not applicable to the factual situation of a given case, the potential liability of the person who entered into a contract in the name of or on behalf of a company may still fall to be determined by common law principles. As previously discussed, the common law principles created a distinction between, on the one hand, a promoter who signed the contract as agent for or on behalf of the company and on the other hand, a promoter who signed the contract in the name of the company. However, in the cases of *Badgerhill* and *Cotronic*, the Court of Appeal, in seeking to apply the common law principles, relied upon the observations of Oliver LJ, who in *Phonogram v Lane* [1982] QB 938 remarked:

> 'Speaking for myself I am not convinced that the common law position ... depends on the narrow distinction between a signature "for and on behalf of" and a signature in the name of a company or association. The question I think in each case is what is the real intent as revealed by the contract? Does the contract purport to be one which is directly between the supposed principal and the other party, or does it purport to be one between the agent himself, albeit acting for a supposed principal, and the other party? In other words, what we have to look at is whether the agent intended himself to be a party to the contract.' (at p 945)

The Court of Appeal, in applying Oliver LJ's comments to the factual situations found in *Badgerhill* and *Cotronic*, concluded that in both cases the relevant contracts had been made with an intention to bind a company and not the individuals who purportedly acted on behalf of the company.

THE REGISTRATION PROCEDURE

The incorporation of a company must be conducted in accordance with the registration provisions contained in the Companies Act 1985. Provided that the registration procedures are followed, and the object of the incorporation is for a lawful purpose, s 1(1) of the CA 1985 allows any two or more persons to form an incorporated company with or without limited liability by subscribing their names to a memorandum of association (the memorandum of association is dealt with in Chapter 7). However, as a result of the UK's implementation of the EC Twelfth Company Law Directive, s 3A of the CA 1985 now provides for the incorporation of single member companies. A single member company may be formed as either a private company limited by shares or a private company limited by guarantee.

The registration of a company involves the delivery of the following documents (together with a registration fee) to the Registrar of Companies:

- the company's memorandum of association;
- the company's articles of association signed by the subscriber(s) named in the memorandum. (It should be noted that a company may be registered without a formal set of articles, in which case the statutory model of articles found in Table A of the Companies (Tables A–F) Regulations 1985 will be deemed to take effect as the company's articles);
- a statement giving particulars of the company's first director(s) and secretary. (Such persons must consent to so act in the capacity prescribed by the particulars.) The statement must also specify the address of the company's registered office;
- a statutory declaration by a solicitor engaged in the formation of the company or a person named as a director or secretary of the company to the effect that the statutory requirements as to registration have been complied with (s 12(3), CA 1985). (If the company is a public company the declaration must provide that the nominal value of the allotted share capital is not less than £50 000 and that the amount paid up on this sum represents not less than one-quarter of the nominal value.)

The refusal to register a company

Prior to the issue of a registration certificate, the Registrar of Companies must be satisfied that the requirements within the statutory registration procedure have been complied with (s 12(1), CA 1985). For example, the Registrar may refuse to register a company where its proposed objects (contained in the memorandum) are illegal or contrary to public policy. (It should be noted that a trade union cannot be registered as a company under s 10(3) of the Trade Union and Labour Relations (Consolidation) Act 1992.)

A case example of the Registrar's refusal to register a company can be found in *R v Registrar of Companies, ex parte More* [1931] 2 KB 197. Here, the Registrar refused to register a company where its objects provided that it would sell lottery tickets in England, on behalf of an Irish lottery; at that time it was illegal to sell lottery tickets in England. The decision of the Registrar to refuse to register a company is, however, subject to judicial review and the Registrar's decision may be reversed. For example, in *R v Registrar of Companies, ex parte Bowen* [1914] 3 KB 1161, the Registrar refused to register a company under the name of 'The United Dental Service Ltd' because the company, in pursuing a dentistry business, was seeking to operate with unregistered dentists. The Registrar objected to the incorporation on the basis that the title of the company's name implied, in its use of the word 'dental', that the dentists employed by the company would be registered dental practitioners. However, the Registrar's decision was reversed on the basis that the word 'dental' did not necessarily imply that the dentists would be registered. (It should be noted that regulations made under s 29 of the CA 1985 now stipulate that a company wishing to be registered with a name which includes the word 'dental' must first obtain the approval of the Registrar of the General Dental Council.)

THE CHOICE OF A COMPANY NAME

A company's name must be stated in its memorandum, and the name with which a company is registered must not be one which is already included in the index of registered company names (s 26, CA 1985). The Registrar of Companies is not responsible for checking the companies name index prior to the registration of a company, the responsibility for that task falls upon the person in control of the company's promotion process. Section 28(2) of the CA 1985 provides that within 12 months of a company's registration the Secretary of State is permitted to direct a company to change its name in circumstances where the choice of name was the same as or too similar to the name of a company already listed on the register.

Where the Secretary of State refuses to exercise his powers under s 28(2), a company which is already in existence may nevertheless challenge the adoption of a name by a newly incorporated company by the means of a passing off action.

The passing off action

The passing off action is a common law remedy. The action may be pursued by any enterprise, be it an incorporated company, a partnership or a sole trader. An action may be commenced in circumstances where a newly formed business adopts the name of an existing enterprise or a name which is similar to an existing enterprise. In order to substantiate a passing off action, it must also be established that the defendant is engaged in a similar type of business activity to the plaintiff. For example, in *Ewing* v *Buttercup Margarine Co Ltd* [1917] 2 Ch 1, the plaintiff operated an unincorporated dairy products business under the name of Buttercup Dairy Co, a dairy business which specialised in the wholesale and retail sale of margarine. The plaintiff commenced a passing off action against the defendant, an incorporated company named the Buttercup Margarine Co Ltd, which had also been formed to operate a wholesale and retail business in margarine. Although the plaintiff had its principal business activities in Scotland, and the defendant operated in Southern England, the passing off action succeeded. The Court of Appeal was of the opinion that the reputation of the plaintiff enterprise was clearly exploited by the defendant company's choice of name and business activity.

MISCELLANEOUS RESTRICTIONS AND OBLIGATIONS IN RESPECT OF THE USE OF A COMPANY NAME

1 Section 26(1) of the CA 1985 prohibits the insertion of the terms limited, unlimited and public limited company (or their Welsh equivalents) into a company's name otherwise than at the end of the company's name.

2 Where the Secretary of State is of the opinion that the use of a specific name may constitute a criminal offence, the use of the name may be prohibited (s 26(1)(d) and (e), CA 1985).

3 If the Secretary of State considers that the use of a company name would imply a connection with HM government or any local government authority or agency, the Secretary of State may refuse to allow the company concerned to register the name in question (s 26(2), CA 1985 and s 2(1), Business Names Act 1985).

4 A business concern is restricted from adopting a name governed by the terms of the Business Names Act 1985. The prohibited names are listed in the Company and Business Names (Amendments) Regulations 1992; such names may only be used where written permission has been obtained from the government body or other association responsible for the protection of the name.

5 In accordance with s 349 of the CA 1985, a company will be liable to a fine where it fails to legibly make mention of its name (including its limited liability status) in all its business letters, notices, invoices, receipts, letters of credit, bills of exchange, cheques and other instruments which confer a monetary obligation on the part of the company.

6 A company's registered name must be clearly and conspicuously affixed or painted on the outside of every office or other premise from where it conducts its business. A company (and every officer of it who is in default) which fails to do so will be liable to a fine (s 348, CA 1985). The abbreviation 'Ltd' for a private limited company and 'plc' for a public limited company will suffice for the purposes of ss 348 and 349 as will the abbreviation 'Co' to represent company. The word 'and' may also be represented by the abbreviation '&'.

7 A business which represents itself (in the last word of its name) to be a limited liability company when in fact it is not a limited liability company is liable to a fine (s 34, CA 1985).

THE SECRETARY OF STATE'S ABILITY TO ORDER A COMPANY TO CHANGE ITS NAME

In accordance with s 32 of the Companies Act 1985, the Secretary of State has the power to order a company to change its name within a period of five years from the date on which the offending name was first registered. The company may, within three weeks of the Secretary of State's direction, apply to the court to set the direction aside. The Secretary of State may exercise this power when of the opinion that the use of the name resulted, or could have resulted in a misleading indication of the business activities of the company – misleading to the extent of causing harm to the public interest. The provision was subject to its first judicial consideration in 1997, namely in *Association of Certified Public Accountants of Britain* v *Secretary of State for Trade and Industry* [1997] 2 BCLC 307. Here Jacob J held that it is for the Crown to establish that a company's name offends the statute. The learned judge in formulating a legal test, concluded thus:

> '... what the court has to do is to decide on the evidence whether the name of the company gives so misleading an indication of the nature of its activities as to be likely to cause harm to the public. It is not sufficient to show that a name is misleading; a likelihood of harm must be shown too. In many cases the latter will follow from the former, but this is not necessarily so: it is difficult to imagine harm, for instance, if a company called Robin Jacob (Fishmongers) Ltd in fact carried on a business of bookbinding.' (at p 311)

It should also be observed that where a company's name was obtained by means of deception, the Secretary of State may also within a five-year period compel the company concerned to alter its name (s 28(3), CA 1985).

Where a company is ordered to change its name, the procedure for doing so is quite straightforward, i.e. by the passing of a special resolution (s 28(1), CA 1985). Nevertheless, the economic dangers inherent in a company having to change its name may be quite serious. For example, after a few years of trading under a specific company name, that name may have become associated with the company's product range to such an extent that a change in corporate name may result in a failure by the general public to associate the product with the newly adopted name of the company, a factor which could adversely affect the company's image and share value.

THE CERTIFICATE OF INCORPORATION

A company is legally incorporated upon the issue of a certificate of incorporation. The certificate of incorporation identifies the company registered by its name and allotted serial number and is conclusive of the fact that all the requirements of the statutory registration procedures have been complied with (s 13(7), CA 1985). The certificate is also conclusive of the status of the company registered, i.e. if the certificate provides that a company is registered as a public limited company then the certificate is conclusive of that matter.

A company, having obtained a certificate of incorporation, is permitted as from the date of the certificate to enter into business activities as a registered company. For example, in *Jubilee Cotton Mills Ltd* v *Lewis* [1924] AC 958, a company's certificate of incorporation was incorrectly dated 6 January 1920, the certificate having not been signed by the Registrar until 8 January 1920. Nevertheless, the House of Lords held that an issue of shares made by the company on 6 January was valid. Notwithstanding that a mistake had been made in respect of the date of the company's incorporation, the certificate's date was, in law, conclusive proof of the fact that the company's incorporation took effect from 6 January 1920.

Except in a case where the Crown (which is not bound by s 13(7), CA 1985) challenges the legality of the objects for which a company was formed, the legal existence of a company cannot be challenged once the certificate of incorporation has been issued. An example of the Crown's ability to challenge the objects of a company can be found in *R v Registrar of Companies, ex parte Attorney General* [1991] BCLC 476. The case involved a company which had been formed with objects which sought to establish a prostitution business. Although the Registrar had previously refused to register the company under the names of 'Prostitute Ltd', 'Hookers Ltd' and 'French Lessons Ltd', the company was finally permitted to be registered under the name of Lindi St Clair (Personal Services) Ltd. Despite the fact that the company had surmounted all the procedural requirements for registration, its objects were clearly contrary to the public interest. As such, the court held that the Registrar had erred in granting the company's registration certificate. Accordingly, the company was struck off the companies register.

Where the Crown successfully brings proceedings to strike a company off the companies register, the company's existence is retrospectively denied. In law, the company will be regarded as an enterprise which never attained incorporation in accordance with the provisions of companies legislation. As such, any outstanding contractual obligations incurred by the business whilst it was on the companies register will be rendered void, i.e. a contract cannot be enforced against a party where that party never attained a legal existence or capacity. (Although this type of situation may be within the theoretical ambit of s 36C(1) of the CA 1985, the judicial interpretation of s 36C(1) would clearly be dismissive of such an action (discussed above).)

The Crown's ability to commence proceedings to strike a company off the register may be harmful to creditors and the practice must be considered to be questionable, especially when an alternative course of action is available under s 122(1)(g) of the IA 1986, i.e. under which a company registered with illegal objects may be wound upon just and equitable grounds, see e.g. *Re International Securities Corporation* (1908) 99 LT 581. To allow the company to be wound up in such circumstances would provide the company's creditors with an opportunity of making a claim against the company's assets. It should be noted that the Crown's powers would also seem contrary to the EC First Company Law Directive (Art 12(3)) which provides that:

> **'Nullity shall not of itself effect the validity of any commitments entered into by or with the company, without prejudice to the consequences of the company's being wound up.'**

Commencement of business

A private company may commence business from the date of its incorporation, whereas a public limited company must, prior to the commencement of its business, wait until it has received a trading certificate (s 117, CA 1985). Where a public company commences business prior to receipt of a trading certificate any party with whom the company dealt will nevertheless be protected, i.e. the contract will not be set aside. However, the company and any officer in default of the provision will be liable to a fine.

Off-the-shelf companies

A registered company may be purchased from an agency specialising in the sale of what are commonly known as off-the-shelf companies. An off-the-shelf company is one which has been incorporated in accordance with the registration provisions of the Companies Act, normally having a minimal share capital (usually two £1 shares). The ultimate purpose for its incorporation being its subsequent sale. The advantage to a prospective purchaser of an off-the-shelf company is the speed, relatively low cost and ease by which a business can attain a corporate form. On the payment of a fee (to the agency supplying the off-the-shelf company) the relevant transfers of shares and company's registers will be conveyed to the purchasers of the company. Notification in the change of address of the company's registered office, company directors and secretary, will then be made. The new shareholders of the company may also, if they so wish, change, in accordance with relevant statutory procedures, the company's name and make any other amendment to the company's constitution as they see fit, for example change the company's objects, the company's articles and the contents of the company's memorandum.

Suggested further reading

Pre-incorporation contracts
Prentice (1973) 89 LQR 518
Green (1984) 47 MLR 671
Griffiths (1993) 13 LS 241

4

THE CLASSIFICATION OF COMPANIES

INTRODUCTION

This chapter examines the various types of corporate entity. In addition, the rules applicable to altering the corporate status of a company are also considered. The relationship between a holding company and its subsidiaries, i.e. the group relationship, is also investigated. The chapter concludes with a brief analysis of the differences between a company and a partnership. For issues relating to the reform of this topic, see the Appendix at p. 373.

TYPES OF COMPANY

Although registered companies only represent about one-third of the UK's population of business structures – partnerships and sole traders are by far the most common form of business medium – the registered company, i.e. a company incorporated as a consequence of compliance with the registration procedures laid down by the Companies Act 1985 (or previous Companies Acts), is by far the most common type of corporate entity. While s 716 of the CA 1985 provides that a company may be formed in pursuance of an Act of Parliament (other than by the Companies Act 1985) or alternatively by royal charter, today the latter two methods of incorporation are rarely adopted. Companies granted corporate status by royal charter are normally institutions with either charitable aims or objectives relevant to the public interest, for e.g. the British Broadcasting Corporation (BBC).

Registered companies

A company registered in accordance with the provisions of the Companies Act 1985 will take one of the following forms:

- a public company limited by shares;
- a private company limited by shares;
- a private company limited by guarantee; or
- a private company which is unlimited.

Prior to 22 December 1980, it was possible to register a fifth type of company, i.e. a private or public company limited by guarantee but with a share capital. While it is no longer possible to register this type of company (see s 1(4), CA 1985), a company which was registered prior to 22 December 1980, as a company limited by guarantee with a share capital, may still operate in that form.

Public companies limited by shares

A company which proposes to operate as a public company must, as from 1980, have been specifically registered as a public limited company. A public company must have at least two shareholders and two directors; a private company need only have one shareholder and one director. Before a public company can trade it must be registered with a minimum share capital of £50 000.

Prior to 1980, a company was classed as a public company if (a) it had a membership in excess of 50, (b) the general public could subscribe for its shares, and (c) no restriction was placed on the transferability of its shares. The pre-1980 position, which had survived since the Companies (Consolidation) Act 1908, was altered by the Companies Act 1980, which implemented the EC Second Company Law Directive. The Directive established a requirement to create a formal distinction between the identification of public and private companies. As a result of the implementation of the Directive by the 1980 Act, a public company had to be identified (at the end of its name) as a public limited company (plc).

In accordance with s 1(3) of the CA 1985, any company which is not registered as a public company is to be construed as a private company. Unlike a private company, a public company may offer its securities to the general public. Whilst a public company is entitled to offer its securities to the general public, it is not bound to do so, but where its shares are so offered, it has the option of applying to have them listed for dealing on the stock exchange (see Chapter 11). Unless a public company registers its own form of articles, its articles will take the form of the Table A articles prescribed by the Companies (Tables A–F) Regulations 1985. A public company's memorandum should follow the format of Table F of the Companies (Tables A–F) Regulations 1985.

Private companies limited by shares

Private companies, limited by shares, represent the vast majority (approximately 98 per cent) of all limited companies registered in the UK. Many private limited companies are small concerns, the shareholders of which are often participants in the management of the company. These small concerns may usually be classified as domestic/family type companies and/or companies formed as a result of the incorporation of a small unincorporated business. The relationship between the shareholders of a small private company is one which is usually built upon mutual trust and confidence. As such, the courts have, in respect to the applicability of company legislation, developed flexible attitudes towards such companies. The judicial approach to small companies is positively influenced by partnership law principles, especially in relation to the interpretation of statutory provisions concerned with the protection of minority shareholders. (The protection of minority shareholders is discussed in Chapter 22.)

Although the vast majority of private companies are small concerns, there is no legal compulsion on the part of a successful private company to re-register as a public company. Indeed, the shareholders of a large and successful private company may wish to retain its private limited liability status so as to exert control over the company's destiny, rather than risking the possibility of losing a controlling interest in the company by altering its status to a public limited company so as to offer shares to the general public. Unlike a public company, a private company cannot offer its securities to the general public (s 81, CA 1985).

The format of a private company's articles will usually follow (but they are not compelled to) the statutory prescribed format of Table A of the Companies (Tables A–F) Regulations 1985. A private company's memorandum should follow the format of Table B of the Companies (Tables A–F) Regulations 1985.

Private companies limited by guarantee

Whilst the majority of private limited companies are limited by shares, a private company may be limited by guarantee. A private company limited by guarantee is one whereby the company's memorandum provides for a liability on the part of the company's members to contribute a fixed sum of money towards the debts of the company (the amount guaranteed), should the company be wound up. A member's fixed sum liability cannot be altered and continues for so long as the member's membership of the company is retained or, in certain circumstances, where the company's liquidation occurs within a year of the member having left the company, see s 2(4) of the CA 1985 and s 74(2) of the IA 1986.

The form of articles and memorandum to be adopted by a company limited by guarantee is prescribed by Table C of the Companies (Tables A–F) Regulations 1985. In the case of a company limited by guarantee and incorporated before 1980, the company may have been incorporated with a share capital; the form of articles and memorandum of a company limited by guarantee and with a share capital is prescribed by Table D of the Companies (Tables A–F) Regulations 1985.

The most appropriate type of company to be registered as a private company limited by guarantee is one with charitable objectives in so far as any profits made by the company will not be distributed as dividend payments, i.e. the company will not normally have any shareholders. The members' capital is kept in reserve and may be called upon in the case of the company's liquidation. Unlike the uncalled share capital of a company limited by shares, the sums of money guaranteed from the company's members are not assets of the company and therefore cannot be used as a means to repay or secure any of the company's debts.

Single member companies

The Companies (Single Member Private Limited Companies) Regulations 1992 (SI 1992/1699) were brought into force on 15 July 1992 to comply with the EC Twelfth Company Law Directive. The regulations give effect to the birth of the single member private limited company. The single member may be either a natural person or a legal person, i.e. the single member may be a corporate entity. The regulations provide that in the absence of any express provision to the contrary, any enactment or rule of law applicable to a private company limited by shares or guarantee, having two or more members, will apply with such modification as may be necessary for companies formed by one person or with only one person as a member (reg 2(1)).

Although Art 2(2) of the Directive makes provision for individual member states to lay down special regulations or sanctions to prevent the possible abuse of the single member company as a corporate form, the UK decided against imposing regulatory conditions, save for the provision that a single member company could not be registered as a public company.

The open-ended investment company

In accordance with the Investment Companies with Variable Capital Regulations 1996 (SI 1996/2827), which came into force on 6 January 1997, a new type of body corporate has been created, namely, the open-ended investment company (OEIC). An OEIC is a company which is permitted to redeem its own shares for cash. The purpose of this type of company is strictly limited to managing a portfolio of investments on behalf of its members. An OEIC may issue more than one class of share and its shares may be traded on an investment exchange. However, an OEIC is not required to have a share capital and does not have par value shares. As its share capital is not of a sufficiently fixed natue, this type of company is exempt from the City of London's Code on Takeovers and Mergers and the Rules Governing Substantial Acquisitions of Shares.

The unlimited company

The unlimited company is a separate legal entity and possesses the characteristics of a corporate entity. However, the members of this type of private company do not have the advantage of limited liability. In many respects a private unlimited company is similar to a partnership concern (discussed below). However, unlike a partnership, the creditors of an unlimited company cannot ordinarily sue the individual members of the company for the repayment of business debts. In order to compel members of an unlimited company to contribute towards the payment of the company's debts, it is necessary for the creditors of the company to seek an order for the company to be wound up.

On the winding up of an unlimited company the members contribute towards the assets of the company in accordance with the terms of the company's memorandum or articles. Where the memorandum or articles have not specified a procedure for such contributions, calls are made equally upon all the contributories; if a member cannot meet the terms of his contribution, the other members of the company will be obliged to make good this loss.

Whilst the liability of the members of an unlimited company is not limited by shares, an unlimited company may have a share capital, in which case the form of the company's articles and memorandum is prescribed by Table E of the Companies (Table A–F) Regulations 1985. On the winding up of an unlimited company with a share capital, calls for contributions to the assets of the company will, in the first instance, be made against those members of the company with capital unpaid on their shares. Where such contributions are insufficient to meet the debts of the company further calls must be made in proportion to the nominal value of each of the contributor's shares. One practical advantage of forming an unlimited company, as opposed to a limited company, is that the many disclosure requirements applicable to limited companies do not apply.

PROPOSED NEW CORPORATE STRUCTURES

The partnership company

Partnership companies are defined by the Department of Trade and Industry (DTI) as private or public companies which share a common characteristic of having employees who hold a substantial proportion of the company's shares. The DTI considers that the meaning of the term 'substantial holding' should vary from company to company, albeit that it should constitute a shareholding of at least 15 per cent. Provision will be made for such a company under s 8A of the Companies Act 1985 (inserted by s 128, CA 1989). Under s 8A(1), the Secretary of State will, by regulation, be able to prescribe a Table G containing articles of association for a partnership company, Table G will be optional.

The limited liability partnership

Legislation for the purpose of establishing a new business structure, the limited liability partnership, will, when enacted, purport to limit a partners liability in respect of a partnership business. However, the legislation is, in accordance with the draft Bill (published in 1998) only applicable to specific regulated professions. The proposed limited liability partnership will be available to a partnership comprising two or more members and will be a body corporate in its own right. Accordingly, its members will have no personal liability for its acts or obligations except as provided for by the statute or under the general law.

In the draft Bill, the DTI sets out its intention that the limited liability partnership will be subject to financial requirements and safeguards akin to those which are applicable to other limited liability concerns. Accordingly, financial and other information will need to be filed on a regular basis, for example, the partnership will be obliged to file accounts with the Registrar of Companies. Further, the delinquent activities of members of the partnership will be subject to similar sanctions to those imposed against company directors, for example, wrongful and fraudulent trading and disqualification.

THE DEREGULATION OF PRIVATE COMPANIES

The modern-day legislative policy has seen a radical departure from a call for the unification of the rules applicable to private and public companies which prevailed in the 1960s. The change of attitude has largely been due to the UK's need to encourage the growth of small private enterprises. The desire to expand the population of small private companies has met with a need to remove certain formal requirements previously applicable to all limited liability companies, requirements which were generally apt to discourage and hamper the creation of the small corporate enterprise. For example, Sch 4, CA 1985 allows small and medium-sized companies to deliver abbreviated accounts to the Registrar.

The Companies Act 1989, whilst not radically altering the applicability of a common set of company law rules for both private and public companies, has nevertheless introduced a legislative programme which in future years is likely to be expanded, with the probability that a distinguishable split will be created between the legislature's treatment of private and public companies. The reforms implemented by the 1989 Act are generally to be welcomed in so far as they reduce the administrative burdens of a private company by, for example, dispensing with the statutory requirement to pass resolutions at general meetings of the company and more significantly by introducing a system of elective resolutions. (The reforms introduced by the 1989 Act are discussed further in Chapter 18.)

Although there would seem to be an obvious need to encourage the expansion of small business enterprises, there is, however, an inherent danger in the apparent legislative move towards the reduction of legislative obligations applicable to the creation and running of small private limited companies. While the founding members of small private companies may be required to give personal guarantees to large lending institutions for moneys borrowed on behalf of their companies, small trade creditors will not generally be afforded such guarantees, neither in most cases will their debts be secured against the company's assets. Therefore, if the 'price' to be paid, in respect of the obligations required for the incorporation and regulation of a limited liability company is diminished, to the extent that the incorporation of vastly unorganised and undercapitalised concerns is unwittingly encouraged, the small trade creditor, an essential constituent of the UK's economy, will undoubtedly be prejudiced. It must always be remembered that while the concept of limited liability is a valuable shield which affords protection to the human constituents of a corporate enterprise against the imposition of personal liability, it is nevertheless a shield which should not be allowed to be transformed into a corporate sword.

The relaxation in the ability to incorporate and administer a limited liability company may also have the effect of devaluing the prestige attributed to the general standing of the concept of limited liability. The trust and confidence of the business community in small private limited companies has, from the time of *Salomon v A. Salomon Ltd*, been tinged with suspicion and further moves to relax its regulation may result in a more emphatic loss of confidence. While, as previously stated, the reforms incorporated in the 1989 Act are to be welcomed, the move towards a more relaxed and distinct regime of private limited companies should be viewed with some caution. To safeguard the value of the concept of limited liability it may, for example, be beneficial to increase the registration fee for incorporation (which in October 1994 was in fact reduced from £50 to £20) and also to follow our European counterparts, all of which, save for Ireland, specify a minimum capital requirement for the incorporation of small limited companies.

Another potential solution could be found in the creation of a new type of incorporated company, a company especially designed and tailored to meet the needs of very small concerns, a type of private company which would trade without a limited liability status. However, the creation of such a company was rejected in a feasibility study carried out by the Law Commission into the reform of company law for private companies (published by the DTI, November 1994). Indeed, other than if private limited companies were required to have a minimum capital requirement, it seems highly improbable whether the incorporation of such a company would, in its removal of the privileges afforded to a limited liability company, ever be viewed by small businesses as an attractive proposition.

GROUPS OF COMPANIES

Notwithstanding that each individually registered company is a separate legal entity responsible for its own actions and liable for its own debts, it is quite a common feature of the UK's corporate structure to find companies which belong to a group structure. A holding company heads a group of companies, a company(ies) which is directly or indirectly under the control of the holding company is termed a subsidiary company(ies). The importance of the holding company/subsidiary relationship is apparent in a number of provisions contained within the Companies Act 1985 and related legislation. Where appropriate, such provisions will be considered within individual chapters of this book.

A holding company/subsidiary relationship is legally defined by s 736 of the CA 1985 (as amended by s 144, CA 1989). Section 736(1) provides that a company is a subsidiary of a holding company if:

- the holding company holds a majority of the voting rights in the company; or

- the holding company is a member of the company and has the right to appoint or remove a majority of the company's board of directors; or
- the holding company is a member of the company and controls alone or in agreement with other shareholders or members of the company, a majority of the voting rights in the company.

In addition, a company will be classed as a subsidiary of a holding company where the company is a subsidiary of another company which is itself a subsidiary of the holding company. A company is classed as a wholly owned subsidiary of another company if its membership is exclusively comprised of a holding company and/or the subsidiaries of the holding company, or persons acting on behalf of the holding company and/or its subsidiaries (s 736(2), CA 1985).

For the purposes of s 736(1), it is provided by s 736A(2) of the CA 1985 that, in calculating voting control, the 'voting rights' are those rights held by the shareholders (or members where a company does nor have a share capital) in relation to their ability to vote at general meetings on all or substantially all matters. The right to appoint or remove a majority of the directors in accordance with s 736(1) is defined by s 736A(3) as the right to appoint or remove directors holding the majority of voting rights at board meetings on all or substantially all matters. A company is treated as having the right to appoint a person to a directorship (of the subsidiary) if the appointment necessarily follows from that person's appointment as a director of the company, or where the directorship is held by the company itself.

The amendments made to s 736 of the CA 1985 by the Companies Act 1989 have rightly transformed the emphasis on determining the existence of a holding company/subsidiary relationship away from a previous reliance on whether control existed as a consequence of a holding company holding more than a 50 per cent share of another company's equity share capital. Prior to the amendment of s 736, the holding company/subsidiary relationship could have existed in a situation where the holding company did not have voting control in the subsidiary, i.e. whilst holding more than 50 per cent of a company's equity share capital, the equity share capital of the company could have been divided into shares carrying different voting rights to the extent that a 50 per cent holding of the share capital did not necessarily equate to a 50 per cent control over voting rights. Conversely, a company, prior to the amendment to s 736 could have escaped being classed as a holding company by holding less than 50 per cent of the company's share capital, irrespective of the fact that it could have controlled the company's voting rights. Thus, the amended s 736, in its adoption of voting control as the principal criteria to determine the holding company/subsidiary relationship, is more realistic in its approach to the determination of control. (It should be noted that under s 736B the Secretary of State has power to amend ss 736 and 736A, CA 1985.)

Accounting purposes

The definition of a group of companies for the purpose of auditing and accounting matters is dealt with by s 258 of the CA 1985 (introduced by s 21, CA 1989). The statutory requirement for a holding company to produce group financial statements has been in force since 1947. The requirement is necessary to produce a true and accurate financial overview of companies which, whilst independent entities, are nevertheless closely related and under the influence of a dominant company. Prior to the implementation of the new s 258 of the CA 1985, the legislature made no distinction between the definition of a holding company/subsidiary relationship for the purpose of group accounts and the definition of a group relationship for other purposes. A distinction was required as a result of the UK's need to comply with the EC Seventh Company Law Directive. The distinction was thought necessary in order to widen the criteria by which companies could be made responsible for the preparation of group accounts in a situation where a company exerted a dominant influence over another business enterprise.

In accordance with s 258, a group relationship is now defined as a parent/subsidiary relationship. Whilst the parent business must be a corporate entity, the subsidiary may be any form of 'undertaking', corporate or otherwise. Section 258 is framed in similar terms to s 736 of the CA 1985, save that s 258 provides additional criteria by which a parent/subsidiary relationship is to be established. In addition to the definitions found in s 736, s 258 provides that a parent/subsidiary relationship exists in a situation where a company has the right to exercise a dominant influence over another company by virtue of provisions contained in the other company's memorandum or articles or by virtue of a control contract (s 258(2), CA 1985). The section also provides for the finding of a parent/subsidiary relationship where a company has a participating interest in another company and actually exercises a dominant influence over that other company, or where both companies are managed on a unified basis (s 258(4), CA 1985). A participating interest will normally amount to a holding of at least 20 per cent of the shares of an undertaking (s 260(3), CA 1985).

Where a parent/subsidiary relationship exists, the group accounts must, as a result of s 227(2) of the Companies Act 1985, be in a consolidated form. The parent company is also obliged to produce its own individual accounts in addition to the consolidated group accounts (see new Sch 4A, CA 1985). It is to be noted that the statutory requirement for a parent company to prepare consolidated accounts ignores the individual and independent characteristics of the subsidiary company as a separate legal entity. Therefore, for accounting purposes, a group of companies is treated as one economic entity.

The membership of a holding company

A subsidiary or a subsidiary's nominee is not permitted to be a member of its holding company and any allotment of shares to the subsidiary from its holding company will be void (see new s 23(1), CA 1985, introduced by s 129, CA 1989). The general prohibition contained in s 23(1) is, however, subject to the following exceptions:

- a subsidiary which was a member of its holding company on 1 July 1948 is permitted to continue as a member of the holding company;
- a company which was not a subsidiary of any other company prior to the enactment of s 144 of the CA 1989 but, which as a result of the new legislation, is now classed as a subsidiary company, may also retain its membership of its holding company;
- s 23(1) of the CA 1985 is not applicable where the subsidiary or its nominee holds shares in the holding company in the capacity of a personal representative or trustee. However, this exception will not apply where the holding company or subsidiary has a beneficial interest under the trust (s 23(2), CA 1985). An interest in the holding company's shares, held only by way of security for the purposes of a transaction entered into by the holding company or subsidiary in the ordinary course of business, which includes the lending of money, will be disregarded for the purposes of determining whether the holding company or subsidiary is beneficially interested;
- the general prohibition contained in s 23(1) does not apply where the subsidiary is concerned as a market maker. A market maker is a person who holds himself out and is permitted by a recognised investment exchange, other than an overseas investment exchange, as willing to buy and sell securities in accordance with the rules of the exchange (s 23(3), CA 1985). It should be noted that as a consequence of the Companies (Membership of Holding Company) (Dealers in Securities) Regulations 1997 (SI 1997/2306) market makers have, in respect of the Stock Exchange Electronic Trading Service (SETS), been replaced by 'intermediaries' for the purpose of buying and selling shares in an electronic order facility. The effect of the amendment will allow intermediaries who are owned by financial institutions, to deal in the securities of their parent company.

It should be noted that where a subsidiary remains a member of its holding company, it will not be permitted to vote at general meetings or at separate class meetings of the holding company.

CHANGING THE STATUS OF A COMPANY

A registered company may at some time during the course of its existence wish or be obliged to change the status with which it was originally registered. For example, a rapidly expanding private company limited by shares, in a desire to secure further capital to finance future growth, may decide that it must, in order to expand, increase its share capital by offering its securities to the general public. In order to legitimately offer its securities to the general public, the company must re-register itself as a public company. Conversely, where a public company's issued share capital falls below the minimum requirement of share capital permitted for a public company, the public company must re-register itself as a private company. The following statutory rules provide the framework by which a company may change its registered status.

Private limited company to a public limited company

A private limited company, other than a private company which is without a share capital, may change its status to become a public company by complying with the procedures laid down by ss 43–48, CA 1985. The procedures require, *inter alia*, the calling of a general meeting of the company to pass a special resolution to effect the company's re-registration as a public company. The special resolution must alter, where necessary, the form of the company's articles and memorandum in order to comply with the statutory requirements for conformity with the articles and memorandum of a public limited company. If the Registrar of Companies is satisfied that a private limited company has complied with all the necessary statutory requirements applicable for its re-registration, the company will be issued with a new certificate of incorporation confirming its status as a public limited company.

Public limited company to a private limited company

In accordance with ss 53–55 of the CA 1985, a public company may alter its status to that of a private company which is either limited by shares or guarantee. A public company may be re-registered as a private company where the general meeting of the company pass a special resolution to that effect. The special resolution must, where necessary, alter the terms of the company's articles and memorandum so as to comply with the registration requirements for a private company.

A public limited company's application to re-register as a private company may be challenged within 28 days of the resolution having been passed to approve the company's change of status (s 54(3), CA 1985). The ability to challenge the application provides a possible safeguard for shareholders who hold shares for investment or speculative reasons, because the loss of public limited status may result in the shareholders having obvious difficulties in realising their investment in the company, i.e. the possible market in which shares can be sold will be severely restricted. Another potential difficulty for this class of shareholder will be the loss of a tangible market value for the shares; the ascertainment of the market value of a share in a private company may prove an especially difficult task (discussed in Chapter 10).

An application made to the court to cancel the resolution to alter the status of a public company may be commenced by holders of not less than 5 per cent in nominal value of the company's issued share capital, or holders of 5 per cent of any specific class of share, or by not less than 50 of the company's members. A shareholder of the company has the right to challenge a proposed change to the company's status provided that the shareholder in question did not consent or vote in favour of the resolution to amend the company's status (s 54(2), CA 1985). On hearing the application to challenge the resolution, the court may order that it should be confirmed or cancelled. The court may also make the order subject to specific terms, for example, it may compel the company to purchase the shares of the dissentient members (s 54(5), CA 1985).

When the Registrar is satisfied that the requirements of the re-registration process have been complied with, the company will be issued with a certificate of incorporation confirming the company's status as a private company (s 55, CA 1985).

Private limited company to an unlimited company

A private limited company may seek re-registration as an unlimited company in accordance with ss 49–50 of the CA 1985. A public limited company cannot re-register as an unlimited company (s 49(3), CA 1985). For a private company limited by shares or guarantee to be permitted to re-register as an unlimited company, the company must have had no previous existence as an unlimited company (s 49(2), CA 1985). To comply with the re-registration formalities, the company must make all the necessary amendments to its memorandum and articles. The entire membership of the company must assent to the change in status (s 49(8), CA 1985) because on the company becoming unlimited the membership will be exposed to the risk of having to make contributions towards the company's debts, should the company become insolvent. Following compliance with the requirements of s 49, the Registrar will issue the company with a certificate of incorporation confirming the company's status as unlimited (s 50, CA 1985).

Unlimited company to a private limited company

Provided that an unlimited company complies with the statutory requirements of s 51 of the CA 1985, it is entitled to re-register as a private limited company. In order to change its status, s 51 requires the unlimited company to pass a special resolution to effect the change. The resolution must state whether the company is to be limited by shares or by guarantee; in either case the resolution must provide for the necessary alterations to be made to the company's articles and memorandum so as to comply with the registration requirements for a limited company.

A company which is re-registered as an unlimited company in accordance with s 49 of the CA 1985 cannot by virtue of s 51 of the CA 1985 be subsequently re-registered as a private limited company. It should be noted that where a company, previously registered as an unlimited company, is wound up within three years of its re-registration as a limited company, both the present and past members of the company may be personally liable to contribute towards its debts (see s 77, IA 1986).

Unlimited company to a public limited company

Where an unlimited company wishes to re-register as a public limited company (s 43, CA 1985), it must comply with the change in status requirements applicable to a change in status from a private to a public limited company and further, the unlimited company must include within the terms of the special resolution, effecting the change, the fact that it is to be limited by shares (s 48(2), CA 1985). If an unlimited company was previously registered as a limited company, it cannot under the procedures contained in ss 43–48 of the CA 1985 be subsequently re-registered as a public limited company.

A COMPARISON BETWEEN REGISTERED COMPANIES AND PARTNERSHIPS

A business partnership is a relationship between persons carrying on a business in common with a view to profit (s 1, Partnership Act 1890). Property vested in a firm belongs to its members and not the partnership business. A partnership, unlike a registered company, is not a separate legal entity, although it may be permitted to sue or be sued in the partnership name. Although the Limited Partnership Act 1907 allows a member of a partnership to attain a limited liability status, a partner with such a status is precluded from taking an active role in the management of the partnership firm. A partnership, unlike a registered company, is contractually bound by an agreement entered into on its behalf by any of its members. For a company to be bound by a contractual relationship, its agents must have been authorised to act by the company's board of directors (see Chapter 9).

In contrast to a company, a partnership does not have perpetual succession. A partner's interest in the partnership business is a property right and whilst this right may be transferred, the transferee will not be admitted as a member of the partnership firm without first obtaining the consent of the partnership's existing members. The acceptance of a new member into the partnership will have the theoretical effect of dissolving the old partnership, i.e. by creating a new one. Where a member leaves a partnership, the retiring member (or his estate) must be paid his share of the partnership business. Again, the partnership in such a case will be theoretically dissolved, although in practice the partnership will, with the consent of the remaining partners, be able to continue its existence.

In an attempt to raise finance, a partnership may seek contributions from its partners in a manner which must be acceptable to all the partnership members. A partnership may raise funds from outsiders and the partners acting collectively may give security for loans in the form of the partnership's assets. It must be noted that a partnership's ability to grant security over its assets is subject to statutory restrictions which prevent individuals and partnerships from creating floating charges over fluctuating assets (the nature of a floating charge is discussed in Chapter 14). Partnerships are further handicapped in respect of raising finance in so far as the majority of business partnerships are only permitted to have 20 members. Exceptions to this rule do exist: the exceptions include firms of solicitors and accountants (see s 716, CA 1985).

One of the principal advantages of forming a partnership business as opposed to the creation of a registered company is that a partnership business does not have to comply with the many formalities required of a registered company. However, it should be noted that the current trend in legislative policy, aimed towards the de-regulation of private companies, may weaken the partnership's advantage in respect of the formality rules. (Also see the proposal to create a limited partnership, discussed above.)

PROPOSALS FOR THE FUTURE REFORM OF THE REGULATION AND STRUCTURE OF COMPANIES

Objectives and themes to enhance proposed changes to UK corporate law were recently set out in the DTI consultation document entitled 'Modern Company Law', the document was published in February 1999. The theme of the consultation paper is one which recognises a need for UK company law to adopt a more modern outlook, to be up to date and to align itself to a more competitive economic outlook. The DTI regards the current framework of company law as one which is steadily becoming obsolete and considers that a general overhaul of corporate law is required.

The DTI has set up a steering committee to review the present law, the review will propose future reforms to the present system and structure of corporate law. The objective of the review is to develop a legal framework, based on the principles reflected in the Companies Act 1985, which cover the birth, existence and death of companies. It will therefore consider procedures for incorporation, the constitutional structure and winding up. In addition, the review will consider rules and sanctions relating to the protection of shareholders, creditors and employees. It is predicted that the final report will be available in 2001.

Suggested further reading

Corporate structures
Freeman (1994) 57 MLR 555
Hicks, Drury and Smallcombe [1995] ACCA Research Report 42
Hicks (1995) 16 Co Law 171
Riley (1995) 58 MLR 595

Group relationship
Schmitthoff [1978] JBL 218

The limited liability partnership
Morris and Stevenson (1997) 60 MLR 538

5

THE INFLUENCE OF THE EUROPEAN UNION ON UK COMPANY LAW

INTRODUCTION

The UK became a member of the European Community in 1972. The UK's membership was implemented in accordance with the European Communities Act 1972 (came into force on 1 January 1973). Since 1992, the pillars of the European Community have collectively become known as the European Union (EU), established by the Treaty of Maastricht in 1992. The EU is, of itself, a political entity without law-making powers. Of the constituent elements (pillars) of the EU, the EC (the European Community, formerly called the European Economic Community) determines Community laws.

THE EC COMPANY LAW HARMONISATION PROGRAMME

In order to pave the way for a greater degree of understanding and co-operation between the member states of the EU, in respect of community trade and the freedom of movement of goods, capital and workers, the freedom of establishment, the mutual recognition of companies or firms and transnational mergers, the EC has strived to bring about a harmonisation programme of national company laws. The spirit of the harmonisation programme is based on principles contained in Art 54(3)(g) of the EC Treaty. The process for harmonisation has been, and continues to be pursued, principally by Council Directives. In principle, a Directive is binding on all member states but only as to the result which it seeks to achieve. Accordingly, it is left to the national legislature to implement the Directive into its own legislation in whatever form and by whatever methods is deemed appropriate (see Art 189(3) of the EC Treaty). While a Directive may afford some flexibility in the manner in which it is implemented, by contrast, where a provision of EC law is prescribed by a regulation, the regulation will be deemed to be directly applicable.

A SUMMARY OF THE EC DIRECTIVES WHICH HAVE HITHERTO BEEN IMPLEMENTED

The First Directive

The First Directive was implemented into UK law by s 9 of the European Communities Act 1972, and covers three specific areas relating to disclosure, validity of obligations and nullity. The Directive has since been incorporated into the Companies Act 1985 by the Companies Act 1989. The primary aim of this Directive is to ensure the protection of shareholders and third parties and to enable two or more member states to carry out transnational operations in an efficient manner with the assurance of legal security.

In relation to disclosure requirements, the Directive is concerned with the co-ordination of general safeguards relating to the disclosure and publicity of company documents. The Directive specifies that companies must disclose and publish their constitutional frameworks together with details of representatives who may lawfully bind the company. Further, a company must publish its financial statements, for example, its profit and loss statement (subject to the Fourth Directive). In respect of protecting third parties, the Directive seeks to prevent abuses of authority by agents or officers of the company (discussed further in Chapter 9) and specifies that persons (promoters) who act for a company prior to its incorporation, will, when the company is incorporated, be jointly and severally liable for obligations which have not been assumed by the company (discussed further in Chapter 3).

The Second Directive

The Second Directive was adopted on 13 December 1976 and contains provisions relating to the classification of companies, rules on the raising of share capital and its maintenance and rules relating to dividends. The provisions were implemented in the UK by the Companies Act 1980 and specifically apply to public limited companies.

In relation to the classification of companies the effect of this Directive is to create a formal distinction in name/title between public companies and private companies. In accordance with the Directive, a public limited company is to be identified as a plc, whereas private companies retain the designation of 'Ltd'. A new definition of the public limited company was enacted (discussed further in Chapter 4).

In respect of rules relating to share capital, the Second Directive adopts provisions which are designed to ensure the preservation of capital by prohibiting reductions through improper distribution to shareholders, and by setting limits on a company's right to acquire its own shares (discussed further in Chapter 12). The Directive also affords protection to shareholders and creditors in relation to an increase or reduction in share capital and further specifies conditions in respect of a company's ability to acquire its own shares.

The Third Directive

The Third Directive was adopted on 9 October 1978 and was implemented in the UK on 1 January 1988 by the Companies (Mergers and Divisions) Regulations 1987 (SI 1987/1991) (see Sch 15B, CA 1985). Its purpose was to introduce a new regime for mergers and reconstructions of public companies. The Third Directive complements the Sixth Directive and covers mergers by acquisition, whereby one or more companies are wound up without going into liquidation and transfer to another all their assets and liabilities in exchange for shares issued to the shareholders of the acquired company or companies. The directive specifies certain disclosure requirements and provides that the merger must be approved by at least two-thirds of the shareholders of the merging companies.

The Fourth Directive

The Fourth Directive was adopted on 25 July 1978 and is incorporated into UK law by the Companies Act 1985. The Fourth Directive, which was amended by the Seventh Directive, prescribes standard (detailed) formats for the preparation and presentation of company accounts. In accordance with this directive, companies have to prepare full accounts for their shareholders, although certain exceptions to the accounting requirements are made in respect of small and medium-sized private companies.

The Sixth Directive

The Sixth Directive was adopted on 17 December 1982 and was implemented in the UK by the Companies (Mergers and Divisions) Regulations 1987 (SI 1987/1991). The Directive, complements the Third Directive and is concerned with rules relating to 'division by acquisition' of public limited companies, i.e. division as opposed to merger, mergers being dealt with by the Third Directive. Accordingly, the Directive applies to the division of public limited liability companies in respect of the practice whereby a public limited company transfers all of its assets and liabilities to a number of other public limited companies in exchange for the issue of shares to the shareholders of the divided company.

The Seventh Directive

The Seventh Directive was adopted on 13 June 1983 and was implemented into UK law by the Companies Act 1989 (in the form of ss 227–230 of the Companies Act 1985). The Directive, which complements the Fourth Directive, is concerned with the preparation, content and publication of group accounts (discussed further in Chapter 4).

The Eighth Directive

The Eighth Directive was adopted on 10 April 1984 and implemented by the UK in accordance with Part II of the Companies Act 1989. The purpose of the Directive is to prescribe minimum qualifications for company auditors, with the objective of enabling auditors to audit the accounts of companies of member states other than the member state in which they qualified. The Eighth Directive supplements the Fourth and Seventh Directives under which the annual accounts of companies must be audited by one or more persons authorised by law to perform that function.

The Eleventh Directive

The Eleventh Directive was adopted on 21 December 1989 and was implemented into UK law by the Oversea Companies and Credit and Financial Institutions (Branch Disclosure) Regulations 1992 (SI 1992/3179) (inserted as s 690A, CA 1985 and Sch 21A, CA 1985). This Directive is concerned with the filing and disclosure requirements (including disclosure of accounts) for branches of companies incorporated in one jurisdiction which carry on business in another. While provisions co-ordinating disclosure requirements are included in the First, Fourth, Seventh and Eighth Directives, such Directives are only applicable to companies (and their subsidiaries) and not branches of companies. Accordingly, the Eleventh Directive completes the gap which would otherwise have existed had branches of companies remained outside the ambit of the disclosure requirements.

Twelfth Directive

The Twelfth Directive was adopted on 21 December 1989 and was implemented into UK law by the Companies (Single Member Private Limited Companies) Regulations 1992. The Directive makes provision for single member private limited-liability companies (discussed further in Chapter 3).

The Works Council Directive

The Works Council Directive forms part of the provisions contained in the 1996 Social Chapter. The purpose of the Directive is to create employee councils in all companies with over 1000 employees. Initially the UK opted out of the Social Chapter but, following a change of government in 1997, that position has now been reversed. The purpose of a works council, which is elected by the company's employees, is to work in close co-operation with management so as to facilitate employee participation in matters connected to, for example, work procedure, working hours, working conditions, etc.

Other Directives

In addition to the aforementioned Directives, the existence of other important Directives should be noted. The said Directives are primarily concerned with the issue of securities in public companies (see Chapter 11) and with matters relating to 'insider dealing' (see Chapter 13). It should also be noted that a Tenth Directive concerned with cross-border mergers of public companies (supplementing the Third Directive) has been adopted by the European Commission.

DRAFT DIRECTIVES

The draft Fifth Directive

The draft Fifth Directive (as amended by a resolution of the European Parliament, 15 January 1982) sets out what, if implemented, would be a radical reconstruction of the board structure for UK companies. Taking its model from the German system, the draft Directive makes provision for employee participation in management functions within certain public companies, i.e. those which alone or with subsidiaries employ 1000 or more persons. The participation envisaged by the draft Directive would be by way of directors appointed from the workforce, a works council or a system established by collective agreement.

To facilitate the introduction of employee participation within the corporate management structure, the draft Fifth Directive envisages a new form of management system. Accordingly, relevant companies will be required to distinguish between directors who manage the company and those directors who supervise the management of the company. In effect, companies will be required to adopt either a two-tier system of management or a one-tier system which allows for a supervisory role to be played by non-executive members of the management board. (The one-tier system is a compromise for those member states unwilling to adopt a two-tier system; in practice both systems will have a very similar effect.)

The draft Directive envisages three principal methods by which a company could choose the representatives for the supervisory tier of management. The most radical form of supervisory board, in respect of the UK's present board structure, is the one whereby the supervisory board would comprise a maximum of one-half company employees with the remaining members being persons elected by the general meeting. The second method is one whereby the supervisory board would be elected by the company's management board, although the appointments would have to be approved by both the general meeting and company employees. The third method envisages the creation of a separate employee representative board having similar powers to the supervisory board but only on matters affecting employees.

In accordance with the draft Fifth Directive, the management board would be obliged to submit a written report to the supervisory board on the progress of the company's business at least every three months. In addition, the management board would have to obtain the approval of the supervisory board when entering into major contracts or instigating major changes in corporate policy. The supervisory board would also have the power to dismiss members of the management board. Salaries of the members of both the supervisory and management boards would be determined independently, i.e. members of either board would not be permitted to set their own salaries.

An interesting component of the draft Fifth Directive is that members of the management board would be precluded from accepting management positions in other companies, thus preventing directors from potentially placing themselves in a conflict of interest position (discussed further in Chapter 17). In addition, the draft Fifth Directive also deals with other matters relating to directors' duties and their enforcement, the conduct and power of the general meeting (discussed further in Chapter 17) and auditors' functions and liability.

The draft Ninth Directive

This draft Directive was concerned with the conduct of groups of companies and in part sought to impose an element of responsibility on holding companies in respect of the actions of their subsidiaries. The proposal for the draft Ninth Directive was introduced in 1984, however, it was never formally adopted and it would now appear that no further steps will be taken to advance its proposals. This may be viewed as unfortunate in so far as a holding company may, at present, exploit the separate legal identities of its subsidiaries at the expense of innocent third parties.

The draft Thirteenth Directive

The draft Thirteenth Directive was adopted in 1989 but has been subject to a number of amendments, the most recent of which was in November 1997. The Directive is concerned with takeovers. The problems with the Directive have involved the reluctance on the part of some member states to accept the concept of the hostile takeover. The UK's objections have predominantly been concerned with the extent of the Directive's legal controls which would inhibit the efficiency of the Takeover Panel under the City of London's present Code on Takeovers and Mergers. The Directive would have a significant effect in the UK where takeover activity is more commonplace than in other member states. The revised version of the Directive introduces disclosure rules for the benefit of employees and shareholders of target companies. The said rules purport to keep employees and shareholders informed of developments once a takeover bid has been made public.

THE PROPOSAL FOR A EUROPEAN COMPANY

As the harmonisation of the EC company law programme gains momentum (albeit that it must be noted that the harmonisation programme is at present moving at a very slow rate), there is a greater possibility that a new European company (a *Sócietas Europaea*) may be created. The idea of the European company was originally conceived in the late 1960s. A draft statute proposing the creation of a European company was first adopted by the EC Commission in 1989 (amended in 1992). The principal aim of the draft statute was one which sought to permit two or more companies based in at least two member states to incorporate a European company, by the formation of either a joint holding company or a joint subsidiary. The company once incorporated would then be registered in the member state in which its principal business operations were to be conducted. The company would be governed by the European statute, although where the statute was silent in relation to a particular aspect of corporate law, the company would be regulated by the national law of the state in which it was registered. The areas of company law that were regulated by the statute included formation, registration, capital, shares and debentures and attached rights, boards and general meetings and their powers, accounts and audit, winding up and liquidation, and worker participation. The matters not covered included, security and the registration of charges, insolvency and receivership, the oppression of minorities and disclosure of interests in shares.

However, there were obvious difficulties with the draft statute, namely, in a situation where the laws applicable to the regulation of the new European company ran contrary to the existing national laws of one or more of the EU member states. For example, in relation to the UK, the proposals relating to management structures contained in the draft Fifth Directive were incorporated into the draft statute notwithstanding that they would have created an unworkable discrepancy between the statute and the UK's national laws.

In April 1996 the text of a new regulation was issued (at half the size of the 1989 version). The new draft regulation, while maintaining the basic spirit and structures embodied in previous drafts, nevertheless purports to remove some of the requirements of previous drafts – these are effectively to be replaced by national law requirements, for example, national law requirements will apply in relation to raising and maintaining capital, accounts, audit and insolvency. The new draft regulations also relax the formation requirements and include a proposal to allow a company with its head office outside the EU to participate in the formation of a European company. This proposal would take effect where the European company is formed under the national law of a member state, has its registered office therein and has a genuine and permanent link with a member state's economy.

The new regulation was influenced by the findings of the Davington Report, a report compiled by a group of industrial experts. The objective of the report was to attempt to find a solution to the disagreements on the worker participation proposals. To this end the report suggests that the terms of worker involvement should be decided by individual companies with priority being given to a framework which would involve free negotiation between employers, employees and their representatives. The report concluded that workers' representatives should be members of the management board or supervisory board and that they should occupy one-fifth of the seats on the management or supervisory board with a minimum of two members. The board would be obliged to inform worker representatives regularly on matters affecting employees and to the progress of the company's business.

However, in response to worker participation proposals contained in the report, the DTI remains somewhat unconvinced, the UK having no tradition of employee representation at board-room level. The DTI concluded that the framework for negotiation as recommended by the Davington Report may deter UK companies from taking advantage of the European company. Further, because the UK government is committed to implementing the European Works Councils Directive, the DTI is not convinced of a need for worker participation, i.e. beyond the requirements of the Works Council Directive.

EUROPEAN ECONOMIC INTEREST GROUPINGS

As a result in 1985 of EC Regulation No 2137/85, it is possible for UK businesses, corporate or otherwise, to enter into an agreement of co-operation with a business or businesses in other member states. An agreement of this nature creates a European Economic Interest Group (EEIG). The purpose in creating the EEIG system was to facilitate co-operation between businesses located in different member states. The businesses, which together form an EEIG, become its members although an EEIG may not exert control over the business activities of any individual member of its EEIG grouping. An EEIG has a separate legal personality, but unlike a registered company, the members of the EEIG are liable for its debts, i.e. it does not possess a limited liability status. An EEIG cannot invite investment from the public.

The registration documentation of an EEIG must include objects which seek to promote economic co-operation between its members although an EEIG must not, in its individual capacity as a separate legal entity, seek to make a profit. An EEIG is not required to have a share capital nor does it need to file annual accounts or reports. Where an EEIG is registered in the UK, UK companies legislation, in so far as it is applicable to the EEIG, will regulate its affairs (see the European Economic Interest Grouping Regulations 1989 (SI 1989/638).

Suggested further reading

The Fifth Directive
Du Plessis and Dine [1997] JBL 23

The EEIG
Drury and Schiebi [1994] JBL 217

6

CORPORATE LIABILITY

INTRODUCTION

This chapter seeks to examine a company's liability for wrongful acts carried out in its name by its officers and corporate servants. The chapter concentrates its attention on an analysis of the conceptual difficulties which are involved in seeking to impose liability on a company for a wrong which requires proof of a requisite 'guilty mind'.

THE NATURE OF THE LIABILITY

A company, in common with other types of employer, may be held vicariously liable for the actions of its servants and agents and may even be held liable where an employee acted contrary to the company's instructions or where the employee carried out his duties in a dishonest manner; see e.g. *Lloyd* v *Grace, Smith & Co* [1912] AC 716. Further, a company may be vicariously liable for the torts of its servants and may, in its own right, be liable for torts of strict liability. In addition, a company may be liable for a tort which involves proof of malice. Malice may be attributed to a company by proving that the company servant who was responsible for the commission of the tort, behaved with malice whilst acting within the course of his employment; see e.g. *Cornfield* v *Carlton Bank Ltd* [1899] 1 QB 392.

However, the ability to attribute a mental state to a company is, in cases where the commission of a criminal or civil wrong involves proof of a defendant's knowledge or intent, far more problematic. A company as an artificial being has no mind or independent will, and as such cannot attain knowledge or form an intention. However, in so far as a company is a distinct legal entity it must be held accountable in law for wrongful acts which are committed in its name. Accordingly, it has been necessary to ascertain a company's knowledge or intent by attributing to it the mental state of its directing mind.

THE DIRECTING MIND OF A COMPANY

To determine the extent of a company's responsibility in relation to the commission of a legal wrong which involves proof of the knowledge or intent of a defendant, the court must ascertain whether the human person responsible for the physical commission of the wrongful act can properly be regarded as

71

a part of the company's directing mind. Where the person in question commands a position within the company's directing mind, the court will impute that person's mental state to the company. For example, in *Lennard's Carrying Co Ltd* v *Asiatic Petroleum Co Ltd* [1915] AC 705, the House of Lords held that a director of the appellant company had occupied such a dominant role in the company's business so as to have acted in the course of his employment as the company's directing mind. The company's business was concerned with the management and maintenance of a ship, a ship which was damaged following the director's failure to correct a fault in the ship's boiler system. The company sought to defend the proceedings on the premise that the damage to the ship had occurred without the company's actual fault or privity, i.e. the state of mind of the company's director was not attributable to the company. The company failed in its defence and was held liable under s 502 of the Merchant Shipping Act 1894 for the plaintiff's loss. In the oft-quoted words of Viscount Haldane LC:

> 'My Lords, a corporation is an abstraction, it has no mind of its own any more than it has a body of its own; its active and directing will must consequently be sought in the person of somebody who for some purposes may be called an agent, but who is really the directing mind and will of the corporation, the very *alter ego* and centre of the personality of the corporation.' (at p 713)

Although the directing mind of a corporation will often be found in a person who is regarded as the *alter ego* of a company (see e.g. the judgments of Lord Parker in *John Henshall (Quarries) Ltd* v *Harvey* [1965] 1 All ER 725 at p 729 and Denning LJ in *Bolton Engineering Co Ltd* v *T J Graham & Sons Ltd* [1957] 1 QB 159 at p 172), it must be stressed that while the *alter ego* of a company will normally be comprised of a company's directors, the directing mind of a company may be found in a different class of person.

The problem of identifying whether a person was a part of the directing mind of a company is more apparent when the culpability for the wrongful act falls upon a person/persons other than the one/ones who had an ultimate responsibility for the particular area of corporate policy in which the wrong occurred, i.e. where the person responsible for a wrongful act cannot properly be regarded as the *alter ego*. Although the individual acts of a company's servants cannot, in terms of the company's potential liability, be attributed to the company (other than by way of vicarious liability), nevertheless, the acts of a company servant may have been undertaken as a result of an implied or actual delegation of authority from the board of directors.

To establish whether a person can be viewed as a part of the company's directing mind, it is often necessary, if not essential, to pierce the corporate veil to examine a company's management structure and chain of command. Such an examination will aid the determination of whether a servant's wrongful act was directly attributable to the company, i.e. whether the servant had or was delegated an authority to act as part of the directing mind or held a position in the corporate structure from which the nature of that position could be construed as being a part of its directing mind. As such, the question as to whether a servant was part of a company's directing mind cannot be resolved by the application of a simple set of rules. The question may only be resolved on a case-by-case basis by analysing the nature of the servant's act and the position which that servant occupied in the corporate structure.

One of the leading authorities on the judicial identification of a company's directing mind is the decision of the House of Lords in *Tesco Supermarkets Ltd v Nattrass* [1972] AC 153. The facts of which were as follows. Tesco was charged with an offence under s 11(2) of the Trade Descriptions Act 1968 (TDA 1968), i.e. for offering to supply goods (in this case a packet of washing powder) at a price higher than the one which had been indicated as applying to the goods in question. (Section 11, TDA 1968 has since been repealed, but a consumer retains protection against misleadingly priced goods by virtue of s 20 of the Consumer Protection Act 1987.) In seeking to defend the action, Tesco relied upon s 24(1), TDA 1968 which provides that, subject to s 24(2), TDA 1968 (see below), a defence may be established where the accused can prove that (a) the commission of the offence was due to the fault of another person or some other cause beyond his control and (b) that he took all reasonable precautions and exercised all due diligence to avoid the commission of the offence by himself or a person under his control. Section 24(2), TDA 1968 requires notification to the prosecutor by the accused of the person who the accused believes was at fault. Tesco complied with s 24(2), TDA 1968 by notifying the prosecutor that the fault in question was attributable to the supermarket's manager. The question to be determined by the court was whether the supermarket manager's fault was directly attributable to Tesco.

At first instance, the magistrates were of the opinion that the store manager was not 'another person' but rather a part of the one entity, the company, i.e. Tesco's defence under s 24(1), TDA 1968 was denied. Although the Divisional Court found the magistrates to have been incorrect in their interpretation of the term 'another person', the court nevertheless concluded that the company had delegated responsibility for the pricing of its goods to its managers and as such the store manager was within the conceptual boundaries of the company's directing mind; Tesco was therefore guilty of the offence charged.

However, on appeal, the decision of the lower courts was overturned by the House of Lords. On the crucial question of whether the company's directing mind could delegate authority, i.e. whether the store manager could (as in the Divisional Court) be construed as a part of Tesco's directing mind, the House were of the unanimous opinion that he could not. Lord Reid, in attempting to define the conceptual boundaries of a company's directing mind, disagreed with cases in which the notion that company servants engaged in the 'brain work' of a company could automatically be classed as part of a company's directing mind. Lord Reid opined that only a company's superior officers, those persons who ultimately controlled the overall corporate policy of an enterprise, could be regarded as a company's directing mind. The store manager did not have the capacity to determine Tesco's corporate policy. Nevertheless, Lord Reid did recognise that a board of directors could –

'... delegate some part of their functions of management, giving to their delegate full discretion to act independently of instructions from them.' (at p 171)

The House, in concluding that Tesco was not guilty of the offence charged, construed s 24(1), TDA 1968 on the premise that it did not impose any form of vicarious liability. A store manager who acted in contravention of corporate policy could not be said to have acted as the company. Therefore, delegation of corporate tasks to a company's store manager could not be interpreted as the delegation of authority in respect of corporate policy. In the words of Lord Diplock:

'To treat the duty of an employer to exercise due diligence as unperformed unless due diligence was also exercised by all his servants to whom he had reasonably given all proper instructions and upon whom he could reasonably rely to carry them out, would be to render the defence of due diligence nugatory and so thwart the clear intention of Parliament in providing it.' (at p 203)

In finding that the store manager was not part of Tesco's directing mind, the House of Lords allowed Tesco's defence under s 24(1), TDA 1968. The identifiable directing mind of Tesco, the company's board of directors, had set up an effective system to avoid the commission of the offence charged under s 11(2), TDA 1968. The directing mind had not delegated any form of discretion to the store manager to act independently of its instructions.

More recently in *El Ajou v Dollar Land Holdings plc* [1994] BCC 143, the Court of Appeal was required to determine whether, for the purposes of establishing a company's liability under a constructive trust, the knowledge of one of its then directors (F) could be imputed to the company. F had knowingly been a party to the fraudulent receipt of moneys which had been acquired as a result of a massive share fraud. The plaintiff in this action sought to trace proceeds from that fraud which had been invested in a property project overseen by the defendant company. The defendant company, the entire share capital of which had been acquired in 1985 by a Liechtenstein foundation, controlled by two US citizens, was managed by S, an appointed agent. S was not however appointed to the company's board of directors which was comprised of three nominees, one of which was F, who also acted as the company's chairman.

The history of the case was as follows. F was asked by S to find an investor for a proposed building project. Having found a willing investor (C), F made the necessary arrangements between C and the company. After negotiations had been completed, F played no further part in the subsequent dealings between C and the company; shortly after he had finalised the agreement, F ceased to be a director of the company. C's investment in the company's property project, of over £1million, represented funds fraudulently obtained from the plaintiff; a fact known to F, but a fact which was not known by S or any of the company's other directors. Indeed, the company's board had never authorised the negotiations between C and F.

At first instance, in determining the question of whether F could, for the purpose of the transaction with C, be regarded as the directing mind of the company, so as to impute the director's (F's) knowledge of the fraud to the company, Millet J ([1993] BCC 698) concluded that the directing mind of the company was S, or S and his American principals, in so far as F had exercised no independent judgement in the matter, i.e. having been instructed by S to secure an investor. However, the Court of Appeal overturned that finding. The Court of Appeal concluded that F had been given the sole responsibility by S to find and conduct dealings with an investor for the property project, a responsibility which F undertook on behalf of the company. Therefore, for the purpose of the investment transaction, F had acted as the directing mind of the company.

Similarly, the House of Lords, in *Re Supply of Ready Mixed Concrete (No. 2)* [1995] 1 AC 456, held that in certain circumstances the knowledge of a company's senior employees may be attributed to the company notwithstanding that such employees sought to bind the company in a manner which was contrary to its corporate policy. This case was concerned with a company which had given an undertaking to the Restrictive Practices Court (in compliance with the Restrictive Trade Practices Act 1976) to refrain from entering into an restrictive arrangement which would amount to a breach of the undertaking. Notwithstanding the undertaking, senior employees of the company, acting within the scope of their employment, entered into a restrictive agreement. The employees acted without the consent of the company's board, which had actively encouraged its employees to abide by the terms of the restrictive agreement. In finding that the actions of the employees could be attributed to the company, which would therefore be found to be in contempt of court, the House of Lords concluded that an undertaking of this nature would have been worthless had the company been able to avoid liability for the acts of its employees, by alleging that the company's board of directors should be construed to have been unaware of the actions of its employees.

In *Meridian Global Funds Management Asia Ltd* v *Securities Commission* [1995] BCC 942 the Privy Council also subscribed to the view that the knowledge of a company employee may, in specific circumstances, be attributed to the company, notwithstanding that the employee in seeking to bind the company acted in abuse of his authority. In this case a company's senior investment manager entered into a security transaction in the name of the company. As a result of the acquisition, the company became a substantial security holder in another company. Contrary to the requirements of the relevant legislation (s 20, New Zealand Securities Act 1988) the company failed to give notice of the acquisition. The failure to give notice was as a result of the senior investment manager's desire to fraudulently attempt to purchase the securities with the objective of selling them on at a profit for himself. It was held that although the company's board of directors had been unaware of the security dealings, the company was nevertheless imputed with the knowledge of its senior manager.

Lord Hoffmann, in giving the judgment of the Privy Council, sought to explain the Privy Council's decision by first setting out rules of primary and then general attribution. The primary rules governed the company in accordance with its constitution or were to be implied by the companies legislation, the general attribution rules were rules based upon principles of agency. Lord Hoffmann concluded that when the said rules were combined, they could normally be applied to determine a company's potential liability for a wrongful act of an employee. However, exceptionally, as in the case before the Privy Council, the rules of attribution would not always forge an answer to determine corporate liability. In such a case, Lord Hoffmann opined that a company's liability, flowing from an act of an employee, could be determined by reference to the language and interpretation of the obligation or rule which the company's employee had contravened. Therefore, according to Lord Hoffmann, the decision in *Tesco Supermarkets Ltd* v *Nattrass* (discussed above) could be explained on the premise that the precautions taken by Tesco's board in seeking to eliminate the improper pricing of goods were sufficient to allow the company to evade liability in so far as the company's actions were adequate for the purpose of satisfying s 24(1), TDA 1968. Similarly, according to Lord Hoffmann, the decision of the House of Lords in *Re Supply of Ready Mixed Concrete (No. 2)* (discussed above) could be reconciled with *Tesco Supermarkets Ltd* v *Nattrass*, because if the company in *Re Supply of Ready Mixed Concrete* had not been found to be in contempt, then the statutory language of the Restrictive Trade Practices Act 1976 would have been worthless.

It is to be observed that Lord Hoffmann's analysis would appear to be a welcome representation of a common-sense approach to the determination of a company's directing mind, albeit that the very nature of a flexible approach may, in reality, do little, despite Lord Hoffmann's reassurance to the contrary (at p 950), to eradicate the inconsistencies and difficulties associated with the ascertaining of whether a servant's act can be equated with that of his master's directing mind. Indeed, the difficulty with the approach advocated by Lord Hoffmann will be in relation to its interpretation and application in those cases where the construction of a relevant statutory provision or other obligation may provide a tentative as opposed to an overwhelming inference of corporate responsibility.

Criminal liability

A company, acting through its directing mind, may be convicted of a criminal offence (other than where the exceptions below apply) irrespective of whether the offence is one of strict liability or one which involves proof of a guilty mind (*mens rea*). As Lord Reid said in *Tesco Supermarkets Ltd* v *Nattrass* [1972] AC 153:

'If the guilty man was in law identifiable with the company then whether his offence was serious or venial his act was the act of the company.' (at p 164)

However, the difficulty in attributing to a company the necessary culpability to warrant the company's conviction for a criminal offence involving *mens rea* is one which has caused much vexation and confusion. Indeed, until 1944, a company had never been successfully convicted of a criminal offence which incorporated *mens rea*. Yet, in that year there were three convictions. The convictions were sustained in: *DPP v Kent & Sussex Contractors Ltd* [1944] KB 146 on a charge of deception, *R v ICR Haulage Ltd* [1944] KB 551 on a charge of conspiracy and *Moore v I Bresler Ltd* [1944] 2 All ER 515 on a charge of fraudulent evasion of tax.

Nevertheless, the ability to attribute the mental state of an individual to the directing mind of a company is still marred by inconsistency in terms of the extent by which a delegation of authority emanating from the 'directing mind' of a company may be interpreted as constituting a sufficient degree of proximity between the individual responsible for the commission of the criminal act and the company. For example, in some cases the directing mind of a company has been held responsible for the acts of its subordinate corporate servants, whereas in other cases the courts have been less willing to extend the directing mind's responsibility for wrongful acts committed by persons who acted without any actual (express or implied) authorisation from the company's board of directors. Examples of cases in which the acts of subordinate corporate servants have been equated with a company's directing mind include: *Moore v I Bresler Ltd* (above) involving a company's branch sales manager; *DPP v Kent & Sussex Contractors Ltd* (above) involving a company's transport officer and *National Coal Board v Gamble* [1959] 1 QB 11, where a weighbridge man's knowledge and intention were attributed to the directing mind of the National Coal Board. An example of a case, other than *Tesco Supermarkets Ltd v Nattrass* (discussed above), where the wrongful acts of company servants were not regarded as the acts of the company's directing mind is *J Henshall Ltd v Harvey* [1965] 2 QB 233 where, in contrast to *National Coal Board v Gamble*, the company was deemed to have no responsibility for its weighbridge man's unlawful act of allowing a lorry to be driven contrary to weight restriction regulations. The company escaped conviction on the ground that, whilst the weighbridge man was a company employee, he was not a corporate officer and as such was absent of any form of corporate responsibility.

Although there may be obvious difficulties in establishing a company's responsibility for a criminal act perpetrated by one of its servants, it is nevertheless possible for a company to be charged and therefore convicted of the most serious crimes. For example, it is possible, following *R v Coroner for East Kent, ex parte Spooner* [1987] 3 BCC 636, for a company to be charged with manslaughter. In this case, the Divisional Court, in hearing an application for the judicial review of a coroner's decision into deaths resulting from the sinking of a passenger ship, 'The Herald of Free Enterprise', expressed the view that on appropriate facts a corporation could be convicted of manslaughter. The owners of *The Herald of Free Enterprise*, P & O European Ferries (Dover) Ltd, were subsequently charged with manslaughter but the case was withdrawn from the jury because of a lack of evidence to substantiate the finding that the directing mind of the company had the necessary *mens rea* to warrant a conviction. However, it should be noted that a conviction for manslaughter has subsequently been recorded against a company; see the *Lyme Bay Canoe* case (noted in [1994] *The Times*, 9 December). Further, it is to be noted that the Law Commission (1996, Consultation Paper 237) has recommended the introduction of an offence of corporate killing. This offence would be committed in circumstances where it was established that the death of a person was attributable to a company's negligence in the conduct and the management of its affairs.

General exceptions to criminal liability

Section 5 and Sch 1 to the Interpretation Act 1978 provide that for the purposes of statutory interpretation a 'person' may, unless otherwise stated, be construed as a corporate entity. However, whilst a company may generally be regarded as an entity to which criminal liability may attach, a company cannot be convicted of a crime where the definition of a criminal act involves the commission of a physical act (*actus reus*) which an artificial entity is legally incapable of performing. For example, an artificial person cannot be convicted of rape, as this offence can only be committed by a male person. Neither may a company be convicted of the offence of conspiracy in circumstances where the persons charged are the company and an officer representing its directing mind. The offence of conspiracy involves at least two independent minds conspiring together, whereas a company and its directing mind are one and the same; see e.g. *R v McDonnell* [1966] 1 All ER 193. However, where a company and a person representing its directing mind are involved in a conspiracy with other persons, the company may be charged with conspiracy; see e.g. *R v IRC Holdings* [1944] 1 All ER 691.

Further, according to the Divisional Court's decision in *Richmond-on-Thames BC v Pinn* [1989] RTR 354, a company cannot be charged with an offence which involves the driving of a vehicle. The court's reasoning for this decision was based on the premise that an artificial person was incapable of the physical act of 'driving'. While it is impossible for a company to drive a vehicle, the court's decision would seem to suggest that a company as an artificial entity should not be convicted of any offence which involves the performance of a human skill or act. The court's reasoning in *Richmond-on-Thames BC v Pinn* must surely be viewed as suspect because the majority of crimes involve the performance of some human skill or act.

Finally, a company may not be convicted of an offence where the punishment for the crime charged is such that a sentence is incapable of being imposed on the artificial corporate entity, for example, life imprisonment on the conviction of a murder charge.

Suggested further reading

Simmonds (1986) 7 Co Law 206
Wells [1988] CLR 788
Burles [1991] 141 NLJ 609
Wells [1993] CLR 551
Clarkson (1996) 59 MLR 557

7

A COMPANY'S MEMORANDUM AND ARTICLES OF ASSOCIATION

INTRODUCTION

The constitutional structure of a company is governed by its memorandum and articles of association. This chapter commences with an examination of a company's memorandum and the powers available to a company to alter clauses contained therein. The chapter then moves on to consider the format of a company's articles and the so-called statutory contract created by s 14, CA 1985. In considering s 14, CA 1985 the chapter examines the powers available to both the company and its membership to enforce and alter obligations created by the articles. For issues relating to the reform of this topic, see the Appendix at p. 373.

THE MEMORANDUM OF ASSOCIATION

The memorandum of a company is primarily concerned with the regulation and outward appearance of the company in respect of its dealings with third parties. Section 3, CA 1985 empowers the Secretary of State to specify by statutory instrument the standard form of memorandum to be adopted by a company. For example, Table B of the Companies (Table A–F) Regulations 1985, prescribes the form of memorandum for a private company whereas Table F prescribes the form of memorandum for a public company. With the exception of certain compulsory clauses the provisions contained within Table B and Table F are not mandatory.

Where a provision in a company's memorandum conflicts with one contained in the company's articles, the provision in the memorandum takes preference; see e.g. *Welton v Saffery* [1897] AC 299. However, where a provision in a company's memorandum is unclear, reference may be made to the company's articles in an attempt to clarify the ambiguity. In accordance with s 2(7) of the Companies Act 1985, a company may not alter the conditions contained in its memorandum unless the purported alteration is permitted by a provision of the Companies Act 1985 (discussed below).

Compulsory clauses

Section 2, CA 1985 provides that the memorandum of a company limited by shares must contain certain obligatory clauses. The obligatory clauses must include the following information:

(a) the name of the company (discussed further in Chapter 3);
(b) the situation of the company's registered office, i.e. whether in England or Wales, Wales or Scotland;
(c) the objects clause of the company. The objects of a company state the business or other activities for which the company is incorporated;
(d) that the liability of the company's membership is limited (s 2(3), CA 1985). The memorandum of a public company must specify that the company is a public limited company (s 1(3)(a), CA 1985);
(e) in the case of a company having a share capital, the company's memorandum must specify the amount of share capital with which it proposes to be registered and also the manner in which the share capital is to be divided into shares of a fixed amount (s 2(5), CA 1985). A subscriber to a memorandum must take at least one share in the company. The exact number of shares taken by a subscriber must be shown against the subscriber's name (s 2(5), CA 1985). In respect of a public limited company, s 11 of the Companies Act 1985 prescribes a minimum share capital requirement. At present this figure is currently fixed at an amount of not less than £50 000 (s 118, CA 1985). (Share capital is discussed further in Chapter 12.)

The alteration of the compulsory clauses

A company may, where permitted, alter the compulsory clauses of its memorandum in the following ways:

(a) *Name.* A company may alter its name by means of a special resolution (s 28(1), CA 1985). It should be noted that a change in a company's name does not affect any rights or obligations incurred by the company whilst operating under its previous name, see e.g. *Oshkosh B'Gosh Inc* v *Dan Marbel Inc Ltd* [1989] BCLC 507 (discussed further in Chapter 3).
(b) *Jurisdiction.* The Companies Act 1985 contains no provision to allow a company incorporated in one jurisdiction to have itself incorporated into another jurisdiction.
(c) *Objects clause.* Section 4, CA 1985 permits the members of a company to alter the company's objects clause by means of a special resolution. It should be noted that by s 5 of the Companies Act 1985, any member who did not vote or consent to a resolution which seeks to alter the company's objects clause may, providing they hold at least 15 per cent of the nominal capital of the company, apply to the court to challenge the purported alteration. The court has the power to invalidate the alteration or accept it in whole or part.
(d) *Status.* Provided that a company acts in accordance with the relevant provisions of the Companies Act 1985, a company may change its status. A private company may become a public company and vice versa (discussed further in Chapter 4).
(e) *Share Capital.* A company may alter its share capital in a number of ways. The methods and requirements for an alteration of a company's share capital are dealt with in Chapter 12.

Alteration of other clauses within the memorandum

Except for its powers to alter the compulsory clauses of a company's memorandum (discussed above), a company is not, subject to one exception, permitted to alter any other clause within its memorandum unless a power to so alter is specifically provided for by a provision contained in companies legislation. The stated exception is that any provision within the company's memorandum which could have been legitimately contained in the company's articles may by s 17 of the Companies Act 1985 be altered by the passing of a special resolution. However, it is to be noted that this exception will not apply where the memorandum of a company excludes its operation.

THE ARTICLES OF ASSOCIATION

A company's articles of association are primarily concerned with matters concerning the internal affairs of the company. For example, a company's articles will normally contain clauses governing matters relating to the regulation of general meetings (discussed in Chapter 18), the appointment and regulation of the powers of company directors (discussed in Chapter 16), class rights attached to shares (discussed in Chapter 10), share capital (discussed in Chapter 12) dividends (discussed in Chapter 12), and accounts and the capitalisation of profits.

Following a company's registration, the Registrar of Companies must be provided with a copy of the company's memorandum and articles. In accordance with s 8(2), CA 1985, if a company does not register its own individual form of articles in compliance with s 7, CA 1985, the contents of the company's articles will be determined by reference to the model form of articles found in Table A of the Companies (Tables A–F) Regulations 1985 (Table A articles). Where a company registers its own set of articles and a matter not dealt with therein is contained within the Table A articles, reference will be made to the Table A articles to determine the matter which was omitted.

Where a company adopts the Table A articles, the form of the Table A articles, in force as of the date of the company's registration will regulate the company's internal affairs. Therefore, a company incorporated prior to 1985, having adopted Table A articles, will, unless the articles were subsequently altered, have articles based on the format of Table A of the 1948 Companies Act. Any provision within a company's articles which is inconsistent with the memorandum of the company or the provisions of the Companies Act 1985 will be invalid. For example, in *Re Peveril Gold Mines Ltd* [1898] 1 Ch 122, the Court of Appeal held the terms of a company's articles to be invalid in so far as they provided specific conditions concerning a shareholder's ability to petition for the winding up of a company, conditions which were contradictory to those stipulated by ss 79 and 82 of the Companies Act 1862 (now governed by s 122, IA 1986).

THE WEIGHTED VOTING CLAUSE

Although a clause contained in a company's articles will be invalid where it seeks to override a provision of companies legislation, it is, nevertheless, perfectly acceptable for a company to insert a clause into its articles the purpose of which is, in a specified situation, to enhance the voting rights of any given member of the company. Accordingly, a weighted voting clause may be adopted to make it virtually impossible, in a practical sense, for a company to pass a resolution in accordance with the companies legislation.

The concept of the weighted voting clause was approved by the House of Lords in *Bushell* v *Faith* [1970] 1 All ER 53. This case involved a small domestic company with a membership comprised of a brother and two sisters; each member held 100 shares. After a series of disagreements between the members, an extraordinary general meeting was called whereupon it was proposed to remove the brother from his directorship of the company. After the meeting the sisters claimed that the brother had been validly removed by a resolution which had polled 200 votes for dismissal as against 100. The brother disagreed on the basis that the articles of the company included a clause (Art 9) which provided:

> 'In the event of a resolution being proposed at any general meeting of the company for the removal from office of any director, any shares held by that director shall on a poll in respect of such resolution carry the right to three votes per share ...'

Applying Art 9, the brother claimed that his sisters had failed to secure the vote to dismiss him by 300 votes to 200.

At first instance, Ungoed-Thomas J found that the brother had been validly removed by the resolution. Ungoed-Thomas J took the view that Art 9 was invalid, because it infringed the statutory power to remove a director by ordinary resolution. However, both the Court of Appeal and House of Lords (Lord Morris of Borth-y-Gest dissenting) disagreed with the learned judge; the validity of Art 9 was upheld. In giving its approval to the weighted voting clause the House of Lords emphasised that such a clause was solely concerned with the allocation of a company's voting rights and as Parliament had never sought to fetter the right of a company to issue a share with special rights or restrictions, it was certainly, in the opinion of their lordships, not for the courts to interfere in this matter.

Therefore, although a weighted voting clause may, in a practical sense, have the effect of restricting the ability of a company to pass a particular type of resolution, it does not offend against the terms of companies legislation, a company's ability to exercise any statutory power by the passing of a requisite resolution remains unfettered, i.e. theoretically, the company may still by the requisite majority (either by ordinary or special resolution) pass the necessary resolution. Yet, the practical effect of the weighted voting clause may be such as to make it impossible to secure a requisite majority of votes so as to enable a resolution to be passed.

THE CONTRACTUAL NATURE OF SECTION 14

Section 14 of the Companies Act 1985 provides:

> 'Subject to the provisions of the [Companies] Act the memorandum and the articles when registered bind the company and its members to the same extent as if they respectively had been signed and sealed by each member, and contained covenants on the part of each member to observe all the provisions of the memorandum and of the articles.'

The wording of the s 14 provision can be traced back to the Companies Act of 1856. Prior to the Companies Act 1985, s 20 of the Companies Act 1948 adopted the wording now found in s 14. Although s 14 is applicable to both the memorandum and articles, the controversy surrounding its interpretation has largely been in respect of provisions contained within a company's articles. The controversy has been in relation to the extent of the contractual nature of the provision.

Although the wording of s 14 stipulates that the articles and the memorandum, when registered, bind the company and its members, the section only provides that the articles and memorandum are binding 'to the same extent as if they respectively had been signed and sealed by each member', i.e. there is no mention of the fact that the company as a separate legal entity is bound as if it had signed and sealed the articles and memorandum. As such, the section fails to recognise the company's separate legal capacity to 'sign and seal' the memorandum and articles. One consequence of this statutory omission is that a debt due to the company from one of its members may be enforced as a speciality debt within a limitation period of 12 years, whereas a debt due from the company to one of its members will only be afforded a limitation period of six years; see e.g. *Re Compania de Electricidad de la Provincia de Buenos Aires Ltd* [1980] Ch 146.

Indeed, it is clear from the reported cases on s 14 (and cases concerned with s 14's statutory predecessors) that the section cannot be interpreted as conferring an equality of rights and obligations which one would normally expect to flow from the law of contract, although in interpreting a company's articles the court must seek to construe them as a commercial or business document so as to give them reasonable business efficacy; see e.g. *Tett v Phoenix Property Ltd* [1986] BCLC 149. Notwithstanding the 'business efficacy' rule, the so-called 'statutory contract' embodied in s 14 is not liable to be set aside on the grounds of misrepresentation, mistake, undue influence or duress. Moreover, terms cannot be implied into the memorandum or articles. For example, in *Bratton Seymour Service Co Ltd v Oxborough* [1992] BCC 471 a company involved in the management of a housing development, comprising a number of properties, sought rectification of an agreement (contained in the company's articles) by which an occupier of property within the developed site, a shareholder of the company, had agreed to contribute a predetermined sum of money for the maintenance of specified parts of the common land attached to the developed property. The company claimed that the rectification of the agreement would accord with the true intentions of the parties, namely that the shareholder concerned should be liable to contribute to all parts of the common areas of the developed property and not just those areas of common land specified in the agreement. The Court of Appeal unanimously held that the rectification of the agreement would not be consistent with the statutory nature of a company's articles, i.e. if the articles were to be rectified, then the alteration of the articles needed to be in accordance with the statutory procedure for the alteration of a company's articles, i.e. in accordance with s 9 of the Companies Act 1985 (discussed below). Dillon LJ stated that:

> '... the articles of association of a company differ very considerably from a normal contract ... It is thus a consequence as was held by this court in *Scott* v *Frank F. Scott (London) Ltd* [1940] Ch 794, that the court has no jurisdiction to rectify the articles of association of a company, even if those articles do not accord with what is proved to have been the concurrent intention of the signatories of the memorandum at the moment of signature.' (at p 474)

In relation to the possibility of a court admitting intrinsic evidence to vary the terms of a company's articles, Sir Christopher Slade commented thus:

> 'If it were to be admissible, this would place the potential shareholders in a limited company, who wished to ascertain their potential obligations to the company, in an intolerable position. They are in my judgement entitled to rely on the meaning of the language of the memorandum and articles of association, as such meaning appears from the language used.' (at p 476)

Obligations enforceable by a company under section 14

Obligations contained within a company's articles which seek to regulate the relationship between the company and its membership are enforceable by the company. An oft quoted illustration of this fact is provided by *Hickman* v *Kent and Romney Sheepbreeders Association* [1915] 1 Ch 881. The case involved a provision in the Association's articles which provided that disputes between the membership and the Association had to be referred to arbitration. It was held that a member of the Association was not entitled to commence court proceedings against the Association without first submitting the dispute to arbitration. The case of *Borlands Trustee* v *Steel Bros* [1901] 1 Ch 279 provides another example. In this case a provision in a company's articles stated that the company might at any time give notice to a member, not holding a senior management post in the company, whereby that member would be obliged to transfer ordinary shares to persons holding senior management posts. The court found that this provision was enforceable by the company as against any member of the company not holding a senior management post.

A company may also rely on provisions in its articles to deny the existence of an internal contractual relationship. For example, in *Kerr* v *John Mottram Ltd* [1940] Ch 657 a member of a company sought specific performance against the company for the sale of shares, a sale which had apparently been agreed to at an extraordinary meeting of the company. Nevertheless, as the minutes of the meeting failed to verify such an agreement it was held that the existence of the contract could be validly denied. This decision was justified on the basis that the articles of the company provided that the minutes of any company meeting were to be conclusive evidence of the business of that meeting.

Obligations enforceable between members *inter se*

Although the obligations created by s 14 may be seen as creating a quasi-contractual relationship between a company and its membership, s 14 fails to indicate whether obligations contained within the articles are directly enforceable between members *inter se*, i.e. can one member sue another to enforce an obligation. Indeed, on a literal construction of s 14, it would only appear to be possible to enforce obligations which affect the rights or liabilities of members in their relationship with each other in accordance with the internal management principle associated with the rule in *Foss v Harbottle* (see Chapter 22), i.e. by enforcing the right through the company; see e.g. *MacDougall* v *Gardiner* (1875) 1 Ch D 13. Accordingly, the wrong would only be enforced where a majority of the membership decided that the company should enter into litigation. Support for the view that members cannot directly enforce obligations against fellow members is to be found in the *obiter* comments of Lord Herschell in *Welton* v *Safferey* [1897] AC 299. His lordship remarked:

> 'It is quite true that the articles constitute a contract between each member and the company, and that there is no contract in terms between individual members of the company; but the articles do not any less, in my opinion regulate their rights *inter se*. Such rights can only be enforced through the company.' (at p 315)

Despite such comments, the more acceptable view would appear to be that members may in specific circumstances directly enforce obligations against fellow members without the need to pursue the action through the company. The principal justification for this view is that the company should not become involved in what would essentially be a dispute between its members, i.e. the company should not be involved in unnecessary litigation. Support for this contention may be found in those cases where pre-emption rights have been enforced between members of a company, i.e. rights contained within a company's articles which provide that where a member wishes or is compelled to sell his shares he must first offer them to existing members of the company; see e.g. *Rayfield* v *Hands* [1960] Ch 1.

However, it should be noted that membership disputes involving obligations which were created entirely outside the framework of the internal corporate relationship are not enforceable in accordance with s 14 in so far as such disputes are not concerned with the constitutional rights of the membership. For example, an obligation involving an independent trading transaction between two members of a company would not be enforceable, even in a situation where the purported dispute was regulated by the terms of the company's articles; see e.g. *London Sack & Bag Co Ltd* v *Dixon & Lugton Ltd* [1943] 2 All ER 767.

Obligations enforceable by the membership against the company

Most of the controversy associated with the interpretation of s 14 concerns the extent by which obligations, contained within a company's articles, may be enforced by the members of the company against the company. If s 14 created a mutual set of contractual rights as between a company and its membership, it would follow that all the provisions of the memorandum and articles would be enforceable. Yet, as previously discussed, s 14 is peculiar in that its contractual effect is not in accordance with what one would normally expect to flow from the law of contract. In *Hickman* v *Kent and Romney Sheepbreeders Association* [1915] 1 Ch 881 Astbury J opined thus:

> 'The wording of [s 14, CA 1985] is difficult to construe or understand. A company cannot in the ordinary course be bound otherwise than by statute or contract and it is in this section that its obligation must be found. As far as the members are concerned, the section does not say with whom they are deemed to have covenanted, but the section cannot mean that the company is not to be bound when it says it is to be bound, as if etc., nor can the section mean that the members are to be under no obligation to the company under the articles in which their rights and duties as corporators are to be found. Much of the difficulty is removed if the company be regarded, as the framers of the section may very well have so regarded it, as being treated in law as a party to its own memorandum and articles.' (at p 897)

While the courts' interpretation of s 14 has had the effect of limiting the enforcement of rights conferred on the membership of a company, the exact scope of this limitation is to some extent unclear. Nevertheless, one class of obligation for which there is no dispute as to a member's right of enforcement are those obligations which may be regarded as pure membership or insider rights. Such rights are common to all the members of any given class of shares. Examples of insider rights include:

- the right of a member to insist that once a company has declared a dividend, that the dividend should be paid in accordance with the terms of the articles (see e.g. *Wood* v *Odessa Waterworks Co* (1889) 42 Ch D 639);
- the ability of a member to enforce a right to a share certificate (see e.g. *Burdett* v *Standard Exploration* (1899) 16 TLR 112);
- on the winding up of a company, after the company has paid its creditors, a member's right to a return of capital; see e.g. *Griffith* v *Paget* (1877) 6 Ch D 511. (Note that a class of preferential shareholders may have priority to a return of capital over other shareholders: see Chapter 10);

- on a valid transfer of shares, the right of a member to have his name entered in the register of members (see e.g. *Re British Sugar Refining Co* (1857) 3 K & J 408).

Another commonly perceived example of an insider right is the entitlement of a member, who holds voting shares in a company, to exercise his vote at company meetings in any way and for whatever purpose he so chooses. The leading authority on the enforcement of the right to vote at a company meeting is *Pender* v *Lushington* (1870) 6 Ch D 70. In this case the articles of a company, the Direct United States Cable Co Ltd, restricted the total voting rights available to its members to the extent that for every ten shares held, a member was entitled to one vote. Irrespective of the number of shares held, no member was entitled to more than 100 votes. The plaintiff (Pender) transferred a number of his shares in the company to nominees who were to use the voting rights attached to the shares to support a resolution which would have had the effect of indirectly benefiting the interests of a rival company in which Pender had a substantial interest. In so transferring the shares, Pender would ensure that many more than the 100 votes he was personally entitled to would be cast in favour of the resolution. At the meeting at which the relevant motion was to be voted on, the chairman of the company disallowed the votes of Pender's nominees with the result that the resolution was lost. The Court of Appeal held that the votes attached to the shares of the nominee's had been improperly rejected. Jessel MR was of the opinion that:

> 'In all cases of this kind, where men exercise their rights of property, they exercise their rights from some motive adequate or inadequate, and I have always considered the law to be that those who have the rights of property are entitled to exercise them whatever their motives may be for such exercise.' (at p 75)

While the ability of a member of a company to exercise a right to vote is an example of an obligation which the courts will normally enforce in accordance with s 14, a view confirmed by the House of Lords in *Carruth* v *Imperial Chemical Industries* [1937] AC 707, it should be noted that a member's entitlement to enforce a right to vote may be lost where a resolution to which the vote related was concerned with a matter of internal procedure, as opposed to a substantive issue affecting the constitutional rights of the membership. For example, in *MacDougall* v *Gardiner* (1875) 1 Ch D 13 a company meeting was held with a view to the plaintiff proposing a motion to dismiss the company's chairman. The company's deputy chairman, who presided over the meeting, accepted a vote on the show of hands to have the meeting adjourned. As a result of the proposed adjournment, the plaintiff demanded a poll (recorded vote). Although the plaintiff demanded the poll in accordance with the terms of the company's articles, the poll on the motion to adjourn the meeting was refused.

In refusing to accept that the plaintiff had been wrongly denied the right to a poll vote, the Court of Appeal emphasised that the plaintiff's action was concerned with an internal procedural irregularity of the company. The procedural wrong (decision to refuse a poll vote) was a wrong committed against the company and not an infringement of the plaintiff's personal rights of membership. The court considered the action to have been ill conceived, Baggallay LJ remarked:

> 'I apprehend that it is not the practice of the court to make declarations of so utterly useless a character as is here asked.' (at p 27)

Although the Court of Appeal clearly rejected the plaintiff's claims, in doing so, it surely ignored the underlying principle at issue in the case, i.e. the ability to enforce the right to vote in accordance with the terms of a company's articles. Had the poll vote been concerned with the actual motion to dismiss the chairman, as opposed to a motion to adjourn the company meeting, it is probable that the outcome of the case would have been a different one. The decision in *MacDougall* v *Gardiner* may be a dangerous precedent to follow in that it most certainly distorts the protection of a basic membership right, i.e. the right to vote (but note that the decision in *MacDougall* was followed in *Cotter* v *National Union of Seamen* [1929] 2 Ch 58).

Perhaps an even more exceptional example of the court's ability to refuse a member's entitlement to vote is to be found in *Standard Chartered Bank* v *Walker* [1992] BCLC 603. In this case the court was asked to grant an injunction to restrain a member (W), who held a substantial but nevertheless minority holding in a public limited company, from exercising his right to vote on a motion which had two purposes. The first purpose was to enable a consortium of banks to instigate a rescue package on behalf of the company, the second sought to remove W from his directorship of the company. As it was almost certain that W would use his votes to block the ordinary resolution required to pass the two part motion, the court, casting off its normal reluctance to involve itself in the internal management of a company, granted an injunction to prevent W from exercising his right to vote.

Although the court's decision could be defended on the premise that an injunction served to protect the very existence of the company, for without the rescue package the continued existence of the company would have been unlikely, it is difficult, if not impossible to reconcile the decision with the principles enunciated in *Pender* v *Lushington*.

Unenforceable membership rights

Although obligations which can be identified as 'insider rights' or 'pure membership rights' are enforceable by the membership of a company, other obligations contained within the company's constitutional documents are generally regarded to be unenforceable; such rights are referred to as 'outsider rights'. Outsider rights are those obligations which do not correspond to the collective constitutional rights of any given class of shareholder. Nevertheless, an 'outsider right' may be indirectly enforceable in a situation where the enforcement of the right necessarily involves the enforcement of an 'insider right' (discussed below) or directly enforceable in a situation where the outsider right is supported by an independent contract, i.e. other than the statutory contract represented by s 14 (see Chapter 7). It should also be noted that while an 'outsider right' is not directly enforceable in accordance with s 14, the 'outsider right' may nevertheless constitute what is termed a membership interest and as such may, if it is infringed, substantiate an action under s 459, CA 1985 (see Chapter 23).

The acceptance of the generally held view that an 'outsider right' is not enforceable in accordance with s 14 owes much to the comments of Astbury J who, in *Hickman v Kent and Romney Sheepbreeders Association Ltd* [1915] 1 Ch 881, laid down three principles of law which he considered governed the provision. These principles have been quoted with approval in many subsequent cases in which the issue of 'outsider rights' has arisen; see e.g. the Court of Appeal's application of the principles in *Beattie v E & F Beattie Ltd* [1938] Ch 708 at p 714. To return to the comments of Astbury J, he stated:

> 'First that no articles can constitute a contract between the company and a third person; secondly, that no right purporting to be given by an article to a person, whether a member or not, in a capacity other than that of a member, as for instance a solicitor, promoter, director, can be enforced against the company; and thirdly, that articles regulating the rights and obligations of the members generally as such do create rights and obligations between them and the company respectively.' (at p 900)

The inspiration for the comments made by Astbury J in respect of 'outsider rights' may be found in cases such as *Eley v Positive Government Security Life Insurance* (1876) 1 Ex D 88 and *Browne v La Trinidad* (1877) 37 Ch D 1. In *Eley*, the articles of the company provided that the plaintiff (E) should be appointed as the company's solicitor for the duration of his life. E was also a member of the company. The Court of Appeal held that E could not enforce the right to lifelong employment as the company's solicitor because the obligation to maintain E in that position was one which did not affect the constitutional rights of the shareholding body, i.e. the obligation was unrelated to rights commonly held by the members of the company.

In *Browne v La Trinidad* the plaintiff (B) made an agreement which was incorporated into the company's articles, whereby, in consideration for the sale of his property to the company, B would become a member of the company and would also be appointed as a director of the company for a minimum period of four years. Although, in accordance with the terms of the sale transaction, B was appointed to a directorship in the company (B never became a member of the company), B was removed from his directorship before the minimum specified period had expired. The Court of Appeal held that even if B had become a member of the company, the right to hold a directorship was not a right which was common to the membership, rather it was an outsider right and as such was unenforceable (see also *Re Tavarone Mining Co (Pritchards case)* (1873) 8 Ch App 956).

The indirect enforcement of 'outsider rights'

As there is no privity of contract (the s 14 contract) between a company and a non-member of the company, it therefore follows that an obligation contained within the memorandum or articles which purportedly confers some form of right on a non-member of the company will be unenforceable. However, where the 'outsider right' is held by a member of the company, the right, whilst unenforceable in respect of the generally accepted interpretation of s 14 (see above), may in certain circumstances be held to be indirectly enforceable.

In those decided cases where outsider rights have been indirectly enforced, the right in question has usually been one associated with the management functions of a company, i.e. the right may be associated with the powers and functions of an organ of the company (board of directors or general meeting) or a constituent part of an organ of the company. For example, in *Quinn & Axtens v Salmon* [1909] AC 442, a member and managing director of a company successfully enforced a term of the company's articles associated with the exercise of rights attached to the office of the company's joint managing directors. The facts of the case were as follows. The company's articles provided that any one of the two appointed managing directors of the company could in certain circumstances veto a decision of the company's board of directors. In accordance with the terms of this provision, the plaintiff sought to exercise his right of veto. The veto was ignored by the company, as a result of which the plaintiff sought an injunction to prevent the company from acting otherwise than in accordance with its articles. The managing director pursued the matter as a member of the company, i.e. he sued *qua* member, and succeeded in obtaining the injunction. The House of Lords, affirming the decision of the Court of Appeal, held that the company, in seeking to discard the obligation, was in effect attempting to bypass rules on the decision-making process of the company; indeed, an attempt which would have had the effect of altering the articles in a manner which was not in accordance with statutory procedure, i.e. by the passing of a special resolution (see s 9, CA 1985). It should be emphasised that the enforcement of the managing director's right was pursued *qua* member, for in accordance with s 14 only a member of the company may enforce the rights contained within the articles.

Other case examples which illustrate the indirect enforcement of outsider rights include *Pulbrook v Richmond Mining Co* (1878) 9 Ch D 610 and *Imperial Hydropathic Co v Hampson* (1882) 23 Ch D 1. In both these cases the articles of the relevant companies contained provisions which sought to restrict the ability of the company to dismiss its directors. In both cases the Court of Appeal held that the restrictions were enforceable by the directors, suing in their capacity as members of their respective companies, in accordance with what is now s 14. (Note that these cases were decided prior to the implementation of s 303, CA 1985.) In the *Pulbrook* case Sir George Jessel MR remarked, in respect of the purported dismissal of the director, that:

'He has the right by the constitution of the company to take part in its management ... It may affect his individual interest as a shareholder as well as his liability as a director.' (at p 612)

A more modern example of the indirect enforcement of an 'outside right' is to be found in *Rayfield* v *Hands* [1960] Ch 1. In this case Vaisey J held that a member of a company should be permitted to enforce a provision of the company's articles which compelled the directors of the company to purchase the member's shares. Vaisey J held that the directors, whilst in a strict sense outsiders, were as members of the company bound by the provisions of the articles. (See also *Re Harmer* [1958] 3 All ER 689, where directors of a company, in pursuing an action as members of the company, obtained a remedy for oppression under s 210, CA 1948. Note that this provision is now represented by s 459, CA 1985.)

Academic theories which have sought to explain the cases in which there has been an enforcement of an outsider right, have resulted in three different lines of thought. The three theories may be identified in the following manner:

Theory A
A member of a company has the right to enforce any obligation contained within the company's memorandum or articles, irrespective of whether the right is an 'insider' or 'outsider right'. However, the member must sue *qua* member.

Theory B
A member of a company has the right to enforce any obligation contained within the company's memorandum or articles, irrespective of whether the right is an 'insider' or 'outsider right'. However, the member must sue *qua* member and the enforcement of the obligation must constitute something more than the enforcement of an internal irregularity.

Theory C
A member of a company has the right to enforce obligations contained within the company's memorandum or articles. Nevertheless, where the member seeks to enforce an 'outsider right' he can only do so where he sues *qua* member and the right is essential to the proper functioning of the company or an organ of the company, i.e. the right in question relates to the ability of a company to function within the constitutional framework of its own regulations and regulations imposed upon it by statute.

It should be made clear that any attempted reconciliation of the academic theories in relation to outsider rights is a difficult, if not improbable task. It must be remembered that the case law in relation to s 14 is, to say the least, often obscure, portraying a level of inconsistency which stems from the very nature of a provision which fails to specify the extent of its contractual effect. However, it is submitted that a common factor in seeking to explain those cases in which outsider rights have been enforced, is the fact that the so-called outsider right has been construed as an essential constituent of a pure membership right. Such an explanation is more akin to Theory C (outlined above). For example, in *Eley* v *Positive Government Security Life Insurance* (1876) 1 Ex D 88 (discussed above), although one could contend (Theory A and B, see above) that the outsider right, the right belonging to the company's solicitor, was unenforceable because it was not pursued *qua* member, it is submitted that a more logical explanation for the failure of the article was because it could not be related to a right commonly held by the membership; the right belonged to the solicitor and no other member of the company. By contrast, in *Quinn & Axten* v *Salmon* [1909] AC 442 (discussed above) the failure to enforce the managing director's power of veto would have affected a membership right ('insider right'), namely to have the business decisions of the company dealt with in accordance with the terms of the company's articles, i.e. if the right had not been enforced the terms of the company's articles would have been flaunted without the authorisation of the general meeting.

Finally, it should be noted that the Law Commission (1997, Report No 246), while recognising the potential problems associated with the interpretation of s 14, nevertheless considered that 'no hardship was being caused by any such difficulty' (at p 105). Moreover, the report considered that there could never be a comprehensive definition of an enforceable membership right under s 14. Accordingly, the Law Commission ruled out any immediate reform of the wording of s 14.

THE POWER TO ALTER A COMPANY'S ARTICLES

By s 9(1) of the Companies Act 1985, a company may alter a provision in its articles by passing a special resolution, i.e. by a three-quarters majority vote of those members who are entitled to vote at general meetings. Alternatively, if Table A articles are adopted (Table A 1985, Art 53), the articles of a company may be altered by the written consent of all the shareholders without the need to convene a company meeting to pass the requisite special resolution (see *Cane* v *Jones* [1981] 1 All ER 533). Indeed, even if Table A, Art 53 is not adopted, then, as a result of the introduction of s 381A of the Companies Act (introduced by the Companies Act 1989), it is now permissible for a private company to pass any form of resolution, to include one which purports to alter a company's articles, by a written resolution (discussed further in Chapter 18).

However, a company may not alter its articles where the effect of the alteration would be inconsistent with the terms of the company's memorandum or with a provision of the companies legislation. For example, in accordance with s 16 of the Companies Act 1985, a company may not, without the prior consent of its members, alter the terms of its articles (or memorandum) to increase its members' liability (also note the restrictions on a company's ability to alter the class rights of its members (see Chapter 10)). It therefore follows that any regulation or article of a company which seeks to fetter a company's ability to alter its articles in accordance with the statutory power of alteration is invalid. In *Allen* v *Gold Reefs of West Africa* [1900] 1 Ch 656 Lindley MR stated that:

> 'The company is empowered by the statute to alter the regulations contained in its articles from time to time by special resolution and any regulation or article purporting to deprive the company of this power is invalid on the ground that it is contrary to statute.' (at p 671)

Determining a valid alteration

For a company's articles to be altered, the alteration must comply with requirements which have been formulated by the courts to safeguard minority interests. As such, an alteration of a company's articles must not be retrospective in its effect, see e.g. *Swaeby* v *Port Darwin Mining Co* (1899) 1 Meg 385. Here the Court of Appeal held that directors could not, by a subsequent alteration to the articles, be deprived of fees payable to them under the terms of the company's articles. Of more general significance is the rule which requires an alteration of a company's articles to be made bona fide for the benefit of the company as a whole. This rule is necessary to prevent a three-quarters majority of the membership from adopting an article by which the majority could seek to gain an advantage, at the expense of the minority of the membership. At first sight this rule may be seen as an exception to a basic principle of company law, namely that a shareholder should be able to exercise his vote in the manner he so pleases. However, strictly speaking, the rule does not curtail this basic principle, it does however enable the court to challenge the outcome of a vote when it is considered to be contrary to the interests and benefit of the company as a whole.

The exact meaning of the term 'the benefit of the company as a whole', in respect of its relevance to determine the validity of an alteration of a company's articles, is unclear. As it is difficult to measure benefit in relation to the company as a commercial entity, i.e. isolated from the interests of those persons who actively participate in the company's business affairs, a more realistic interpretation of the term 'the benefit of the company as a whole' may be to consider 'the shareholders as a whole'.

In order to determine whether an alteration of a company's articles is *bona fide* for the benefit of the company, the courts have generally adopted a two-part test. The first part of the test is subjective and requires a determination of whether or not a three-quarters majority of shareholders in seeking an alteration to the terms of a company's articles did so with the honest belief that the alteration would benefit the company as a whole. The second part of the test is objective in nature and requires the court to consider whether or not the alteration of the company's articles was undertaken in good faith without the intention of producing a discriminatory effect on minority interests. Due to the general reluctance of the courts to interfere in the business decisions of a company, the majority of the decided cases emphasise the importance and predominance of the subjective element of the test; see e.g. *Shuttleworth* v *Cox Bros & Co Ltd* [1927] 2 KB 9 and *Rights & Issues Investment Trust Ltd* v *Stylo Shoes Ltd* [1965] 1 Ch 250.

While the effect of an alteration to a company's articles may cause some disadvantage to minority interests, disadvantage alone is not in itself sufficient to warrant a declaration that the alteration was invalid. For example, in *Allen* v *Gold Reef* [1900] 1 Ch 656, the articles of a company were altered to allow the company to have a 'first and paramount lien' for debts owing by any member of the company upon all shares held in the company. Prior to the alteration the lien only extended to shares that had not been fully paid up. In fact, the alteration in the company's articles only affected one member of the company, the said member being the only holder of ordinary shares which had been fully paid up. Whilst it was unfortunate, in that the practical effect of the alteration was to disadvantage this shareholder, the Court of Appeal upheld the validity of the alteration on the grounds that it was beneficial to the company as a whole; the alteration was not considered to have a discriminatory effect because in a theoretical sense it applied equally to all members who held ordinary shares which had been fully paid up.

In applying the objective part of the test, the court must divorce itself from a consideration of the personal motives which may have influenced a three-quarters majority of the membership to accept the proposed alteration. The court must weigh up the advantages and disadvantages of the alteration and in doing so consider the affect of the alteration in relation to the rights of those who claim to have been prejudiced. However, the court must balance the interests of the minority against the potential benefit which the alteration may have been calculated to have on the company as a whole. An example of the factors to be considered in the application of the objective test is to be found in *Greenhalgh* v *Arderne Cinemas* [1951] Ch 286, where Evershed MR stated that:

'... the case may be taken of an individual hypothetical member and it may be asked whether what is proposed is, in the honest opinion of those who voted in its favour, for that person's benefit.' (at p 291)

Evershed MR went on to state that the alteration would be impeached if:

'... the effect of it was to discriminate between the majority shareholders and the minority shareholders, so as to give the former an advantage of which the latter were deprived.' (at p 291)

However, it is to be observed that the above interpretation of the objective test is not without a fundamental flaw, namely, its application would be highly improbable in a situation where a company's membership was split between two opposing factions of the company's membership, i.e. where there was no middle ground, no hypothetical member. (By analogy, see *Clemens* v *Clemens* [1976] 2 All ER 268, discussed in Chapter 19.)

In cases where the courts have invalidated a proposed alteration of a company's articles, the alteration has been set aside on the premise that its intended effect was aimed at producing an inequitable division in rights as between holders of shares of the same class. For example, in *Dafen Tin Plate v Llanelly Steel Ltd* [1920] 2 Ch 124 a company altered its articles to enable members who held a majority stake in the company an absolute right to purchase the shares of any minority shareholder. The reason for the alteration was to prevent a specific minority shareholder, who had transferred business interests to one of the company's competitors, from retaining his membership of the company. Whilst the purpose behind the alteration may have been for the benefit of the commercial entity, the terms of this alteration were too wide. The alteration had the effect of giving those members of the company who held a majority stake, the right to expel a minority shareholder without valid excuse.

The above case may be contrasted with *Sidebottom v Kershaw, Leese & Co* [1920] 1 Ch 154, where the alteration of a company's articles also had the effect of giving the directors of the company the right to purchase the shares of any member of the company. However, unlike in *Dafen Tin Plate*, the amended article expressly specified that the purchase of a member's shares could only take place in a situation where a member carried on a competing business.

A further case example of where the court invalidated a proposed alteration of a company's articles is *Brown v British Abrasive Wheel* [1919] 1 Ch 290. Here, the company sought to alter its articles so as to compel a minority holding of 2 per cent to sell its shares to a group of majority shareholders who held the remaining 98 per cent of shares in the company. The reason for the proposed alteration was to encourage the majority to inject more capital into the company with the purpose of saving it from liquidation: the majority shareholders had promised to inject the necessary capital, providing the minority were compelled to sell their shares. Astbury J held the alteration to be unjust, the learned judge commented:

> 'I find it very difficult to follow how it can be just and equitable that a majority, on failing to purchase the shares of a minority by agreement, can take power to do so compulsorily.' (at p 297)

While the alteration may have been seen as unfair to the interests of the minority, it is nevertheless questionable whether or not the potential survival of the company was in this instance more important than the interests of a very small minority holding (by analogy, see e.g. *Standard Chartered Bank v Walker* [1992] BCLC 603).

Finally, it should be noted that where the alteration of a company's articles results in a membership interest being subjected to unfairly prejudicial conduct, it may in the member's interest be preferable to pursue an action under s 459 of the Companies Act 1985 (see Chapter 23). By analogy, it is interesting to note the Privy Council's decision in *Caratti Holding Co Pty Ltd v Zampatti* (1978) 52 ALJR 732. Here, the Privy Council held that a clause in a company's articles which permitted a majority shareholder to purchase the shares of a minority shareholder at par value, when the share value was greatly in excess of the par value, was oppressive to the minority's interest. Indeed, a minority shareholder's task of seeking to establish grounds for an action for unfairly prejudicial conduct is likely to be a less daunting proposition than attempting to substantiate a finding that the alteration of articles was not conducted *bona fide* for the benefit of the company as a whole.

ENFORCEABLE OBLIGATIONS WHICH FALL OUTSIDE THE SCOPE OF S 14 OF THE COMPANIES ACT 1985

Directors' service contracts

A member of a company (or a non-member) may enter into a separate enforceable contractual agreement with the company, the terms of which would have been unenforceable had they been included within the company's memorandum or articles. A separate contractual agreement of this type allows terms, otherwise regarded as outsider rights, to be enforced by the means of the separate contractual agreement. A typical example of a separate enforceable contractual agreement which, if it had been contained within the company's articles, would have been viewed as giving rise to an outsider right, is a director's service contract. An independent service contract will allow a director to pursue an independent claim for damages in a situation where the company breaches the terms of the agreement. It should be noted that where a director's service contract is silent as to a specific matter, for example, the length of the service contract, the relevant term may be implied into the independent service contract where the term was included within the company's articles (see e.g. *Re New British Iron Co, ex parte Beckwith* (1898) 1 Ch 324 and *Read* v *Astoria Garage (Streatham) Ltd* [1952] Ch 637).

It should be observed that the appointment of a person to a directorship is not of itself evidence of an independent contract between the director and company (see e.g. *Newtherapeutics Ltd* v *Katz* [1991] Ch 226), although upon being appointed to a directorship, the newly appointed director will be bound by the provisions of the company's memorandum and articles even in a situation where the director is not a member of the company. See e.g. *Re Anglo Austrian Printing & Publishing Union* [1892] 2 Ch 158 where Bowen LJ stated:

> '... the company puts forward the terms of the articles as the terms by which it will be bound; and the director by becoming and acting as a director of the company accepts that position.' (at p 168)

In circumstances where a director has a separate service contract and terms of the company's articles are impliedly incorporated into the service contract, a valid alteration of the company's articles will have the effect of altering the implied terms of the service contract, i.e. the new terms of the articles will be impliedly incorporated into the director's service contract. For example, in

Shuttleworth v *Cox Brothers & Co Ltd* [1927] 2 KB 9 the company's articles provided that its directors were to be appointed for life unless they were disqualified from holding office in any of six prescribed ways. The company's articles were subsequently altered by adding a seventh condition. A director, to which the seventh condtion applied, sought a declaration to the effect that the alteration was invalid in so far as it could not have a retrospective effect on the terms under which he was appointed to hold office. In upholding the company's ability to invoke the seventh condition and thereby dismiss the director, the Court of Appeal concluded that in so far as the articles had been legitimately altered, the director had no grounds of complaint.

Where, however, a director's service contract expressly contains terms which are also included within the company's articles, an alteration of the articles will not have the effect of altering the terms contained within the director's service contract. In such a case the terms of the service contract remain separate and severable from those contained within the altered articles.

Remedies for a breach of an independent contract

Where the terms of an independent contract seek to exclude the company from exercising a statutory power, for example, the alteration of the company's articles, can a company breach the agreement and impugn its contractual obligation? Indeed, if a company is unable to contract out of exercising a statutory power, should an agreement purporting to achieve that objective be declared invalid, or should the agreement be valid to the extent that a breach of its terms is permissive of a claim in damages? Alternatively, is it possible to restrain a company by means of an injunction from acting in accordance with the terms of a statutory power where an independent contractual obligation actually precludes the company from exercising the statutory power?

In seeking to answer the above questions, it is first important to point out that a company cannot within the terms of its articles, forgo its right to alter its articles. However, other than where a statutory power specifically provides that its effect cannot in any way be impugned by the articles or **otherwise** (see e.g. s 303, CA 1985), it would appear quite legitimate for a independent contractual agreement to include a provision which purports to restrain a company from exercising a specified statutory power, such as, the alteration of its articles.

Accordingly, a contractual agreement may be binding where its effect is to prevent the company from altering its articles; see e.g. *Punt* v *Symons & Co Ltd* [1903] 2 Ch 506. However, will a breach of the contractual agreement give rise to the usual remedies associated with a breach of contract? In *Punt* v *Symons & Co Ltd* the remedy for the breach of the agreement was restricted to a claim for damages. Nevertheless, in *Baily* v *British Equitable Assurance Co* [1904] 1 Ch 374, the Court of Appeal, in distinguishing *Punt* v *Symons & Co Ltd*, implied that the remedy for a breach of such an agreement should not be so restricted. Cozens-Hardy LJ stated:

'... It would be dangerous to hold that in a contract of loan or contract of service or contract of insurance validly entered into by a company there is any greater power of variation of the rights and liabilities of the parties than would exist if, instead of the company, the contracting party had been an individual. A company cannot by altering its articles, justify a breach of contract.'
(at p 382)

Although the decision of the Court of Appeal was subsequently overturned by the House of Lords ([1906] AC 35) on the basis that there had never been a contractual agreement to the effect that the company would not alter its articles, it is to be observed that the House of Lords did not seek to challenge the findings of the Court of Appeal in respect of its conclusions relating to the effect and consequences of a breach of the contract. Indeed, the Court of Appeal's findings were followed in *British Murac Syndicate* v *Alperton Rubber Ltd* [1915] 2 Ch 168, where an injunction was granted to prevent a proposed alteration of a company's articles.

However, in *Southern Foundries Ltd* v *Shirlaw* [1940] AC 701, the House of Lords came to the conclusion (albeit in *obiter* comments) that an injunction should not be granted to prevent a company from altering its articles, notwithstanding that the company would be in breach of contract by acting on new articles; a breach which could accordingly be remedied by an award of damages. Indeed, it is submitted that the approach adopted in *Southern Foundries* represents the correct interpretation of the consequences to be attached to a breach of a contractual agreement which purports to preclude a company from exercising its right to exercise a statutory power. Accordingly, a company should not be prevented from breaching the contractual obligation in so far as it should not be prohibited from acting in accordance with a statutory power, a power of which the other contracting party will most probably be aware. Nevertheless, a company should not be allowed to breach a contractual obligation without fear of the imposition of some form of penalty, namely, it should in such a case, be made liable to a claim in damages.

MEMBERSHIP AGREEMENTS

In addition to those terms of a company's articles which purport to regulate the relationship of members *inter se*, the shareholders of a company may lawfully bind themselves by way of an independent membership agreement, to act or vote in a specific way on issues governed by the terms of the agreement; see e.g. *Greenhalgh* v *Mallard* [1943] 2 All ER 234.

The existence of a membership agreement is a common feature in small private companies and usually purports to bind the entire, or a substantial majority of, the existing membership of the company. The agreement seeks to regulate matters of internal management so that those members who are a party to the agreement unanimously agree to vote on specific issues in a predetermined way (see *Breckland Group Holdings Ltd* v *London & Suffolk Properties* [1989] BCLC 100, discussed further in Chapter 19).

Although an effective membership agreement (an agreement which is comprised of a majority of the company's membership) affords a degree of certainty as to the outcome of issues governed by the terms of the agreement, the terms of a membership agreement may prove to be a handicap where, for example, a member, as a party to the agreement, refuses to sanction a decision to pursue a policy falling outside the terms of the membership agreement. For example, with the passage of time, a majority of those members who are party to a membership agreement may consider that a term contained therein should no longer be pursued, thereby rendering it essential to dispense with its continued adoption. However, if just one member who is a party to the agreement disagrees, it is possible that the terms of the agreement may be enforced by injunction (discussed below) – a situation which could be most detrimental to the company concerned.

The effectiveness of a membership agreement, in terms of its ability to influence the outcome of any given vote, will normally be dependent on the number of members who are bound by its terms. Problems relating to the validity of a membership agreement may arise in a situation where the vast majority of a company's membership are bound by an agreement, the terms of which conflict with a company's freedom to act in accordance with one of its statutory powers, for example, the statutory power to alter the terms of its articles by the passing of a special resolution. Where a provision in a company's articles contradicts the terms by which a statutory power can be exercised, the provision will be invalid (see e.g. *Re Peveril Gold Mines Ltd* [1898] 1 Ch 122), but can the same be said of a provision contained within a membership agreement?

In *Russell v Northern Bank Development Corporation Ltd* [1992] 1 WLR 588, the House of Lords upheld the validity of a membership agreement by which all the current members of a company were bound. The company had five shareholders who, as parties to the agreement, contracted to refrain from increasing the company's share capital, save in a situation where all parties to the agreement consented in writing to increase the share capital. When subsequently the board of the company proposed a motion to increase the company's issued share capital, one of the shareholders challenged the motion's validity on the premise that it contradicted the terms of the membership agreement. The four shareholders who were in favour of the motion counter-claimed for a declaration that the membership agreement was invalid in so far as it purported to restrict the statutory power of the company to create further capital.

The power to alter the company's memorandum, in respect of the company's capital clause, was governed by Art 131(1) of the Companies (Northern Ireland) Order 1986 (a copy of s 121(1), CA 1985). In accordance with this statutory power the company was permitted to alter its share capital if it was authorised to do so by the terms of its articles. Article 1 of the company's articles adopted the regulations contained in Part II of Table A in Sch 1 to the Companies Act (Northern Ireland) 1960. Regulation 44 of Table A (a copy of reg 32 of Table A Companies (Tables A–F) Regulations 1985) provided that the company could increase its share capital by means of an ordinary resolution.

Although the House of Lords, overruling the decision of the Court of Appeal (MacDermott LJ dissenting) [1992] BCLC 431, recognised that the membership agreement would have been invalid if it had been contained in the company's articles, it nevertheless formed the opinion that the agreement was separate and distinct from the company's articles (confirming the view expressed by MacDermott LJ in the Court of Appeal). The membership agreement was construed as one of a purely personal nature. Lord Jauncey, expressing the unanimous opinion of the House, quoted with approval (at p 593) a passage from Lord Davey's judgment in *Welton* v *Saffery* [1897] AC 299, namely:

> 'Of course, individual shareholders may deal with their own interests by contract in such a way as they may think fit. But such contracts, whether made by all or some only of the shareholders, would create personal obligations, or an *exceptio personalis* against themselves only, and would not become a regulation of the company, or be binding on the transferees of the parties to it, or upon new or non-assenting shareholders.' (at p 331)

However, in so far as the membership agreement sought to bind the company (the company was also a signatory to the agreement), the House held the agreement to be as obnoxious as if contained in the company's articles. The company had in effect agreed not to exercise its statutory powers for a period which would last for so long as any of the members who were a party to its terms remained as shareholders of the company. Nevertheless, as the membership agreement between the company's shareholders was independent and severable from the purported agreement with the company, the agreement, in so far as it affected the rights of the shareholders *inter se*, was binding.

The significance of the decision of the House of Lords in *Russell* v *Northern Bank Development Corporation Ltd* should not be underestimated. Although neither the company nor the future membership of the company was bound by the membership agreement, the practical effect of the decision is one which restricts the company from acting in accordance with its statutory powers. Whilst the fetter on the company's ability to act in pursuance of a statutory power is of a temporary nature, i.e. for so long as those party to the agreement commanded a sufficient majority of votes, the effect of the obstruction is such as to distort the intention of the relevant companies legislation. A motion to pass a resolution which conflicts with the terms of a membership agreement may only be passed with the consent of those who are a party to the agreement. Accordingly, the danger represented by the decision of the House of Lords in *Russell* is that it opens up the possibility of a member of a company, as a party to a membership agreement, having the capacity to obtain an injunction to prevent other members of the agreement who wish to act otherwise than in accordance with its terms. As such, where a membership agreement comprises the vast majority of the company's shareholders, an injunction seeking compliance with the terms of the agreement could clearly, albeit indirectly, fetter the company's ability to exercise a statutory power. Indeed, the statutory framework within which companies operate may be rendered subservient to the terms of membership agreements. Moreover, in an extreme case, a company may become a slave to the terms of a membership agreement thereby existing in an isolated independence from the statutory framework into which it was born. Finally, it is submitted that a far more logical, albeit more passive remedy, for a breach of a membership agreement would be for an aggrieved shareholder to pursue an action for damages or seek some other form of redress under s 459 of the Companies Act 1985.

Suggested further reading

Theory A
Gregory [1981] 44 MLR 526

Theory B
Wedderburn (1957) CLJ 194 and (1958) CLJ 93

Theory C
Goldberg [1972] 35 MLR 362 and [1985] 48 MLR 158
Prentice [1980] 1 Co Law 179

Alteration of articles
Rixon [1986] 86 MLR 446

Independent contracts and membership agreements
Sealy [1992] CLJ 437
Davenport (1993) 109 LQR 210
Shapira (1993) 109 LQR 210
Griffin [1993] NLJ 589
Savirimuthu (1993) 14 Co Law 137
Riley (1993) 44 NILQ 34
Ferran [1994] CLJ 343

8

A COMPANY'S CONTRACTUAL CAPACITY

INTRODUCTION

The validity of a corporate transaction is dependent upon the contractual capacity of a company and issues relating to directors' authority. This chapter seeks to explain matters pertinent to the former; directors' authority is discussed in Chapter 10.

The area of company law which forms the subject matter of this chapter has been the subject of substantial reform in the guise of the Companies Act 1989. Whilst the effect of the Companies Act 1989 will be discussed in some detail, this chapter commences by considering the historical development of rules relevant to corporate capacity. An understanding of the historical development of this area of the law will hopefully help the reader appreciate why issues relating to corporate capacity have, throughout the history of company law, been the source of much confusion and why, eventually, such vexation resulted in reforming legislation. For issues relating to the reform of this area, see the Appendix at p. 373.

CORPORATE CAPACITY – THE *ULTRA VIRES* RULE

The determination of a company's capacity to enter into contractual obligations was historically dominated by the *ultra vires* rule. The rule provided that a contractual transaction which went beyond a company's corporate capacity was to be treated as a void transaction. If void, not even the unanimous consent of the company's shareholders could validate the transaction.

The roots of the *ultra vires* rule emanate from those cases concerned with statutory companies which were formed to, for example, construct public utilities, such as railways and canals. Such companies were restricted in the pursuit of legitimate business activities by the particular statute which granted them corporate status. Any act by a statutory company which contravened a limitation placed upon its capacity would be deemed *ultra vires* and void; see e.g. the House of Lords' decision in *Eastern Counties Rlwy* v *Hawkes* (1855) 5 HLC 331.

In 1855, as a result of the introduction of a limited-liability status for joint stock companies, the legislature considered it necessary to offer some means of protection for corporate creditors so as to curb the potential danger of investing capital in enterprises which, as a consequence of their limited-liability status, offered investors minimal protection should the company fall into a state of insolvency, i.e. the limited-liability status of companies precluded the personal resources of a company's membership from being used to repay corporate debts. The legislature introduced provisions into the Companies Act of 1856, whereby companies were obliged to register objects clauses; these clauses were to be included within a company's memorandum of association. An objects clause had to specify a company's intended business purposes. Accordingly, prior to entering into a credit agreement with a company, a creditor could inspect the company's objects clause to discover its business purposes, an investigation which may have influenced a creditor's decision to advance loan funds.

In *Ashbury Railway Carriage and Iron Co v Riche* (1875) LR 7 HL 653 the House of Lords construed the 1862 Companies Act (which had replaced the 1856 Act) in a restrictive manner, to hold that any matter not expressly or impliedly authorised by a company's objects clause would be one which went beyond the capacity of the company. This strict interpretation of the 1862 Act was also subject to the application of the *eiusdem generis* rule of construction. This rule limited the scope of any of the company's set objects. Accordingly, objects which were ancillary to the company's main object were to be construed in conjunction with the main object. Therefore, in *Ashbury*, an object which permitted the company to act as 'general contractors' could not be read as implying that the company could engage in a business as finance agents, although arguably the term 'general contractors' could have covered that activity. Instead, the object which permitted the company to act as general contractors was construed in relation to the company's main object, namely, the company's principal business purpose of mechanical engineering. Thus, the company could only act as general contractors in connection with the business of mechanical engineering. By acting as finance agents, the company had acted *ultra vires*, so the transaction was void.

The justification for the House of Lords' strict interpretation of the Companies Act 1862, and indeed the rationale for the *ultra vires* rule, was couched in terms of both shareholder and creditor protection. The *ultra vires* rule, protected shareholders in so far as they could seek an injunction to restrain the company from entering into an *ultra vires* transaction, or if a company's main object (substratum) had failed, by allowing a shareholder to petition to the court for a winding up order; see e.g. *Re German Date Coffee* (1882) 20 Ch D 169. Alternatively, where a company acted beyond its capacity, the members of the company, by the passing of an ordinary resolution, could avoid the contract and seek the return of the subject matter of the contract, or where that was not possible, sue the party (the constructive trustee) with whom the contract had been made.

Somewhat surprisingly, unsecured creditors, unlike shareholders, had no rights pertaining to the enforcement of the *ultra vires* rule, although a secured creditor having taken a charge over the company's property was given the right to seek an injunction to restrain the company from entering into an *ultra vires* transaction; see e.g. *Cross v Imperial Continental Gas Association* [1923] 2 Ch 553.

The development of the *ultra vires* rule

While giving some form of protection to both shareholders and creditors, the *ultra vires* rule was not conducive to commercial business in so far as a person contracting with a company was deemed to have constructive notice of the company's objects clause. Accordingly, a company's objects clause, as a document available for public inspection, was deemed to have been inspected and the knowledge contained therein was deemed to have been known by persons contracting with the company, irrespective of whether or not any inspection of the document had actually taken place. Therefore, a person who dealt with a company could not subsequently complain if a transaction to which he was a party conflicted with the company's objects clause; the transaction could be avoided by the company. (It should be noted that at first instance in *Bell Houses Ltd* v *City Wall Properties* (1966) 1 QB 207 Mocatta J suggested that a third party could also invoke the *ultra vires* rule against a company. However, in subsequent cases this suggestion was never followed. On appeal, the decision of Mocatta J was overturned, but on different grounds.)

In an attempt to rectify the restrictive nature of the *ultra vires* rule, the courts were, in subsequent cases, to weaken the strict approach taken by the House of Lords in *Ashbury*. For example, in *A–G* v *The Great Eastern Railway Co Ltd* (1880) 5 App Cas 473 the House of Lords held that a company could pursue a course of business which was reasonably connected to its stated objects or, for that matter, could employ a power, for example, the power to borrow money for the purpose of its business, regardless of the fact that the particular power was absent from the company's objects clause. (The powers of a company, often contained within the objects clause, were tools to be employed to assist the fulfilment of stated objects.)

In 1904, came one of the most significant decisions in connection with the weakening of the impeachable nature of the *ultra vires* rule, namely, *Re David Payne & Co Ltd* [1904] 2 Ch 608. Here the Court of Appeal, in affirming the decision of Buckley J, inflicted what should have been a fatal blow to the *Ashbury* interpretation of the rule. Prior to *Re David Payne* it was considered that where a company employed a legitimate power but for a purpose not within its stated objects, then the exercise of the power would be *ultra vires* and void. In *Re David Payne* that view was discarded by exclusively restricting the question of whether a power use was *ultra vires*, to the issue of corporate capacity. Accordingly, the questions to ask were: was the power in question capable of being used to pursue the corporate objects? Did the capacity to employ the power exist? Therefore, where a company was legitimately able to exercise a corporate power, the use of that power would be valid (*intra vires*) even if ultimately the purpose for its use was for an activity outside the company's objects clause.

In *Cotman* v *Broughman* [1918] AC 514 the House of Lords, albeit reluctantly, struck another nail into the coffin of the *ultra vires* rule by refusing to invalidate an objects clause, the effect of which eradicated the main objects (or substratum) rule enunciated in the *Ashbury* case. The objects clause in *Cotman* failed to comply with the legislature's requirement that the memorandum should identify the objects of a company in a plain and unambiguous manner. The House of Lords in giving its tacit approval to the *Cotman* objects clause, opined that once an objects clause had been approved by the Registrar, such approval was conclusive evidence that all the requirements of the Companies Act had been complied with (this is now governed by s 13, CA 1985).

In *Cotman*, although the House of Lords suggested that through the vigilance of the Registrar, similar clauses to the one found in *Cotman* should not be permitted, the House's suggestion was not adhered to. The *Cotman* type clause became a regular feature of objects clauses. Due to the removal of the substratum rule (main objects rule) companies began to include a multitude of business objects within their objects clauses to hopefully expand their corporate capacity and preclude the possibility of a transaction being challenged on the basis of the *ultra vires* rule. Nevertheless, it should be noted that the power of a shareholder to petition for the winding up of a company on the basis that the company's main object had failed, remained in tact. (However, it is to be observed that in *Re Kitson & Co Ltd* (1946) 1 All ER 435 the Court of Appeal diluted the substratum rule by providing that a company may not necessarily have one main object but may, in fact, have two.)

In *Bell Houses Ltd* v *City Wall Properties* [1966] 2 QB 656 the scope of a company's objects clause was further extended by the approval of a clause which authorised the company to carry on any business whatsoever which, in the opinion of the directors, could be advantageously carried out by the company in conjunction with or ancillary to any of the ventures specified in the objects clause.

The confusion between *ultra vires* and an abuse of powers

In relation to corporate capacity a transaction, although not *ultra vires*, may nevertheless have been entered into as a result of an abuse of the powers afforded to directors. The legal consequences flowing from such a transaction were explained in *Re David Payne*, namely, a transaction within the capacity of a company may be voidable where the third party had actual notice that the transaction had been used to pursue something which constituted an abuse of a director's power (the third party with actual notice would be liable as a constructive trustee; constructive trustees are discussed further in Chapter 17).

Unfortunately, the correct rationale of *Re David Payne* became confused with the concept of *ultra vires*. The confusion between *ultra vires* transactions and those which had taken place as a result of an abuse of directors' powers became commonplace. For example, in *Re Lee Behrens & Co Ltd* [1932] 2 Ch 46, a case concerned with an implied power to grant pension policies to employees and their spouses, Eve J, in considering whether the issue of a particular pension policy had been beyond the capacity of the company, declared that two questions had to be asked and answered in the affirmative before the transaction could escape the consequences of the *ultra vires* rule, namely, was the transaction *bona fide?* Secondly, was the power used for the benefit and to promote the prosperity of the company?

In reality, the above questions had no relevance to the issue of capacity (*ultra vires*) but were connected with whether directors of the company had abused their powers in allowing a particular transaction to proceed. Therefore, in declaring the pension policy in *Re Lee Behrens & Co Ltd* to be void on the premise that negative answers had been supplied to the two questions, Eve J clearly erred in his construction of the determination of a company's corporate capacity. The investigation into corporate capacity should not have been concerned with the state of mind of the officers of the company. In *Re Lee Behrens* the implied power was capable of being used to pursue the objects of the company and as such should not have been declared *ultra vires*.

Regrettably, the decision in *Re Lee Behrens* became widely accepted as an authority for determining whether a power use by a company incorporated an abuse of corporate capacity, thus rendering the power use to be *ultra vires*. The judgment of Eve J was applied in cases such as *Re Jon Beauforte Ltd* [1953] Ch 131, *Parke* v *Daily News Ltd* [1962] Ch 927, *Re Ward M Roith Ltd* [1967] 1 WLR 432 and *Introductions* v *National Provincial Bank* [1970] Ch 199.

The principles associated with *Re David Payne* were to remain clouded in confusion until the decision of Pennycuick J in *Charterbridge Corporation Ltd* v *Lloyds Bank* [1970] 1 Ch 62. Here, a company's (Castleford) ability to mortgage its property to a bank in order to secure the indebtedness of a group of other companies, to which Castleford belonged, was called into question. Castleford, having taken a mortgage over its property, subsequently sold the property to the Charterbrige Corporation, but did so prior to repaying the mortgage to the bank. As the mortgage remained unpaid, the bank claimed the property in accordance with its mortgage terms. Charterbridge, which had been unaware of the existence of the mortgage, contended that notwithstanding that the power to mortgage property had been contained within Castleford's objects clause, the mortgage transaction should nevertheless be viewed as *ultra vires* because it had not been entered into for the benefit of Castleford, but merely to support other companies in the group of companies to which Castleford belonged.

Accordingly, Pennycuick J had to decide whether the benefit of the mortgage in relation to its benefit to the company was an issue of any relevance to the determination of an *ultra vires* transaction. Pennycuick J held that as the power to mortgage was one which was capable of being used to pursue Castleford's objects, the use of the power could not be *ultra vires*. In other words, Eve J's benefit test had no application to the determination of whether or not the transaction was *ultra vires*. The confirmation of Pennycuick J's decision was provided in subsequent cases, namely, *Re Halt Garages* [1982] 3 All ER 1016, *Re Horsley & Weight* [1982] Ch 442 and *Rolled Steel Products Ltd* v *British Steel Corporation* [1986] Ch 264. In this latter case, the Court of Appeal finally put to death any confusion that might have remained in relation to directors' powers and the *ultra vires* rule. The Court of Appeal killed off any suggestion that the doctrine of *ultra vires* was interwoven with issues relating to directors' powers. Accordingly, transactions which involved a dispute over the exercise of directors' powers, a director's authority to exercise delegated powers or a director's duty to exercise powers bona fide and for a proper purpose, had no place in the determination of a company's capacity to act.

STATUTORY REFORM OF THE *ULTRA VIRES* RULE

In many respects, the courts acted to curtail the severity of the *ultra vires* rule, albeit that at times the judicial suppression of the rule had been inconsistent and fraught with ambiguity. In contrast and for many years, the legislature was slow to act in respect of reforming the rule. The first statutory intervention was in fact made following the recommendations of the Cohen Committee Report in 1945 (Cmnd 6659). In accordance with the Companies Act 1948, Parliament permitted companies to alter their objects clause by the passing of a special resolution (today this provision is contained within s 4, CA 1985). Whilst this statutory reform gave companies more flexibility and scope to alter the direction of their corporate purposes, it obviously did not protect third parties in situations where a company entered into a new type of business venture without having first altered its objects clause. If, however, the Cohen Committee recommendations had been enacted in full, the position would have been different; the committee had suggested that in relation to transactions with third parties, companies should have the powers of a natural person, i.e. in effect the *ultra vires* rule would have been abolished in respect of third-party transactions. In relation to shareholder protection, the committee had been in favour of retaining the safeguards offered to shareholders by the *ultra vires* rule.

In 1962, the Jenkins Committee (Cmnd 1749) proposed an even wider reform to the *ultra vires* rule by suggesting that the doctrine of constructive notice be abolished. However, the committee's recommendations were not heeded. The statutory overhaul of the *ultra vires* rule was to remain sidelined until, as a result of the United Kingdom's entry into the European Community, the UK legislature was press-ganged into action. To permit English law to comply with the requirements of Art 9 of the EC First Company Law Directive, s 9 of the European Communities Act 1972 was introduced; Art 9(1) provided that:

> 'Acts done by the organs of the company shall be binding upon it even if those acts are not within the objects of the company, unless such acts exceed the powers that the law confers or allows to be conferred on those organs.'

Section 9 of the European Communities Act 1972 later became s 35 of the Companies Act 1985. Section 35(1) (prior to its amendment by the Companies Act 1989), provided that:

'In favour of a person dealing with a company in good faith any transaction decided on by the directors is deemed to be one within the capacity of the company to enter into and the power of the directors to bind the company is deemed free of any limitation under the memorandum and articles.'

At first, it was considered by many commentators that s 35(1) had achieved the desired effect of abolishing the *ultra vires* rule in relation to third-party dealings; s 35(2) sought, in compliance with Art 9(2), to abrogate the constructive notice rule in circumstances where the conditions of s 35(1) had been satisfied. Certainly, in those cases where the wording of s 35 was applicable, the removal of the *ultra vires* rule had been achieved. However, whilst the intention of s 35 had been to comply with Art 9 in its entirety, the language of s 35, CA 1985 failed to achieve that objective; see e.g. *International Sales and Agencies Ltd* v *Marcus* [1982] 3 All ER 551 where the court questioned whether the words 'dealing' and 'transaction' covered gratuitous dealings, and *Barclays Bank Ltd* v *TOSG* [1984] BCLC 1 where Nourse J questioned the meaning of the term 'good faith'. (This latter case reached the House of Lords [1984] AC 626, but no comments were made in respect of the analysis of the term 'good faith'.)

As a result of the problems associated with the wording of s 35, the ghost of the *ultra vires* rule remained. Whilst the threat of the *ultra vires* rule prevailed, companies in drawing up their objects clauses, continued to create elaborate and well-defined clauses. Third parties who entered into contracts with companies were still advised to scrutinise and check the contents of objects clauses. The *ultra vires* rule which had persistently hampered contractual freedom between companies and third parties, continued to be of great nuisance value.

THE EFFECT OF THE COMPANIES ACT 1989

In accordance with the proposals of the Prentice Report 1986 (a Department of Trade and Industry investigation into the legal and commercial implications of abolishing the *ultra vires* rule), s 110 of the Companies Act 1989 amended s 35 of the Companies Act 1985. The effect of the amendment was one which, in relation to a company's dealings with third parties, finally abolished the *ultra vires* rule. Section 35(1) (as amended) now provides as follows:

'The validity of an act done by a company shall not be called into question on the ground of lack of capacity by reason of anything in the company's memorandum.'

Although s 35 would have been more appropriately worded if it had stated, '... an act would not be called into question by reason of anything which had been **excluded** from a company's memorandum', it is clear that the statutory intention of the section is to abrogate the *ultra vires* rule in respect of third-party interests, i.e. to comply with Art 9. While a company is not (contrary to the recommendations of the Prentice Report) theoretically possessed of the capacity of a natural person, capacity is nevertheless unrestricted by the contents of its memorandum; note, however, that the authority of individual directors may be restricted by the company's articles or by the board of directors, a restriction which might potentially diminish the ultimate ability of a company to enter into a particular transaction (discussed further in Chapter 9).

Although the Companies Act 1989 does not remove the need for an objects clause, it does seek to avoid the practice of prolonged clauses by introducing a standard type of clause for the purpose of permitting companies to pursue any activity within a commercial context (s 3A, CA 1985). For existing companies, the option to adopt this new form of clause is exercised by the passing of a special resolution. By adopting an objects clause in line with s 3A, it should be noted that where companies wish to place a limitation on their power to exercise such objects (limitations on the exercise of objects were found in cases pre-1989 Act; see e.g. *Simmonds* v *Heffer* [1983] BCLC 298 and *Rosemary Simmons Memorial Housing Association Ltd* v *UDT Ltd* [1986] 1 WLR 1440), then such a limitation will have to be separately provided for within the terms of a '3A type' of objects clause.

Where limitations on objects are included, such limitations will not however deflate the commercial capacity of a company in its dealings with third parties, s 35(1) prevents this from happening. However, limitations contained in the objects clause will regulate the board of directors in relation to the board's own powers, and a transaction falling foul of a stipulated limitation whilst not *ultra vires* a third party, will render any director acting contrary to the terms of the limitation (subject to a special resolution of the general meeting ratifying the director's act) to any potential liability which may result from the transaction (see, s 35(3), CA 1985, discussed below). Similarly, corporate powers which are not covered by the s 3A definition but which the company wishes to include within its objects clause may also need to be expressly provided for; such powers would possibly include the ability to make charitable or political donations.

Although the consequences of pursuing corporate purposes, other than those specified within the objects clause, would not as a result of s 35(1) render the transaction void, it should be observed that the wording of s 35(3) does provide a somewhat contradictory picture, in that it states:

> 'It remains the duty of the directors to observe any limitations on their powers flowing from the company's memorandum; and action by the directors which but for subsection (1) would be beyond the company's capacity may only be ratified by the company by special resolution. A resolution ratifying such action shall not affect any liability incurred by the directors or any other person; relief from any such liability must be agreed to separately by special resolution.'

In circumstances where a transaction exceeds the company's capacity as a consequence of an improper exercise of directors' powers (powers contained within the memorandum), prima facie s 35(3) would appear to provide that the transaction should be unenforceable, save where the general meeting passed a special resolution to adopt it. Nevertheless, such an interpretation must be flawed because s 35(3) expressly acknowledges that the transaction in question would have been unenforceable 'but for section 35(1)'. In other words, a transaction which falls outside a company's corporate capacity, having taken place as a result of an abuse of directors' powers (powers which are contained within the memorandum), will, in respect of third-party interests, retain its validity as a result of s 35(1).

The purpose of s 35(3) would thus seem to be restricted to a situation whereby the **company** itself seeks to enforce a transaction which is beyond the directors' powers and outside the scope of the company's capacity (i.e. as opposed to where a third party seeks to enforce a transaction under s 35(1)). Where a company does seek to enforce such a transaction, it must adopt the irregular transaction by a special resolution. A resolution ratifying such an action will not affect any liability incurred by the directors (for breach of powers) or any other person; relief from any such liability must be agreed to separately by an additional special resolution.

By retaining the concept of an objects clause, the 1989 Act maintains one of the initial justifications of the *ultra vires* rule, namely, shareholder protection. Indeed, the ability of a shareholder to prevent the company from pursuing a transaction outside its objects clause is expressly maintained by the 1989 Act (introduced as s 35(2), CA 1985). Section 35(2) provides that:

> '**A member of a company may bring proceedings to restrain the doing of an act which but for subsection(1) would be beyond the company's capacity; but no such proceedings shall lie in respect of an act done in fulfilment of a legal obligation arising from a previous act of the company.**'

Nevertheless, a severe limitation on the ability of a shareholder to so intervene is made where the company's act is in furtherance of an existing legal obligation: such actions may not be avoided. During the parliamentary passage of the Companies Act 1989, Lord Wedderburn of Charlton (speaking in the House of Lords) raised a salient observation in relation to the term 'legal obligation'. His lordship stated that a company would always have to enter into some form of legal obligation prior to the commencement of a commercial act. Therefore, the performance of a commercial transaction which would otherwise have been beyond a company's capacity will be outside the ambit of shareholder control, i.e. it is highly unlikely that a shareholder (other than shareholder/director) will have any knowledge of the proposed transaction so as to intervene to prevent it from having contractual force. Accordingly, as soon as the transaction is agreed upon, the legal obligation, for the purposes of s 35(2), will have been created. Indeed, although the legislature's intention in its use of the term 'previous legal obligation' may have been one which was designed to spread a wider net of protection for shareholders, it would appear that if such an intention ever existed, it has nevertheless been swallowed up by the statutory language in which s 35(2) is presented.

One shareholder right which would definitely appear to have been lost, following the implementation of s 35(1), is a shareholder derivative action (discussed in Chapter 22) in respect of the return of corporate property following a breach of corporate capacity. The concept of third parties holding property as constructive trustees in such a situation would appear to have disappeared as a consequence of the newly formulated s 35(1), i.e. a company cannot invalidate a transaction which falls exclusively within the ambit of s 35(1).

Suggested further reading

Confusion between powers and objects in relation to the ultra vires *rule*
Baxter [1970] CLJ

Article 9 of the EC Act 1972
Prentice (1973) LQR 518
Sealy and Collier [1973] CLJ 1

Reform of the ultra vires *rule pre-1989*
Pennington (1987) 8 Co Law 103

The effect of the 1989 Act
Griffin [1991] NILQ 38
Poole (1991) 12 Co Law 43
Ferran (1992) 13 Co Law 124, 177

9

THE AUTHORITY OF DIRECTORS AND OTHER OFFICERS TO BIND THE COMPANY

INTRODUCTION

This chapter seeks to examine the rules relating to the authority of directors and other authorised persons in relation to their ability to enter into binding transactions on behalf of a company. The chapter commences by explaining the agency rules applicable to the delegation of corporate authority. The chapter then considers the significant reforms which have been made to this area of company law by the Companies Act 1989. The reader should be warned that the aforementioned reforms are complex and at times vague. It is hoped that future case law will provide some answers to aid the interpretation of the reforming legislation. For issues relating to the reform of this topic, see the Appendix at p. 373.

THE AGENCY RELATIONSHIP

Whether an individual officer of a company is possessed of an authority to bind the company in a contractual relationship with a third party will be dependent upon the rules of agency. Prior to s 9 of the European Communities Act 1972 (previously discussed in Chapter 8), the formation of an agency relationship was dependent upon the potential scope of an officer's authority to act as determined by the company's constitutional documents, i.e. the memorandum and articles. Where a third party relied upon an officer's authority to bind a company, the third party's case would fail if the type of authority alleged was outside the ambit of the company's constitution. The third party was deemed to have constructive notice of the contents of the memorandum and articles. However, as a consequence of the 1972 EC Act and subsequent legislation, culminating in the Companies Act 1989, the relevance of the memorandum and articles, as the ultimate source of a company's capacity to delegate authority, is no longer of crucial importance. Provided that a third party acts in good faith, the power of the board of directors to bind the company or authorise others to do so is, as a result of s 35A(1) of the Companies Act (introduced by the Companies Act 1989), deemed to be free of any limitation under the company's constitution.

Notwithstanding that s 35(1) of the Companies Act 1985 provides that the validity of a corporate transaction cannot be called into question by anything contained in a company's memorandum, it must be emphasised that in order to retain its validity a corporate transaction will need to be authorised by the board of directors or a company officer acting with the delegated authority of the board.

Types of authority

There are two principal forms of valid authority: actual authority – which may be either express, implied, or usual (real) – and ostensible (apparent) authority.

Actual authority

The board of directors acting as a collective body is invested with the powers of the company, i.e. the company is the principal in the agency relationship. Subject to a contrary intention within a company's articles, the actual authority to exercise the powers of the board or part of those powers may be delegated to individual directors, a committee of directors or to directors occupying an executive position, for example, a director appointed to the post of managing director; see Table A, Art 72. Furthermore, the board of directors may give powers of attorney delegating the exercise of any of its powers to any person; see Table A, Art 71.

The delegation of actual authority takes place as a result of a resolution passed by the board to appoint a director or committee of directors to take charge of certain company powers. A delegation of the board's actual authority in any matter, is termed an express actual authority. The delegation of actual authority may also be implied. For example, where a director is expressly or impliedly appointed to a particular executive position, the director concerned will have an implied authority to bind the company in a manner consistent with the powers associated with that position, i.e. a usual (real) authority. An executive position to which an implied actual authority is attached may be subject to express restrictions, which have been imposed by either the board or the company's articles. Prior to the Companies Act 1989, a third party was deemed to have constructive notice of any restrictions placed on a director's authority by the company's constitution. However, in accordance with the rule in *Royal British Bank* v *Turquand* (1856) 6 E & B 327 (discussed below), a third party, when dealing with a company, was not bound to ensure that all the internal regulations of the company had been complied with in respect of the exercise and delegation of authority, i.e. the third party was not deemed to have notice of matters of internal management which sought to impose restrictions upon a director's authority. Where the *Turquand* rule was operative, the third party was permitted to rely on the authority of the director as determined in accordance with his usual authority, i.e. the authority usually associated with the particular type of executive post occupied by the director in question.

An oft quoted case example of the operation of implied actual authority is *Hely Hutchinson* v *Brayhead Ltd* [1968] 1 QB 549. This case concerned the extent and determination of an authority vested in a company chairman to bind a company to a contract, in a situation where the chairman had not sought the prior approval of the company's board. The Court of Appeal found that as the chairman was accustomed, often without consultation with other board members, to commit the company to contracts, his actions were akin to those of a *de facto* managing director. In common with the chairman's previous dealings, the remaining members of the board had not sought to curb the chairman's powers. As such, the court held that the chairman's authority to contractually bind the company could be implied from the executive position he was allowed to occupy, i.e. as the company's *de facto* managing director.

Ostensible authority

Unlike actual authority, which operates on the basis of an express or implied delegation of authority from the company (the principal) to an officer of a company (the agent), ostensible authority operates as a result of a representation from the company (the principal) to a third party. The representation is to the effect that a particular person (the agent) possesses the necessary authority to bind the company. An officer of a company who possesses ostensible authority will have no actual authority to perform the act to which the ostensible authority relates.

In effect, ostensible authority will be established where there has been a representation from the board of directors or duly authorised executive, which expressly or by conduct acknowledges the right of the company's agent to bind the company in a particular matter. The third party must rely upon the representation and must alter his position as a consequence of that reliance. For example, in *Freeman & Lockyer* v *Buckhurst Park Properties Ltd* [1964] 2 QB 480, Kapoor (K), a director of the defendant company (C) entered into a contract with the plaintiffs (P), without first seeking the approval of the three other members of C's board. The board subsequently refused to honour the terms of the contract on the ground that K had no authority to enter into the contract. The Court of Appeal held that whilst K had never been appointed to an executive position, i.e. a position which carried an actual authority to bind the company in the contractual relationship with P, the board were nevertheless aware of K's managerial activities, i.e. K had been left in charge of the day-to-day management of the company. As such, P was justified in relying on K's ability to bind the company.

It will be observed that the cases of *Freeman & Lockyer* v *Buckhurst Park Properties Ltd* and *Hely Hutchinson* v *Brayhead Ltd* are, in many respects, similar. Whilst the latter case was one concerned with implied authority, the distinction between implied authority and ostensible authority may on occasions be a very fine one. It is suggested that in *Freeman Lockyer* the reason why the court was unwilling to find an implied authority was because K had never formally or impliedly been appointed to an executive management post. The acquiescence of the individual members of the board to K's activities did not amount to a valid authority that K should manage the day-to-day business of the company in a position akin to that of a managing director.

A case example which establishes the flexibility of the concept of ostensible authority is *First Energy Ltd* v *Hungarian International Bank Ltd* [1993] BCC 533. Here the Court of Appeal held that a bank's senior manager had, from his position as a senior employee of the bank, an ostensible authority to communicate to the plaintiff the bank's apparent approval of the plaintiff's proposed transaction. The court so held, notwithstanding that the bank had not given its approval to the transaction and regardless of the fact that the plaintiff was aware that the manager did not have any actual authority to approve the transaction without first having obtained permission from the bank's head office. Although the Court of Appeal accepted that the bank manager would not ordinarily have had an ability to self-authorise transactions without the approval of his head office (by analogy, see e.g. *Armagas Ltd* v *Mundogas SA* [1986] 2 All ER 385), the court found that in the instant case the bank's head office (the principal) had nevertheless clothed its agent with the trappings of authority in a manner capable of inducing the plaintiff to rely on the existence of the agency relationship. It had done so by, for example, allowing the bank manager in previous dealings between the bank and the plaintiff, to instigate negotiations on behalf of the bank and to communicate the bank's acceptance of short-term credit facilities to the plaintiff. The plaintiff had relied upon the bank manager's ostensible authority in its dealings with the bank; the bank manager having been held out as having a type of usual authority to bind the bank in respect of the type of transaction in question. Indeed, it would have been nonsensical and contrary to commercial reality had the court reached a contrary judgment, because had it done so, it would have resulted in a bizarre conclusion, namely that the plaintiff would have been expected to seek the approval of the bank's head office whenever it sought to confirm a communication in relation to a proposed transaction, a communication which had been given to it by one of the bank's own senior managers.

It should also be noted, for the purpose of establishing ostensible authority, that where the representation of authority relied upon by a third party is contained within the company's constitutional documents, then reliance on the contents of the documents must have been as a direct result of the third party's actual notice of them; the concept of constructive notice will not avail a third party in this context (see e.g. *Rama Corporation Ltd* v *Proved Tin & General Investments Ltd* [1952] 2 QB 147).

THE INDOOR MANAGEMENT RULE
(THE *TURQUAND* RULE)

The indoor management rule, which is derived from the case of *Royal British Bank* v *Turquand* (1856) 6 E & B 327, provides that when dealing with a company, a third party is not bound to ensure that all the internal regulations of the company have been complied with in respect to the exercise of an authority to bind the company. The operation of the rule is subject to a number of exceptions, namely:

- a third party with actual knowledge of the fact that a transaction is outside the authority conferred by the company's constitution cannot plead the rule (see e.g. *Howard Patent Ivory Manufacturing Co* (1833) 38 Ch D 156);
- a third party cannot rely on the rule in circumstances where he is an insider, i.e. an officer of the company (see e.g. *Morris* v *Kansen* [1946] AC 459);
- where there are suspicious circumstances surrounding the authorisation of a transaction and the third party should reasonably have been aware of such circumstances, the third party will not be able to rely on the rule (see e.g. *Underwood* v *Bank of Liverpool & Martins Ltd* [1924] 1 KB 755);
- the rule will not operate where the contractual authorisation was a forgery (see e.g. *Ruben* v *Great Fingall Consolidated* [1906] AC 439);
- finally, where the necessary authorisation for a transaction requires the passing of a special resolution, a third party will be deemed to have notice of the outcome of the resolution in so far as this type of resolution requires public registration (see e.g. *Irvine* v *Union Bank of Australia* (1877) 2 App Cas 366).

While the indoor management rule is applicable to the internal procedures necessary to validate any given exercise of authority, for example, it would be applicable in a situation where an ordinary resolution was required to validate an exercise of authority, the rule taken on its own cannot extend to issues relating to the ability of a board of directors to confer ostensible authority. Thus, a third party is not entitled to rely on the indoor management rule for the purpose of assuming that an officer had been given an authority by the board to act in excess of his actual or usual authority.

A case example which illustrates the relationship between the *Turquand* rule and ostensible authority is *Mahony* v *East Holyford Mining Company* (1875) LR 7 HL. This case involved a claim by a company to the effect that its bank had paid moneys from the company's account without due authorisation. The bank, in making payments from the company's account, had done so in the belief that it was following the conditions laid down in the company's articles; the articles prescribed that payments should only be made when cheques had been signed by two directors and then countersigned by the company secretary. The difficulty in this case was that no director or company secretary had actually been appointed by the company. However, the persons who purported to authorise the payments for the company were nevertheless allowed to do so by the company. The House of Lords held that the bank was allowed to assume (as it had no actual notice to the contrary) that the internal regulations of the company had been complied with, and that appointments to the positions of corporate responsibility had been made (operation of indoor management rule). The House found that the acquiescence of the company in its failure to deny that the officers had authority to act created a representation upon which the bank could rely (ostensible authority).

THE EFFECT OF THE COMPANIES ACT 1989

Prior to its amendment by the Companies Act 1989, s 35(1) of the Companies Act 1985 was not exclusively confined to questions relating to the validity of a purported *ultra vires* transaction. Indeed, s 35(1) was of importance whenever the authority of a director was called into question. Where the section was applicable (note the problems created by the wording of the section; see Chapter 8) the board of directors' authority to bind the company was deemed free of any limitation placed upon it by the company's memorandum and articles. Accordingly, a third party could rely on the authority of the board of directors provided that the third party acted in good faith. Section 35(2) of the 1985 Act abolished the concept of constructive notice in so far as s 35(1) was applicable.

As well as severely restricting the ambit of the *ultra vires* rule, the Companies Act 1989 (s 108(1)), in its attempt to produce a climate of contractual freedom, has sought to further limit the restrictions placed upon the authority of company directors. The reforms applicable to directors' authority are aimed at complementing those made in connection with matters relating to the overall scope of a company's capacity to enter into contractual relationships. The 1989 Act has amended and introduced new sections into the relevant parts of the 1985 Act. A new s 35A(1) of the Companies Act 1985 provides:

> 'In favour of a person dealing with a company in good faith, the power of the board of directors to bind the company, or authorise others to do so, shall be deemed to be free of any limitation under the company's constitution.'

In accordance with s 35A(1), the status of the board may be described as the guardian of its principal's (the company's) ability to delegate authority. In an attempt to surmount the difficulties associated with the interpretation of the wording used in old s 35(1) (discussed in Chapter 8), a new s 35A(2)(a) of the Companies Act provides that a person will deal with a company if he is 'a party to any transaction or other act to which the company is a party'. As such, the section should be construed as not only being applicable to commercial actions. In addition, s 35A(2)(b) and (c) clarify the meaning of 'good faith' by providing that a person is not to be regarded as having acted in bad faith solely as a result of knowing that a corporate act was beyond the powers of the directors under the company's constitution; indeed a person is presumed to have acted in good faith unless the contrary is proved (this clearly extends the protection afforded by the *Turquand* rule). However, it is somewhat unfortunate that no guidance is given as to what constitutes bad faith. It should also be observed that although s 35A(1) uses the term 'limitations under the company's constitution', the term 'constitution' is in accordance with s 35A(3) given an extended meaning, in so far as it includes limitations deriving from a resolution of the general meeting, a meeting of any class of shareholders and limitations derived from a membership agreement. In the unlikely event of a third party being unable to rely on s 35A, a transaction involving a breach of director's authority may nevertheless be ratified by ordinary resolution. However, note that the ratification of a transaction which was entered into with an authority which exceeds a limitation on the board's powers, as specified within the memorandum, may only be achieved by a special resolution of the general meeting (s 35(3), CA 1985).

The legislature's decision not to confer individual directors with the authority to bind the company as of right was in sharp contrast to the recommendations of the Prentice Report (1986). However, in this respect, the legislature's decision to not adopt the Prentice Report's proposals was perhaps understandable. The radical departure from the traditional position of ultimate authority as vested in the board of directors would have meant that a director responsible and with authority to bind the company in, say, contract type X, would have had an equal and independent right to bind the company in contract type Y. The director's ability to bind the company in contract type Y would have existed without any form of delegation of authority from the board and would have bound the company to the contract, despite the fact that the director may not have had any expertise in business matters related to contract type Y.

Although the Companies Act 1989, in its retention of the board as the ultimate source of authority, denies individual directors an unfettered right to contractually bind the company, s 35A allows individual directors the right to bind the company where the director's act is the result of a delegation of authority from the board. The power to so bind the company is deemed free of any limitation under the company's constitution (new s 35A(3), CA 1985). Therefore, a company officer, with authority delegated from the board to, for example, bind the company in contract type Y, will be able to so bind the company, irrespective of whether the company's constitution prohibits the company from entering into a type Y contract and irrespective of the fact that the director's position conferred no usual authority to bind the company to the transaction.

In respect of shareholders' rights, shareholders retain the power to prevent transactions from taking place, where, if the transaction had been allowed to proceed, the board would have exceeded its authority (new s 35A(4), CA 1985). However, where a contract is to be performed in fulfilment of a previous legal obligation, no shareholder intervention will be possible (see Chapter 8 for a discussion on the meaning of 'previous legal obligation'). It should be noted that the board or a person authorised by the board will remain personally liable to the company in respect of a transaction which was entered into outside the scope of the company's constitution (new s 35A(5), CA 1985). However, if a third party acts in good faith, no shareholder action (save for the limited right under s 35A(4)) will be able to prevent the enforcement of a contract with a company where the contract was entered into by a duly authorised officer of the company, even in a situation where the contract type is not permitted by the company's constitution or where the enforcement of the contract might otherwise have been regarded as a fraud on minority interests. Indeed, the minority shareholders' position is weakened by the fact that a third party's actual knowledge of a limitation on a director's authority to enter into a contract will not necessarily preclude the third party from having acted in good faith (new s 35A(2), CA 1985).

Unlike the wording of the old s 35 of the Companies Act 1985, the effect of the Companies Act 1989 has been to abrogate the constructive notice rule without any form of restrictive limitations. Under the old s 35 the abolition of the constructive rule had no effect unless the contract in question was of a commercial nature and was one decided upon by all the directors (see Chapter 8). However, although a third party is not deemed to have constructive notice of an act which is beyond the company's constitution, he must nevertheless assure himself that the person with whom he dealt was authorised to act by the board. This is impliedly confirmed by new s 35B, CA 1985 which states:

> 'A party to a transaction with a company is not bound to enquire as to whether it is permitted by the company's memorandum *or as to any limitation on the powers of the board of directors to bind the company or authorise others to do so.*' (emphasis added)

Although s 35B removes a third party's need to concern himself about the existence of a limitation on authority, the section nevertheless impliedly preserves the requirement for an authority to have existed, i.e. the transaction must still be sanctioned by the board or a duly authorised person.

The abolition of the constructive notice rule, in so far as it affects the ability of an authorised person to bind the company, is, nevertheless, subject to one exception, namely, where the board enter into a contract with an insider, i.e. a director or connected person, and the board exceed any limitations on its powers under the company's constitution, the transaction will become voidable at the company's option. As such, insiders are not to be protected by the abolition of the constructive notice rule and will not be able to seek the protection of ss 35A and 35B. The insider and any director of the company who authorised the contract will remain personally liable to account to the company for any gain made or loss incurred as a result of the transaction (new s 322A, CA 1985). Where, however, an innocent bona fide third party acquires rights as a result of the insider transaction, the company will, in such a case, be unable to avoid it.

The removal of the doctrine of constructive notice to all areas of company law, save for company charges, was to be made as a result of s 142(1) of the Companies Act 1989, which sought to create a new s 711A of the Companies Act 1985. However, this provision has not (yet) been enacted. Interestingly, s 711A(2), CA 1985 provided that the abolition of the constructive notice rule would –

'... not affect the question as to whether a person is affected by notice of any matter by reason of a failure to make such enquiries as ought reasonably to be made.'

The wording of s 711A(2) was perhaps vaguely constructed and appeared to be in conflict with s 35B of the Companies Act 1985. Nevertheless, in so far as the section relates to questions of corporate capacity and directors' authority, it is suggested that it may be construed as reinforcing the fact that it remains a third party's responsibility to ensure that a purported company agent has some form of authority to act on behalf of the company in the area of corporate policy in question.

The position of the *Turquand* rule after the Companies Act 1989

In abolishing the doctrine of constructive notice, the Companies Act 1989 has to some extent extinguished the need for the *Turquand* rule. However, the *Turquand* rule may still be of assistance in matters concerning the board's delegation of authority. For example, where the board delegates authority to a company agent, but in doing so places internal restrictions on the ability of the agent to carry out his functions (a matter not covered by s 35A(3), CA 1985), then in accordance with the *Turquand* rule, the third party will not, unless he has actual notice, be deemed to have knowledge of such restrictions. The *Turquand* rule will also continue to be of assistance in those cases where no valid appointment of a company officer has been made, notwithstanding that the company's constitution provides for such appointments; see e.g. *Mahony* v *East Holyford Mining Co* (1875) LR 7 HL (discussed above).

Suggested further reading

The effect of the 1989 Act
Griffin [1991] NILQ 38
Griffin (1991) 12 Co Law 98
Poole (1991) 12 Co Law 43
Ferran (1992) 13 Co Law 124, 177

10

THE LEGAL NATURE AND CHARACTERISTICS OF HOLDING SHARES IN A LIMITED COMPANY

INTRODUCTION

A company which is limited by shares is founded on an undertaking by its members to contribute capital in consideration for the issue of shares. The aim of this chapter is to explain the legal characteristics associated with the various types of share capital. In addition to identifying the legal characteristics attributed to the various types of shares, this chapter briefly discusses share valuations and the powers of both the court and Secretary of State to impose restrictions on rights associated with share ownership. The issue of shares in public companies is specifically dealt with in Chapter 11. The maintenance of a company's share capital is dealt with in Chapter 12.

THE LEGAL CHARACTERISTICS OF A SHARE

The extent of a shareholder's undertaking to contribute capital to a company and the shareholder's right to participate in dividend distributions and vote at general meetings are all related to the number and class of shares held in the company. As soon as share capital is contributed, it becomes the property of the company and as such the company is not to be regarded as a debtor in respect of its repayment or restoration.

A commonly quoted definition relating to the legal nature of a company share is that advanced by the judgment of Farwell J in *Borland's Trustee* v *Steel Bros & Co Ltd* [1901] 1 Ch 279. His lordship stated:

> 'A share is the interest of a shareholder in the company measured by a sum of money, for the purposes of liability in the first place and interest in the second, but also consisting of a mutual set of covenants entered into by all the shareholders *inter se*.' (at p 288)

In respect of the above quotation, 'the sum of money' is the price attached to a share. Following the advancement of the full purchase price for a share, a person's liability to contribute capital ceases. The minimum amount by which the share may be purchased from the company is termed the nominal value of the share (see e.g. *Ooregum Gold Mining Co of India* v *Roper* [1892] AC 125). Where a company offers to sell shares at a price in excess of their nominal value, the monetary difference between the price paid for the shares and the nominal value is termed the 'share premium' and must be placed in a share premium account (discussed below).

The extent of a shareholder's interest is measured by the number and class of shares purchased. A shareholding interest is comprised of all the legal rights of membership contained within a mutual set of covenants: the company's memorandum and articles of association. However, the exact scope of a membership interest is likely to extend beyond strict legal rights; the extent of a membership interest will be dependent upon the nature of the shares and the type of company in which they are held. (The scope of a membership interest is discussed in Chapter 23.)

Unless a company is unlimited or limited by guarantee, its memorandum must indicate the amount of share capital which the company is permitted to issue (authorised share capital clause), together with the manner in which the capital is to be divided into shares of a fixed amount (s 2(5), CA 1985). The nominal capital of a public company must not be less than £50 000. A company is not permitted to issue shares beyond its authorised share capital limit, although where a company's articles permit, the authorised share capital may be altered in accordance with s 121(1) and (2) of the Companies Act 1985. Where a company adopts the standard Table A articles, Table A, Art 32 provides that alterations to the authorised share capital clause may be instigated by an ordinary resolution, although if the company is a private company, the alteration powers contained within s 121 may be employed without the need to call a general meeting, i.e. provided that the members of the company unanimously agree to the alteration in writing.

IDENTIFYING A MEMBER OF A COMPANY

A person may become a member of a company in one of four ways:

- by subscribing to the memorandum on the incorporation of the company;
- by making a successful application to a company for shares;
- by purchasing shares from an existing member of a company; or
- by acquiring shares as a result of a member's death or bankruptcy.

While the terms 'member' and 'shareholder' are quite often interchangeable, it is nevertheless possible to be a member but not a shareholder of a company. For example, a company limited by guarantee has members, but it does not normally have shareholders. Conversely, it is possible to be a shareholder but not a member of a company. For example, the holders of what are termed 'bearer shares' are classed as shareholders, but although shareholders, they may not necessarily be members of the company. Holders of bearer shares are entitled to specific shares identified in a share warrant. Subject to any contrary provision within the articles, the bearer of a share warrant is entitled to have his name entered in the register of members only upon the surrender of the share warrant (s 188, CA 1985).

The register of members

Section 352 of the Companies Act 1985 provides that every company must keep a register of its members, giving details of their names, addresses and the extent of each member's shareholding in the company. The subscribers to a company's memorandum are deemed to have agreed to become members of the company and upon the company's registration must be entered as members in the company's register of members (s 22(1), CA 1985). Section 22(2) of the Companies Act 1985 further provides that every other person who has otherwise assented to become a member and whose name is entered in the register of members, is a member of the company. For a person to assent to become a member of a company it is unnecessary to establish a binding contract between that person and the company. Accordingly, a person's membership of a company will *prima facie* be conclusive where, irrespective of the absence of a binding contract, a person's name (if he has assented) is added to the register (see e.g. *Re Nuneaton Borough AFC Ltd* [1989] BCLC, 454). However, it should be noted that in *POW Services Ltd* v *Clare* [1995] 2 BCLC 205, Jacob J held that notwithstanding that the conditions may have been met in relation to s 22(2), a person's membership of a company could nevertheless be denied, as of right, in circumstances where, for example, that person became a member of the company in contravention of a term(s) of the company's articles.

Where the details entered in the register of members are incorrect in some material respect, they may be challenged in accordance with s 359 of the Companies Act 1985. In order for a person to successfully challenge an entry, it is necessary to establish a legitimate interest in the shares to which the entry relates. A legitimate interest may be defined as one which is in the best interests of the company as a whole. For example, in *Re Piccadilly Radio plc* [1989] BCLC 683, the court refused to correct an entry in the register relating to the transfer of shares, notwithstanding that the shares had been transferred in breach of the company's articles (however, note the decision of Jacob J in *POW Services Ltd* v *Clare*, discussed above). The court refused to sanction a rectification of the register because those seeking to rely on s 359 sought to protect their own membership interests rather than the interests of the company. Those members who sought to challenge the transfer of shares did so in order to prevent the transfer of shares to a party opposed to a takeover bid in which they, the objecting members, had a personal interest, i.e. those members who sought to rely on s 359 did so for a collateral and improper purpose.

The case of *Re Thundercrest Ltd* [1994] BCC 857 does, however, provide an example of a successful application under s 359. The case concerned a proposed allotment of a rights issue of shares. The company's three shareholders, who were also the company's only directors, had all expressed a willingness to participate in the issue, however, one of the shareholders, P (the plaintiff) failed to reply to the letter of provisional allotment. The letter had, in accordance with the terms of the company's articles, been sent by post, by recorded delivery. As a result of P's failure to reply to the offer letter (although the letter was correctly addressed, P never received the offer letter), the two other shareholders (the defendants) wrongly assumed that P had decided to decline to participate in the rights issue. The shares previously meant for P were therefore allotted between the defendants.

The issue was declared invalid in accordance with s 359 in so far as the period of notice allowed for the acceptance of the offer had, contrary to s 90(6), CA 1985, been less than the prescribed 21 days. Although the offer letter was properly posted in accordance with the terms of the company's articles and despite the existence of a provision in the company's articles which allowed the notice for the acceptance period to expire after 'a set time period' (the time period for acceptance of this rights issue was set at 18 days), Paul Baker J observed that the company's articles provided that the relevant legislation (s 90(6)) would apply unless it was inconsistent with the articles. As the terms of the company's articles did not **specifically** make mention of a definite expiry period in relation to the acceptance of an allotment offer, Paul Baker J held that the expiry period should be governed in accordance with s 90(6). It was insufficient that the company's articles had permitted the company to set an expiry period, other than the one specified by s 90(6). Further, the learned judge considered that the defendants' case had been prejudiced in so far as P's offer letter had been returned by the post office to the company's office prior to the allotment of the shares, i.e. the defendants should have been aware that P had never received the letter. Accordingly, the company's register was modified to cancel the said shares.

ISSUING SHARES

Shares are issued (allotted) by a company as a result of a resolution from the company's board of directors; the board must be vested with the power to issue shares, a power which is usually contained within the company's articles. An authority to allot shares will last for a maximum of five years whereupon it may, if so desired, be renewed by the general meeting. Alternatively, the power to issue shares may be authorised by an ordinary resolution in general meeting (s 80, CA 1985). However, it should be noted that a private company may, in accordance with s 80A of the Companies Act 1985, elect by ordinary resolution to authorise directors to allot shares to a maximum specified amount over a fixed or indefinite period. This authority may be revoked by general meeting (discussed further in Chapter 18).

A director who knowingly and wilfully contravenes, permits or authorises a contravention of s 80 is liable to a fine. However, a person who purchases shares which have been issued without a proper authority, i.e. in accordance with s 80, will nevertheless obtain a good title in respect of the issued shares (s 80(10), CA 1985). It should be noted that a company cannot allot shares to itself; see e.g. *Trevor v Whitworth* (1887) 12 App Cas 409.

Where shares are issued with the appropriate authority, the issue may nevertheless be voidable in circumstances where it was deemed to be for an improper purpose, for example, where the underlying purpose of the issue was to manipulate voting control as opposed to raising additional share capital (discussed further in Chapter 17). In appropriate circumstances a share issue could also be avoided where it constitutes a fraud on minority interests (see Chapter 22), or alternatively where its effect was to unfairly prejudice the interests of the members generally or a part of the membership, i.e. contrary to s 459, CA 1985 (see Chapter 23).

Purchase of shares in a private company

Although a private company may seek offers for its shares from persons other than existing members, it is nevertheless a common feature of a private company's articles to find a clause which purports to restrict the manner in which the company's shares are held, for example, the ownership of shares may be restricted to the existing members of the company or their relatives. It should be noted that it is an offence for a private company to make an offer of its shares to the general public (s 81, CA 1985), although under s 170 of the Financial Services Act 1986 (as amended by s 199, CA 1989), the Secretary of State for Trade and Industry may, by order, prescribe circumstances in which a private company will be permitted to advertise securities (the nature of the advertisement will be restricted and be of a private character). In addition, a private company, if authorised to so act by the Secretary of State, may be allowed to issue investment advertisements in circumstances where the securities to be advertised are of a type which are not, in the opinion of the Secretary of State, likely to attract the attention of the general public and where it is expected that the shares would be purchased by persons who were sufficiently capable of understanding any risks involved in respect of the purchase.

Nominee holdings

Shares may be registered in the name of a nominee; the nominee will hold the shares directly or indirectly for some other party. While the owner of shares may wish to register them in the name of a nominee for a legitimate reason, the use of nominees may disguise a more sinister purpose. For example, nominee holdings may mask an attempt by the true owner of the shares to secretly purchase sufficient capital to instigate a takeover bid. The Companies Act 1985 seeks to remedy any potential abuse of nominee holdings (Part VI, CA 1985 as amended by s 134, CA 1989). For example, under s 198 of the Companies Act 1985, notification of known interests in voting shares in a public company must be communicated to the company concerned within two days of the obligation arising. An 'interest' normally means a holding of 3 per cent in the shares of the company. The provisions contained within Part VI of the Companies Act 1985 are supplemented by the powers of investigation afforded to the Department of Trade and Industry (see Chapter 24).

THE PAYMENT FOR COMPANY SHARES

Except in a situation where a company allots bonus shares to its existing members (discussed below), or where it resolves to extinguish any amount owing on shares which were at that time not fully paid up, then in accordance with s 99 of the Companies Act 1985, the acquisition of a company's shares and the payment of any premium on the shares must be by means of a monetary consideration, i.e. shares must be paid for with cash or something to which a monetary value can be attached. Whilst a private company may accept an undertaking for the future performance of services in consideration for the sale of shares, a public company may not do so (s 99(2), CA 1985). Further, a public company may not allot shares for a consideration which includes any form of undertaking which is to be or may be performed more than five years after the allotment (s 102, CA 1985).

While the full purchase price of a share can be paid for in instalments (partly paid shares), a public company may not issue a share unless at least 25 per cent of its nominal value and the whole of any premium payable on it has been made (s 101(1), CA 1985). An exception to this rule is provided for by s 101(2) of the Companies Act 1985, namely, shares may be allotted in pursuance of an employee's share scheme (discussed below).

Where the consideration to be provided for the purchase of shares in a private company is other than a cash consideration, the court will not generally enquire as to the adequacy of the consideration; see e.g. *Re Wragg* [1871] 1 Ch 796. However, the court may intervene where the consideration is clearly inadequate, i.e. if it appears that some form of fraud or bad faith has been involved (see e.g. *Hong Kong & China Gas Co v Glen* [1914] 1 Ch 527). However, where a public company accepts payment in exchange for an allotment of shares, otherwise than in cash, the company must normally obtain a valuation or validation of the value of the consideration in question (s 103, CA 1985). Section 103, CA 1985 is applicable save in a situation where a company allots:

- bonus shares;
- shares to the shareholders of another company in exchange for the transfer or cancellation of shares in that other company; or
- shares to the shareholders of another company in exchange for the acquisition of the assets and liabilities of that other company.

Other than where one of the above exceptions applies, the valuation or validation must be undertaken by an independent person who must be qualified as an auditor (s 108(1), CA 1985). A copy of the independent report must be sent to the proposed purchaser of the shares. Where a contravention of the aforementioned provisions take place and shares are allotted, the allottee will be personally liable to pay an amount up to the nominal value of the shares, plus a part or whole of any premium on the shares. The allottee will be liable except in circumstances which indicate that he was unaware of any form of contravention. The court may exercise its discretion under s 113 of the

Companies Act 1985 to exempt the allottee from the whole or any part of the liability.

Share certificate

The articles of a company often provide for the form and contents of the company's share certificate; see e.g. Table A, Arts 6 and 7. A share certificate is not a document of title to shares but rather it is prima facie evidence of title. Share certificates must be issued by a company within two months of the allotment of shares (s 185, CA 1985).

Share transfers

A share may be transferred in accordance with the terms of a company's articles. The articles of a private company often include a clause which restricts a member's ability to transfer shares. The articles of a private company may even give the directors of the company a power, in defined circumstances, to compel a member to transfer shares; see e.g. *Sidebottom* v *Kershaw, Leese & Co Ltd* [1920] 1 Ch 154 (discussed in Chapter 7).

A more common restriction on the transfer of shares is one which provides a right of pre-emption, i.e. a member who wishes to sell shares must first offer them to existing members of the company. Where a member wishing to sell shares is compelled to sell to an existing member of the company, the company's articles will normally contain a valuation procedure. The valuation of shares will normally be undertaken by the company's auditor. Other than where fraud is alleged, the valuation cannot normally be challenged (see e.g. *Jones* v *Sherwood Computer Services plc* [1992] 1 WLR 277), albeit that an aggrieved member may in an appropriate case seek a just and equitable winding up order against the company (see s 122(1)(g), IA 1986, discussed in Chapter 23). An appropriate case would be where the member's entitlement to a proportion of the company's realised assets amounted to a sum in excess of the valuation figure (see e.g. *Re Abbey Leisure* [1990] BCC 60, discussed further in Chapter 23). In addition, a member of a company may in appropriate cases, pursue an action in negligence against the person responsible for the share valuation (see e.g. *Whiteoak* v *Walker* [1988] 4 BCC 122).

A company's articles may also provide that the directors of the company may, at their absolute discretion, refuse a transfer of shares or only approve one on specified grounds. Where this power of veto exists, the company will be required to give notice of any refusal to register shares within two months of the presentation of the transfer (s 183(5), CA 1985). Where such notice is not given, as in *Re Swaledale Cleaners Ltd* [1968] 1 WLR 1710 and more recently in *Re Inverdeck Ltd* [1998] BCC 256, then, in accordance with s 359 of the Companies Act 1985, a person to whom the shares were transferred will be entitled to an order requiring the company to register the transfer of shares. If, in accordance with a company's articles, a refusal to transfer shares may only take place in specified circumstances, the specified circumstances must be met, prior to the company's refusal to register a transfer (see e.g. *Re Bede Steam Shipping Co Ltd* [1917] 1 Ch 123).

Transfer procedure

The procedure for transferring shares is normally set out in a company's articles (see e.g. Table A, Arts 23–28). In addition to any regulatory provision contained within the articles, for example, in a private company compliance with pre-emption rights, the regulation of fully paid-up share transfers is provided for by the Stock Transfer Act 1963. Transfers of partly paid shares are outside the ambit of the 1963 Act. A company's power to refuse to register a transfer of shares is one which must be exercised bona fide for the benefit of the company; see e.g. *Tett* v *Phoenix & Investment Co Ltd* [1984] BCLC 599.

Prior to April 1997, the transfer of securities listed on the stock exchange operated via a computerised system called the Talisman system. This system was introduced following the Stock Exchange (Completion of Business) Act 1976. Under this system, transactions on the London Stock Exchange were partly based on computerised trading, however, the completion of the transfer of title to securities was effected manually. The implementation of a totally paperless system for the transfer of listed securities was proposed in 1981, a system to facilitate the Stock Exchange being brought into line with the major European markets. Section 207 of the Companies Act 1989 was passed to enable regulations to be made containing the necessary changes to the law governing the transfer of securities by a computerised system. An initial computerised system which was to be known as the Taurus system was abandoned in March 1993, after a meeting of the London Stock Exchange considered that its cost would be too expensive. Nevertheless, a less onerous system, known as CREST, was developed and put into operation in July 1996; it replaced the Talisman system over a nine-month transition period. The CREST system is not compulsory and is only applicable to a company which has been approved as a 'participating issuer'. (See the Uncertificated Securities Regulations 1995 (SI 1995/3272).)

TYPES OF SHARES

A company may create different types of shares, i.e. the legal rights of a particular type of share (class rights) may vary from those of other types of shares issued by the company. The legal rights attached to shares may be seen as comprising:

- rights as to dividend payments;
- voting rights; and
- rights to the return of capital on an authorised reduction of capital or on a winding up of a company.

The legal rights of any given type of share are determined by either, the terms of a company's constitution, i.e. the memorandum or articles, or by the terms of the particular share issue.

Deferred/management/founders' shares

This type of share may be issued to the founders of a company. The right to a dividend payment is deferred on a founder's share, i.e. the dividend payment is held back until a dividend payment has been made to the company's other shareholders; the holders of founder shares are then entitled to the remainder of whatever amount the company has reserved for dividend payments. Founders' shares are now rare, especially in public companies where strict Stock Exchange listing requirements have curtailed their existence. These stricter rules were introduced to curb promoters of public companies from exploiting their positions, i.e. promoters were often able to take founders' shares to a value in excess of the value of their services to the company.

Employee shares

Many companies operate schemes whereby company employees are encouraged to take up shares. Employee share schemes allow the workers in a company to participate in the profits they help create. In addition to giving the employees a right to a share of the company's profits, employee share schemes may be seen as a means of motivating the workforce to attain higher profit levels. Section 743 of the Companies Act 1985 defines an employees' share scheme as a scheme for the benefit of the *bona fide* employees or former employees of the company, the company's subsidiary or holding company, or a subsidiary of the company's holding company or, the wives, husbands, widows, widowers or children or step children under the age of 18 of such employees or former employees.

Where shares are offered to the employees of a company, the general pre-emption rules contained within s 89 of the Companies Act 1985 (discussed below) are not applicable, i.e. a company is not required to first offer the shares, designated for the employees, to existing members of the company. However, where a general allotment of shares is proposed, the pre-emption rules operate in favour of the employee share scheme, i.e. part of the general issue of shares must first be offered to holders of existing employee shares.

Ordinary shares

Where a company's shares are issued without being divided into different classes, the shares will be ordinary (equity) shares. If a company issues shares which have specific class rights (discussed below), any remaining shares to which the specific rights are not attached will be construed as ordinary shares. The greatest part of a company's share capital will normally consist of ordinary shares. An ordinary share is usually the only type of share to carry votes at general meetings of the company's shareholding body. Where a company declares a dividend payment, the dividend payable on ordinary shares will usually be determined in accordance with the performance of the company and therefore will vary according to the fortunes of the company. Dividends payable on ordinary shares are paid after dividends have been paid to preference shareholders (discussed below).

It is permissible for a company, if authorised by its constitution, to issue different types of ordinary shares. Ordinary shares may be created as non-voting shares, shares with limited voting rights, or shares with enhanced voting rights. For example, a company's ordinary shares may be divided into distinct classes, for example, a class A ordinary share and a class B ordinary share. Although both class A and class B shares may carry the same rights in respect to dividend payments, the class A share may carry 100 votes per share whereas the class B share may only carry one vote per share; see e.g. *Holt v Holt* [1990] 1 WLR 1250.

It is also possible for a company to create ordinary shares which, in specific circumstances, carry enhanced voting rights. For example, the voting rights attached to the shares held by a director of a company may, in accordance with the terms of the company's articles, be increased in circumstances where the general meeting propose to remove the said director from office; see e.g. *Bushell v Faith* [1970] AC 1099 (discussed in Chapter 7).

Preference shares

A preference share is a share to which certain preferential rights are attached. Although there is no statutory definition to expose the specific nature of this type of share, the most common distinctive attribute attached to a preference share is the preferential payment of dividends in priority to other types of shares. However, as noted below, this may not be the only preferential type of right attached to a preference share. A company may also issue convertible preference shares; these type of preference shares, subject to the terms of their issue, can, at the option of the shareholder, be converted into ordinary shares.

The determination of the extent of the legal rights attached to a preference share will be dependent upon the construction of that part of a company's constitution which governs the particular share issue. The terms of the relevant regulations (or terms of the specific terms of the share issue) exclusively define the rights attached to a class of shares; see e.g. *Scottish Insurance Corporation Ltd v Wilsons & Clyde* [1949] AC 462. In the absence of specific regulations to determine the rights attached to a particular type of share, the rights of the holders of all classes of shares (ordinary and preference shareholders) are deemed to be the same; see e.g. *Birch v Cropper* (1889) 14 App Cas 525.

The voting rights attached to preference shares are normally defined so that preference shareholders are only entitled to a right to vote in circumstances where their dividend payments are in arrears, or in a situation where a proposed variation of the rights attached to the preference share is advanced. Where the voting rights of preference shareholders are not so defined, the principle in *Birch* v *Cropper* will apply, i.e. preference shareholders will be accorded the same voting rights as the holders of ordinary shares.

Preferential right to dividend payments

The holder of a preference share may be entitled to a fixed rate of return (fixed dividend) or alternatively, the rate of return may be fixed with an additional payment to represent a share in the company's profits. This latter type of preference share is called a participating preference share. The right of participation is limited to an entitlement to share in any surplus profits, i.e. to be paid after a dividend has been paid to the company's ordinary shareholders. For the preference share to have been created as a participating preference share, the company's constitution must specify that the preference share was so created; see e.g. *Will* v *United Lankart Plantations Co Ltd* [1914] AC 11.

The preference shareholder's entitlement to a fixed payment will be dependent, in any given year, on the company's ability to declare a dividend. The entitlement to a fixed payment may be either cumulative or non-cumulative. Where the payment is of a cumulative nature and the company is unable to pay a fixed payment in any one year, it must make up the difference at some future date, i.e. when it is able to declare a dividend. Unless the terms of a preference share issue state otherwise, there is a presumption that a preference share is cumulative; see e.g. *Webb* v *Earle* (1875) LR 20 Eq 556. Where a company is in liquidation, the entitlement of the company's preferential shareholders to any outstanding amount owed in respect of a cumulative dividend payment, will be dependent upon whether the company's constitution made provision for such payments. Where a company's constitution does specifically provide for such payments, any arrears owing to preference shareholders will be paid out of the company's remaining surplus assets, following prior payment of the company's debts. If a company's constitution contains no specific provision of entitlement, it will be assumed that preference shareholders are unable to claim arrears of dividend; see e.g. *Re Crichton's Oil Co* [1902] 2 Ch 86.

Preferential rights to capital assets

On the winding up of a company or upon a reduction of capital (discussed in Chapter 12), a company's preference shareholders may, by the terms of the company's constitution or share issue, be given a preferential right to the return of their capital investment and/or a right to participate in the distribution of a company's surplus assets. Whether a specific right exists as to the return of capital or the ability to participate in surplus assets is a question which will be determined by a construction of the company's constitution, or terms of the share issue. Where the company's regulations make it clear that preference shareholders have no preferential right to the return of capital or the right to participate in the distribution of surplus assets, then effect will be given to such a term. Where the company's regulations simply afford a preferential return of capital, the company's regulations will be exhaustive of that right, i.e. the preference shareholders will take a preference in the return of their capital investment but will not be entitled to participate in a division of any surplus capital, i.e. assets that remain after the company's creditors have been paid and after all shareholders have had their initial capital investment in the company returned to them (see e.g. *Scottish Insurance Corporation* v *Wilsons & Clyde Coal Co Ltd* [1949] AC 462). Where no provision is made within the regulations for the distribution of capital or surplus assets, all shareholders of all classes will participate equally; see e.g. *Birch* v *Cropper* (1889) 14 App Cas 525, where Lord Macnaughten, expressing the unanimous view of the House of Lords stated:

> **'Every person who becomes a member of a company limited by shares of equal amount becomes entitled to a proportionate part in the capital of the company, and, unless it be otherwise provided by the regulations of the company is entitled as a necessary consequence, to the same proportionate part in all the property of the company, including its uncalled capital.'** (at p 543)

However, difficulties in respect of the entitlement of preference shareholders to participate in the surplus assets of a company have nevertheless arisen in circumstances where a company's surplus assets include accumulated income, income which prior to the company's liquidation could, by the terms of the company's constitution, have only been distributed to the company's ordinary shareholders. Whilst any accumulated income should, following a company's liquidation, be considered to be a part of the company's surplus assets, i.e. dividend payments to ordinary shareholders are no longer made when a company is in liquidation, in *Re Bridgewater* [1891] 2 Ch 317 the Court of Appeal took a contrary view. The court's decision in *Re Bridgewater* was founded upon the premise that, irrespective of a company's liquidation, certain non-capital assets of the company could retain their character as income and as such the income could only be converted into capital if an intention to that effect had been made clear by the company's constitution. Whilst the decision in *Re Bridgewater* avoided the anomaly of income meant only for distribution amongst ordinary shareholders being distributed to both ordinary and preference shareholders, it is suggested that the decision impugns the logical assumption that in liquidation the rights of the company's shareholders should no longer be governed by regulations specifically formulated to regulate the company whilst it was a going concern. Indeed, subsequent cases (see e.g. *Re Isle of Thanet Electricity Supply Co Ltd* [1950] Ch 161 and *Dimbula Valley (Ceylon) Tea Co Ltd* v *Laurie* [1961] Ch 353) would appear to confirm the view that unless specifically provided for by the company's constitution, the rights of shareholders on the liquidation of the company cannot be calculated according to rights which were applicable to them prior to the company's liquidation.

THE CLASS RIGHTS ATTACHED TO SHARES

The rights attached to a particular type of share are termed class rights and may be determined by reference to the contents of a company's constitution (see e.g. Table A, Art 2), created by the terms of a particular share issue or by a special resolution of the general meeting (see *Re Old Silkstone Collieries Ltd* [1954] Ch 169, discussed below) and further may, in accordance with *Harman* v *BML Group Ltd* [1994] 2 BCLC 674, be created by the terms of a shareholders' agreement.

In *Harman* v *BML Group Ltd*, the Court of Appeal (overturning a decision of Paul Baker QC sitting as a deputy High Court judge) upheld the validity of a quorum provision contained in a shareholders' agreement to which all the members of the company were party. The agreement provided that the holder of B shares (Z or his proxy) had an absolute right to be present at all shareholder meetings. The capital of the company was divided as between the holders of 'A' ordinary shares of which C and D held a majority (X and Y held a minority of the 'A' shares), and the holder of the 'B' ordinary shares (Z held all of this class). The class A and B shares carried equal rights. C and D held an overall majority of the company's ordinary shares and voting rights. In 1993 a dispute arose between C and Z, whereby Z alleged that C and D had perpetrated a fraud against the company. As a consequence of this dispute, an extraordinary meeting was convened by Z; the meeting was convened with the intention of passing a motion to dismiss C and D from their directorships. The meeting (lasting for only one minute) resulted in C and D being dismissed from their directorships; the vote was taken by a show of hands. Z, X and Y having voted in favour of the motion; the meeting was closed before C and D could seek the right to a poll vote, a vote which they would not have lost in so far as they held the majority of the voting shares.

As a result of their dismissal, C and D sought to convene a meeting of the shareholders to reverse the decision taken at the extraordinary meeting. Z refused to attend the meeting, which therefore would, in accordance with the shareholder agreement, have been rendered invalid, if it had proceeded. C and D therefore sought to hold a meeting pursuant to s 371 of the Companies Act 1985 (discussed further in Chapter 18) which would have allowed them to convene the meeting irrespective of the shareholder agreement and as such without Z in attendance. The Court of Appeal concluded that an order under s 371 would have overridden Z's class rights and would therefore have been inappropriate.

In addition, class rights may also be created where, by the terms of a company's constitution, rights have been conferred on a particular member of the company in that member's capacity as a shareholder. In such a case the class rights exist notwithstanding that they have not been specifically attached to the shares held by the member. For example, in *Cumbrian Newspapers Group Ltd* v *Cumberland & Westmorland Herald Newspaper & Printing Co Ltd* [1987] Ch 1 the plaintiff acquired a 10.67 per cent holding in the defendant company (Cumberland) and, as a condition of the acquisition,

Cumberland's articles were altered to confer the plaintiff with specific rights designed to prevent an outside party from acquiring control of Cumberland. Irrespective of the fact that the rights were not attached to the shares acquired by the plaintiff, Scott J held that such rights were class rights. As such, the rights could only be altered pursuant to the statutory procedure laid down by s 125, CA 1985 (see below).

It should be noted that shares which are prima facie issued on the same terms may also be impliedly subdivided by the court into separate classes, even in circumstances where no specific rights or benefits were conferred on a particular shareholder. The implied creation of class rights is rare and will only take place in very well-defined circumstances. An example of the implied subdivision of shares into separate classes is to be found in *Re Hellenic & General Trust Ltd* [1976] 1 WLR 123.

THE VARIATION OF CLASS RIGHTS

A company may wish to vary the rights attached to a particular class of its issued shares. The procedure which governs a company's ability to vary class rights is regulated by s 125 of the Companies Act 1985. The complex rules contained within this section are summarised below. Prior to an analysis of s 125, it is first necessary to determine whether a change in the terms of a particular share issue does in fact amount to a variation of class rights.

What amounts to a variation of class rights?

The Companies Act 1985 provides little guidance as to the definition of what amounts to a variation of class rights, save that s 125(7) provides that an alteration of a provision contained in a company's articles for the variation of the rights of a class of shareholders, or the insertion of such a provision into the articles is to be construed as a variation of class rights. Section 125(8) further provides that references to a variation of class rights are to be read to include an abrogation of such rights. However, it does not always follow that a cancellation of class rights will have the effect of varying those rights. For example, in *Re Saltdean Estate Co Ltd* [1968] 1 WLR 1844 a company resolved to reduce its capital by paying off the company's preference shareholders, i.e. returning the preference shareholders' capital investments in the company. The company was profitable and the preference shareholders had been accorded a right of participation in the company's profits. As a consequence of returning the preference shareholders' capital, the preference shares were cancelled. The preference shareholders alleged that the company's action amounted to a variation of class rights. The court held that the return of capital to the preference shareholders, thereby ending their right to participate in the company, could not be regarded as a variation of the preference holders' class rights. On the contrary, the reduction of the company's capital and the subsequent return of capital was in accordance with the class rights of the preference shareholders as defined by the company's articles. Although the company's articles provided that the consent of a class meeting was required for a proposal which would affect, modify, deal with or abrogate in any manner the rights and privileges of that class of preference shareholders, the articles also provided that holders of preference shares should be the first class of shareholders to have capital returned in the event of the company being wound up.

However, it is to be observed that in *Re Saltdean*, the preference shareholders' right to a return of capital was expressed to be on the winding up of the company and not upon a reduction of capital. Nevertheless, it would appear that the ability of a company to reduce its capital and pay off preference shareholders is *prima facie* an implied consequence of a preference shareholder's preferential right to the return of capital in the event of the company being wound up. This view was impliedly confirmed by the House of Lords in *House of Fraser plc* v *ACGE Investments Ltd* [1987] AC 387.

However, in cases involving the determination of whether preference shareholders have a right to a return of capital, it is essential to construe the company's constitution or the terms of the share issue, a point illustrated by the Court of Appeal's decision in *Re Northern Engineering Industries plc* [1994] 2 BCLC 704 (affirming the first instance decision of Ferris J, [1993] BCLC 1151). The said case involved a proposed reduction of a company's capital by paying off preference shares and cancelling them. The company's articles provided that the rights of any class of shares would be varied by a reduction of the capital paid up on the shares. The company contended that its articles did not apply to the proposed cancellation of preference shares because the articles only had effect where there was a reduction of capital as opposed to a cancellation of the shares. It was held that a cancellation of shares necessarily implied a reduction of share capital. As the variation of the preference shareholders' rights had not been put to a separate meeting of the preference shareholders in accordance with s 125 of the Companies Act 1985 (see below), the court refused to confirm the reduction in capital.

In determining whether a variation of class rights has taken place the courts have drawn a distinction between the rights of a class of shareholders and the enjoyment of those rights. Therefore, to establish a variation of class rights, the rights of a class of shareholders must be fundamentally and specifically altered. Where a company acts merely to affect the rights of a class of shareholders without expressly altering such rights, that particular corporate act will not be construed as a variation but merely as affording a change in the enjoyment of those rights. For example, in *Greenhalgh* v *Arderne Cinemas Ltd* [1946] 1 All ER 512 the company's share capital was divided between two classes of shares: one class of 2s (10p) shares and the other of 10s (50p) shares. Both classes of share carried one vote each. An ordinary resolution was passed which had the effect of subdividing the shares valued at 10s each (50p) into shares of 2s each (10p); each new share was to carry one vote. The resolution increased the voting power (5x) of shareholders who previously held the 10s (50p) shares. The plaintiff, Greenhalgh (G), objected to the subdivision of the 10s (50p) shares on the ground that its effect was to vary his class rights, i.e. prior to the resolution, G, who held the bulk of the 2s (10p) shares, had control of over 40 per cent of the membership votes, whereas, after the resolution his voting powers were reduced to less than 10 per cent of the votes. The court held that no variation of the rights appertaining to G's 2s (10p) shares had taken place, so the resolution had not specifically altered G's rights. G still had the same quantity of 2s (10p) shares, each share still carried one vote. Whilst the effect of the resolution resulted in G's loss of control of over 40 per cent of the votes, the resolution had not altered the specific nature of the rights attached to the 2s (10p) shares. (See also *White v Bristol Aeroplane Co Ltd* [1953] Ch 65 and *Re John Smith's Tadcaster Brewery Co Ltd* [1953] 1 All ER 518.)

Indeed, case examples which illustrate an actual variation of class rights are quite rare. However one such example is *Re Old Silkstone Collieries Ltd* [1954] Ch 169. This case involved a colliery which had been nationalised, i.e. the colliery had been taken over from private ownership by the National Coal Board. However, the company which operated the colliery remained in existence to collect compensation payable as a result of nationalisation. Although the company reduced its capital, by returning a part of the preference shareholders' capital investment, the company nevertheless resolved that all its shareholders would participate in the forthcoming compensation award. Despite such assurances, a further reduction in capital was proposed, the effect of which would have resulted in the cancellation of the class of preference shares. The court held that such a proposal would, if implemented, have amounted to a variation of class rights in that the preference shareholders had been promised a right to participate in the compensation payments. The proposed variation was declared unfair and as such the court refused to sanction the further reduction of capital.

Other examples of a variation of class rights would include:

- a proposal whereby one type of share would be converted into another type of share, for example, where a company sought to convert ordinary shares into preference shares and vice versa;
- where a company sought to alter the voting rights, dividend rights or capital rights attached to a particular class of share.

Section 125 of the Companies Act 1985

Where a company proposes to vary the rights of a particular class of shareholder it must, prior to implementing the variation, comply with the procedures contained within s 125. Section 125(6) provides that a meeting held to consider a variation of class rights must consist of a quorum of the holders of (or representing by proxy) at least one-third of the nominal value of the class of share concerned; the meeting must be attended by at least two members of that class (other than an adjourned meeting, where the attendance requirement is one member (or proxy) of the class concerned). The precise procedure for a variation of class rights is determined in accordance with the following requirements:

Class rights contained in the memorandum

Where the rights of a particular class of share are contained within a company's memorandum, such rights may be varied in accordance with the following procedures.

1 If the procedure for the variation of class rights is contained within the memorandum, the rights may be varied in accordance with that procedure providing the variation is not concerned with the giving, variation, revocation or renewal of an authority for an allotment of shares under s 80 of the Companies Act 1985, or with a reduction of the company's share capital under s 135 of the Companies Act 1985 (see s 125(3), CA 1985). Where the variation of rights is connected with the above matters, the procedure for the variation must be carried out in accordance with s 125(2) of the Companies Act 1985. Section 125(2) provides that the holders of three-quarters in nominal value of the issued shares of the class to be varied must consent in writing to the variation. Alternatively, an extraordinary resolution passed at a separate meeting of the holders of the class may sanction the variation; by s 125(6)(b) a member of the class may demand a poll vote. In addition, the company must comply with any further requirement (however imposed) in relation to the variation of the class rights.

2 Where class rights are contained in the memorandum but the variation procedure for the particular class rights is contained within the articles, the procedure within the articles will be followed providing the variation procedures contained therein were in existence as of the date of the company's original incorporation. Nevertheless, despite the alteration procedures having been contained within the articles as of the date of the company's original incorporation, the procedure for the variation of class rights will not be adhered to where the class rights to be varied accord with those contained in s 125(3)(c). Class rights concerned with those matters mentioned in s 125(3)(c) may only be varied in accordance with the procedure laid down in s 125(2) (see above).

3 If the rights of a particular class of share are contained within the memorandum but neither the memorandum nor the articles of the company make any provision for the procedure whereby those rights may be varied, then, in accordance with s 125(5) the class rights may only be varied by the unanimous agreement of all members of the company.

Class rights contained otherwise than in the memorandum

Where rights are attached to a class of shares otherwise than by the memorandum, then the variation procedure will be as follows.

1 If the variation procedure for the class rights is contained within the articles or memorandum, such rights will, subject to s 125(3)(c) (see above), be varied in accordance with the terms of the articles or memorandum.

2 Where the class rights are contained otherwise than in a company's memorandum and no variation procedure exists within the articles, the rights of the class may be varied in accordance with s 125(2), CA 1985 (see above).

The minority's right to object to a variation of class rights

Where a decision is taken by a separate meeting of the class of shareholders to sanction a proposed variation of class rights (s 125(2), CA 1985), and a minority of the class objects to the terms of the variation, the minority shareholders may, provided that they hold 15 per cent of the issued shares and did not consent to or vote in favour of the variation, apply to the court to have the variation cancelled (s 127, CA 1985). An application to the court under s 127 has the effect of suspending the variation of class rights until such a date as the court decides whether it is to confirm the variation. The objecting minority of the class must apply to court within 21 days of the decision affirming the terms of the variation. In deciding whether to affirm the variation, the court must consider the extent to which the variation would affect the class. Where its effect would be to cause unfair prejudice to the class as a whole, the variation will not be sanctioned. (The meaning of unfair prejudice for the purpose of determining an application to cancel a variation of class rights may, by analogy, be likened to the definition afforded to 'unfairly prejudicial conduct' found within s 459, CA 1985 (see Chapter 23).

In reaching a decision to affirm a variation of the rights of a specified class of shares, the members of the class concerned must exercise their power to vote bona fide for the purpose of benefiting the class as a whole. As such, a conflict of interest may arise in a situation where a member (X) of a company holds, for example, both class A and class B shares and where a proposed variation of class A shares, whilst detrimental to the general interests of holders of A shares, would nevertheless, personally benefit X, in so far as the variation would benefit the holders of B shares. In such a case should the member vote for the greater good of the class or to benefit his own personal interests?

The above problem arose in *Re Holders Investment Trust Ltd* [1971] 1 WLR 583. The case involved a proposed reduction of capital, whereby the company proposed to replace the company's existing preference shares with unsecured loan stock. The cancellation of the preference shares would have benefited the holders of the company's ordinary shares in so far as their dividend payments would no longer have been diminished by the prior payment of interest to preference shareholders. The majority of the holders of preference shares who also held a majority holding of the company's ordinary shares voted in favour of the proposal. The minority holders of the preference shares opposed the variation. The court, in refusing to sanction the variation, held that the principal consideration for a member of a class of shares in deciding whether to affirm a variation of class rights was the overall benefit of the class.

THE CLASSIFICATION OF SHARE ISSUES

Rights issue (pre-emption rights)

When a company issues shares, the issue may be subject to a pre-emption right that the shares must, in the first instance, be offered to existing members of the company (a rights issue), i.e. prior to being offered to non-members of the company (note that the pre-emption right will not apply to employee share schemes, discussed above). The rules which currently govern such pre-emption rights owe much to the implementation of the EC Second Company Law Directive (discussed in Chapter 5). The Directive was implemented by the Companies Act 1980. Although the Directive was concerned with the regulation of rights issues in public companies, the rules enacted in the Companies Act 1980 were applied equally to private companies. The rules have since been incorporated into the Companies Act 1985 (ss 89–96, CA 1985).

By s 89(1) of the Companies Act 1985, where a company offers an issue of equity securities (ordinary shares) for cash, it must, in the first instance, make the offer to its existing ordinary shareholders. A 'rights issue' must be made in direct proportion to the number of shares held by each ordinary shareholder. A private company may exclude s 89(1) by a provision contained within its memorandum or articles (s 91, CA 1985).

Company directors (of both public and private companies), if authorised to allot shares in accordance with s 80 of the Companies Act 1985, may be empowered to disapply or modify the effect of s 89(1) either generally or in relation to a particular allotment (s 95, CA 1985). To disapply or modify such rights generally, the directors must have been given an authority within the company's articles or alternatively must have been authorised to do so by a special resolution. In relation to a specific allotment of shares the general meeting may, by special resolution, decide that s 89(1) should not be applied to the specific allotment. Alternatively, the general meeting may decide that s 89(1) should only apply in some modified form.

A contravention of s 89(1) (subject to the above exceptions) will render every officer of the company who knowingly authorised or permitted the contravention to take place, jointly and severally liable to compensate any member of the company to whom an offer of shares should have been made (s 92, CA 1985).

An issue of shares at a discount

A company is not, subject to limited exceptions, permitted to issue shares for a consideration which is less than the nominal value of the shares (s 100(1), CA 1985). A person who has purchased shares at a discount will be liable to pay to the company an amount equal to the discount, plus interest (s 100(2), CA 1985). The exceptions to s 100(1) are as follows:

- a debenture, which is subsequently converted into a share may be issued at a discount, provided that the right to convert the debenture was not an immediate right; and
- property which is exchanged for shares in a private company may be of a lesser value than the nominal value of the shares issued (discussed above).

An issue of shares at a premium

Shares may be issued at a premium, i.e. the selling price of the share may exceed its nominal value. Where a company issues shares at a premium, a sum equal to the amount of the premium payment must be transferred into a special account called the share premium account (s 130, CA 1985).

Where a company acquires the shares of another company in exchange for the issue of its own shares and the nominal value of the issue of its own shares is less than the value of the shares acquired, then the difference between the two values must be transferred to the share premium account.

A bonus issue

A bonus issue of shares is facilitated by a company using reserve funds to pay up unissued shares. The shares are then distributed as a bonus issue to the existing members of the company; the total number of bonus shares that each shareholder receives will be dependent upon the proportion of shares currently held in the company.

Redeemable shares

A redeemable share is a share which the company may, at its option, buy back from the shareholder at some specified date in the future (redemption date). The reason a company may wish to issue this type of share may be connected to the company's desire to raise short-term capital. A company which is authorised by its articles, is permitted by s 159 of the Companies Act 1985 to issue redeemable shares, provided that the issue does not represent the totality of the company's share capital. Section 159A (introduced by s 133, CA 1989) provides that the date (or dates) on which the shares may be redeemed must be specified in the company's articles or, if the articles so provide, fixed by the directors; in the latter case the date(s) must be fixed before the shares are issued. Any other circumstances in which the shares are to be or may be redeemed must also be specified in the company's articles. The repayment of the redeemable shares cannot be deferred beyond the redemption date, although subject to the shares having been fully paid up, the shares may be redeemed at the option of the company or shareholder at a date prior to the one specified by the terms of redemption.

In redeeming shares, s 160 of the Companies Act 1985 provides that the company must redeem the shares out of its distributable profits or out of the proceeds of a new share issue. However, it should be noted that a private company may in certain circumstances redeem shares out of its own capital (discussed in Chapter 12). Where shares are redeemed out of a company's distributable profits, an amount equal to the amount by which the company's issued share capital is diminished on the cancellation of the shares must be transferred to a reserve fund known as the capital redemption reserve (s 170, CA 1985).

THE VALUATION OF SHARES

On occasions, it will be necessary for a court to determine the valuation of shares, for example, a valuation of shares may be required to assess a person's liability to capital gains tax or inheritance tax. Where the particular shares to be valued are listed shares, their value may often be calculated according to their current quoted market price. However, as the vast majority of companies are not listed, it is often necessary for the court to attempt to calculate the valuation of the company's share.

Shares which are the subject matter of a court's valuation must be valued in an objective manner. The objective test employed will, unless the articles provide for a contrary procedure, be conducted on the basis of a sale as between a willing but not anxious vendor and a willing but not anxious purchaser. The crucial factors which determine any share valuation are the size of the shareholding and the expected dividend and asset realisation of the shares in question. In relation to private companies, an important consideration will be whether the company's articles purport to restrict the potential market for the sale of the shares; see e.g. *Holt* v *IRC* [1953] 1 WLR 1488. Whilst the valuation of shares can never be an exact science (see e.g. *Holt* v *Holt* [1990] 1 WLR 1250) the following guidelines are often employed by the courts.

1 Where the block of shares to be valued carries enough votes to enforce a winding up of the company, i.e. 75 per cent or more votes, the most likely method of valuation will be determined in accordance with the value of the company's assets. This method of valuation entails a valuation of the net corporate assets of the company. The number of shares to be valued is then represented as a percentage of the value of the total net assets to give the pre-liquidation valuation figure, for example, if 80 out of an issued share capital of 100 shares are to be valued and the company in question has net assets to the value of £10 000, the valuation figure would be £8000 (divided by 80 which would equal £100 per share). Where the company is to be wound up, a deduction in the valuation figure will be made so as to take account of the liquidation costs; see e.g. *M'Conel's Trustees* v *IRC* [1927] SLT 14.

2 The asset valuation method may still be employed where the block of shares to be valued falls below 75 per cent, i.e. a figure necessary to enforce a winding up of a company. In such cases, a discount on the asset

valuation will be made in accordance with the size of the holding. A majority holding of 50 per cent or more will warrant a discount in the region of 5 per cent, whereas a minority holding of, for example, 10 per cent may warrant a reduction of up to 20 to 30 per cent.

3 An alternative method for the valuation of shares is one which is determined according to the earning capacity of the shares to be valued, i.e. the calculation of the potential dividend entitlement of the shares. In assessing the value of dividends it will be necessary for a court to forecast expected profits. In so determining the potential dividend yield of a share, it is seldom practicable to look more than two to three years ahead. For private companies the court will normally estimate the dividend yield for the last three to five years prior to the date of valuation; see e.g. *Re Lynall* [1972] AC 680. Forecasts that the future profits of a company will be markedly different from recently recorded profits will be treated with caution. Where the expected future profits of a company are minimal or perhaps non-existent, the share valuation will normally be reduced to take account of the relative lack of marketability which the shares will possess. As with the asset valuation method, the smaller the shareholding interest, then the greater will be the reduction in the final valuation figure of the shares.

It should be noted that in determining the value of shares in cases under s 459 of the Companies Act 1985, the court will consider matters other than those outlined above (discussed in Chapter 22).

INVESTIGATIONS INTO SHARE OWNERSHIP

Section 442 of the Companies Act 1985 (as amended by s 62, CA 1989), permits the Secretary of State to appoint inspectors to investigate the share ownership of a company. Members of a company may apply to the Secretary of State to instigate such an investigation. If an application is made by 200 or more members of a company, or by members holding 10 per cent or more of the company's issued shares, then, unless the Secretary of State considers the application to be vexatious or considers that an alternative type of action under s 444(1) of the Companies Act 1985 is more appropriate, he must appoint inspectors. The type of action governed by s 444(1) is one whereby the Secretary of State may require of any person information appertaining to the ownership of shares. As a result of action taken under s 442 or s 444, the Secretary of State may impose a freezing order on the relevant shares (s 445, CA 1985) (see below).

Where the company is a public limited company, the company itself may seek information as to whether at any time within the last three years a person had (or still has) an interest in its voting shares (s 212, CA 1985); see e.g. *Re Lonrho plc (No 3)* [1989] BCLC 480. Shareholders holding 10 per cent or more of the voting shares in a public limited company may call for the board to exercise these powers. The information obtained must be recorded on the company's register of interest in shares.

FREEZING ORDERS

The courts or the Secretary of State may order that restrictions be placed upon the ownership rights attached to specified shares. Where an order is made, it is referred to as a freezing order. A breach of a freezing order constitutes a criminal offence (s 455, CA 1985).

The Secretary of State's powers to make a freezing order are determined in accordance with s 445 of the Companies Act 1985. This section may be used in accordance with the Secretary of State's powers of investigation into the ownership of specified shares (see above) or under s 210(5), CA 1985, i.e. where a person has been convicted of failing to disclose a substantial interest in the shares of a company. Further, the courts may impose a freezing order on specific shares in circumstances where a public company has failed to receive an adequate response to a request for information under s 212, CA 1985.

The effect of a freezing order (ss 454–457, CA 1985) is to:

- prevent the shares from being transferred;
- restrain the votes attached to the affected shares from being exercised;
- suspend rights of pre-emption attached to the affected shares; and
- prevent dividends from being paid and capital (except where the company is in liquidation) from being returned to the holders of the shares.

As a result of s 135 of the Companies Act 1989, inserted as s 216(1A) of the Companies Act 1985, the court may modify the extent of the effect of a freezing order in circumstances where it considers that the consequences of a full order would unfairly affect the rights of third parties.

Suggested further reading

Pickering (1963) 26 MLR 499
Pennington (1989) 10 Co Law 140

Share freezing orders
Milman and Singh (1992) 13 Co Law 15

Class rights/variation
Reynolds [1996] JBL 554

11

THE ACQUISITION OF SHARES IN A PUBLIC COMPANY

INTRODUCTION

The purpose of this chapter is to explain the rules applicable to the regulation of an offer of shares in both listed and unlisted public companies. As such, this chapter will seek to expose the recent effect of the UK's implementation of the EC Prospectus Directive. This chapter will also consider the available remedies for loss or damage arising from a purchase of shares in a public limited company, in circumstances where the company's offer of such shares, contained a false or misleading statement.

LISTED SECURITIES

Other than a purchase of shares on the Stock Exchange, the most likely method of acquiring shares in a public company will be to apply to a company's advertisement (contained within a prospectus or listing particulars) for the sale of its shares. Acceptance of the offer takes place when the company gives notice to the applicant that an allotment has been made to him. Listed securities are securities which have been admitted to listing on the London Stock Exchange, the principal market in the UK for security transactions. Securities include shares and debentures and certificates which represent property rights or contractual rights in shares and debentures.

Prior to 1984, listing on the Stock Exchange was almost exclusively regulated by the Stock Exchange's own Listing Rules. In 1984, in addition to the Exchange's Listing Rules, three EC Directives – the Admissions Directive (No 79/279), the Listing Particulars Directive (No 80/390) and the Interim Reports Directive (No 82/121) – were implemented in the form of the Stock Exchange (Listing) Regulations 1984. The regulation of prospectuses for unlisted securities was left to provisions contained within the Companies Act 1985. The Financial Services Act 1986 aimed to consolidate the regulation of listed and unlisted securities in one Act; Part IV of the 1986 Act dealt with listed securities to which the aforementioned EC Directives applied and Part V related to unlisted securities. However, Part V was never brought into force, the principal reason being the UK's need to comply with the subsequent EC Prospectus Directive (89/298). The Prospectus Directive has now been implemented by the Public Offers of Securities Regulations 1995 (SI

1995/1537) ('the 1995 Regulations'). Part IV, FSA 1986 has also been subjected to some technical alterations as a result of the 1995 Regulations.

The 1995 Regulations, as amended by the Public Offers of Securities (Amendment) Regulations 1999 (SI 1999/734) and the Public Offers of Securities (Amendment) (No 2) Regulations 1999 (SI 1999/1146), provide a new and wider regime for the control of public offers of corporate securities offered within the UK (the amendment regulations having effect from 10 May 1999). The 1995 Regulations apply where securities are offered to the general public for the very first time, irrespective of whether a listing is required; offers of securities include offers for a cash or a non-cash consideration. The ultimate aim of the Prospectus Directive is to encourage the creation of a European market with common rules for the regulation of dealings in securities.

Admission to the Official List

Under ss 142–144 of the Financial Services Act 1986, applications for listing must be made in the manner determined by the Stock Exchange, i.e. in accordance with the Listing Rules (commonly referred to as the 'Yellow Book'). The Listing Rules comprise a comprehensive set of requirements for the listing of securities. The Listing Rules are too extensive to be repeated in this text. However, a summary of the main requirements of the rules (in relation to an issue of shares) include details of the applicant's:

- registered name, registered office, directors, auditors, solicitors and other persons involved in the preparation of the issue together with the responsibilities undertaken by those so involved in the issue of the securities;
- the details of the share issue together with information related to the company's issued and paid-up share capital and the classes of shares into which it is divided. This information must include the names of any person who holds 3 per cent or more of the issued share capital;
- the company's trading record must be included and this record must be for a period of at least three years for which audited accounts must be available. In addition, for accounting periods beginning on or after 31 October 1995, a company must include within its annual report and accounts a statement by the directors to the effect that the business is a going concern; and
- a detailed record of the company's management team and their business interests. If the company has been in existence for less than five years, details of the company's promoters must also be included.

Further, the company's directors must make a declaration to the effect that, to the best of their knowledge and belief, the information which they have provided for the purpose of the issue is correct.

As a result of the 1995 Regulations, the offer document which must comply with the listing rules is, for a first-time offer of listed securities, referred to as a prospectus and not, as was previously the case, listing particulars.

However, other than where the 1995 Regulations apply, the offer document may still be referred to as listing particulars. For example, the document will still be referred to as listing particulars where the offer is not a first offer of the relevant securities or where existing securities are introduced into the London Stock Exchange from the Unlisted Securities Market or Alternative Investment Market.

Unless an issue falls within the exemptions provided by Sch 3 of the 1995 Regulations, inserted into the Financial Services Act as Sch 11A (the exceptions are discussed below, in the context of unlisted securities), the production of a prospectus is mandatory where the issue of securities is being offered to the general public for the first time. An advertisement to sell securities to the general public is deemed an offer to sell such securities albeit that in contract law an advertisement for sale is normally regarded as an invitation to treat. Although there is no precise definition of what will constitute an offer to the public, it is to be noted that the 1995 Regulations (reg 6) provide that:

> 'an offer which is made to any section of the public, whether selected as members or debenture holders of a body corporate, or as clients of the person making the offer, or in any other manner, is to be regarded as made to the public.'

Section 146 of the Financial Services Act 1986 imposes an overriding duty on the applicant to disclose all the information which investors and their professional advisers would reasonably require and reasonably expect to find for the purpose of making an informed assessment of the creditability of an issue. Where a significant change in the circumstances of any matter relevant to the determination of information contained in the prospectus or listing particulars occurs before dealings in the securities commence, the publication of a supplementary prospectus is required to explain such changes (s 147, FSA 1986). However, under s 147(3) liability may be evaded for non-compliance with the production of a supplementary prospectus where the issuer can establish that it was unaware of the change in circumstances which would have otherwise necessitated the need to publish the supplementary prospectus.

The Stock Exchange is responsible, in the case of an offer for listed securities, for vetting applications for the publication of a prospectus or listing particulars. Under s 144(2), as amended by the 1995 Regulations, the prospectus or listing particulars must, prior to being published, be submitted in draft to the Stock Exchange for their formal approval. In circumstances where the Stock Exchange considers the application to be detrimental to the interests of investors, the application may be refused; albeit that such a decision may be subject to judicial review. Section 154 allows the Stock Exchange to control the nature of advertisements in relation to the issue of a prospectus or listing particulars in the case of an application for listing; the Stock Exchange must approve all such advertisements.

UNLISTED SECURITIES

In 1980, the London Stock Exchange created the Unlisted Securities Market (USM) in an attempt to encourage the trading of securities in those public companies which were not sufficiently established or willing to offer securities on the listed market. Initially, acceptance onto the unlisted market was more relaxed in terms of its procedural requirements than entry onto the listed market. However, as a consequence of less stringent standards of admission into the principal markets of other EU countries (following the passing of two EC Directives (89/298 and 87/345)) the lowering of standards for admission onto the listed market became an inevitable consequence of the London Stock Exchange's desire to remain competitive with other EU markets. As a result, the regulatory distinction between the listed and unlisted markets was significantly reduced. Indeed the distinction became almost redundant. As a consequence of the removal of a greater part of the distinction between the two markets, a new market has been created in its place, namely, the 'Alternative Investment Market' (AIM). This new market officially opened in June 1995 and will basically perform the same function as that which had originally been perceived for the USM.

Admission to the Alternative Investment Market

The principal requirements for admission are as follows:

- the company must be incorporated in accordance with the national laws of the country in which it was registered and must be allowed to offer securities to the public;
- the securities to be traded on the market must be freely transferable;
- the company must appoint and retain a nominated adviser and a nominated broker;
- the company must accept continuing obligations with regard to such matters as preparation of accounts, completion of transfers of securities and dealings in securities by directors and employees.

Regulating public offers of unlisted securities

Public offers of unlisted securities are now regulated by the Public Offers of Securities Regulations 1995 ('the 1995 Regulations') where the convertible securities are to be offered to the general public for the first time; previously such offers were regulated by the Companies Act 1985 (convertible securities are defined by reg 3(1)(b), and naturally include shares and debentures). To comply with the 1995 Regulations, the company issuing the securities must publish a prospectus which, during the duration of the offer, must be made available to the general public at a UK address; no charge must be levied for the prospectus (reg 4(1)).

Prior to its publication, the prospectus must be delivered to the Registrar of Companies for registration (reg 4(2)). In addition to including detailed disclosures about the issuer and the securities to be offered in the issue (1995 Regulations, Sch 1), the 1995 Regulations (reg 9(1)) provide, with the exception of pre-emptive issues falling within reg 8(4) and issues previously made within the preceding 12 months (reg 8(6)), that the issuer must include within the prospectus all such information which would enable investors to make an informed assessment of the issuers assets and liabilities, its profits and losses, the financial state and immediate prospects of the issuer and the specific rights to be attached to the securities subject to the offer (unless the Stock Exchange considers the publication of certain information to be detrimental to the issuer (reg 11(3)).

An offer of securities 'for the first time' includes securities which are of the same class as securities which have previously been offered by the offeror to the public in the UK. However, where the number or value of the securities to be offered is less than 10 per cent of the number or value of the securities already offered, and detailed and up-to-date information about that class of securities is available, i.e. information which would otherwise have complied with Sch 1 of the 1995 Regulations, then in accordance with reg 8(5), the need to issue a prospectus in respect of such securities will be dispensed with.

The 1995 Regulations apply if the offer is for a cash or non-cash consideration and are also applicable to a situation where the offer is made other than in writing. The scope of the 1995 Regulations extends to a situation where the shares are being offered other than by the issuing company, for example, they will apply to a shareholder or underwriter of an issue, albeit that the necessary disclosure requirements in relation to the issuing company will, as one might expect, be less severe than if the company itself was purporting to make the offer of the securities (see reg 11(2)).

Exceptions to the 1995 Regulations

Offers of securities which are not within the ambit of the 1995 Regulations are listed in reg 7. These exceptions are applicable to both listed and unlisted securities and where relevant deem that the exempted offer may be instigated without the production of a prospectus. The list of exceptions is extensive and includes the following types of offers:

- where the securities are offered to persons acting in the course of a business which is involved or may reasonably be expected to be involved in the acquisition, holding, managing or disposing of investments: for example, commercial banks and listed investment trusts;
- where the securities are offered to persons in the context of their trades, professions or occupations;
- if the securities are offered to no more than 50 persons. The possibility of exploiting this exception by subdividing the issue so that, for example, a first issue of securities to 50 persons could immediately be followed by a second, third, etc. issue to 50 persons is dealt with by reg 7(6). This regulation precludes such exploitation by prohibiting an offer of a class of

securities which would otherwise have fallen within this exception where, during the previous 12 months, another offer of the same class of securities had been open to either the general public or had been made in accordance with this exception. It is also to be noted that offers of securities made to trustees of a trust or members of a partnership are deemed to be offers to a single entity (person);

- where the securities are offered to members of a club or association (whether or not incorporated) in circumstances where it can be reasonably ascertained that the members share a common interest in the club or association and the purpose to which the proceeds of the offer will be put;

- where the securities are offered in connection with a bona fide invitation to enter into an underwriting agreement in respect of them;

- if the securities are those of a private company and are offered to existing members or their families, existing employees or their families or holders of its debt securities. (It should be noted that a private company is generally prohibited from offering shares to the general public.);

- where the securities are offered to a restricted circle of persons, who would, to the knowledge of the offeror, be reasonably aware of the risks involved in taking up the offer. (This exception may apply where there is an issue of securities by a private company if the issue is other than to family members, etc.);

- where the securities of a private company are offered in accordance with pre-emption requirements in the company's articles or an agreement between holders of securities in the company;

- if the offer comprises a bonus issue, i.e. shares issued on a fully paid up basis to a company's shareholders. For the purpose of this exception, 'shareholders' include any person who held shares in the company up to 60 days prior to the date of the offer;

- where the securities are offered by an incorporated company (or employee trust) to its employees or former employees, or the spouse or children (under the age of 18) of the company's employees or former employees. In addition, the exemption will apply where employees are made offers of securities in a company which is a member of the group of companies to which the employer belongs;

- if the securities are offered to the UK government, local authority or public authority;

- where the total consideration to be paid for the issue does not exceed ECU 40 000 (approximately £33 000 at current rates). Regulation 7(6) prohibits an offer of a class of securities which would otherwise fall within this exception where, during the previous 12 months, another offer of the same class of securities had been open to either the general public or had been made in accordance with this exception;

- if the securities are offered in connection with a takeover offer or a merger as defined by the 'Merger Directive' (78/855). In relation to takeovers involving offers for UK companies, the definition of a takeover is that as provided by Part XIIIA of the Companies Act 1985, namely, a takeover

150

offer means 'an offer to acquire all the shares, or all the shares of any class or classes, in a company (other than shares which at the date of the offer are already held by the offeror), being an offer on terms which are the same in relation to all the shares to which the offer relates or, where those shares include shares of different classes, in relation to all the shares of each class'. The definition of a takeover for takeover offers of companies outside the UK extends the definition in Part XIIIA of the Companies Act 1985 and applies to offers to acquire substantially all or a specified proportion of the shares (or class of shares) of the target company;

- where the securities offered are Euro-securities and no advertisement relating to the offer is issued in the UK other than an advertisement falling within Art 8 of the Financial Services Act 1986 (Investment Advertisements) (Exemptions) (No 2) Order 1995 (SI 1995/1536) or Art 11 of the Financial Services Act 1986 (Investment Advertisements) (Exceptions) Order 1996 (SI 1996/1586).

Mutual recognition of prospectuses

The 1995 Regulations, by implementing the EC Prospectus Directive into UK law, give effect to the mutual recognition of prospectuses or listing particulars across the EU. Therefore, provided that a prospectus or listing particulars, in compliance with the Listing Particulars Directive, have been vetted in the course of satisfying a member state's regulations, the securities which form the subject of the prospectus or listing particulars may be offered or admitted to listing in other member states. Under s 156A of the Financial Services Act 1986 (introduced into the FSA by the 1995 Regulations), a prospectus relating to unlisted securities can be submitted to the London Stock Exchange for its approval in compliance with the mutual recognition provisions; if the UK is one of the member states in which the securities are to be offered. The information to be contained in such a prospectus will, for vetting purposes, be governed by the Listing Rules and not the 1995 Regulations. However, such prospectuses will not be required to be translated nor will they need to include taxation information relevant to the UK.

COMPENSATION FOR A FALSE OR MISLEADING STATEMENT CONTAINED WITHIN A PROSPECTUS OR LISTING PARTICULARS

A person who subscribes to a public offer of listed or unlisted securities may, when that person has suffered loss or damage in acquiring the securities to which the offer document relates, seek compensation from the person or persons responsible for the offer document. Compensation will be payable where the damage or loss resulted from any untrue or misleading statement or omission which should, in accordance with the relevant statutory provisions, have been included within the prospectus or listing particulars (see reg 14 of the 1995 Regulations for unlisted securities; s 154A, FSA 1986 (introduced by Sch 2(3), 1995 Regulations) for listed securities; s 150, FSA 1986 for listing particulars). Liability is not dependent upon whether the subscriber placed reliance upon the misstatement or had knowledge of any omission. Liability also extends to supplementary listing particulars and prospectuses.

Defences

Various defences are available to a person or persons who would otherwise have been liable for a false or misleading statement or omission in the offer document or any supplementary document. The defences are applicable irrespective of whether the securities to be offered are listed or unlisted securities. The defences are contained in s 151 of the Financial Services Act 1986 in respect of listing particulars and in s 154A of the Financial Services Act 1986 (introduced by Sch 2(3), 1995 Regulations) in the case of a prospectus required by the Listing Rules. For a prospectus issue in relation to unlisted securities the defences are listed in reg 15 of the 1995 Regulations. The defences are as follows.

1 The person or persons responsible for the offer document may escape liability where it is established that the subscriber was aware that the offending statement was indeed untrue or misleading or had knowledge that a matter which should have been included in the offer document had in fact been omitted.

2 The person or persons responsible for a false or misleading statement or omission may also escape liability where the statement or omission was of an innocent nature, i.e. the person or persons responsible for the misrepresentation or omission, having made such enquiries as were reasonable to make in the circumstances, reasonably believed at the time when the statement was delivered for registration that it was true or, in the case of an omission, that the offending omission would have been unnecessary had it been included within the offer document. The belief in the accuracy of the offer document must continue up until the time when the securities were acquired.

3 Liability will not be incurred where loss resulted from a statement (included in the offer document) which was made by an official person or taken from a public document, provided that the statement was proved to have been accurately and fairly produced.

4 Liability may be evaded for not producing a supplementary offer document where it is established by a person responsible for the original offer document that the alteration of an inaccuracy contained therein, did not, as a result of a reasonably held belief, merit the production of the supplementary document. It should nevertheless be noted that an error as contained in the original offer document may of itself still give rise to a primary liability (see s 151, FSA 1986 or reg 14 of the 1995 Regulations).

5 Liability may be evaded even where the person or persons responsible for the offer document had knowledge of an innocent but nevertheless mis-

leading statement or omission prior to the purchase of securities provided that:

(a) the securities were acquired before it was reasonably practicable to have brought the correction to the attention of persons who were likely to acquire the securities; or

(b) that a reasonable, albeit unsuccessful, attempt (for example publishing the error in the national press) had been made to bring the correction to the attention of persons likely to acquire the securities; or

(c) the securities to which the statement or omission had been applied were acquired after a reasonable lapse of time and if the securities were dealt in on an approved exchange, the person or persons responsible for the offer document were unaware of the misstatement or omission until after the commencement of those dealings.

It is to be observed that the part (c) defence begs the question as to the period of time deemed necessary to substantiate a reasonable time lapse and also, if applicable, the point in time at which the person or persons responsible for the misstatement or omission, having discovered the error after the commencement of dealings in the securities, should have disclosed that fact. Where, for example, the relevant misstatement or omission was discovered by the person or persons responsible for the offer document shortly after the commencement of dealings but, despite such a discovery, no attempt was made to publicise or correct the error at that time and subsequently, a reasonable period of time elapsed before the error was generally made public, it would appear that the defence, if read literally, would still apply where the shares were purchased after a reasonable period of time but prior to the publication of the error. This must surely be a flaw in the legislation, as it could encourage non-disclosure of the error in the offer document. Further it would indeed appear contradictory to the spirit of the ability to qualify for a defence under the above headings (a) and (b).

Further, a person responsible for an offer document containing an untrue or misleading statement may escape liability where such a person proves reasonable reliance on the accuracy of a statement made by and with the consent of an expert; the skill and knowledge of whom could not have been reasonably doubted by the person responsible for the offer document. The belief must continue up until the time the securities were acquired. However, liability may still be evaded in circumstances where:

(a) the securities were acquired before it was reasonably practicable to have brought the expert's incompetence or lack of consent to the mistaken statement to the attention of persons who were likely to acquire the securities; or

(b) that a reasonable, albeit unsuccessful, attempt (for example by publishing the error in the national press) had been made to bring the mistake to the attention of persons likely to acquire the securities; or

(c) the securities to which the expert's statement had been applied were acquired after a reasonable lapse of time and where the securities were dealt in on an approved exchange the person or persons responsible for the offer document continued to believe in the accuracy of the expert's statement and the expert's consent to the statement appearing in that document until after the commencement of those dealings.

Again, it is regrettable in relation to (c) that the legislation fails to make any mention of the period of time deemed necessary to substantiate a reasonable time lapse and also, if applicable, the point in time at which the person or persons responsible for the offer document should disclose the fact that the expert's statement/omission was inaccurate.

Persons responsible for a prospectus or listing particulars

The persons who are deemed responsible for the publication and contents of an offer document are defined by s 152 of the Financial Services Act 1996 in relation to listing particulars, s 154A (introduced by Sch 2(3), 1995 Regulations) in relation to a prospectus required by the Listing Rules and by reg 13 of the 1995 Regulations in respect of a prospectus issue of unlisted securities. The definitions will also apply to supplementary prospectus or listing particulars. The definitions of persons who are deemed to be responsible are as follows:

- the issuer of the securities to which the offer document relates or the offeror of the securities where they are issued other than by the issuer. However, where securities are issued other than by the issuer, the offeror will not be deemed to be responsible where the prospectus was primarily drawn up by the issuer or where the offeror is making the offer in association with the issuer;
- where the offeror of the securities is not the issuer of those securities but the offeror is an incorporated company, any person who is a director of that company at the time when the prospectus is published;
- any director of an issuer which is an incorporated company at the time when the listing particulars (or prospectus for listed securities) are submitted to the Stock Exchange or, in the case of unlisted securities, when the prospectus is published. An exception is provided where the issuer had not made or authorised the offer contained in the offer document. Further, a director of an issuer is exempted where the offer document was published without his knowledge or consent and on becoming aware of its publication he gave public notice of the fact that it was published without his knowledge or consent. It would appear from the terms of the 1995 Regulations that this latter exception would not apply where the securities were offered other than by the issuer, i.e. where a person is the director of the offeror of securities in a situation where the offeror is not the issuer;
- any person who accepts and is so stated as accepting in the listing particulars or prospectus, responsibility for, or for any part of the particulars or prospectus;

- any person who does not fall within any of the above definitions is nevertheless responsible for authorising the contents of, or any part of, the particulars or prospectus.

THE STATUTORY REMEDIES AND THE CALCULATION OF DAMAGES

As a consequence of the 1995 Regulations, the statutory remedy for an untrue or misleading statement contained in a prospectus offering unlisted securities is now aligned to the statutory remedy for an untrue or misleading statement contained within a prospectus or particulars offering listed securities. Prior to the 1995 Regulations, a prospectus offering unlisted securities was governed by s 67 of the Companies Act 1985. Under s 67, compensation was payable where the loss or damage was sustained to any person who subscribed for shares or debentures in a public company on the faith of a prospectus which contained any untrue statement. Therefore, in effect, a subscriber could only bring an action under s 67 where reliance had been placed on the accuracy of the contents of a prospectus. The person or persons responsible for the issue of a prospectus (but not the issuing company) were liable where the false or misleading statement was established (s 67(2), CA 1985).

As the law now stands, after the implementation of the 1995 Regulations (see reg 14), compensation is payable to any person who suffered damage or loss as a result of acquiring securities which were advertised in the prospectus. Accordingly, the class of persons to whom compensation is payable would appear wider than under s 67, where the class of persons capable of claiming compensation was restricted to the subscribers of the share issue, i.e. persons who purchased the securities directly from the issuing company. Under the present law, it will suffice for the purpose of claiming compensation, for a person to establish that he purchased securities which had been advertised in the prospectus. Therefore, there would appear to be no specific requirement that the purchaser of the securities was a subscriber to the issue, i.e. in a contractual relationship with the issuing company. This extends the scope of the remedy beyond similar legislation which is concerned with providing a remedy for false and misleading statements, see, for example, the Misrepresentation Act 1967.

As with s 67, any compensation payable under the 1995 Regulations (and Part IV, FSA 1986) is likely to be calculated on principles based upon the tort measure of calculating damages, i.e. by attempting to put the plaintiff back in the position he was in prior to the untrue or false statement. The tort measure of damages having been historically applied to the term 'compensation'; see e.g. *Clark* v *Urquhart* [1930] AC 28. Therefore, for example, where shares are purchased at £1000 but as a consequence of a false or misleading statement were, at the time of their sale, only worth £500, the damages recoverable would amount to £500. The value of the shares purchased must be determined, as of the date of their acquisition, i.e. in the above example the value would be £500; see *Davidson* v *Tulloch* (1860) 3 Macq 783. Accordingly, although a false and misleading statement in a prospectus or listing particulars may result in a gradual but continuous fall in the value of shares, in the above example, the shares may fall to a value of, say, £100, the court will not, in its assessment of compensation, ordinarily take account of the slide in the value of the shares as from the date of their acquisition. In relation to the above example, damages would still only be calculated at £500 (and not £900). Prior to the House of Lords' decision in *Smith New Court Securities* v *Scrimgeour*, the above rule operated in relation to the valuation of shares, notwithstanding that the misrepresentation was of a fraudulent nature and despite the fact that in assessing damages for the tort of deceit it is possible for the court, subject to the loss being too remote, to award damages for consequential losses flowing from an untrue statement; see e.g. *Doyle* v *Olby (Ironmongers) Ltd* [1969] 2 All ER 119. Indeed, by analogy, contractual misrepresentations of both a fraudulent and negligent character which have invoked the implementation of the Misrepresentation Act 1967 have led the courts to award damages for losses which occurred after the date of the plaintiff's reliance on the offending misrepresentation; see e.g. *Naughton* v *O'Callaghan* [1990] 3 All ER 191 and *Royscot Trust Ltd* v *Rogerson* [1991] 3 All ER 294.

However, following the decision of the House of Lords in *Smith New Court Securities Ltd* v *Scrimgeour Vickers (Asset Management) Ltd* [1996] 4 All ER 769, it would now appear permissible for a court, when valuing shares purchased as a consequence of a fraudulent misrepresentation, to consider events which actually occurred prior to the acquisition of the shares, i.e. where such events would have been relevant to determining the valuation of the shares prior to their acquisition. The facts of the case were as follows. The plaintiff (SNCS) purchased shares in Ferranti International Signal plc. The plaintiff purchased the shares through the defendant (SV) who sold the shares as an agent for Citibank NA (C). Shortly after the sale, the price of Ferranti shares fell dramatically. SNCS subsequently sold the shares, but lost over £11 million on the sale. SNCS claimed damages from SV and C on the premise that it had been induced to purchase the shares as a consequence of a fraudulent misrepresentation, namely, SNCS was induced to purchase the shares as a result of being informed by a director of SV (acting for C) that two other reputable bidders were willing to make bids for the shares.

At first instance ([1992] BCLC 1104), Chadwick J held that the fraudulent misrepresentation had the effect of creating a false market in the shares. In determining the true market value of the shares, the learned judge considered events prior to the acquisition as relevant to the calculation of the value of the shares. The significant event in question being that the price of Ferranti shares (at the time of SNCS's acquisition) had itself been inflated by a fraudulently misleading preliminary announcement as to Ferranti's end of year profits. The eventual effect of the fraudulent announcement, i.e. a reduction of the price of a Ferranti share, only became apparent after SNCS's acquisition of the Ferranti shares.

Chadwick J found that the shares, which had been purchased by SNCS at a price of 82.25p per share, had an apparent market value of 78p at the date of their acquisition, however, having taken into account the fraudulent announcement as to Ferranti's end of year profits, the true market value of the shares had only been 44p per share (a figure based on the price of the shares prior to the fraudulent announcement relating to the end of year profits). As such SNCS received damages of 38.25p per share.

Although the Court of Appeal ([1994] BCLC 212) agreed that SNCS's claim for damages should be upheld as a result of the fraudulent misrepresentation relating to the additional bidders for the shares, the court strongly disapproved of the valuation method employed by Chadwick J. The Court of Appeal refused to accept that when valuing shares it was correct to take account of events unknown to both parties at the time of the transaction. Accordingly, the Court of Appeal valued the shares in accordance with the ascertainable market value of the shares at the time of the sale. As a result, the amount of damages payable to SNCS was reduced from 38.25p per share to 4.25p per share. The Court of Appeal's reasoning was based on the fact that if the valuation was to take account of the fraudulent announcement of Ferranti's end of year profits, the defendants would, in effect, have been deemed accountable for a diminution in the value of the shares in circumstances where they had played no part in, or had any knowledge of such a deception.

The House of Lords, in reversing the decision of the Court of Appeal, concluded that damages in the tort of deceit, in respect of the valuation of shares, could be calculated on the basis of an assessment of any consequential loss which had been suffered by SNCS as a result of acquiring the Ferranti shares. Accordingly, the valuation could take account of the value of the Ferranti shares prior to the inflationary effect on that value by the fraudulent announcement of Ferranti's end of year profits. In effect, the House concluded that it was possible to assess the loss flowing directly from the transaction without any reference to the date of the transaction or indeed any particular date. The House so concluded, despite the fact that in cases such as *Doyle* v *Olby* (*Ironmongers*) *Ltd* the assessment of damages had been calculated for all the actual damage **directly flowing from the fraudulent inducement**. In *Smith New Court* the House of Lords extended the calculation of damages to cover events prior to the fraudulent inducement. Accordingly, the level of damages awarded in favour of SNCS was restored to the level provided at first instance.

Rescission

Where a person acquires securities in a public company or for that matter a private company in reliance on a fraudulent, negligent or innocent misrepresentation in relation to the offer of those securities (an omission may also be classed as a misrepresentation) proceedings may, if the offeree so desires, be taken to rescind the contract. A person may only exercise a right of rescission against the company issuing the securities where the company allotted the securities in question. In other cases the right to rescind may be exercised against the offeror of the securities. Following rescission, the purchase price of the securities plus any interest will be returned to the offeree. A person's right to rescind the contract may be lost where the offeree, after becoming aware of the misrepresentation, acted in a manner to affirm the contract, or where there was an unreasonable delay in seeking to rescind the contract, or where the issuing company went into liquidation.

It should be noted that the rule of law established in the case of *Houldsworth* v *City of Glasgow Bank* (1880) 5 App Cas 317, namely, that any claim for damages against a company may only be sustained if the contract relating to the security issue is rescinded, was expressly overturned by s 111A of the Companies Act 1985 (introduced by s 131(1), CA 1989).

SHARES PURCHASED FOLLOWING A NON-CONTRACTUAL REPRESENTATION

Where, following a misleading statement made by a company, a purchaser is induced to acquire securities in that company, other than securities actually offered in a prospectus or listing particulars, the purchaser will be unable to claim a statutory remedy against the company or its directors. However, a purchaser of such securities may be able to obtain a remedy for the misstatement in two distinct situations. The first situation is where it is possible to establish an action in deceit, i.e. it would be necessary for the purchaser to prove that, as a direct result of a fraudulent misstatement, he had been induced to take the shares. Alternatively, the purchaser may be able to commence an action based upon negligent misstatement, i.e. where it is established that the company owed the purchaser a duty of care.

In *Hedley Byrne Ltd* v *Heller Ltd* [1964] AC 465 the House of Lords established the rule that a duty of care would arise in a situation where there was a 'special relationship' between the parties: a relationship establishing a sufficient degree of proximity. The ability to establish the relationship being dependent upon evidence indicative of the representee's reasonable reliance upon the misstatement. However, the potential scope of the proximity test was to be subsequently suppressed by the House of Lords in *Caparo Industries plc* v *Dickman* [1990] 2 AC 605, where Lord Oliver expressed its definition in the following manner:

> 'What can be deduced from the *Hedley Byrne* case, therefore, is that the necessary relationship between the maker of a statement or giver of advice ("the adviser") and the recipient who acts in reliance upon it ("the advisee") may typically be held to exist where (1) the advice is required for a purpose, whether particularly specified or generally described, which is made known, either actually or inferentially, to the adviser at the time when the advice is given; (2) the adviser knows, either actually or inferentially, that his advice will be communicated to the advisee, either specifically or as a member of an ascertainable class, in order that it should be used by the advisee for that pur-

pose; (3) it is known either actually or inferentially, that the advice so communicated is likely to be acted upon by the advisee for that purpose without independent inquiry, and (4) it is so acted upon by the advisee to his detriment. That is not, of course, to suggest that these conditions are either conclusive or exclusive.' (at p 637)

In accordance with the above statement, it may in part be concluded that the proximity test may now, in respect of the representee's detrimental reliance on a misstatement, only be satisfied where the representee relied upon the misstatement for a purpose which must have been ascertainable and within the representor's reasonable contemplation at the time the misstatement was made, and further that the representor must have been aware that the misstatement would be relied upon by the representee. The effect of the above analysis may be to place a much more onerous burden on the representee in terms of establishing a negligent misstatement. For example, in *Al Nakib Investments (Jersey) Ltd v Longcroft* [1990] 3 All ER 330 it was held that while the directors of a company owed a duty of care to persons who subscribed for shares in reliance on a prospectus, no such duty was owed to a person who purchased shares in the company on the open market, albeit that the purchase was made in reliance upon the contents of the said prospectus. In applying the test advanced in *Caparo Industries plc v Dickman* to the facts of the *Al Nakib* case, Mervyn Davies J concluded that a duty of care was not to be attached to a situation where a statement had been made for a particular purpose but was used for another purpose. Accordingly, the purpose of the prospectus was to invite offers for shares subject to the prospectus issue and not a subsequent purchase of shares on the open market. (Yet, note the probable effect of reg 14 of the 1995 Regulations – discussed above.)

In contrast to the decision in *Al Nakib Investments (Jersey) Ltd v Longcroft*, it is to be noted that a far more liberal interpretation of the decision in *Caparo Industries plc v Dickman* may be implied from the judgment of Lightman J in *Possfund Custodian Trustee v Diamond* [1996] 2 All ER 774. Here the learned judge, in refusing to strike out a claim concerning a misstatement contained in a company's prospectus, but a claim based upon a market acquisition of the shares, concluded that the plaintiff's contention that the prospectus had an implied purpose of seeking to encourage the purchase of shares in the market (in addition to its principal purpose of inviting shares in accordance with the terms of the prospectus), may, if that claim was sustainable, have been of a sufficient character to result in the plaintiff's ability to establish a duty of care.

Suggested further reading

Pre-1995 regulations
Welch (1985) 6 Co Law 247
Griffin (1991) 12 Co Law 209

12

THE CLASSIFICATION AND MAINTENANCE OF SHARE CAPITAL

INTRODUCTION

This chapter seeks to explain the manner in which the Companies Act 1985 purports to regulate the maintenance of a company's share capital. Prior to an exposition of the capital maintenance rules, a classification of share capital will be undertaken. The chapter is concluded by a brief examination of the rules pertinent to the regulation of dividend payments. For issues relating to the reform of this area, see the Appendix at p. 373.

THE CLASSIFICATION OF SHARE CAPITAL

A company's share capital is measured in monetary terms and represents an amount which when contributed becomes part of the company's overall capital assets. However, this rather simplistic definition ignores the different uses to which the term 'share capital' may be employed. The term 'share capital' may be used in the following contexts.

Authorised share capital

A company's authorised share capital represents the total nominal value of shares which may be issued in the company. The sum which represents the authorised share capital is fixed by the company's memorandum (the capital clause). A public company must have an authorised capital of at least £50 000 (s 118, CA 1985).

Issued capital

That part of a company's authorised share capital which has been issued to its shareholders is referred to as the company's issued share capital. A public company must have an issued share capital of £50 000, i.e. if a public company has an authorised share capital of £50 000, it must issue all of its share capital.

Unissued share capital

The difference between the nominal value of a company's authorised share capital and the nominal value of its issued share capital, minus any amount of issued capital which has not been called up by the company, represents the sum of the company's unissued share capital.

Called-up share capital

Called-up share capital is the sum of consideration which the holders of a company's shares have been required to pay to the company in return for the issue of the company's shares.

Uncalled share capital

The difference between the nominal value of a company's issued share capital and the value of the company's called-up share capital represents the sum of the company's uncalled capital. Any amount outstanding on the issue of partly paid-up shares will form a part of the company's uncalled share capital. Although the majority of companies issue fully paid-up shares, a partly paid issue may on occasions prove to be a more attractive proposition to a potential investor, i.e. payment for the shares will be spread over a period of time as opposed to a demand from the company for one initial payment.

Paid-up share capital

The total amount of consideration actually contributed for a company's shares is termed its paid-up share capital.

Reserve capital

In accordance with s 120 of the Companies Act 1985, the members of a company may by special resolution decide to set aside a part of the company's uncalled share capital as a fund for the payment of unsecured creditors should the company be wound up. This reserve fund of capital cannot be reconverted back into uncalled capital or be used by the company as security for a loan. The reserve capital fund can, however, be reduced with the consent of the court (see s 135, CA 1985, discussed below).

Capital reserve accounts

The most common type of capital reserve accounts are (a) the share premium account, (b) the capital redemption reserve and (c) the revaluation reserve. Sums in a capital reserve fund cannot be used to pay dividends, though they may be used to finance an issue of bonus shares. A company's capital reserves should be contrasted with its revenue reserves, the latter represent a company's retained profits. Retained profits, unlike reserve capital, may be used to pay dividends.

(a) The share premium account

A company share has a nominal value; a share cannot be issued at a discounted value below that of its nominal value. However, a share may be issued for a consideration in excess of its nominal value, i.e. the share may be issued at a premium. The difference in value between a share's nominal value and any premium paid on the share must be transferred to the company's share premium account (s 130, CA 1985).

(b) The capital redemption reserve

In accordance with ss 160 and 162 of the Companies Act 1985, a company may in certain circumstances redeem or purchase its own shares out of its distributable profits. As a result of such a purchase or redemption, the company's capital will be reduced by the extent of the loss in the value of the shares purchased or redeemed. Therefore, in order to maintain its capital balance, the company must place in its capital redemption reserve an amount equal to the reduction in share capital (s 170, CA 1985).

(c) Revaluation reserve

A revaluation reserve represents an amount by which the value of a company's assets have increased. An amount equal to an increase in the value of a corporate asset should be transferred to the company's revaluation reserve.

MAINTENANCE OF SHARE CAPITAL

A company's share capital represents the shareholders' investment in the company, it comprises the total sum received from the issue of shares, together with any sums held in the company's share premium account or other statutory capital reserve such as the capital redemption reserve. In relation to accounting procedures, the company's share capital represents a notional liability, i.e. in theory, on the winding up of the company it must be returned to shareholders.

A company's net assets must be maintained in conjunction with the company's notional liability. A company's share capital represents a measure by which asset values should correspond. However, unlike share capital, a company's net assets are prone to economic fluctuations in value, for example, the values attached to a factory or piece of land are likely to be dependent upon external economical and political factors. As such, the values attached to a company's share capital and a company's capital assets are in reality unlikely to be the same. Where the sum representing the total of a company's share capital is in excess of the company's net assets, there may be a presumption that the company is insolvent, however, this may not necessarily be the case because in such a situation the value of a company's real assets may still exceed its real liabilities (discarding the notional liability to shareholders). Nevertheless, in the case of a public company s 142 of the Companies Act 1985 deems that if the company's net assets fall to an amount which is equal to or below half of its called up share capital the company must, within

28 days of that fact becoming known to one of the company's directors, convene an extraordinary general meeting for not later than 56 days thereafter. The meeting must consider the steps, if any, which should be taken to correct the situation.

While a company is a going concern, its capital cannot be returned to shareholders in the form of dividend payments. A company's capital assets are used to generate future wealth and profit, such profit may be distributed to shareholders in the form of dividend payments. A company's capital assets represent security upon which loan funds may be raised. The rules which regulate the maintenance of a company's share capital (the yardstick measure of a company's capital assets) are primarily designed to protect the interests of corporate creditors; the formulation of such rules owe much to the implementation of the EC Second Company Law Directive.

Increasing share capital

A company, if permitted by the terms of its articles, may alter the conditions of its memorandum (capital clause) to effect an alteration in share capital (s 121, CA 1985). Table A, Art 32 provides that an alteration in accordance with s 121 may take place by the passing of an ordinary resolution. Where, in effecting an alteration, a company increases share capital, it must, within 15 days of having passed the resolution to authorise the increase, give notice to the Registrar. The notice must include details of any conditions subject to which the new shares have been issued.

Reduction in share capital

A company may wish to reduce its share capital for a number of legitimate reasons, for example, the company's net assets may have fallen to a value below that of its share capital. A reduction of share capital is not normally a detriment to a company's shareholders; one of the objectives of writing off share capital may be to enable the company to resume paying dividends or to continue to pay dividends at a higher rate. However, in so far as the reduction of share capital may have some commercial effect on the saleable value of the share, a reduction in share capital may adversely affect the shareholder.

The group of persons for which a reduction in a company's share capital is most likely to cause anxiety is the company's creditors, i.e. the effect of a reduction in capital is to deplete the company's recognised measure of capital: should the company fall into liquidation, the pool of assets out of which creditors may be paid would, in theory, be reduced. A company, if it wishes to reduce its issued share capital, must first be authorised to do so by its articles (authorisation is contained within the Table A articles by Art 34). An authorisation within the company's memorandum is insufficient; see e.g. *Re Dexine Patent Packing and Rubber Co* (1903) 88 LT 791. Secondly, the company in general meeting must pass a special resolution to effect the reduction. Finally, the company must obtain the court's approval (s 135, CA 1985).

In accordance with s 135(2), a company will normally be capable of reducing its share capital in one of three ways. First, it may extinguish or reduce liability on its partly paid shares. Secondly, it may cancel paid-up share capital which has been lost in relation to available assets, i.e. by reducing the nominal value of its shares. Thirdly, a company may, either with or without extinguishing or reducing liability on any of its shares, pay off any of the paid-up share capital which is in excess of its needs. For example, a company may choose to return to its ordinary shareholders, say, 10p for every fully paid-up £1 share; instead of repaying in cash, the company may allot debenture stock to its shareholders.

In relation to the second method described above, i.e. by cancelling paid-up share capital which has been lost, in respect to the value of corporate assets, this method avoids having to retain profits to replace lost capital; see e.g. *Carruth* v *Imperial Chemical Industries Ltd* [1937] AC 703. In *Re Jupiter House Investments Ltd* [1985] 1 WLR 975 Harman J held that to prove a loss of capital the loss should be construed as permanent and not a temporary loss in the value of a capital asset. Nevertheless, Harman J took the view that where the loss could not be proved to be permanent, the company could, albeit in exceptional circumstances, attain court approval for a reduction where it had set aside a non-distributable reserve to ensure that if the loss of capital was recovered it would not be distributed in the form of dividend payments. However, it should be noted that in *Re Grosvenor Press plc* [1985] 1 WLR 980 Nourse J took a contrary view by declaring that although a fall in the value of a capital asset may only be temporary, there remained no compelling reason, except in exceptional circumstances, for the court to require a reserve to be set aside.

The courts' primary concern, in deciding whether to affirm a company's reduction of share capital, will be to consider the effect of the reduction upon the company's ability to repay its debts (s 136, CA 1985); see *Poole* v *National Bank of China* [1907] AC 229. Where a proposed reduction of share capital would have the effect of reducing liability in respect of unpaid share capital or where the reduction would result in the payment of paid-up share capital to shareholders, creditors of the company are entitled to object to the reduction in accordance with s 136(3) to (6) of the Companies Act 1985. However, under s 137, where the court is satisfied that the effect of the reduction in capital would not leave the company's creditors in a perilous position, it may confirm the reduction or may impose upon it, such terms and conditions as it sees fit.

In addition to considering the effect of a reduction of capital upon a company's creditors, the court must, in appropriate cases, consider the effect of the reduction upon the various classes of company shareholder; see e.g. *Re Ratners Group plc* [1988] 4 BCC 293. The court must determine whether the reduction of capital would have the effect of varying the rights of a class of shareholder. For example, where preference shareholders are entitled to a repayment of capital in preference to ordinary shareholders, upon a reduction of a company's paid up capital, the preference shareholders should be paid in full, prior to any payment to the ordinary shareholders. The consent of a class of shareholders must be obtained where a proposed reduction of capital would result in a variation of class rights (s 125, CA 1985, discussed in Chapter 10).

REDUCTION OF SHARE CAPITAL AS A CONSEQUENCE OF A REDEMPTION OR PURCHASE OF A COMPANY'S SHARES

Section 143 of the Companies Act 1985 provides statutory confirmation of a long established principle of company law in relation to a company's capacity to expend capital. The principle was expressed by Lord Herschell in *Trevor* v *Whitworth* (1887) 12 App Cas 409:

> 'The capital may, no doubt, be diminished by expenditure upon and reasonably incidental to all the objects specified. A part of it may be lost in carrying on the business operations authorised. Of this all persons trusting the company are aware, and take the risk. But I think they are right to rely, and were intended by the Legislature to have a right to rely, on the capital remaining undiminished by any expenditure outside these limits, or by the return of any part of it to the shareholders.' (at p 415)

The purpose behind s 143 is to prevent the return of capital to shareholders and hence the general depletion of capital funds. Nevertheless, exceptions whereby companies may purchase or redeem their own fully paid-up shares, thus returning capital to shareholders, are contained within the Companies Act 1985 (see below). A company may also acquire its own fully paid-up shares otherwise than for valuable consideration, for example by way of gift; a public company which acquires shares in this manner must dispose of them or sell them within three years of the acquisition (s 146, CA 1985).

In *Acatos & Hutcheson plc* v *Watson* [1995] BCC 450, for the first time in English law, it was necessary for the court to consider whether a company (A) in purchasing the entire issued share capital of another company (B) had infringed s 143 in so far as B's sole asset comprised a holding of 29.4 per cent of the issued share capital in A. In other words, in purchasing the entire issued share capital of B, A would, albeit indirectly, have been purchasing an overriding interest in its own shares, i.e. B's 29.4 per cent stake in A. The background to this case was as follows. B had been used by members of A (including H, A's chairman and chief executive) as a means to acquire shares in A, with the intention that H and other members of B would eventually make a takeover bid for A. However, notwithstanding that such an intention was abandoned, it was nevertheless discovered that B's holding in A created an adverse effect on the level of trading in A's shares. Accordingly, the members of B were anxious to eliminate B's shareholding in A, as indeed were directors of A. The most obvious solution would have been to put B into liquidation with its holding in A returned to B's shareholders (B had no outstanding creditors). However, such a scheme would have attracted a substantial tax burden.

Accordingly, an alternative method was advanced, whereby A proposed to purchase the share capital of B's members in exchange for an issue of its own shares to the members of B. Therefore, B would retain its shares in A, but the independent status of B would, in practice, be removed in so far as it would become a wholly owned subsidiary of A. In addition, A proposed to alter the rights attached to the shares held by B, to the extent that the shares would carry no votes or rights to dividend payments. Basically, while B would technically continue to exist, it would do so in a lifeless state with no power or future capacity in terms of voting rights to influence the affairs of its newly adopted holding company.

In sanctioning the validity of the proposed agreement, Lightman J opined that the share purchase did not infringe s 143 because A did not intend to purchase its own shares but rather it sought to purchase the shares belonging to the members of B. Although the purchase impliedly meant that A would purchase an outright interest (as B Ltd's holding company) in its own shares, Lightman J considered that this was not the same as an express purchase of its own shares. Lightman J also found that the transaction, in so far as B, as a subsidiary of A, would hold shares in its holding company, did not transgress s 23 of the Companies Act 1985 (discussed in Chapter 12) because the shares held in A, by B, had been rendered devoid of any voting rights. Finally, Lightman J concluded that the proposed purchase of shares in B would have no adverse effect on the creditors or shareholders of A plc. Lightman J construed the purchase as being in the best interests of all concerned parties.

Although the decision taken by Lightman J in *Acatos & Hutcheson plc* v *Watson* would seem to have served the interests of all the parties concerned (with the possible exception of the Inland Revenue), it must however be viewed with some caution in terms of future precedent. The truth of the matter is that the practical if not the theoretical result of the transaction was one whereby A acquired its own shares, albeit that the acquisition was a result of an indirect procurement of the shares.

EXCEPTIONS TO SECTION 143 OF THE COMPANIES ACT 1985

Redemption

A company's ability to redeem its own shares provides a fundamental exception to s 143. Shares may only be redeemed if they have been fully paid up. On the redemption of shares the company's issued share capital will be reduced by the nominal value of the redeemed shares. The rules regulating redeemable shares are to be found in s 160 of the Companies Act 1985.

Purchase procedures

Despite s 143, and where a company is authorised to do so by its articles (1985 Table A, Art 35 so authorises) a company may, in accordance with specified circumstances, be permitted to purchase its own shares. Where a company is so permitted, the funds for the purchase must be either taken from the company's profits or alternatively from the proceeds of a new issue of shares; the new issue having been specifically made for the purpose of purchasing the company's existing shares (see ss 161(a) and 162(2), CA 1985). Additionally, a private company may, in an off-market purchase (see below), purchase its own shares from capital, in which case once purchased, the shares will be cancelled and the company's share capital reduced.

Where shares are purchased (or redeemed) wholly or partly out of profits, then a transfer of funds equal to the par value of the shares must be made to the capital redemption reserve. Any premium payable on the shares must normally be paid out of profits. However, where a company's shares were initially issued at a premium, any premium attached to the shares on the date of purchase by the company may be paid out of the proceeds of an issue of new shares up to an amount not exceeding the lesser of:

(a) the total amount of premium obtained from the shares when they were first issued; and

(b) the amount standing to the credit of the share premium account at the time of issue. This amount includes any premium obtained on the new issue.

(a) Market purchase

A market purchase of shares affects public companies and is a purchase made on a recognised UK investment exchange (a public company may also make an off-market purchase under s 163(1)(b), CA 1985 (discussed below)). A company may authorise a market purchase if it is given authority to do so by the general meeting; the general meeting may authorise the transaction by ordinary resolution. In addition, the company must comply with the statutory procedures contained within s 166 of the Companies Act 1985, i.e. the resolution granting the authority to purchase must specify a maximum number of shares to be acquired and the maximum and minimum prices to be paid for the shares. The resolution must also specify a date when the authority will expire; the maximum duration for the authority is 18 months. A copy of the resolution authorising the share purchase must be sent to the Registrar within 15 days of it having been passed. (Note that s 166 provides an exception to the general rule concerning the notification of resolutions to the Registrar; normally only special resolutions must be filed with the Registrar.)

In accordance with Stock Exchange requirements, a market purchase of 5 per cent or more of a company's share capital, within a period of 12 months, must be made either by way of tender or a partial offer to all the company's existing shareholders. Purchases below this limit may be made through the market if the price paid is not more than 5 per cent above the average of the middle market quotations taken from the Official List for the ten business days prior to the date of purchase.

(b) Off-market purchase

An off-market purchase comprises a purchase of shares otherwise than on a recognised UK investment exchange or, if the shares were purchased on a recognised investment exchange, in a situation where the shares purchased had not been subject to a marketing arrangement (see s 163(1), CA 1985). An off-market transaction is normally executed by private contract between a company and one of its existing shareholders.

An off-market purchase must be approved by a special resolution of the general meeting (s 164(1) and (2), CA 1985); a copy of the proposed purchase contract should be made available for inspection by the company's membership 15 days prior to the meeting at which the motion to approve the contract is to be heard. The member of the company with whom the contract is made is not permitted to vote on the motion. Where the company is a public company, the authority contained in the resolution will last no longer than a period of 18 months (s 164(4), CA 1985). It should be noted, following the decision of Lindsay J in *Re R W Peak (King's Lynn) Ltd* [1998] BCC 596, that an informal resolution cannot be used to validate a purchase by a company of its own shares.

A contract of purchase may be contingent giving either the company or member, or both, an option to purchase. If a company provides consideration for an option to purchase, the consideration must be taken from its distributable profits (see ss 165 and 168, CA 1985). The company in making an off-market purchase must deliver a return to the Registrar. The return must notify the Registrar of the details of the transaction and be delivered no later than 28 days from the date of purchase. A copy of the purchase contract must be kept at the company's registered office for a period of ten years (s 169(4) and (5), CA 1985). In relation to a public company, the Registrar must be informed of the aggregate amount paid for the shares, together with details of the maximum and minimum prices paid for each class of share which has been purchased (s 169(2), CA 1985).

Court orders for the purchase of shares

In addition to a voluntary purchase by a company of its own shares, a company may be ordered by the court to purchase shares from one of its members; see e.g. ss 54(6) and 461, CA 1985.

PAYMENT FOR A COMPANY'S OWN SHARES OUT OF CAPITAL (PRIVATE COMPANIES)

Provided that a private company is authorised to do so by its articles (note that no such authority is contained within the Table A articles), it will, in accordance with s 171 of the Companies Act 1985, have a capacity to use capital as a means of redeeming or purchasing its own shares, otherwise than by making payment from its distributable profits (defined in s 172, CA 1985) or the proceeds of a fresh issue of shares; see ss 160 and 162 of the Companies Act 1985. However, a private company may only expend capital if the company's distributable profits are of an insufficient value to facilitate the redemption or purchase. A private company which expends capital for the purpose of purchasing its own shares will not require the authorisation of the court, but it will require its general meeting to pass a special resolution to authorise the expenditure (s 164(2), CA 1985). A member who holds shares to which the motion to purchase shares applies is not permitted to vote on the resolution. A company's purchase or redemption of shares from capital will be unlawful unless the company complies with the statutory procedures laid down in ss 173 to 175 of the Companies Act 1985.

Any expenditure for the purchase or redemption of shares which is to be taken from capital is referred to as 'the permissible capital payment' (s 171(3), CA 1985). The calculation of the permissible capital payment will, in accordance with s 171(6), include a sum representing the proceeds of an issue of shares for the purpose of the redemption or purchase of the company's own shares. Where the permissible capital payment for shares redeemed or purchased is less than their nominal value, the amount of the difference must be transferred to the company's capital redemption reserve (s 171(4), CA 1985). If however, the permissible capital payment is greater than the nominal amount of the shares to be acquired, then the amount of any capital redemption reserve, share premium account or fully paid share capital of the company, and any amount representing unrealised profits standing to the credit of any revaluation reserve, may be reduced by a sum not exceeding the amount by which the permissible capital payment exceeds the nominal amount of the shares (s 171(5), CA 1985).

If a company uses capital to purchase its own shares, the directors of the company are required to make a statutory declaration to the effect that despite the company's expenditure from capital it is still capable of meeting its debts throughout the year immediately following the purchase (s 173(3), CA 1985). The declaration, which must be made within the week before the special resolution to authorise the payment from capital, must be accompanied by an auditor's report to support the terms of the declaration. Any member who did not vote in favour of the resolution or any creditor of the company may, within five weeks of the date of the special resolution authorising payment from capital, apply to the court for an order to prohibit the payment (s 176(1) and (2), CA 1985). Under s 177, the court may, on the hearing of an application under s 176, adjourn the proceedings in order that an arrangement may be made for the company to compensate the dissentient members or the claims of the dissentient creditors (s 177(1)) and/or, the court may make an order under s 177(2) either confirming or cancelling the resolution which gave effect to the purchase or redemption of the company's own shares. In addition, under s 177(3) the court may order that the company purchase the shares of any dissentient member.

Where a company redeems or purchases its shares out of capital, but within a year immediately following the capital expenditure falls into liquidation and cannot pay its debts, the directors of the company who were responsible for the declaration of solvency, together with the person from whom the shares were redeemed or purchased, will be liable to contribute towards the assets of the company. A director may escape liability if it is shown that he had reasonable grounds to believe in the accuracy of the declaration (s 76, IA 1986). However, where a director made a declaration without grounds to believe in its accuracy, the director concerned may be liable to a fine or imprisonment, or both (s 173(6), CA 1985).

FINANCIAL ASSISTANCE GIVEN TO A THIRD PARTY FOR THE PURCHASE OF A COMPANY'S SHARES

The general rule

Section 151 of the Companies Act 1985 provides a general prohibition against a company giving financial assistance (whether directly or indirectly) for the purpose of aiding a person's acquisition of shares in the company or the company's subsidiary. Under s 151(2), the prohibition is extended to cover cases in which the shares have already been acquired, i.e. the company cannot give financial assistance to a third party for the purpose of reducing or discharging liabilities incurred as a result of the acquisition. The purpose of s 151 is to protect creditors and shareholders from the consequences which may flow from a company's capital assets being abused to confer financial assistance for the purchase of the company's own shares. Financial assistance may be defined in a number of ways: for example, by way of gift, guarantee, loan, etc. (s 152(1), CA 1985); see e.g. *Belmont Finance Corporation* v *Williams Furniture Ltd (No 2)* [1980] 1 All ER 393 and *Charterhouse Investment Trust Ltd* v *Tempest Diesels Ltd* [1985] 1 BCC 99, 544.

Section 151 is, however, subject to exceptions, which are provided for by s 153. Where applicable, the exceptions allow the giving of financial assistance for share acquisitions (discussed below). The exceptions apart, the giving of financial assistance is not merely prohibited, but it is also punishable as a criminal offence. The company itself may be fined, and any director or officer in default may be fined and/or imprisoned for a maximum of two years (s 153(3) and Sch 24). Under s 8 of the Accessories and Abettors Act 1861, any other person who knowingly took part in such a transaction (including the recipient of the assistance) may be liable as an accessory to the offence. Furthermore, since the giving of financial assistance is unlawful, any security or guarantee offered by or to the company as part of such an arrangement will be void; see e.g. *Heald* v *O'Connor* [1971] 1 WLR 497.

Exceptions to the general rule (s 153, CA 1985)

Section 153(1) allows a company to give financial assistance for the purchase of its shares or shares in its holding company in a situation where the company's principal purpose in providing the assistance was as an incidental part of some larger purpose, i.e. the purpose for the assistance was not in itself driven by a desire to facilitate the acquisition of shares. Section 153(2) further provides that an exception will exist where the company's principal purpose in giving assistance was not to reduce or discharge any liability incurred by a person for the purpose of acquiring shares in the company or its holding company, notwithstanding that the reduction or discharge of any such liability was an incidental part of some larger purpose of the company. In respect of qualifying under both s 153(1) and (2), the assistance must have been given in good faith and must have been in the interests of the company.

Section 153(3) to (5) provides additional exceptions to s 151. Section 153(3)(b) states that s 151 will have no application in respect of an allotment of bonus shares. Section 153(4) permits certain companies to give financial assistance in the form of loans in circumstances where the lending of money is a part of the company's usual business activities. Section 153(4)(b) as amended by s 132, CA 1989 also provides that a company may offer financial assistance for the purchase of its shares in respect of an employee share scheme, provided that the assistance is given in good faith and in the interests of the company. In respect of public companies, s 153(4) is only applicable where the company has net assets which are not reduced as a result of assistance being given or, to the extent that those assets are reduced, the assistance provided is taken from distributable profits (s 154, CA 1985).

In relation to private companies, s 155 of the Companies Act 1985 creates a further and far-ranging exception by providing that a private company is possessed of a general authority, by the passing of a special resolution in general meeting, to authorise financial assistance for the purchase of its own shares or shares in its holding company; the holding company must also be a private company and the group of companies, controlled by the holding company, must have no public company within its ranks. In accordance with s 155, financial assistance may be given providing the company's net assets are not, as a result of the assistance reduced or, to the extent that they are reduced, the assistance is provided out of distributable profits. The special resolution authorising financial assistance must be passed within a week of the date on which the directors of the company made a statutory declaration as to the company's immediate solvency (see below).

In accordance with s 157(2), where a special resolution has been passed to effect the grant of financial assistance, an application may be made to the court by the holders of not less than 10 per cent in nominal value of the company's issued share capital, or any class of the issued share capital, for the cancellation of the resolution, providing the application is not made by a member who consented to or voted in favour of the resolution. In addition, the application must be made within four weeks of the passing of the resolution (s 158, CA 1985).

Where, in accordance with s 156, a private company gives financial assistance for the purchase of its own shares, the directors of the company must make a statutory declaration to the effect that they are of the opinion that the company will remain solvent for a period of 12 months from the date on which the financial assistance was given (s 156(1)–(3)). The directors' declaration must be supported by a report from the company's auditors which must confirm that the directors' assessment of the company's financial state is reasonable (s 156(4)).

Judicial interpretation of the exception rules

In *Brady* v *Brady* [1988] BCLC 579 the House of Lords was called upon to determine a number of issues pertinent to the interpretation of the financial assistance rules and their exceptions. The case involved a family business which was carried on by two brothers (J and B). The business had successfully been in operation as a private limited company (Brady) since 1959; it was also comprised of a number of subsidiary companies. J and B were the sole directors of Brady; the company's issued share capital was split as between B, who held 46.68 per cent and J, who held 46.66 per cent, the remaining 6.66 per cent of the issued share capital was held by T Ltd, a subsidiary of Brady. Up until 1982, the Brady group flourished, but in that year the group encountered trading difficulties. The group's difficulties were largely expounded by a management deadlock between J and B.

In an attempt to resolve the management deadlock, an agreement was reached whereby the assets of the group were to be split between the two brothers. It was decided that the assets would be split without liquidating Brady. In order to facilitate the reorganisation, the business interests of the group were to be merged and eventually split in equal proportions between two new companies, M Ltd, which was to be controlled by J, and A Ltd controlled by B. The reorganisation was to initially take place via the transfer of the Brady assets to M Ltd, M Ltd would then issue loan stock to A Ltd, i.e. representing an equal share of the group's assets. The loan stock was to be redeemed by the subsequent transfer of assets from M Ltd to A Ltd.

However, before the scheme was completed, B became dissatisfied with the proposed division of assets and as a result refused to abide by the terms of the agreement. As a consequence of B's refusal to honour the agreement, J sought an order for specific performance. In his defence, B claimed (amongst other matters) that the transfer of assets from Brady to M Ltd, assets which would eventually be used to discharge M Ltd's debt to A Ltd (the redemption of its loan stock), constituted an illegal transaction.

B's assertion that the transaction was illegal rested in part on the premise that the transaction was contrary to s 151(2), i.e. Brady would have given financial assistance to M Ltd so as to reduce M Ltd's liability in respect of its acquisition of Brady shares. J contended that the transaction was within the ambit of the exception to s 151 as provided for by s 153(2). At first instance the court found in favour of J and ordered specific performance. However, the Court of Appeal disagreed ([1988] BCLC 20) (Croom-Johnson LJ dissenting) on the applicability of the s 153(2)(b) exception. The majority of the Court of Appeal concluded that the assistance to M Ltd had not been given in good faith nor for the benefit of Brady, in so far as it had been a gratuitous disposition and was therefore contrary to the company's objects and thus *ultra vires*.

On appeal to the House of Lords, the House disagreed with the Court of Appeal's findings in relation to the interpretation of good faith and corporate benefit. Lord Oliver, expressing the unanimous opinion of the House, explained the reasons why Brady's decision to give financial assistance was one which could be couched in terms of having been taken in good faith and in the best interests of the company. His lordship opined:

> 'In the circumstances of this case, where failure to implement the final stage of the scheme for the division of the two sides of Brady's business is likely to lead back to the very management deadlock that it was designed to avoid and the probable liquidation of Brady as a result, the proposed transfer is not only something which is properly capable of being perceived by Brady's directors as calculated to advance Brady's corporate and commercial interests and the interests of its employees but is indeed, viewed objectively, in the company's interest.' (at p 597)

Nevertheless, somewhat surprisingly, the House of Lords (contrary to the findings of both the High Court and Court of Appeal) took the view that Brady's principal purpose in giving financial assistance to M Ltd was not an incidental part of some larger purpose so as to satisfy the terms of s 153(2)(a). Lord Oliver feared that the term 'larger purpose' if construed liberally, could be viewed as a 'blank cheque' for the purpose of avoiding s 151. In interpreting the term 'larger purpose' in the context of the *Brady* case, Lord Oliver stated as follows:

> 'The purpose and the only purpose of the financial assistance is and remains that of enabling the shares to be acquired, and the financial or commercial advantages flowing from the acquisition, whilst they may form the reason for forming the purpose of providing assistance, are a by-product of it rather than an independent purpose of which the assistance can properly be considered to be an incident.' (at p 599)

Accordingly, Lord Oliver viewed the assistance given to M Ltd by Brady for the purchase of Brady shares as devoid of a larger purpose.

While Lord Oliver's narrow construction of the term 'larger purpose' restricts the ease by which s 153(2) may be used as a means to avoid s 151, as a consequence of his comments it is somewhat difficult to imagine a situation in which s 153(2) would be applicable; it is suggested that Lord Oliver's restrictive interpretation went too far in its desire to protect the s 151 provision. Surely, in *Brady* the purpose of the assistance was to ultimately facilitate the reorganisation of the group; it is suggested that the financial assistance would in fact have been devoid of any meaningful purpose had this not been the case (see the comments of Croom-Johnson LJ: [1988] BCLC 20 at p 32.)

Nevertheless, despite the House of Lords' findings, it allowed J's appeal. As Brady was either able to provide the assistance out of distributable profits or the effect of the proposed transaction would not have reduced Brady's assets, the exception to s 151 – as represented by s 155(2), CA 1985 – was fulfilled.

Future reform

In October 1993, the Department of Trade and Industry (DTI) issued a consultative document in relation to a proposed relaxation of the rules relating to compliance with the statutory rules contained in ss 151 to 158 of the Companies Act 1985. The consultative document, while recognising the need for protective measures aimed at preventing the abuse of the financial assistance rules, took the view that the current prohibitions were too restrictive and inflexible.

In order to inject more flexibility into the exception to the rule represented by s 151, the consultative document recommended the replacement of the 'larger purpose' exception contained in s 153. The consultative document considered that this exception should be replaced with one which allowed financial assistance to be permitted where the predominant reason for assistance was undertaken in the best interests of the company, the assistance having been given in good faith. The consultative document also favoured a second type of exception, namely, to allow financial assistance in a situation where to do so would not materially reduce the net assets of the company.

In November 1996, the DTI commenced a further consultation exercise on proposals to reform the law on financial assistance. The result of that exercise was published in April 1997. The DTI, in confirming the findings of the October 1993 consultation document, concluded that the 'larger purpose' test, expounded in *Brady* v *Brady* should be abolished and replaced by a 'predominant reason' test, but that such a test would have to be drafted in a manner which would avoid the narrow construction applied to the 'larger purpose' test.

The 1997 DTI recommendations also sought to amend or reform other aspects of the financial assistance rules and exceptions. For example, the DTI suggested that companies which gave financial assistance should not be subject to criminal sanctions and that a defence should be made available to company officers who were subject to prosecution. Further, the DTI recommended that a transaction should not be void solely on the grounds that it constituted unlawful financial assistance.

While a move to relax the cumbersome 'larger purpose' test as expounded in *Brady* v *Brady* [1988] BCLC 579 is to be welcomed, it is submitted that in applying the proposed test of 'predominant reason' it will be necessary, in order to attempt to counter any potential abuse of the exception, to provide that a decision to confer financial assistance should have been first approved by the company in general meeting (possibly by special resolution). It is suggested that the management of a company should not be afforded too much freedom in the determination of considerations relating to the best interests of the company in respect of deciding whether, in any given instance, financial assistance should have been given for the purchase of the company's shares.

DISTRIBUTION OF PROFITS – THE PROVISION FOR DIVIDEND PAYMENTS

A dividend payment may be seen as the return on a shareholder's investment for the purchase of shares in a company, i.e. dividend payments represent a share in company profits. A dividend is usually payable to a shareholder in proportion to the nominal value of the shares held in the company, but it should be noted, in accordance with s 281 of the Companies Act 1985, that the memorandum or articles of a company may place restrictions on the payment of dividends.

The provision for the regulation of a company's payment of dividends is usually made within the company's articles, e.g. Table A, Art 102 specifies that a company may by ordinary resolution declare a dividend, but that no dividend shall exceed an amount recommended by the company's directors; see *Scott v Scott* [1943] 1 All ER 582. In deciding whether to recommend the payment of a dividend, the directors must act in the best interests of the company.

When a dividend is declared, it represents a debt due from the company to its shareholders. Although a company is not bound to declare a dividend, it should be noted that if the company is capable of doing so, the failure to declare a dividend may unfairly prejudice the interests of its members, thus giving rise to an action under s 459 of the Companies Act 1985; see e.g. *Re Sam Weller & Sons Ltd* [1990] BCLC 80 (discussed in Chapter 23).

A dividend cannot be paid from a company's capital assets and may only be paid out of the profits available for distribution to shareholders (s 263, CA 1985). Public companies are subject to additional restrictions. Section 264 provides that a public company may only make a distribution of its profits if the amount of its net assets is not less than the aggregate of its called-up share capital plus undistributed reserves, and further the distribution must not reduce the amount of those assets to less than the aggregate.

If the directors of a company decide not to declare a dividend or to declare a reduced dividend, the company may retain its profits in the business; indeed, most companies retain at least a proportion of their profits to inject back into future business projects. The directors of a company may create reserves (taken from what would have been distributable profits) and such reserves may be capitalised and used for the purpose of allocating bonus shares (see Table A, Art 110). Dividend payments must, unless the contrary is specifically provided for in the company articles, be paid in cash, though it should be noted that Table A, Art 105 allows a company to pay dividends other than in cash.

Where a dividend is declared in contravention of s 263 or s 264, then, in accordance with s 277, any member who was aware or had reasonable grounds for believing that there had been a contravention of the statutory procedures will be liable to repay the dividend payment to the company; see e.g. *Precision Dippings Ltd v Precision Dippings Marketing Ltd* [1986] Ch 447. Further, the directors of the company, in declaring the dividend, will have acted in breach of duty and in abuse of their powers and, as such, will prima facie be liable to make good any loss incurred by the company.

Suggested further reading

Pickering (1965) 81 LQR 248
Sterling (1987) 12 Co Law 169
Doran [1991] 12 Co Law 99

13

INSIDER DEALING AND RELATED MATTERS

INTRODUCTION

Insider dealing can be defined for most purposes as the misuse of unpublished 'inside information' relating to a company for the purpose of gaining an unfair advantage in transactions involving company shares or other company securities. It will typically involve the sale of securities by a company officer, employee or professional adviser who knows, on the basis of such information, that the price of those securities is about to fall, or the purchase of securities by an insider who knows that they are about to rise. It is most frequently associated with Stock Exchange transactions and it is in relation to such transactions that most of the controlling legislation is directed.

Insider dealing is in certain circumstances punishable as a statutory offence, and may sometimes give rise to civil liability, but there are limits to the reach of either sanction. Before examining these in more detail, it may be helpful to look briefly at some of the factors that may influence share prices, because it will be to such matters that inside information will generally relate.

INFLUENCES ON SHARE PRICES

Although company shares or debentures must be issued with specific nominal values, their actual market value (i.e. the price at which they are bought or sold) may vary from day to day, and will be influenced by a range of market forces. There may indeed be some relationship between the market price of a company's shares and the value of its net assets, but it would be wrong to assume that if a company has net assets of, say, £10 million and has issued 10 million shares, the shares must necessarily be valued at £1 each. Investors will be interested in prospects for future growth and (to a lesser extent) dividends, but will not usually be keen to buy shares in a company which has been trading or performing poorly, even if it has ample capital assets. Conversely, expectations of strong future growth may propel the price of a company's shares to a level well above that suggested by asset values alone. The winning or losing of a major contract may therefore have a large and immediate influence on the company's share prices. So too may the announcement of better or worse than expected trading results. Much depends here on what kind of result the markets were expecting. Thus, the announcement of a £10 million trading loss can actually precipitate a *rise* in that company's share prices, if dealers had previously marked down their prices in anticipation of even worse results, and a £10 million profit may cause a fall in prices if they had expected it to be £20 million.

Prices may also be influenced by national or international events that lie beyond the company's own control: currency or interest-rate fluctuations, wars, disasters, recessions and changes of governments may all play their part in the rise or fall of a company's share price. This can most easily be seen in relation to those public companies whose shares are traded on the Stock Exchange. Dealers on the Exchange continually adjust their prices to take account of all relevant factors. In private companies (or in unquoted public ones), there will be no publicly quoted price for shares, but market forces may still influence the price that a vendor might hope to obtain from a sale. It should, for example, be possible to get a good price for a substantial block of shares in a well run company where business is good and future prospects encouraging, but in times of recession especially, it may be impossible to find a buyer for a minority stake in a badly managed and loss-making private company.

Paradoxically, a decline in share values to a level well below the value of a company's assets may make it an attractive target for a potential takeover bidder, who may be willing to offer existing shareholders a better price for their shares than they could hope to obtain under normal trading conditions. It is for this reason that the announcement or mere expectation of a takeover bid almost invariably precipitates a surge in the price of the target company's shares, and 'insiders' who know of an as yet unpublicised takeover proposal may be tempted to take advantage of that knowledge, before this price surge occurs.

The unfair advantage of inside knowledge

Investing in company securities can be a risky business. They can appreciate in value much more quickly than money placed in a savings account, but their value can also fall. The more knowledge that investors have concerning the companies in which they intend to invest, the better their chances become of making profits. It is for this reason that strict rules govern the publication and contents of listing particulars or prospectuses when shares are to be issued to the public (see Chapter 11). Disclosure of information is seen as being vital to the cause of investor protection, and thus to the maintenance of investor and market confidence. This cause is not helped, however, if some buyers or sellers (the insiders) possess advance knowledge of matters which will seriously affect future prices, but which for the time being remain undisclosed and therefore unknown to other investors.

It is not always easy to identify specific 'victims' in cases of insider dealing, particularly where shares are traded on an investment exchange. Such transactions do not ordinarily take place between individual investors, and nobody is likely to be tricked into buying or selling shares which he or she would not otherwise have bought or sold to or from someone else. Investors deal with firms that are members of the exchange, and these firms also deal with each other. If, for example, investor X decides to sell his 5000 shares in Megacorp plc, he will instruct his stockbroker or bank to make the sale on his behalf. A broker must sell at the best price he can obtain on the market, but X may specify a minimum price below which shares must not be sold. Similarly, if investor Y is seeking to buy Megacorp shares, he will buy them through his own broker or bank. On the London Stock Exchange, the shares of listed companies are bought and sold from dealers (or 'market makers') on the exchange who will at any given time offer a lower price for shares they are prepared to buy (their bid price) than for identical shares they are prepared to sell (their offer price). Dealers, who may also act as brokers, compete to quote the best prices. These prices are continuously updated in response to news and demand and are displayed on numerous computer screens under the SEAQ (Stock Exchange Automated Quotation) system, so uncompetitive quotes will attract no custom.

If a company (in the example, Megacorp plc) is one of the UK's largest companies (primarily those which make up the FTSE 100 index), bid and offer orders can be matched automatically under what is known as the SETS, or electronic order book system. A slightly different system is used for shares in smaller companies traded on the Stock Exchange's Alternative Investment Market (AIM). Whichever system is used, however, shares sold to an 'insider' prior to a dramatic rise in their value are likely to be shares which would in any case have been sold at a similar price to other investors, and shares sold by such an insider may in any case have been resold to a third party prior to any slump in their market value.

This spurs some lawyers and economists to argue that insider dealing should not be a crime at all. Such arguments were first advanced by the law and economics movement in the United States, where insider dealing has been legally controlled since the 1930s. In *The Economics of Legal Relationships*, for example, Manne argued that if directors or other insiders were allowed to trade on the basis of their inside knowledge, this would produce gradual adjustments in share prices as markets react to increased buying or selling (which pushes prices up or down) and as the inside information gradually becomes general knowledge. In contrast, a public announcement of price-sensitive information that has hitherto been kept as a carefully guarded secret may trigger a sudden and possibly damaging surge or drop in the market price. Insider dealing would, in other words, produce a 'more efficient market'.

The opinions expressed by writers such as Manne arguably overlook or neglect the fact that the real victims of uncontrolled insider dealing are likely to be the reputations of the markets and the confidence of potential investors, who may come to feel that investing on such markets is akin to playing poker with opponents who know the markings on the backs of the cards as well as the fronts. Insider dealing on regulated markets therefore appears to be prohibited for the sake of maintaining public confidence in those markets, rather than for the sake of protecting individual investors. Significantly, the position in relation to private transactions that do not go through regulated markets and do not use or involve professional intermediaries is largely untouched by the current legislation, and the position there is still governed only by general equitable principles (discussed below).

'Rigging' or misleading the markets

Compared to insider dealing, 'market rigging' is a more obvious fraudulent activity, and one that has been outlawed for much longer. In contrast to the insider who exploits natural market movements by keeping one step ahead of them, the 'rigger' attempts to precipitate, or in some cases prevent, price movements, either by circulating false information or by creating a misleading and artificial demand for shares or other marketable securities.

This can, in some cases, involve explicit lies and deception. In the notorious case of *R* v *de Berenger and Others* (1814) 105 ER 536, false rumours were circulated concerning the supposed death of Napoleon Bonaparte, in order to boost the value of government securities (then known as 'consuls') held by the defendants. Those responsible were convicted of a conspiracy to effect a public mischief. This form of conspiracy no longer exists (Criminal Law Act 1977, s 5), but a charge of conspiracy to defraud would still be possible on such facts, as would a charge under s 47(2) of the Financial Services Act 1986 (below).

Conspiracy to defraud is a common law offence, the essence of which consists of an agreement by two or more persons dishonestly to cause or risk loss to another, or dishonestly to deprive another of some right or advantage to which he might be entitled (see *Scott* v *Metropolitan Police Commissioner* [1975] AC 819 and *Adams* v *R* [1995] BCLC 17). The offence created by s 47(2) of the Financial Services Act 1986 is more specific and requires no conspiracy. It provides as follows:

> 'Any person who does an act or engages in any course of conduct which creates a false or misleading impression as to the market in or the price or value of any investments is guilty of an offence if he does so for the purpose of creating that impression and of thereby inducing another person to acquire, dispose of, subscribe for or underwrite those investments or to refrain from doing so or to exercise, or refrain from exercising, any rights conferred by those investments.'

It may be that practising a successful deception of the *de Berenger* kind on today's markets would require a degree of audacity and sophistication (to say nothing of resources) that would be beyond the abilities of any likely perpetrator, but it is clear that more narrowly focused attempts to distort the price of a particular company's shares may still occur, and may indeed be facilitated by the ever increasing reliance on computers and electronic information systems, which may be vulnerable to abuse.

In the prosecutions that followed the takeover of the Distillers Group by Guinness plc, it was alleged that Guinness directors had used their company's very considerable resources to support the market price of its own shares (e.g. by paying other persons to buy and/or retain those shares). This, it was alleged, stimulated artificial demand and forced up the market price for the purpose of making the Guinness takeover bid more tempting to the Distillers shareholders, who were being offered Guinness shares in exchange for their old ones. Such conduct, if proved, would also have contravened s 151, Companies Act 1985 (discussed in Chapter 12), which makes it unlawful for a company to give financial assistance to persons who are acquiring its own shares, but it should be noted that in relation to major new issues, a limited form of manipulation for the purpose of 'price stabilisation' may be permitted by rules made under s 48(7) of the Financial Services Act.

Option dealing by directors, etc.

Section 323 of the Companies Act 1985 prohibits directors or shadow directors from buying either 'put' or 'call' options relating to the shares of their own company, its subsidiary or holding company, or subsidiaries of the same holding company, if those shares are listed on any stock exchange in Britain or elsewhere. Under s 327, the s 323 prohibitions are extended to the spouses and infant (i.e. minor) children or step-children of such directors. Breach of the prohibitions is punishable by a fine and/or up to two years' imprisonment, but it is a defence for someone charged by virtue of s 327 to prove that he had no reason to know of his spouse's or parent's status as a director of the company in question.

Put and call options entitle their holders to require other parties to buy or sell relevant shares at a specified price and within a specified time. Option dealing is therefore a form of speculation, rather than a form of investment. It is akin to a gamble on the future price of the shares concerned. The purchaser of an option to acquire, say, 100,000 Megacorp shares at £2.25 each will clearly not exercise his option if the market price falls to £2.20, but may make a handsome profit by so doing if the price rises within the specified period to, say, £2.50 per share.

Directors of the companies concerned are clearly likely to have inside knowledge as to the probability of future price movements, and would therefore be in a position to unfairly exploit such knowledge through option dealing. This risk is so obvious that the prohibition against dealing in options is made absolute in their case. The prosecution would not have to prove that a defendant actually had inside knowledge of any likely future price movement, and the offence is, to that extent, distinct from that of insider dealing. The rationale behind it is, however, largely the same, and it should be noted that suspicious instances of option dealing by persons who fall outside the scope of ss 323 and 327 may sometimes be prosecuted for insider dealing contrary to the Criminal Justice Act 1993 (below).

The above rules control the buying and selling of options, but do not preclude companies from providing their directors or other executives with share options as part of a salary and remuneration package. If the company prospers and its share price rises, the options rights may well prove to be more valuable than the director's basic salary. In recent years, the excessive value of some directors' option rights has called into question the whole issue of directors' remuneration.

INSIDER DEALING AS A CRIMINAL OFFENCE

Historical background

Insider dealing was first made an offence by the Companies Act 1980, and the relevant provisions were largely re-enacted in the Company Securities (Insider Dealing) Act 1985. This original legislation, which has now been repealed and superseded by provisions contained within Part V of the Criminal Justice Act 1993, created an unnecessarily complicated series of offences, which were spread between several lengthy sections of the legislation. There were really only two or three different kinds of criminal behaviour, but different provisions would apply depending on what kind of insider was involved.

The basic offence was contained within s 1(1) of the Insider Dealing Act. This prohibited individuals who had specified connections with a company from dealing in that company's securities on a recognised stock exchange whilst in possession of confidential, unpublished and price-sensitive information relating to the securities concerned. Section 1(1) did not, however, apply to those connected with Company X, who knew of Company X's proposed takeover of Company Y, and acquired Company Y shares in anticipation of future price rises. This kind of insider dealing was covered instead by s 1(2). Insider dealing by public servants (such as DTI officials) whose jobs give them access to price-sensitive information was meanwhile left to separate provisions within s 2, and deals transacted through off-market dealers were left to s 4. The actions of so-called 'tippees' (defined as persons who had obtained information directly or indirectly from insiders, knowing this to be unpublished and confidential information) were left to two separate subsections within s 1, but tippees of public servants were covered by the same s 2 provisions as the public servants themselves!

It is not unusual for company legislation to be criticised for unnecessary complexity or verbosity, and in this respect the Insider Dealing Act was in any event a relatively mild offender. The repeal and replacement of this legislation was eventually dictated by the need to comply (albeit belatedly) with a European Community Directive on Co-ordination of Insider Dealing Regulations (89/592/EEC). This required the extension of insider dealing controls to cover dealings in a wider range of securities, including government stock (gilts), local authority debt securities, 'futures' and contracts for differences (these last being effectively bets on future fluctuations in share or stock indices). The DTI took the view that, if major changes were in any event necessary, the opportunity should be taken to reform the insider dealing laws as a whole. This was done in Part V of the Criminal Justice Act 1993, which came into force on 1 March 1994.

The basic offence

In contrast to the legislation it replaces, the Criminal Justice Act 1993 uses just one short section (s 52) to state the offence. Section 52(1) and (3) provide that an *individual* (not a company) who has information as an insider commits the offence of insider dealing if he deals in securities that are price-affected in relation to that information and does so on a regulated market or acts as or in reliance on a professional intermediary. Section 52(2) adds that the offence can also be committed (a) by encouraging another person to so deal (whether or not that other person is aware of the situation) or (b) by improperly disclosing insider information.

The remaining 12 sections and two schedules define the relevant terms, provide defences and state the penalties applicable. The resulting structure (which is similar in many ways to that adopted in ss 1–7 of the Theft Act 1968) is manifestly more logical than that which existed under the Insider Dealing Act, but it could further have been improved by placing all the applicable defences in the main body of the Act (as is normal in criminal legislation), rather than spreading them confusingly between the main body and the schedules.

Definitions for the purpose of s 52(1)

The prosecution must be able to prove in any case of alleged insider dealing under s 52(1): (a) that relevant securities were involved, (b) that the accused dealt in them, (c) that he did so whilst in possession of information as an insider, (d) that the securities were price-affected in relation to that information, and (e) that the dealing concerned took place *either* on a regulated market *or* with the involvement of a professional intermediary. In the absence of defence concessions, the prosecution must prove each of these elements beyond reasonable doubt. Only then might it become necessary for the defence to seek to establish one of the statutory defences set out in s 53 and Sch 1.

1 Securities
Securities are defined for the purpose of the new offence in Sch 2. This complies with the EC Co-ordination Directive (above) by extending to government and local authority debt securities, financial futures, depository receipts, traded options and contracts for differences, as well as to shares, warrants and debt securities or debentures issued by companies. As to options, see also ss 324 and 327 of the Companies Act 1985.

2 Dealing
Dealing is defined in s 55 of the Criminal Justice Act as meaning the acquisition or disposal of securities, or the direct or indirect procuring of such acquisition or disposal by another person.

Acquisition and disposal are then defined in turn so as to include agreements to acquire or dispose of securities, or contracts which create such securities. This definition covers cases in which the insider arranges for his nominee or agent to do the dealing, even if the nominee or agent is a company. The principal offender must be an individual, but the person whose acts are procured need not be, nor need that person be party to the offence.

3 Information as an insider

This is dealt with in s 57, which provides that a person has information as an insider if and only if he knows it to be inside information and knows that he has acquired or obtained it from an inside source.

These terms are then defined in turn by other provisions of the Act. To find the definition of 'inside information' one must refer back to s 56, which provides that it means information which:

(a) relates to particular securities or to a particular issuer (e.g. a company) rather than to securities or issuers generally;
(b) is specific or precise;
(c) has not been made public; and
(d) would significantly affect prices, if it were published.

To have this information from an 'inside source', the accused must be a director, employee or shareholder of a company (but not necessarily of the same company) or of another issuer of securities or must alternatively have access to that information by virtue of his employment, office or profession (s 57(2)(a) or knowingly obtain his information from a person in one of those categories (s 57(2)(b). This definition is wide enough to cover 'tippees', and also covers insiders in company X who know that it is going to bid for company Y and buy shares in Y in anticipation of the price rise that will inevitably follow announcement of the bid. There is therefore no need, as there was under the Insider Dealing Act, for separate offence-creating provisions dealing specifically with such conduct. It does not matter whether the insider or tippee deliberately sought to obtain such information or whether it was unsolicited (see *A–G's Reference (No 1 of 1988)* [1989] BCLC 193).

Critics of the new insider dealing legislation originally expressed concern over the fact that breach of confidentiality – an essential ingredient in the old insider dealing offences – is not mentioned anywhere in the Criminal Justice Act. What then of the position of market analysts or other experts, who might possess price-sensitive information derived from their own researches, rather than from any tip-offs or leaks, but nevertheless obtained by virtue of their professions? Would such persons find themselves barred from dealing or from passing on their knowledge to their clients? And what of market makers or dealers who may become aware through their work of major market transactions that may influence subsequent prices?

Part of the answer to such fears would seem to lie in s 58, which provides, *inter alia*, that information may be regarded as having been made public, even if it can be acquired only by observation, or by persons exercising diligence or expertise. Section 58 also provides that information is made public if it is derived from information that has been made public. Analysts whose work is based on the study of published information should remain able to trade freely on that basis. Analysts who work on the basis of leaks from insiders may of course be in a very different position.

Market makers or dealers who become aware through their work of unpublished price-sensitive 'market information' (typically relating to major acquisitions or disposals of securities) may be left in a more uncertain position, and their subsequent actions may need to be judged against imprecise concepts of reasonableness or good faith, under special defences contained in Sch 1 to the Act (as to which, see under 'defences' below).

4 Price affected

Securities are 'price affected' by inside information if that information would be likely, on publication, to have a significant effect on prices or values (s 56(2)–(3)). This is a question of fact, not one of law, and the facts of each case must be assessed on their own merits.

5 Regulated markets

These are defined by the Insider Dealing (Securities and Regulated Markets) Order 1994 and currently include, not only those markets established by the London Stock Exchange, but also the international electronic NASDAQ market and markets established under stock and investment exchanges throughout the European Community and the European Economic Area. Exchanges dealing in financial futures and derivatives (such as LIFFE and OMLX) are also covered.

6 Professional intermediaries

These are defined in s 59. The involvement of a professional intermediary is relevant to liability only in the case of off-market transactions, and the definition is wide enough to include professional market makers in OTC (over-the-counter) transactions, usually involving shares in small public companies which do not have a proper market quotation or listing. Face-to-face transactions involving no such intermediaries (such as a privately negotiated sale of shares within a private family company) remain wholly outside the scope of the legislation, but it should be remembered that any false reasons given for sales or purchases (e.g. 'I'm only selling because I need the money for my sick mother ...') could give rise to prosecutions for offences under the Theft Act 1968.

Jurisdictional limitations

One more issue must be considered before turning to special defences under the Act, namely that of territorial extent. This is dealt with in the Criminal Justice Act 1993, s 62 – the gist of which is that there must be some territorial link with the United Kingdom. *Either* the dealing itself must take place on a UK regulated market (defined as the two London Stock Exchange markets, together with LIFFE, OMLX and Tradepoint, which provides an alternative market for the shares of a number of listed companies) *or* some other crucial element of the offence must take place within the UK. Thus, it would suffice if D in London discloses inside information to E in New York, who then deals on a regulated market in Frankfurt or Paris.

Defences

Defences to prosecutions for insider dealing are set out in s 53 and in Sch 1 to the Act. Sch 1 does not interpret or qualify s 53 (as one might expect such a schedule to do). Instead, it adds further defences that, it seems, could not be accommodated in the main body of the Act. Nevertheless, both provisions represent an improvement on the old law, under which it was far from clear where the burden of proof actually lay. (See e.g. *R v Cross* (1990) 91 Cr App R 115.) It is clear that the burden of proving the new defences lies on the accused. This burden may (as with all such defence burdens) be satisfied on the balance of probabilities: the court must be satisfied that the defence is probably true, but it need not be entirely convinced by that defence.

It must be remembered that the ability to prove a s 53 or Sch 1 defence will not be relevant unless the basic definitional elements of the offence itself can be proved by the prosecution. Where, for example, D is alleged to have been guilty of insider dealing as a tippee, it is for the prosecution to prove, not only that D held inside information when he dealt, but also that he knew it to be inside information. If this cannot be proved, then he cannot be regarded as an insider under s 57 and cannot be guilty under s 52, whatever the position under s 53.

The defences take up two pages of legislation, and cannot fully be summarised here. In essence, they deal with situations in which the accused was not seeking to profit or avoid loss by means of his inside information, was not seeking to help anyone else to profit by it, or was otherwise doing his job in good faith. If, for example, a new company director buys shares in his company merely in order to satisfy a minimum shareholding requirement stipulated by the company's articles of association, he will not be guilty of insider dealing, even if he holds inside information at the time. His innocence will be all the more obvious if the inside information points to a likely *fall* in the price of shares he buys. Acts done in accordance with price stabilisation rules (e.g. in relation to Euro-security issues) are also expressly exempted from liability under the new legislation.

Encouraging others to deal: s 52(2)(a)

Under s 52(2)(a), an individual who has unpublished price-sensitive information as an insider will be guilty of insider dealing if he encourages another person to deal in the affected securities in a way that he himself would be forbidden to do. This is not the same as procuring acquisition or disposal under s 52(1) because, for the purpose of s 52(2), no actual dealing need occur. Encouragement is enough in itself, even if the other person flatly refuses to act. Nor need any inside information be disclosed. It would be enough for an insider to say to a friend, 'Megacorp shares look a good buy at the moment; why don't you get some?' It would be a defence, however, for the accused to prove that he honestly believed the inside information had already been published or that no illicit profit would be made (s 53(2)).

Unlawful disclosure of inside information

Under s 52(2)(b), the improper disclosure of inside information to someone who has no right to receive it (e.g. disclosure to one's spouse or golfing partner) is deemed to amount to insider dealing. It need not be coupled with any encouragement to deal, nor need any such dealing ever occur. This apparently draconian provision is however subject to possible defences under s 53(3), under which the accused may, for example, escape conviction by proving that he did not expect any insider dealing to result from his indiscretion.

Prosecutions and penalties

The maximum penalty for insider dealing is imprisonment for up to seven years, and/or a fine at the discretion of the court. Prosecutions require the consent of the Director of Public Prosecutions or the Secretary of State for Trade and Industry, but need not be brought by either of these. It is accordingly possible for the Stock Exchange to bring prosecutions if the relevant consent can be obtained. Disqualification from involvement in company management may be added to these penalties under the Company Directors Disqualification Act 1986 (*R* v *Goodman* [1993] 2 All ER 789). The conviction of an individual who is authorised to conduct investment business may also lead to the revocation of that authorisation, and the consequent loss of his livelihood.

CIVIL LIABILITY FOR INSIDER DEALING

In *Percival* v *Wright* [1902] 2 Ch 421, the directors of a coal mining company were offered some shares in the company, which they purchased from the plaintiffs at an agreed price of £12.10s (£12.50) each. The shares were not listed on any Stock Exchange, and so the price was determined by an independent valuation, but neither the valuer nor the plaintiffs were aware that the directors were negotiating a possible sale of the colliery itself, at a price far higher than that indicated by the £12.10s per share valuation. When the plaintiffs eventually heard of the negotiations, they sought rescission of the share transfer, but it was held that the directors had been under no duty to disclose any information concerning the negotiations, and the action failed.

Percival v *Wright* is sometimes taken as authority for the proposition that directors owe no fiduciary duties to shareholders, and sometimes as authority for the proposition that insider dealing involves no risk of civil liability, but it would be dangerous to rely on the validity of either proposition. Directors and other company officers are in a fiduciary position as against the company itself, and in certain circumstances (although perhaps not in all) they may come to owe duties to members of the company as well (see Chapter 17). It is also possible for a client of a person who is authorised to conduct investment business under the Financial Services Act 1986 to bring an action for damages against that authorised person, under s 62 of the Act, if it can be proved that the latter's breach of the insider dealing legislation has caused the client loss. These possible grounds of liability will be considered in turn.

Liability to the company

It is unusual for the company itself to suffer anything more than embarrassment as a result of insider dealing on the part of its directors or officers, and there does not seem to be any reported case under English law in which a company has even attempted to sue one of its officers for insider dealing, but it is nevertheless probable that an insider dealer's company could sue him, on the basis of the equitable rules governing the fiduciary relationship between them. As explained in Chapter 17, it is a well-established rule of equity that a fiduciary, such as a company director, may only profit from his position to the extent that is expressly authorised by the person to whom his fiduciary duty is owed (in this case, the company). Any unauthorised profit derived from his position must be deemed to belong, in equity, to that person, and it was held by the House of Lords in *Boardman* v *Phipps* [1967] 2 AC 46 that this rule extends to profits derived from the use of valuable information acquired in a fiduciary capacity. It does not matter whether the company (or other person to whom the duty was owed) was ever in a position to exploit the information, nor does it matter that its exploitation was incapable of causing it any harm. It is, in effect, the same doctrine as that applied in *Regal Hastings Ltd* v *Gulliver* [1967] AC 134 (see Chapter 17), and it might be thought that its application in insider dealing cases would be rather less controversial or unjust than was its application in *Regal Hastings* itself.

The lack of reported cases is not, however, surprising. Where insider dealing by directors or other corporate officers is revealed, the company may well be keen to secure the resignation of those responsible, and in the case of listed companies, the regulatory bodies may insist upon it. A criminal prosecution may result in a disqualification order lasting several years, but if the company's main loss is to its reputation or image, it will probably prefer to ensure that the case is forgotten as soon as possible. A prolonged civil action in the courts is not the way to achieve this.

There is nevertheless at least one American case in which a company forced directors to disgorge their ill-gotten insider gains: *Diamond* v *Oreamuno* (1969) 248 NE 2d 910, a decision of the New York Court of Appeals. The directors of a company sold their shares on the market at US $28 per share, shortly before publication of disastrous trading figures precipitated a collapse of the price to $11, and were held liable to account to the company for the difference. The lesson here is perhaps that civil action by the company becomes more likely when the shares concerned are off-loaded just before a collapse. Such off-loading may leave the company with a number of bitter and angry shareholders, whilst at the same time weakening the position within the company of the insider dealers themselves.

Liability for breach of duty to shareholders

An individual with inside information does not necessarily owe any civil duty to shareholders or potential future shareholders whose investments might be affected, but some insiders might find themselves in a position where such duties will arise. Thus, in *Allen* v *Hyatt* (1914) 30 TLR 444 the directors of a company offered to assist the other shareholders by procuring the sale of their shares to an outside buyer. They obtained and exercised options to purchase the shares, but then made a substantial profit for themselves by reselling them at a much higher price. Distinguishing *Percival* v *Wright* [1902] 2 Ch 421, the Privy Council held that the directors had held themselves out as agents for the shareholders, and were accountable to the shareholders on the basis of that agency relationship.

Allen v *Hyatt* might be seen as a case turning on its own rather unusual facts, but a somewhat wider principle appears to be behind the decision of the New Zealand Court of Appeal in *Coleman* v *Myers* [1977] 2 NZLR 225 and that of Browne-Wilkinson V-C in *Re Chez Nico* (*Restaurants*) *Ltd* [1991] BCC 736. In *Coleman* v *Myers* it was held that directors of a private family company owed fiduciary duties to its shareholders, as a result of the shareholders' high degree of dependence upon their information and advice, and of the role of the directors in procuring the transactions in question. Approving of this decision and doubting that of *Percival* v *Wright*, Browne-Wilkinson V-C in *Chez Nico* (*Restaurants*) agreed that, 'fiduciary duties, carrying with them a duty of disclosure, can arise, which place directors in a fiduciary capacity *vis-à-vis* the shareholders' ([1991] BCLC at p 750).

Actions under ss 61 and 62 of the Financial Services Act 1986

Under s 62 of the Financial Services Act 1986, a person authorised under that Act to carry on investment business in the United Kingdom may be liable in damages to a person who has suffered loss as a result, *inter alia*, of a contravention of rules or regulations made under Part I, Chapter V of the Act. The Conduct of Business Rules, made by the Securities and Investments Board (now the Financial Services Authority) require authorised persons to comply with applicable insider dealing legislation, and if such persons are knowingly party to insider dealing, they may be sued for breach of statutory duty by any private investor who has suffered consequent losses. Actions by persons other than private investors are restricted under s 62A of the Act.

Under s 61, the Financial Services Authority may itself apply to the court in order to seek an order that might 'remedy the contravention'. This may involve depriving an insider of illicit profits and compensating other investors who can be shown to have been 'adversely affected'.

Rescission or avoidance of contracts

Section 63 of the Criminal Justice Act 1993 provides that 'no contract shall be void or *unenforceable* by reason only of s 52'. This contrasts with the wording of the repealed Insider Dealing Act, which provided only that contracts would not be rendered void or *voidable*. In *Chase Manhattan Equities Ltd* v *Goodman* [1991] BCLC 897 Knox J held that the earlier provision was intended to do nothing more than prevent the unscrambling of completed Stock Exchange transactions, and that uncompleted contracts tainted with insider dealing would not be enforceable by the guilty party, by virtue of the principle, *ex turpi causa not oritur actio* (a legal action cannot be based on a wrongful cause). It seems that the re-wording of the replacement provision can only have been intended to overcome and reverse the effect of that precedent. In other words, an insider might be able to enforce an executory contract for which he could be jailed! On the other hand, such a contract may still be unenforceable if some other kind of illegality or fraud can be proved to taint it.

DISCLOSURE AND INVESTIGATION OF SHAREHOLDINGS AND DEALINGS

The control of insider dealing and related evils depends to a significant effect on the keeping of accurate records relating to potentially significant share transactions. These include dealings transacted by company directors and certain dealings transacted by other major investors, including those whose own dealings may be modest, but who are acting in concert with others for the purpose of obtaining or consolidating control over the company.

Disclosure by directors

Section 324 of the Companies Act 1985, together with Sch 13 to that Act, lays down rules requiring directors or shadow directors to notify their companies in writing of any relevant shares or debentures held on taking office and of subsequent transactions affecting those holdings. Relevant shares include those in related companies, such as holding or subsidiary companies. Section 328 extends the disclosure requirement to cover the holdings of spouses and minor children of directors, and it is clear from Sch 13 that the disclosure requirement extends even to the price paid or received for the shares. This is obviously not the kind of disclosure that a director would wish to make if he were engaging in insider dealing, but non-compliance with these requirements is itself a criminal offence, punishable by a fine and/or up to two years' imprisonment, and may sometimes be easier to prove than insider dealing. In some cases, disclosure will also be required, in a different form, on the basis that the director is also a substantial shareholder or is acting in concert with others.

The information supplied to the company must then be kept on a register, as provided by ss 325 and 326 of the Companies Act 1985, and where the shares or debentures are listed on a UK investment exchange, the exchange must itself be notified in accordance with s 329. The obligation to notify the exchange is the company's, and when notified, the exchange may publish it in whatever manner it deems appropriate.

Disclosure by substantial shareholders and concert parties

Part VI of the Companies Act 1985 sets out detailed provisions relating to the disclosure of substantial interests in the relevant (i.e. voting) share capital of public companies. Disclosure of such interests (including the combined interests of persons acting in concert with a view to acquiring or tightening control of the company) helps to ensure fair dealing in relation to takeover bids, and it is in relation to takeover bids that cases of insider dealing most frequently occur.

The basic rule is that acquisition by one person of an interest in 3 per cent or more of a public company's voting shares (or 3 per cent of any one class of voting shares) gives rise to a duty of disclosure (ss 198–199). The duty of disclosure extends to subsequent transactions, whether the percentage of shares held is increased or decreased, and ceases only after the company has been notified that it has fallen below the 3 per cent limit. Three per cent of the voting shares of a major listed company may in fact be an enormous block of shares, worth millions of pounds, and the effect of disclosure clearly becomes more significant the larger the disclosed holdings become. Non-compliance with disclosure requirements is, once again, punishable by a fine and/or imprisonment (s 210). For investment and unit trusts or collective investment schemes holding shares in listed companies, the applicable limit was raised to 10 per cent by the Disclosure of Interests in Shares (Amendment) Regulations 1993.

A person will be taken to be interested in shares held by his spouse or minor children, or by another company effectively controlled by him (s 203), and where a number of persons agree to act in concert with a view to acquiring shares in a given company (the target company), they may be deemed to form a 'concert party', in which case each would be deemed to have an interest in the holdings of the others (ss 204–205). In other words, disclosure would become mandatory once the total shareholding of the different party members reaches 3 per cent. Effective compliance with the disclosure requirement would also require full identification of the concert party and its members, thus making it impossible for control of a company to be achieved by stealth, before other shareholders or the market can react to it.

191

There are detailed and complex (some would say impenetrable) rules governing the quantification of relevant interests and the exact definition of a concert party, but the real problem in such cases is that an undisclosed concert party may be very hard to detect or to prove once its existence is suspected, particularly where its membership is based abroad and where the shares are registered in the names of nominees for the true, beneficial, owners. To this end, a public company may launch an investigation into the ownership of its shares (s 212), under which it may (*inter alia*) write to certain shareholders, requiring them to state whether any other person has an interest in the shares, and whether that person is a member of a notifiable concert party. Failing a satisfactory answer to such enquiries, the company may seek the appointment of inspectors by the DTI, for the specific purpose of enquiring into the ownership of the company (ss 442–443, CA 1985: see further Chapter 22).

If in either case the investigation is blocked or frustrated by the non-compliance of shareholders to whom enquiries are directed, a powerful sanction is available in the form of a 'freezing order', which may be imposed by the court under s 216 or by the Secretary of State under s 445. This prevents the exercise of transfer, voting, pre-emption or dividend rights in respect of the shares concerned (ss 454–457). A similar order may be imposed by the Secretary of State following a s 210 conviction for non-disclosure of a requisite interest in shares.

Where the rights of innocent third parties are unfairly affected by the imposition of such sanctions, their application may be modified or rescinded in so far as those parties are concerned (s 456(1A), inserted following the unsatisfactory position previously revealed in *Re Lonrho plc* [1988] BCLC 53).

Investigations into suspected insider dealing

The most significant investigation provisions in this context are those contained in ss 177–178, FSA 1986. These empower the Secretary of State to appoint inspectors where it appears to him that there are circumstances suggesting possible breaches of the insider dealing legislation. Refusal to co-operate with the appointed inspectors may be referred by them to the High Court, and if the court is satisfied that there was no reasonable excuse for the refusal, it may fine or imprison the persons concerned, as if they had been guilty of contempt of court. The Secretary of State may also be directed by the court to exercise his powers under s 178, effectively revoking or restricting an authorised person's authority to conduct investment business.

The scope of these provisions was illustrated in *Re an Enquiry under the Insider Dealing Act* [1988] AC 660, where a financial journalist was held to be in contempt of court through his refusal to disclose the sources of an article he had published, concerning leaks of insider information from the Monopolies and Mergers Commission, Office of Fair Trading and DTI. He had argued that he was justified in protecting his sources under s 10 of the Contempt of Court Act 1981, but the House of Lords held that this provision could not justify or excuse his non co-operation once it had been proved that disclosure was necessary for the prevention of future crime.

In theory, a guilty individual who is questioned by inspectors under s 177 of the FSA may be forced to incriminate himself. Incriminating answers may then be used in evidence against him at a subsequent trial (s 177(6)), whilst the deliberate or reckless furnishing of false information may be punishable under s 200(1). The rules relating to self-incrimination during such investigations have, however, been held to be inconsistent with the United Kingdom's obligations under Art 6 of the European Convention on Human Rights (see *Saunders* v *United Kingdom* [1998] 1 BCLC 362). This does not in itself invalidate or overrule such rules (and will not do so even after the Human Rights Act 1998 has been brought into force), but has led the Secretary of State to adopt a policy of not relying upon such evidence in future criminal trials. It may still be used, however, in disqualification proceedings under the CDDA 1986 (i.e. these are not criminal proceedings, see *R* v *Secretary of State for Trade, ex parte McCormick* [1998] BCC 379).

Stock Exchange Listing Rules

The rules prescribed by legislation and case law are supplemented, as far as listed companies are concerned, by those of the Stock Exchange's Listing Rules. The most significant feature of these rules, as far as insider dealing is concerned, is that they require prompt disclosure to the Stock Exchange itself of various kinds of price-sensitive information, so that it may be published as soon as possible. Once this has been done, the opportunity for misuse of such information will clearly evaporate.

Appended to the Listing Rules is the *Model Code for Securities Transactions by Directors*, which listed companies are expected to adopt. This, *inter alia*, requires directors to give prior notice to their company of any proposed share dealing, and to abstain from dealing at all within a period of two months preceding announcements of yearly or half-yearly results.

The Listing Rules are mandatory for listed companies and for persons who wish to act as directors of listed companies, and in many respects they go well beyond what the general law requires. The smaller Alternative Investment Market is less closely controlled by the Stock Exchange authorities, but the Traded Securities (Disclosure) Regulations 1994 require companies whose securities are traded on that market to inform the public as soon as possible if any major new developments occur which are not public knowledge but which may have a significant effect on market prices for its securities. Non-compliance may result in the Stock Exchange suspending all trading in that company's shares, in accordance with duties imposed on it by these 1994 regulations.

Suggested further reading

Dine, J. (1994) *Criminal Law in the Company Context*, Chapter 3. Aldershot: Dartmouth

Background to and analysis of the 1993 Act
Alcock (1994) 15 Co Law 67

Fiduciary duties and insider dealing
Loss (1970) 33 MLR 34
White (1995) 16 Co Law 163

Reform of CA 1985, s 323
Law Commission Report No. 261, Part II (pp 133–144)

14

LOAN CAPITAL

INTRODUCTION

The availability of credit facilities is an integral part of the commercial world in which limited companies operate. Banks and other financial institutions which operate credit facilities often demand security to counter the potential risk of default; security normally takes the form of a charge on the assets of the debtor company. The purpose of this chapter is to explain the various credit facilities available to companies and the forms of security offered to company creditors. Priority interests in respect of competing security interests and the registration of charges is dealt with in Chapter 15. This chapter does not seek to explore insolvency regimes and procedures, in so far as such an exploration would inevitably involve an exposition of substantive matters of insolvency law – a task which, in the author's opinion, is best reserved for a book which is specifically concerned with principles of insolvency law.

THE DEBENTURE

A document which purports to acknowledge a credit arrangement between a company and a creditor is commonly referred to as a debenture. There is no precise legal definition of a debenture save that the term relates to a document creating or evidencing a debt; see e.g. the judgment of Bowen LJ in *English & Scottish Mercantile Investment Trust* v *Brunton* [1892] 2 QB 700. The Companies Act 1985 makes no attempt to define a debenture, although s 744 provides that a debenture includes debenture stock, bonds and any other securities of a company, whether constituting a charge on the assets of a company or not. A debenture holder is entitled to obtain payment of the sums due to him, whether they be principal or interest; the prescribed rate of interest which is stipulated in the debenture must be paid to the debenture holder irrespective of whether or not the debtor company is in profit.

Many of the statutory rules which regulate the issue of shares (discussed in Chapter 10) apply equally to an issue of debentures (see Part IV, CA 1985). For example, it is an offence for a private company to offer debentures to the public (s 81, CA 1985). However, unlike an issue of shares, and provided that debentures do not confer an immediate right of conversion into shares (see e.g. *Campbell's case* (1876) 4 Ch D 470), a company may offer debentures at a discounted price (see e.g. *Moseley* v *Koffyfontein Mines Ltd* [1904] 2 Ch 108).

Where debentures are offered on the basis that at some future date they may be converted into shares, the directors of the issuing company must be authorised by the general meeting, or by its articles, to make such an issue (s 80, CA 1985). Convertible debentures must first be offered to existing shareholders or debenture holders before being offered to the general public (ss 89 and 94, CA 1985).

Debentures are normally redeemable within a specified time period. However, although equity generally prevents the clogging of the right to redeem, debentures may be perpetual or only redeemable on the occurrence of a very remote event (s 193, CA 1985); see e.g. *Knightsbridge Estates Trust Ltd* v *Byrne* [1940] AC 613. Unless there is a provision within a company's articles to the contrary, a company may re-issue debentures which have been redeemed (s 194, CA 1985).

The ability of a company to issue debentures will end on the appointment of a receiver or on the winding up of the company. A company may continue to issue debentures up until the appointment of a receiver, even in a situation where an application for a receiver's appointment has been made; see e.g. *Re Hubbard & Co Ltd* (1898) 79 LT 665.

Debenture stock

As with a company share, a debenture is transferable; it may be sold on by its original holder. Nevertheless, a debenture may only be transferred in its original form, i.e. a debenture for £100 cannot be sold off in units of £10. However, an issue of debentures can be made in the form of debenture stock, i.e. the company may create a loan fund out of which a holder of the stock obtains a certificate for, say, £1000 worth of the loan fund (debenture stock). The holder of the loan stock is then able to transfer units of whatever minimum denomination (in the above example, £100) has been attached to the particular debenture stock issue. Where debenture stock is issued, holders of the stock will, in terms of priority of repayment of the funds invested in the stock, take equally, i.e. *pari passu*. Where a company issues loan stock, it is usual for it to enter into a trust deed with a trustee company. The purpose of this trust relationship is to confer on the trustee the power to enforce the conditions laid down in the debenture in favour of the holders of the stock, i.e. the beneficiaries of the trust agreement.

SECURITY INTERESTS

When a company wishes to raise finance, especially long-term finance, it will almost inevitably be obliged to give security for the amount it wishes to borrow. An action by a secured creditor to realise a security interest will not normally be possible until the debtor company fails to meet its obligations under the terms of debenture contract. However, where a company borrows money by way of an overdraft facility, the overdraft may be expressed to be repayable on demand.

The mortgage/legal charge

The essential characteristic of any mortgage, be it of a legal or equitable nature, is that it is a conveyance of an interest in property with a provision for redemption. A legal mortgage may be created over personal or real property. In the case of a legal mortgage taken over land, the mortgage may only be created in one of two ways. First, it may be created by a transfer of the property for a terms of years absolute, i.e. a lease, which is subject to a provision providing that the lease will terminate when the mortgagor (debtor) repays the debt owed to the mortgagee (creditor). Secondly, and more commonly, a mortgage may be created by a charge by deed expressed to be by way of legal mortgage; this is often referred to as a legal charge. With the second method, the mortgagee (chargee) obtains no estate in the land secured by the mortgage, but by s 87(1) of the Law of Property Act 1925, should the mortgagor fail to make the repayment of sums due under the mortgage, the chargee may take possession of the mortgaged property.

A mortgage may also be of an equitable character. For example, where a mortgage of land is created in writing other than by deed, or the mortgage is not evidenced by any form of document, but the party seeking to enforce the mortgage can establish some form of part performance such as the deposit of title deeds, then the mortgage will be of an equitable character. A mortgage will also be of an equitable nature where the interest which forms the subject matter of the mortgage is itself of an equitable as opposed to a legal nature, for example a beneficial interest under a trust. Under s 53(1) of the Law of Property Act 1925, a transfer of an equitable interest in property must be in writing and signed by the transferor or his duly authorised agent. The remedies for enforcing a legal or equitable mortgage are: foreclosure, sale, possession or the appointment of a receiver, though there are procedural differences between the enforcement of remedies available for the two different types of mortgage.

The fixed/specific charge

A fixed charge (often referred to as a specific charge) is generally regarded as a type of mortgage and is equitable in its character. However, unlike a mortgage, a fixed charge does not involve a conveyance of any interest in the assets which form the subject matter of the security, but merely gives the chargee certain rights over the charged property.

In order to create a fixed charge over a corporate asset, the asset in question must be identifiable, although it need not be in existence at the time the charge was created; see e.g. *Re Yorkshire Woolcombers Association Ltd* [1903] 2 Ch 284, i.e. the property to which a fixed charge may attach can be future property. The holder of a fixed charge obtains certain rights in relation to the secured assets, rights which may be pursued in the event of default by the chargor (company creating the charge). As with any charge, the precise rights of the chargee are to be found within the document (debenture) creating the charge.

Subject to the requirements of registration (discussed in Chapter 15), a fixed charge confers an immediate security over the charged property. A company having created a fixed charge over its property cannot sell or deal with the charged asset without first obtaining the permission of the fixed charge holder. In *Re Yorkshire Woolcombers* [1903] 2 Ch 284 Vaughan Williams LJ stressed that it was quite inconsistent with the nature of a specific charge for the chargor to be at liberty to deal with the relevant property as he pleased. His lordship stated:

> 'I do not think that for a "specific security" you need have a security of a subject matter which is then in existence. I mean by "then" at the time of the execution of the security; but what you do require to make a specific security is that the security whenever it has once come into existence, and been identified or appropriated as a security, shall never thereafter at the will of the mortgagor cease to be a security. If at the will of the mortgagor he can dispose of it and prevent its being any longer a security, although something else may be substituted more or less for it, that is not a specific security.' (at p 294)

Property which is subject to a fixed charge and which is sold on to a third party without the chargee's consent will remain subject to the charge unless the third party is a *bona fide* purchaser without notice of the existence of the charge. However, providing the charge is registered, the third party will be deemed to have notice of its existence.

The floating charge

Although it is advisable for a person entering into a loan or credit agreement with a company to secure the advancement of funds by means of a fixed charge or mortgage, a company may have already created a fixed charge or mortgage over the particular asset with which the subsequent creditor wishes to secure his loan. In such circumstances, priority issues may deem that it is not in the subsequent creditor's interests to secure his loan by means of a second fixed charge or mortgage (priority issues are discussed in Chapter 15). Indeed, the merits of taking a second mortgage/fixed charge will depend upon the value of the asset in relation to the amount of credit which the first fixed charge or mortgage purported to secure. Where circumstances are such so as to render the creation of a subsequent fixed charge or mortgage ineffectual, a creditor may secure his loan by means of the floating charge.

The floating charge is a device which can only be given as security for a debt incurred by a limited company. It was a device created by the Court of Chancery; its origins may be traced back to the *Panama* case (1870) 5 Ch App 318. The nature of a floating charge is such that the charge does not attach itself to a specific corporate asset until an event termed, 'crystallisation' occurs. The floating charge is created over a class of assets which by their very nature are deemed to lack a degree of permanence, thus preventing them being readily identified, i.e. the assets are of a constantly changing nature. The impractical implication of trying to create a fixed charge over such assets being that the holder of the fixed charge would have to be continually renewing the terms of his charge so as to keep pace with the changing nature of the assets. In addition, if such assets were to be the subject of a fixed charge, the company would be put under a most difficult condition of having to notify and seek the permission of the holder of the fixed charge whenever it wished to dispose of an asset forming part of the chargee's security.

Property to which a floating charge is likely to be attached will include, stock, plant, tools and other transient assets of a company. While companies legislation provides no exhaustive definition of the term 'property', the term should, in accordance with the decision of the House of Lords in *Sharp* v *Woolwich Building Society* [1998] BCC 115, be construed as comprising property in which, at the least, a beneficial interest was held. It is common for a floating charge to be expressed to encompass the whole of the company's undertaking, i.e. the charge will, following its crystallisation, be intended to take priority over assets other than those which are subject to a fixed charge or mortgage. Where a company's assets are of a variable nature, a charge on the company's undertaking is normally expressed to be by way of floating charge, however, a company with assets comprised of only one major fixed asset, for example, an office block, may create a fixed charge on this property; this, in effect, will constitute a fixed charge on the company's undertaking.

Therefore, the floating charge is created over assets of a shifting nature; the sale of such assets is one of the means by which the company will be able earn income from which it can meet its obligations under the terms of the debenture by which the floating charge was created. In *Illingworth* v *Houldsworth (Re Yorkshire Woolcombers Association Ltd)* [1903] 2 Ch 284, Romer LJ tentatively identified the floating charge as possessing the following characteristics:

- a charge on all of a class of assets of the company present and future;
- a class of assets which in the ordinary course of a company's business would be changing from time to time;
- a charge which would allow the company to carry on its business in the ordinary way, i.e. the company would have the ability to trade in the assets which were subject to the floating charge.

Characteristics of the floating charge

It is normal practice in a contract of floating charge to include within its terms express clauses which stipulate that: the company will not deal with its assets otherwise than in the normal course of its business, and that the company will not grant a further charge over the charged asset which would rank, in terms of priority, ahead of the floating charge. This latter clause may be seen as somewhat contradictory to the first clause in that it restricts a company from dealing with its assets in the ordinary course of business, namely, it precludes the company from creating further charges ranking above the floating charge. Nevertheless, the validity of this type of clause (the negative pledge clause) has remained unchallenged and is now regarded as a standard and unexceptional term of most floating charge contracts. Indeed, a threatened breach of either clause would entitle a chargee to obtain an injunction to prevent the breach or, where the actual security interest was threatened by a potential breach, it may entitle the chargee to apply to the court for the appointment of a receiver; see e.g. *Re London Pressed Hinge Ltd* [1905] 1 Ch 576.

Crystallisation of the floating charge

A company may continue to deal with assets which are the subject of a floating charge right up until the time the charge crystallises; see e.g. *Re Borax* [1901] Ch 326. A floating charge will crystallise when a creditor takes action (normally by the appointment of an administrative receiver) to realise the security as a result of the happening of a specified event, i.e. the event will be specified within the debenture document. Alternatively, crystallisation may be triggered by an event implied by law. Specified events implied by law are the winding up of the company, the appointment of a receiver (by another secured creditor) and the cessation of the company's business; see *Re Woodroffes (Musical Instruments) Ltd* [1985] BCLC 227 and *Re The Real Meat Co Ltd* [1996] BCC 254. The class of assets which have been made subject to the floating charge become identifiable on the crystallisation of the charge; the floating charge crystallises into an equitable fixed charge (see e.g. *Re Griffin Hotel* [1941] Ch 129).

Automatic crystallisation

A clause in a debenture contract which provides that a floating charge is to crystallise into an equitable fixed charge on the happening of a specified event without the need for the creditor to make claim to the assets subject to the charge by, for example, appointing an administrative receiver, is termed an automatic crystallisation clause. The legal effectiveness of such a clause was once doubted but the judicial acceptance of the automatic crystallisation clause is now well established, having been established on the premise that the court should seek to give effect to the contractual intention of the parties subject to the charge.

The principal criticism levied against the concept of automatic crystallisation is based upon public policy issues. (See, in particular, the Report of the Review Committee on Insolvency Law and Practice (Cmnd 8558 (1982)), paras 1570–82.) The criticism concerns the fact that no registration procedure is in place for the crystallisation of automatic crystallisation clauses; see the comments of Berger J in *R v Consolidated Churchill Cooper Corporation Ltd* [1978] 5 WWR 652 (the problem of automatic crystallisation in relation to priority issues is discussed further in Chapter 15).

The judicial acceptance of automatic crystallisation clauses has been a gradual one. In *Re Brightlife Ltd* [1986] BCLC 418 Hoffmann J was of the opinion that automatic crystallisation clauses would be effective in circumstances where very clear language had been used to create a term of the debenture giving effect to the process of automatic crystallisation. Hoffmann J interpreted the decision of the House of Lords in *Government Stock & Other Securities Investment Co Ltd v Manila Rlwy Co Ltd* [1897] AC 81 as indicative of the view that the potential validity of an automatic crystallisation clause should be sought by the construction of the term purporting to create it. He supported the decision of the New Zealand court in *Re Manurewa Transport Ltd* [1971] NZLR 909, which gave effect to the contracting party's freedom to include a term within a debenture which permitted the automatic crystallisation of the floating charge. Hoffmann J stated:

> 'It seems to me fallacious to argue that once the parties have agreed on some terms which are thought sufficient to identify the transaction as a floating charge, they are then precluded from agreeing to any other terms which are not present in the standard case.' (at p 427)

The acceptance of the validity of an automatic crystallisation clause was again confirmed by Hoffmann J in *Re Permanent Housing Holdings Ltd* [1988] BCLC 563. For a more recent case example confirming the judicial acceptance of automatic crystallisation clauses, see *Griffiths v Yorkshire Bank plc* [1994] 1 WLR 1427 (discussed further in Chapter 15).

The advantages and disadvantages of the floating charge

The principal advantage of the floating charge is that it allows a company to offer a secured form of loan without seriously restricting the company's ability to carry on its business. Conversely, the company's ability to offer this security interest attracts creditors who might otherwise have been reluctant to offer finance. Although a creditor, having taken a floating charge, will not have his loan secured to the same degree as if secured by a fixed charge or mortgage, the floating charge security interest is better than none at all. The negative pledge clause, as yet, offers little practical advantage to a creditor who inserts such a clause into the debenture document, i.e. for the purposes of priority rights, a subsequent chargee is not deemed to have constructive notice of the clause. Nevertheless, if s 95 of the Companies Act 1989 is ever to be implemented (as s 399, CA 1985), the prescribed particulars to be delivered to the Registrar (of which a subsequent chargee is deemed to have constructive notice) may include a negative pledge clause. However, it is to be observed that while such a change would be welcomed in respect of the chargee who takes a first floating charge over a class of assets, registration of a negative pledge clause may restrict the ability of a company to create subsequent charges over a particular class of assets already subject to a charge containing a negative pledge clause, thus restricting a company's ability to raise finance.

Another important advantage in taking a floating charge is that it will enable its holder to appoint an administrative receiver (defined by s 29(2) of the Insolvency Act 1986) to realise the security interest. The appointment of an administrative receiver will not require the approval of the court although the appointment will carry extensive powers (see Sch 1 of the Insolvency Act 1986). In addition, it prevents (without the receiver's consent) the subsequent appointment of an administrator. An administrator is appointed by the court and has extensive statutory powers to oversee the affairs of a company in financial difficulty; the administrator's powers include the right to sell corporate assets which are subject to a charge.

A theoretical disadvantage of the floating charge, which in some cases may become a practical disadvantage, is that the security interest is dependent upon a class of assets which, in terms of their volume and therefore value, may depreciate to a level which falls below the amount of the loan secured by the charge. A further flaw with the floating charge is that, unlike a fixed charge, a receiver seeking to enforce the security interest must set aside funds from the sale of the charged assets to meet the prior demands of preferential creditors (discussed in Chapter 15).

Avoidance of floating charges

In accordance with s 245 of the Insolvency Act 1986, a floating charge may be invalidated where it was created in the 12 months prior to the onset of the chargor's insolvency, unless the charge was created in consideration for money paid at the same time as or after its creation. The charge may be invalidated where at the time of its creation the company was unable to pay its debts or, as a result of the transaction creating the charge, the chargor company became unable to pay its debts. In the case of a charge created in favour of a person who was connected with the company, the charge will be deemed invalid where it was created two years prior to the company's insolvency, unless it was created in consideration for money paid at the same time as or after its creation.

Distinguishing the floating and fixed charge

First, it is important to note that it would be most incorrect to distinguish a floating charge from a fixed charge solely in terms of the fact that the asset over which the floating charge operates may be used in the company's ordinary course of business. An asset subject to a fixed charge will also be used in the pursuit of a company's business activities. In reality, the distinguishing factor between a floating and fixed charge is the capacity of the company having created a floating charge, to dispose or deal with the charged asset unless and until the charge crystallises; see e.g. *Re G E Tunbridge Ltd* [1994] BCC 563. Accordingly, it may be feasible for a fixed charge to exist in circumstances where there is a well defined, but nevertheless, limited right on the part of the chargor to deal with assets subject to the charge, always providing that the consent of the chargee is required before the chargor is permitted to dispose of assets made subject to the charge; see e.g. *Re Cimex Tissues Ltd* [1995] 1 BCLC 409. In *Evans* v *Rival Granite Quarries Ltd* [1910] 2 KB 979, Buckley LJ stated:

'A floating security is not a specific mortgage of the assets, plus a licence to the mortgagor to dispose of them in the course of his business, but it is a floating mortgage applying to every item composed in the security, but not specifically affecting any item until some event occurs or some act on the part of the mortgagee is done which causes it to crystallise into a fixed security.' (at p 999)

Conversely, a charge may still be construed to be floating in character despite the fact that it contains some form of restriction (albeit that the restriction must be very limited) on the chargor's ability to freely dispose of the assets charged in the ordinary course of the company's business. For example, a floating charge may well contain a negative pledge clause, the intended effect of which is to restrict the chargor from creating future charges over the charged assets which would rank ahead of or *pari passu* with the floating charge. It should be noted that in *Re Cosslett (Contractors) Ltd* [1997] BCC 724 the Court of Appeal held that, in determining the nature of a floating charge, it was essential to consider whether the chargor retained control over the charged assets, rather than having an absolute freedom to employ the charged assets in the ordinary course of its business. Millett LJ observed that:

'The essence of a floating charge is that it is a charge, not on any particular asset, but on a fluctuating body of assets which remain under the management and control of the chargor, and which the chargor has the right to withdraw from the security despite the existence of the charge. The essence of a fixed charge is that the charge is on a particular asset or class of assets which the chargor cannot deal with free from the charge without the consent of the chargee. The question is not whether the chargor has complete freedom to carry on his business as he chooses, but whether the chargee is in control of the charged assets.' (at p 734)

A fixed or floating charge? The problem cases – book debts

The general priority position of floating charges (discussed in Chapter 15) deems it less advantageous for a creditor to take security in the form of a floating charge. As such, the floating charge may be regarded as a 'second class' type of security interest. If at all possible, creditors will wish to take security in the form of a fixed charge. Indeed, as result of the status of the floating charge, creditors have sought to extend the potential scope of the fixed charge. However, in purporting to secure a loan by way of a fixed charge, creditors have often fallen short of achieving that purpose and in such cases the court's construction of the debenture will result in the charge being construed as but a floating charge. The courts must construe a debenture contract to detect the true nature of the charge. Therefore, a debenture which attempts to create a fixed charge and which may expressly refer to the charge as being fixed may in reality be construed as having only created a floating charge; see e.g. *Royal Trust Bank* v *National Westminster Bank plc* [1996] 2 BCLC 682.

A charge taken over a company's book debts represents a security interest in the uncollected debts owed to the company and the realised proceeds of such debts. Although a charge over book debts cannot attach itself to the proceeds part of the secured assets until such a time as the debts are realised, a security interest in acquired property operates as a present interest where it is intended to take immediate effect, subject only to its acquisition by the debtor. Therefore, as from the date of its creation, a charge over book debts is of a continuous nature applying to both the unrealised debt and the realised proceeds of the debt. Once book debts have been realised, the asset over which the charge was originally taken will be substituted by the proceeds of the book debt, unless the terms of the charge provide otherwise.

The decision of Hoffmann J in *Re Brightlife* [1987] Ch 200 provides the classic example of a charge taken over a company's book debts being construed as a floating charge despite the fact that the terms of the charge purported to create a fixed charge. The case concerned a security interest which had been expressed to be by way of a first specific charge over the present and future book debts of a company named Brightlife Ltd. In accordance with the terms of the charge, Brightlife Ltd was prohibited from selling, factoring or discounting its book debts and from dealing with its book debts otherwise than in the ordinary course of getting in and realising the same.

In so far as the terms of the charge failed to restrict Brightlife Ltd from disposing of the proceeds of its book debts for the purpose of its ordinary business activities, then clearly the nature of the charge over the proceeds of debts, collected prior to the appointment of the liquidator, was the natural subject of a floating charge. However, as the chargor was fundamentally prohibited from dealing with the unrealised debts, the effect of the charge over the uncollected book debts conveyed more of a resemblance to a specific charge than that of a floating charge.

Hoffmann J explained his finding that the security interest should be construed as a floating charge on the basis that, irrespective of the restrictions placed upon the chargor's ability to sell, factor or discount the unrealised debts, the nature of a floating charge allowed some form of restriction to be placed on the company's ability to deal with the charged assets; the most normal form of restriction being a negative pledge clause; see also *Re Armagh Shoes Ltd* [1982] NI 59 and *Norgard v DFCT* (1987) ACLR 527.

A somewhat contradictory decision to the one arrived at in *Re Brightlife* is to be found in the decision of Slade J, in the earlier decided case of *Siebe Gorman & Co Ltd* v *Barclays Bank* [1979] 2 Lloyds Rep 142. This case concerned the interpretation of a debenture contract which purported to create a specific charge over the present and future book debts of a company named R. H. McDonald Ltd, the charge having been created in favour of Barclays Bank. The debenture contract provided that during the continuance of the security interest the company was obliged to pay the proceeds received from all present and future book debts into its account held at Barclays Bank and that subject to the prior consent of the bank in writing, the company would not charge or assign the 'same' in favour of any other person.

The charge was construed as a specific charge, notwithstanding that the proceeds of book debts were to be paid into the company's current account, an account normally associated with current day-to-day business expenditure. Nevertheless, restrictions were imposed upon the company's ability to withdraw funds from its current account during the continuance of the company's general indebtedness to the bank. Therefore, any credit balance on the current account, which included a sum collected from the discharge of the company's book debts would not, without the bank's written consent, be capable of being withdrawn from the account.

However, doubt may nevertheless be attached to the practical consequences of the decision in *Siebe Gorman*, in so far as the parties to the charge must have contemplated that whilst in credit to the bank, the company would be at liberty to draw on its current account to satisfy its everyday commercial commitments. Nevertheless, if *Siebe Gorman* is considered to be a controversial decision, subsequent findings of a fixed charge having been created over book debts have shown an even more liberal approach to the finding of a fixed charge. For example, in *Re a Company (No 005009 of 1987)* [1989] BCLC 13 Knox J found that a charge over book debts had been created as a specific charge on the premise that the proceeds of the book debts were to be paid into an account held with the chargee (bank). The charge was so construed, despite the fact that it contained no restrictions (unlike in the *Siebe Gorman* case) in relation to the chargor's capacity to use moneys within the account for the purpose of pursuing its ordinary course of business. Also see the Court of Appeal decision in *Re Atlantic Computer Systems plc* [1990] BCC 859 and the decision of Vinelott J in *Re Atlantic Medical* [1992] BCC 653 – both cases provide emphatic examples of the adoption of a liberal approach to the construction of a security interest as a fixed charge.

A more satisfactory manner of creating a charge to have the effect of establishing a specific charge over book debts may be found within the terms of a charge considered by the Supreme Court of Ireland in *Re Keenan Bros Ltd* [1986] 2 BCC 98, 970. Here, the terms of a debenture sought to create a specific charge over the book debts of Keenan Bros Ltd in favour of Allied Irish Banks Ltd (AIB). The terms of the charge specified that the company could not, without the prior consent of AIB, purport to waive, assign or otherwise deal with the book debts in favour of any other person. The charge also obliged the company to pay all moneys received, in respect of realised book debts, into a designated account held with AIB; an account which had been opened for the sole purpose of collecting the proceeds of book debts. Once realised, the proceeds of the book debts were to be paid into a special account and as such were isolated and identifiable as separate funds; if necessary the specific funds could have been monitored to ensure they were not withdrawn to satisfy the company's ordinary commercial requirements (also see *Re CCG International Enterprises* [1993] BCLC 1428).

In the cases examined above, it was a common feature of the judicial construction of the charges over book debts that they should be construed as indivisible, i.e. the charge was either fixed or floating. However, the decision of the Court of Appeal in *Re New Bullas Trading Ltd* [1994] BCLC 485 may have had the effect of altering the judicial perception of the charge as being of an indivisible nature. The case concerned an application by administrative receivers regarding the order of priority by which payments should be made to a company's secured creditors. The sums available for distribution comprised the realised proceeds of the company's book debts, the debts having been uncollected prior to the appointment of the administrative receivers.

A secured creditor of the company claimed priority in respect of the discharge of moneys loaned to the company, a loan partially secured by a charge over the company's book debts. The terms of the charge prohibited the company from selling, factoring or discounting the book debts and provided that all outstanding book debts were to be the subject of a specific charge, the proceeds of which were to be paid into a nominated account. The charge further provided that on the realisation of the debts the proceeds were to be dealt with in accordance with the chargee's instructions. In the absence of instructions, sums paid into the account were to be released from the specific charge to become subject to a floating charge.

At first instance, Knox J construed the charge over the book debts in accordance with the accepted judicial interpretation of such charges, i.e. the charge was indivisible and in so far as the charge allowed the company a capacity to deal with the proceeds of the debts in the ordinary course of its business, it was floating in its nature. In reversing the decision of Knox J, the Court of Appeal held that the security interest had been intended to operate as a specific charge in relation to the unrealised book debts and a floating charge in respect of the proceeds of the debts. The court's acceptance of the divisible nature of the charge necessitated the recognition of a procedure by which the assets secured by the specific charge could be transferred to the floating charge and to this end the court gave weight to the parties own intentions as to how the transfer of assets would be achieved.

It should be stressed that the decision in *Re New Bullas* was taken on the basis that the express terms of the charge sought to create a specific charge over uncollected debts and a floating charge over the proceeds of the debts. The wording of the charge in *Re New Bullas* accorded with what the court considered to be the natural division of a charge over book debts, thereby creating two distinct parts to the charge. Accordingly, a charge which purports to create a fixed charge over uncollected debts and a floating charge over the proceeds of the debts must specifically spell out such an intention within the terms of the debenture, otherwise it will fail to create the divisible charge; see e.g. *Re Westmaze Ltd* [1999] BCC 441.

Suggested further reading

The nature of a charge
Pennington (1960) 23 MLR 630
Boyle (1985) Co Law 277
Ferran [1988] CLJ 213

Naser (1994) 15 Co Law 12
Worthington [1994] CLJ 81

The problem with charges over book debts
Goode (1994) 110 LQR 592
Griffin (1995) 46 NILQ 163

15

THE PRIORITY RIGHTS OF CREDITORS AND THE REGISTRATION OF CHARGES

INTRODUCTION

The purpose of this chapter is to discuss the priority rights of competing corporate creditors. A consideration of the registration procedure is also undertaken.

PRIORITY RIGHTS

Where a receiver or liquidator of a company is entrusted with the responsibility of selling a corporate asset(s) to discharge the debts of a company, the realisation of such an asset(s) may be insufficient to discharge the amount loaned by individual creditors. To determine whether a particular creditor is entitled to be paid in priority to other creditors it is necessary to examine the rules which govern the priority interests of competing charge holders.

Priority between fixed charges

A duly registered legal or equitable fixed charge, acquired *bona fide* for value without notice – for example, a legal or equitable mortgage of a legal estate in land (created under ss 85(1) or 86(1) of the Law of Property Act 1925) – will take in priority to a subsequently created and registered legal or equitable fixed charge. Where a charge is registered over corporate assets, any subsequent chargee having taken security over the same assets is deemed to have notice of the earlier charge. However, if the earlier created legal or equitable fixed charge was not duly registered, the holder of the subsequently created and registered legal or equitable fixed charge would take priority over the first created charge. It should be noted that notwithstanding the absence of a registration system for crystallised floating charges, a company cannot create a fixed charge ranking in priority to a crystallised floating charge.

Where a company creates a legal fixed charge over its property but subsequently sells the property to a third party, the property will remain charged in the hands of the new owner, even if the third party did not have notice of the existence of the fixed charge. Where a company creates an equitable fixed charge over its property, but later sells the property, the property will remain charged in the hands of the new owner if, at the time the property was purchased, the new owner had notice of the chargee's interest.

Priority between fixed and floating charges

By its very nature, a floating charge will not attach itself to any particular asset until the date of its crystallisation. As such, a fixed charge which is created over a particular asset, an asset to which the floating charge may attach at the date of its crystallisation, will, if it is duly registered, take in priority to the floating charge. (See e.g. *Re Hamilton Windsor Ironworks Co Ltd* (1879) 12 Ch D 707 and see s 464(4), CA 1985.)

A subsequently created fixed charge will take priority over an earlier created floating charge, even if the floating charge expressly includes a covenant on the part of the company not to create a charge ranking in priority or *pari passu* with the floating charge, i.e. provided that the subsequent fixed charge was created without actual notice of the covenant; see e.g. *English & Scottish Mercantile Investment Trust* v *Brunton* [1892] 12 Ch D 707. While the subsequent charge holder will be deemed to have constructive notice of the earlier created floating charge, he will not be deemed to have constructive notice of the covenant (negative pledge clause); see e.g. *Wilson* v *Kellard* [1910] 2 Ch 306.

Priority in relation to competing floating charges

Where a company creates more than one floating charge over a class of assets, the floating charge (if it is duly registered) which was the first in time, will normally have priority. This priority rule applies even where the first floating charge did not include a negative pledge clause; see e.g. *Re Benjamin Cope & Sons Ltd* [1914] Ch 800. However, in the case of two competing charges, it would appear, from the decision of Morrit J in *Griffiths* v *Yorkshire Bank plc* [1994] 1 WLR 1427, that if the later registered floating charge crystallises prior to the crystallisation of the first registered floating charge, then it will take priority, in so far as it will have been converted into an equitable fixed charge before the first charge was so converted. It should also be noted that where a company creates a first floating charge and that charge contains a negative pledge clause expressed to govern a specific class of the assets so charged, then a subsequent floating charge which stipulates that it is to take priority over the first floating charge in respect of the class of assets to which the negative pledge clause is not applicable, will take priority over that class; see e.g. *Re Automatic Bottle Markers Ltd* [1926] Ch 412.

The payment of preferential creditors

The preferential debts of a company are listed in Sch 6 to the Insolvency Act 1986. Preferential debts rank equally amongst themselves. They are categorised as follows: debts due to the Inland Revenue, debts due to customs and excise, social security contributions, contributions to occupational pension schemes, remuneration of employees, and finally, levies on coal and steel production.

Section 196 of the Companies Act 1985 (as amended by Sch 13, IA 1986) and s 40 of the Insolvency Act 1986 deal with the priority position of preferential creditors where a company is not in the course of being wound up. Section 175, IA 1986 is concerned with the priority position of preferential debts when a company is in the process of being wound up.

A company not in the course of being wound up

Section 40 of the Insolvency Act 1986 applies in the case of a company where a receiver is appointed on behalf of the holders of any debentures of the company secured by a charge which, as created, was a floating charge. If the company is not at the time in the course of being wound up, its preferential debts shall be paid out of the assets coming into the hands of the receiver in priority to any claims for principal or interest in respect of the debentures.

Therefore, in accordance with s 40, where a debenture was created by a company as a floating charge, a receiver appointed before a winding up order had been made to realise the assets secured by the charge, must first discharge the debts of the company's preferential creditors in priority to the claims of the floating charge holder, irrespective of whether or not the floating charge crystallised prior to the appointment of the receiver. Where possession of the assets are taken by or on behalf of the debenture holder without the appointment of a receiver, the position is as above, namely, preferential debts must be paid in priority to the claims of debenture holders which were created as floating charge securities (s 196(1), CA 1985, amended by Sch 13, IA 1986).

Accordingly, the company's preferential creditors will be paid out of the assets coming into the hands of the receiver in priority to any claims in respect of the holder of a debenture secured by means of floating charge. Prior to the implementation of s 40, it had been thought that a floating charge could take in priority to the claims of preferential creditors in a situation where the floating charge crystallised into a fixed equitable charge before the appointment of a receiver, i.e. a fixed charge takes in priority to preferential creditors; see e.g. *Re Permanent House Holdings Ltd* [1988] BCLC 563. However, following the implementation of s 40, it now seems highly unlikely whether a crystallised floating charge will take such a priority. Yet, the decision of Morrit J in *Griffiths v Yorkshire Bank plc* [1994] 1 WLR 1427 would appear to paint a contradictory picture. Here, Morrit J was of the opinion that s 40 was only applicable to a crystallised charge where the holder of that charge had appointed a receiver, i.e. s 40 was not applicable where a receiver had been appointed by another charge holder.

Notwithstanding that the literal interpretation afforded to s 40 by Morrit J may have some force, clearly the effect of such an interpretation is one which creates a loophole in the section's application, a loophole which must have never been intended by the legislature. Indeed, in *Re H & K (Medway) Ltd* [1997] 2 All ER 321 Nueberger J came to the conclusion that s 40 should and indeed could be interpreted in a manner which allowed for its application in a situation where the holder of a crystallised floating charge had not been responsible for the appointment of the receiver. The learned judge held that on its true construction, the expression 'the debentures' as contained in s 40(2), was a reference to any debentures of the company secured by a charge which, as created, was a floating charge, and not merely a reference to debentures under which a receiver had been appointed. Indeed, this interpretation makes much sense in so far as it prevents the potential abuse of the provision in a situation where the holders of two competing floating charges (the charges having automatically crystallised) reach an agreement whereby one of the charge holders appoints a receiver so that the other charge holder escapes the consequences of s 40 by taking in priority to the company's preferential creditors.

In a situation where a company creates a composite charge, i.e. a fixed charge over specified identifiable assets and a floating charge over the rest of the company's undertaking, it would appear that a receiver need only apply the assets subject to the floating charge to meet the priority demands of the preferential creditors and not the totality of the assets over which the composite charge was expressed, i.e. the assets over which the fixed charge was created would be free from the claims of the preferential creditors; see e.g. *Re Lewis Merthyr Consolidated Collieries Ltd* [1929] 1 Ch 498.

A company in the course of being wound up

Where a company is in the course of being wound up, the preferential debts must also be paid in priority to debts that were expressed to be secured by means of a floating charge (s 175, IA 1986). However, the payment of the preferential debts, out of funds realised from the sale of assets subject to a floating charge, will themselves be subject to the prior claim of the winding up expenses; see e.g. *Re Barleycorn Enterprises Ltd* [1970] Ch 465.

Under a composite floating and fixed charge, where the assets subject to the fixed charge are sold and realise a surplus over the debt secured by the composite charge, then according to the case of *Re G L Saunders Ltd* [1986] 1 WLR 215, the surplus should first of all be made available for the purpose of payment to any subsequent fixed charge holders and then the liquidator (liquidation expenses), in priority to the company's preferential creditors.

An agreement to alter priority rights

While it may be difficult to appreciate situations in which a creditor with a charge over corporate property (the first chargee) should wish to transfer his priority interest in favour of another creditor, the other creditor having an inferior priority ranking charge over the same property as the first chargee, in practice, a contractual agreement between the first and second chargees to effect such an alteration in the priority position may afford some advantage to the first chargee. The first chargee's priority rights may be transferred without the need to seek the approval of the company having created the charge; see *Cheah Theam Swee* v *Equiticorp Finance Group Ltd* [1992] BCC 98 (Privy Council).

A further example of the workings of a priority agreement is *Re Portbase* (*Clothing*) *Ltd* [1993] BCC 96. Here the holder of a fixed charge entered into a contract with the holder of a floating charge with the effect that the fixed charge would be postponed to rank in priority immediately after the floating charge. Chadwick J held that the effect of so transferring the priority interest did not transfer the fixed charge holder's priority in respect of payment ahead of preferential creditors to the floating charge holder. The holder of the fixed charge took payment after the holder of the floating charge holder who took payment after the preferential creditors.

UNSECURED CREDITORS

An unsecured creditor is in a very weak position when it comes to the disposal of corporate funds for the purpose of the settlement of debts. An unsecured creditor's claim for the recovery of moneys advanced to a company will be based upon the contractual rights attached to the agreement between the parties. Pending judgment, an unsecured creditor has no claim to a debtor's property. Where judgment has been obtained in favour of the unsecured creditor, the debtor's property cannot be sold to realise the amount of the debt unless a court order has been obtained to sanction the sale.

An unsecured creditor has two basic remedies while the company is still a going concern. First the unsecured creditor may sue for the principal and interest and obtain judgment from the court. Failure on the company's part to meet the judgment will then allow the judgment creditor to seek a court order for the sale of the company's property. Where a judgment creditor has obtained judgment against the company and the goods have been seized and sold by the appointed sheriff, a creditor with a floating charge secured over the assets subject to the judgment order will lose priority in favour of the unsecured creditor. Secondly, the unsecured creditor may petition the court to have the company wound up in accordance with s 122(1)(f) of the Insolvency Act 1986, i.e. on the ground that the company is unable to pay its debts (see s 123, IA 1986). However, in such a case the creditor would only receive payment after the company's secured creditors.

THE REGISTRATION OF CHARGES

A company, in charging property, will not normally give up physical possession of the secured property. Accordingly, future creditors may be duped into believing that the property remains unencumbered and as such there is a danger that a creditor may advance funds to a company on the strength of its apparent but nevertheless illusionary wealth. Therefore, to protect creditors, government-administered registers have been devised for the purpose of recording non-possessory charges on the following types of property:

- British ships – (Merchant Shipping Act 1894);
- registered land – (Land Registration Act 1925);
- registered trade marks – (Trade Marks Act 1938 and the Trade Marks Act 1994);
- registered designs – (Registered Designs Act 1949, as amended by the Copyright, Designs and Patents Act 1988);
- unregistered land – (Land Charges Act 1972);
- aircraft and hovercraft registered in UK – (Mortgaging of Aircraft Order 1972);
- UK patents – (Patents Act 1977).

In addition to the above registration requirements, a non-possessory charge on almost any kind of property belonging to a registered company will be required to be registered with the Registrar of Companies, under the Companies Act 1985.

The registration system

At present, the registration system for company charges is governed by Part XII of the Companies Act 1985. Part IV of the Companies Act 1989 contained a significant number of recommendations for the reform of the present registration system; many of the proposals for reform having been based upon suggestions put forward by the Diamond Report, 'A Review of Security Interests in Property' (1989). However, the proposed introduction of Part IV of the Companies Act 1989 was subject to much criticism and doubt, having been regarded as a cost-cutting exercise without any real and lasting benefits to its users and one which failed to do justice to the full recommendations of the Diamond Report. The criticism and doubts focused, in part, on the fact that the new legislation would not have had a retrospective effect, therefore its implementation would in effect have created two registration systems operating side by side, an obvious recipe for confusion. Although Part IV of the Companies Act 1989 will now never be implemented in its entirety, certain changes to the present registration system, based upon Part IV of the 1989 Act, may be enacted at a future date. However, the exact scope of these changes remains somewhat unclear (see the DTI consultation document on the registration of company law charges, 17 November 1994). As such, the discussion of the registration system will proceed by first setting out the various statutory rules in accordance with the current position, the discussion will then consider the proposed reforms as contained in Part IV of the Companies Act 1989.

Registration

Section 395 of the Companies Act 1985, places a company under an obligation to register a charge with the Registrar within 21 days after the date of its creation. The term 'charge' is not defined. Section 93, CA 1989 sought to define a charge as any form of security interest (fixed or floating) over property (including future property) other than an interest arising by operation of law; for example a lien over goods arises by operation of law. The specific nature of a security interest was not defined by Part IV of the 1989 Act. As such it was unclear whether a charge to secure a non-monetary obligation would have been registrable under the 1989 Act proposals. Under the present system (pre-1989 Act) it is unlikely whether such an interest would create a registerable charge; see e.g. *Stoneleigh Finance* v *Phillips* [1965] 2 QB 537.

Charges that require registration

Charges that require registration are listed in s 396(1) (CA 1985), namely:

(a) a charge for the purpose of securing an issue of debentures;
(b) a charge on uncalled share capital of the company;
(c) a charge created or evidenced by an instrument which, if executed by an individual, would require registration as a bill of sale;
(d) a charge on land or any interest in land other than a charge for rent or any other periodical payment;
(e) a charge on book debts of the company;
(f) a floating charge on the company's undertaking or property;
(g) a charge on calls made but not paid;
(h) a charge on a ship or aircraft, or any share in a ship;
(i) a charge on goodwill, trade marks, patent, copyright, etc.

The list of charges which would have required registration under the amending provisions of Part IV of the 1989 Act would have slightly altered the present list. Part (i) would have been expanded to include any intangible movable property. Part (e) would have been expanded to include book debts which had been assigned to the company and part (f) would have been expanded to include a charge on the whole or part of the company's property. Under Part IV of the 1989 Act, part (c) on the current list would have been replaced to the extent that a charge would have become registrable where it was created over goods or any interest in goods. However, a charge would not have been registrable where the chargee was entitled to possession either of the goods or of a document of title to them. Goods would have included a ship or aircraft. A pledge, i.e. the transfer of personal property to a creditor to secure repayment of a debt would not, as under the present system, have been registrable; see e.g. *Wrightson* v *MacArthur & Hutchinsons Ltd* [1921] 2 KB 807.

Under Part IV of the 1989 Act a charge would not have been excluded from the registration procedure merely because it allowed the chargee to take possession of the goods on default of payment (see, s 93, CA 1989). However, it is unclear whether this provision would have required registration in the case of retention of title clauses, hire purchase contracts, conditional sale agreements or finance leases, in so far as it is unlikely whether such devices would ever have been interpreted as charges for the purposes of the Act. However, if Part II of the Diamond Report had been introduced into the 1989 Act in its entirety, then it is probable that all the aforementioned categories of contract would have been classed as registrable (see Diamond Report, Part II, paras 23.6 and 23.7).

In registering a charge, s 401 of the Companies Act 1985 requires specific information to be registered, for example, the date of the creation of the charge, the amount secured by the charge, short particulars of the property charged and the persons entitled to the charge.

Book debts

Although the term 'book debt' is not defined by the Companies Act 1985, the Diamond Report suggested that a book debt should be defined as 'debts due or to become due to the company in respect of goods to be supplied or services rendered or to be rendered by the company in the course of the company's business' (see Diamond Report, para 23.9.22). Under the present and the proposed registration system under the 1989 Act, a charge on an insurance policy is not to be treated as a charge on book debts, in so far as the debt on the insurance policy is a contingent debt; see e.g. *Paul & Frank Ltd* v *Discount Bank (Overseas) Ltd* [1967] Ch 348. Further, a negotiable instrument given to secure the payment of any book debts of a company which is used by way of security for an advance to the company, is not treated as a charge on the book debts of the company (s 396(2), CA 1985).

While it has become common practice for the Registrar to accept, for registration purposes, charges taken over a company's bank account, there is no statutory provision which indicates that a company's bank account should be regarded as a book debt owed to the company so as to render it the subject matter of a charge. Indeed, the judicial view would seem to indicate that a company's bank account (while in credit) should not be regarded as a book debt; see e.g. Hoffmann J in *Re Brightlife* [1987] Ch 200.

The registration certificate

Under the present system, the registration certificate is deemed to be conclusive evidence that the requirements of the Companies Act have been satisfied. The Registrar has the ultimate responsibility for checking the contents of particulars sent to him. It is for the Registrar to decide what charges have been created; where the Registrar makes a mistake as to the contents of the particulars he may be liable for any loss suffered as a consequence of the mistake.

In accordance with Part IV of the 1989 Act, the Registrar would have been relieved of the responsibility and any potential liability for certifying the registration of particulars. The registration certificate would only have been considered to be conclusive evidence of the fact that the specified particulars had been delivered to the Registrar no later than the date stated in the certificate; it was to be presumed, unless it was established to the contrary, that the specified particulars were not delivered earlier than that date. Under the 1989 Act any person would have been able to require the Registrar to provide a certificate stating the date on which any specified particulars of, or other information relating to a charge, had been delivered to him.

Under the present system, the actual instrument creating the charge must be delivered to the Registrar within 21 days of the charge's creation. However, under Part IV of the 1989 Act, it would have been the duty of a company creating the charge, or acquiring property subject to a charge, to deliver the prescribed particulars of the charge in the prescribed form, to the Registrar for registration within 21 days of the charge's creation, or in the case of acquiring property subject to a charge, the date of acquisition.

Failure to register the charge

Under the present registration system a company and any officer of the company in default in failing to register a charge will be punishable by fine. The failure to register may be taken into account in any disqualification proceedings which are instigated against a director. The proposed registration system contained in the 1989 Act did not attempt to alter these penalties for non-compliance.

In accordance with the terms of the present system, a charge which has not been registered within the requisite period but which should have been will be void against the liquidator and any creditor of the company, although the obligation to repay the money secured by the charge is not invalidated by a failure to register; indeed, it becomes immediately repayable. Under Part IV of the Companies Act 1989, if the particulars of a charge had not been registered within the requisite period then in circumstances where a relevant event occurred after the creation of the charge, whether before or after the end of the 21-day period, the charge was to be void as against:

(a) an administrator or liquidator of the company; or
(b) any person who for value acquired an interest in or right over property subject to the charge.

In connection with (a), the relevant event was the beginning of insolvency proceedings, and for (b) it related to the acquisition of that right. Where a relevant event occurred on the same day as the charge was created, the relevant event was to be presumed to have occurred after the charge was created, unless the contrary was proved. It should be stressed that in respect of Part IV of the Companies Act 1989, a charge would no longer have become immediately void after the 21-day period had elapsed. As under the present system, the obligation to repay the money secured by the charge would not have been invalidated by a failure to register.

Late delivery/rectification

Section 404 permits rectification of the register in circumstances where the court is satisfied that an omission or misstatement of any particular was accidental, or due to inadvertence or to some other sufficient cause, or is not of a nature to prejudice the position of creditors or shareholders of the company, or that on other grounds it is just and equitable to grant relief.

Under the present system, the only way in which particulars may be registered after the elapse of the 21-day period is as a result of a court order (also under s 404, CA 1985); see e.g. *R v Registrar of Companies, ex parte Central Bank of India* [1986] 2 QB 1114. In considering an application under s 404, there must be evidence which justifies the court in allowing registration out of time; the court must consider whether it is just and equitable to give relief and it must consider the effect on other creditors if it were to allow late registration (see e.g. *Re Telomatic Ltd* [1993] BCC 404).

Under Part IV of the 1989 Act, it was proposed that if the prescribed particulars had been delivered later than the 21-day period, the charge would only have become void against a liquidator or administrator of the company where insolvency proceedings began within:

(a) two years after the creation of a floating charge, created in favour of a person connected with the company;
(b) one year in the case of other floating charges;
(c) six months in any other case.

A charge would only have become void where a company was unable to pay its debts on the date the particulars were delivered, or in a situation where the company was unable to pay its debts as a consequence of the transaction under which the charge was created.

The effect of errors

Under the present system, the certificate of registration is conclusive, i.e. errors in the filed particulars of a charge do not prevent enforcement of the rights contained therein; see e.g. *Re Nye* [1971] Ch 1052. Had Part IV of the 1989 Act been enacted, a charge containing errors would have been void to the extent of rights not disclosed by the registered particulars; errors would, however, have been capable of being corrected. A charge which contained an error would have been void against an administrator, liquidator of the company or any person who acquired an interest in the property subject to that charge at a time when the particulars were inaccurate in a relevant respect. Nevertheless, the court would have been given a discretion in determining whether the charge was void, a discretion which could be employed in circumstances where it was satisfied that the error had not caused any prejudice to:

(a) any unsecured creditor of the company;
(b) a person who became an unsecured creditor whilst the charge details were incorrect; or

(c) in the case of an interested person, where that person did not rely on the validity of the unregistered particulars.

Under Part IV of the Companies Act 1989, a prior created charge would not have been void as against a later charge for want of registering relevant particulars unless some or all of the relevant particulars of the later charge were delivered for registration within 21 days of that charge's creation, or before complete and accurate relevant particulars of the earlier charge were delivered for registration. For example, if charge X was created on 1 June and a later charge, charge Y, was created over the same property on 1 August and by 1 October particulars of neither charge had been delivered to the Registrar, then at this stage charge X would not be void as against charge Y. However, if say on the 1 November complete particulars had been delivered in respect of charge Y, charge X would (no particulars having been delivered) have become void as against charge Y.

Notice of matters disclosed on the register

It must be noted that the proposed abolition of deemed (constructive) notice, which was to be introduced by the Companies Act 1989, as s 711A of the Companies Act 1985, would not have applied to a person taking a charge over corporate property. Therefore, a prospective chargee would, as is the case under the current system of registration, have had notice of any matter disclosed on the register.

The company register

In accordance with ss 406 and 407 of the Companies Act 1985, a company must keep at its registered office, a copy of every instrument creating a charge, irrespective of whether the charge must be registered in accordance with the Companies Act 1985. The register is open to public inspection. A failure to enter a charge on the register will not invalidate the charge but the company and any officer of the company in default will be liable to a fine.

EXAMPLES OF INTERESTS WHICH DO NOT CREATE REGISTRABLE CHARGES

Hire purchase agreements

Where a company has acquired goods on hire purchase terms (HP), ownership in those goods will not pass to the company until it has fulfilled all of its obligations under the HP agreement. A company cannot create a charge over goods subject to a HP agreement in so far as while the HP agreement is in force, the company is not the legal owner of the goods. Nevertheless, the position is not quite so straightforward where goods acquired under a HP agreement are affixed to land belonging to a company, land over which the company has created a mortgage or charge. In circumstances where the goods subject to the HP agreement were affixed to the land before the security interest was created, then ordinarily the HP firm may repossess the goods where there is a breach of the hire purchase agreement. However, this general rule will not be applied where the security interest is in the form of a legal mortgage, for in this case, if the holder of the mortgage had no notice of the HP agreement when the mortgage was created, he will be allowed to treat the affixed goods as part of the land over which the security was created; see e.g. *Hobson* v *Gorringe* [1897] 1 Ch 182.

Where goods subject to a HP agreement are attached to land over which a specific mortgage of land of a legal or equitable nature had been previously created, the mortgagee will be entitled to count the goods as part of his security interest; see e.g. *Longbottom* v *Berry* (1869) LR 5 QB 123.

The retention of title clause

A retention or reservation of title clause, sometimes referred to as a *Romalpa* clause, is a contractual provision inserted into a contract of sale which seeks to allow the seller to retain title in the goods he sells. The seller reserves title in the goods until such a time as the buyer has fulfilled certain conditions contained within the contract of sale. In terms of priority interests, a supplier of goods with a valid retention of title clause, will, in the event of a company going into receivership or liquidation, be paid moneys owing to him in priority to a creditor secured by means of a registrable charge. Where a seller successfully reserves the right of ownership in goods, the buyer will be unable to create a charge over the goods, i.e. it is impossible for the buyer to create a charge over something which he does not legally own. The legal effect of a valid retention of title clause is therefore similar to a hire purchase (HP) contract, save that under a HP contract the prospective buyer of the property has no legal right to pass title in the goods. By contrast, a term will be implied into a contract containing a valid retention of title clause to the effect that the prospective buyer of the goods will have the legal right to pass title in the goods.

The ability of a seller to retain title in goods, is given legal effect by the Sale of Goods Act 1979. Section 17 of the Act states:

'Where there is a contract for the sale of specific or unascertained goods the property in them is to be transferred to the buyer at such time as the parties to the contract intend it to be transferred.'

Section 19 of the Sale of Goods Act 1979 provides:

'Where there is a contract for the sale of specific goods or where goods are subsequently appropriated to the contract, the seller may, by the terms of the contract or appropriation, reserve the right of disposal of the goods until certain conditions are fulfilled; and in such a case, notwithstanding the delivery of the goods to the buyer, or to a carrier or other bailee or custodier for the purposes of transmission to the buyer, the property in the goods does not pass to the buyer until the conditions imposed by the seller are fulfilled.'

Whilst the practice of a seller retaining title in goods can be traced back to the nineteenth century, the scope of this contractual device has been extended in more recent times. The development and subsequent debate over the ambit of the retention of title clause can be directly attributed to the decision of the Court of Appeal in *Aluminium Industrie Vaasen BV* v *Romalpa Aluminium Ltd* [1976] 2 All ER 552. The facts of *Aluminium Industrie Vaasen BV* v *Romalpa Aluminium Ltd* are as follows. A Dutch company (AIV) supplied aluminium foil to the defendant company (R). The sales contract was subject to a retention of title clause, which included:

(a) an all moneys restriction, i.e. no property in the goods was to pass until all the goods supplied had been paid for;
(b) a condition that foil supplied by AIV should, until its use in the manufacturing process, be stored separately;
(c) a stipulation which provided that objects made from the foil as supplied by AIV would become the property of AIV as security for the payment of moneys owing to AIV;
(d) a restriction which stated that until all debts owing to AIV had been paid, R would hold the unused foil and products made from the foil supplied, in the capacity of a fiduciary owner; and
(e) a condition that if R sold the foil, or goods manufactured from the foil, to a sub-buyer, AIV would have a claim on the proceeds of such sales or, alternatively, the right to take over any claim that R might have against such sub-buyers for debts arising from the sale of foil or products manufactured out of the foil.

R went into receivership owing AIV £122 000. R's receiver certified that R held £50 000 worth of unused foil which had been supplied by AIV and that a further £35 000 had been received from the sale of such foil; these funds had been placed in a separate bank account. On the basis of clauses (a), (b) and (d) (see above), AIV claimed the right to recover the unused foil from R's premises. In reliance upon clause (e), AIV also claimed the right to the £35 000 held in the bank account. As R had not used the foil to manufacture other goods, clause (c) did not come into play.

The Court of Appeal held that AIV were entitled to claim both the unused foil and the proceeds of the sub-sales of the foil. In respect of AIV's right to claim the proceeds of the sub-sales of foil it was necessary for AIV to establish that the retention of title clause created a fiduciary relationship between the contracting parties, so as to enable AIV to argue that they were entitled to an equitable tracing order in respect of the £35 000, i.e. that R held the £35 000 in a form of trust for the benefit of AIV (see e.g. *Re Hallets Estate* (1880) 13 Ch D 696 and more recently, *Re Fleet Disposal Services Ltd* [1995] BCC 605). In deeming that there was a fiduciary relationship between the contracting parties on the basis of a finding of agency, Roskill LJ stated:

'If an agent lawfully sells his principal's goods he stands in a fiduciary relationship to his principal and remains accountable to his principal for those goods and their proceeds.' (at p 563)

However, it is to be noted that, somewhat surprisingly, R conceded that it had acted as a bailee for the foil, thus confirming the notion that property in the foil had not passed and hence strengthening the argument that AIV and R had, indeed, intended to create a fiduciary relationship. A fiduciary relationship was found despite the fact that AIV had extended a 75-day credit period to R, a fact which suggested that R would not have immediately been liable to account for the proceeds of sale, a consideration which in itself appeared contrary to the establishment of a fiduciary type of relationship. Another controversial facet of the case was that the establishment of a fiduciary relationship implied that R would have had to account for all moneys received from the sub-sales of the foil, i.e. any profit received from the sub-sales would have been held for the benefit of AIV. Such a notion would appear quite peculiar in a commercial type relationship in the sense that, would R have entered into a contractual relationship which forbade it from dealing with profits obtained from the sale of the foil? Surely AIV was only entitled to the proceeds of sale in so far as necessary to discharge the amount of moneys owed to them by R?

Deciding whether a clause seeking to reserve title is a valid retention of title clause

There seems little doubt, but note the case of *Re Andrabell* [1984] 2 All ER 407, that if a contract of sale contains a retention of title clause which does no more than to retain the legal ownership in goods until such a time as the full purchase price of the goods have been paid for, that such a clause will, in accordance with s 19 of the Sale of Goods Act 1979, be upheld as reserving title in the property; see e.g. *Clough Mill* v *Martin* [1984] 3 All ER 982. However, it should be noted that a clause which purports to retain equitable and beneficial ownership will not reserve title in the property; see e.g. *Re Bond Worth* [1980] Ch 228 and *Stroud Architectural Systems Ltd* v *John Laing Construction Ltd* [1994] BCC 18. Difficulties in respect of the effect and validity of a purported retention of title clause have occurred in the situations described below.

The all moneys restriction

A retention of title clause may purport to retain ownership in goods which have already been paid for by the buyer. For example, a contract for the sale of goods may consist of the consignment of goods: A, B, C and D. The buyer may have paid in full, for goods A and B but not for goods C and D. In this given example, the effect of an 'all moneys restriction' contained within a retention of title clause would, if upheld, be that the seller would retain ownership in goods A, B, C and D until payment for all four goods had been met. Thus, even though the buyer had paid for goods A and B he would not have acquired the legal title in those goods until the amount owing in respect of goods C and D had been discharged.

Although it is arguable that a seller's claim to retain title in goods which have already been paid for by the buyer would render the contract of sale void as a result of a total failure of consideration (note that The Cork Committee Report 1982 (Cmnd 8558) proposed that an all moneys clause should not be given effect and accordingly treated as creating a registrable charge), the validity of an 'all moneys clause' was supported by the House of Lords in *Armour & Anor* v *Thyssen Edelstahlweke AG* [1990] BCC 929. In supporting the potential validity of such a clause, the House of Lords placed a strong emphasis on the correctness of giving effect to the intentions of the parties as taken from the contractual agreement. Lord Keith, expressing the unanimous opinion of the House of Lords observed:

> 'In the present case the parties to the contract of sale clearly expressed their intention that the property ... should not pass ... until all debts due ... had been paid. In my opinion there are no grounds for refusing to give effect to that intention ... Counsel ... argued that the word 'conditions' in s 19(1) must be read as excluding any condition which had the effect of creating a right of security over the goods. I am, however, unable to regard a provision reserving title to the seller until payment of all debts due to him by the buyer as amounting to the creation by the buyer of a right of security in favour of the seller. Such a provision does in a sense give the seller security for the unpaid debts of the buyer. But it does so by way of a legitimate retention of title, not by virtue of any right over his property conferred by the buyer.' (at p 928–9)

A manufactured goods restriction

A restriction, whereby the seller purports to retain title in goods manufactured from those supplied under the contract of sale, has fallen to be considered by the courts on a number of occasions. As yet, there is no reported case in which the validity of such a restriction has been upheld. The principle justification for not giving effect to the validity of such a clause is that goods which have been supplied by the seller and which have been through the manufacturing process, inevitably lose their original identity. Accordingly, the resulting manufactured goods can no longer be identified as those over which the retention of title clause was placed; see e.g. *Borden UK* v *Scottish Timber Products Ltd* [1981] Ch 25, *Re Peachdart Ltd* [1984] Ch 131, *Hendy Lennox Ltd* v *Grahame Puttick Ltd* [1984] 1 WLR 485, *Clough Mill* v *Martin* [1984] 3 All ER 982, *Modelboard Ltd* v *Outer Box Ltd* [1992] BCC 945, *Ian Chisholm Textiles Ltd* v *Griffiths* [1994] BCC 96 and *Chaigley Farms Ltd* v *Crawford, Kaye & Grayshire Ltd* [1996] BCC 957. In this latter case, a farmer sought to incorporate a retention of title clause in a contract for the sale of livestock. The clause provided that until the animals had been paid for in full, the farmer would retain title in the livestock. The purchaser sent the livestock for slaughter. Garland J held that the retention of title clause could have no effect in so far as the livestock were not of the same character following their slaughter, i.e. carcasses of animals were not the same 'goods' as animals in their living state.

A proceeds of sale restriction

A proceeds of sale restriction which is contained within a retention of title clause is one which purports to restrict the buyer's ability to deal with the proceeds of sale, i.e. a clause which allows the seller to trace the proceeds of sale. Such clauses may afford the seller a right to the proceeds of sale of the original goods or may be extended to allow the seller a right to the proceeds of a sale of goods manufactured from the goods supplied under the original sales contract. Save for the decision in *Aluminium Industrie Vaasen BV* v *Romalpa Ltd* [1976] 1 WLR 676, there is no other authority in which a restriction of this nature has been accepted, otherwise than by creating a charge on the goods; see e.g. *Re Bond Worth* [1979] 3 All ER 919, *Pfieffer Weinkellerei Weineinkauf GmbH & Co* v *Arbuthnot Factors Ltd* [1988] 1 WLR 150, *Compaq Computers Ltd* v *Abercorn Group Ltd & Ors* [1991] BCC 484 and *Modelboard Ltd* v *Outer Box Ltd* [1992] BCC 945.

In *Modelboard Ltd* v *Outer Box Ltd* Michael Hart QC, sitting as a deputy High Court judge, was called upon to determine the nature of an agreement between a seller (S), and purchaser (P) in respect to a term of a sale contract which provided that P would sell finished goods manufactured from goods supplied by S, as agents and bailees for S, and that the entire proceeds of sale would be held on trust for S and kept separate from P's other moneys. Despite the clear intention of the language of the term, i.e. the creation of an agency/bailee relationship, Michael Hart QC construed this term in the light of commercial reality and as such found that its intention could not have been to vest the total purchase price paid for the finished goods (which would include the profit made by P, over and above the contract price paid to S), in the hands of S. Accordingly, the purported existence of a fiduciary relationship as between P and S in respect of the entire proceeds of sale was denied. S's interest in the proceeds of sale was found to be an interest by way of charge which was rendered void as a consequence of its non-registration.

Criticism of the potential effect of a retention of title clause

The principal criticism of the concept of the retention of title clause is that there is no requirement to register such a clause. Accordingly, a creditor wishing to take a charge over corporate assets will find it difficult to establish whether the assets which are to be the subject of the charge are already the subject of a retention of title clause. As such, the very nature of a retention of title clause may be considered to be unfair, i.e. chargeholders are relegated, in terms of priority rights, by the prior claims of the holder of a retention of title clause. The legal effect, in terms of the priority advantage of a retention of title clause, may also be considered unfair in that charges expressed to be created over future assets of a company will be relegated, in terms of priority rights, behind a later created retention of title clause, i.e. the goods which were subject to the later created retention of title clause may otherwise have represented part of the future assets of the company.

Summary

The courts in cases after *Romalpa*, have sought to concentrate their attention on the substance and commercial reality of a purported retention of title clause, with the effect that in the overwhelming majority of cases, retention of title clauses have been construed as devices which have failed to create a fiduciary relationship between the parties. Indeed, many retention of title clauses have been construed to be unregistered charges. For example, in *Compaq Computers Ltd* v *Abercorn Group Ltd* [1991] BCC 484, Mummery J opined that:

> 'In determining whether any given agreement creates a charge, equity looks to the substance and reality of the transaction. What on the face of it may appear to be ... an out-and-out disposition of a beneficial interest in property by way of trust, may in fact be by way of security only, with a right of redemption and therefore, in the nature of a charge ...' (at p 493)

The trust device

As a general rule, a creditor who invests funds into a company will not be deemed to have become the beneficiary of any trust relationship with the company. Nevertheless, the courts have in exceptional circumstances recognised the possibility of a creditor inserting a trust device into a contract, the effect of which is to create a trustee–beneficiary relationship between the contracting parties. The validity of a trust device will afford a creditor a priority in the funds governed by the trust, ahead of other creditors who may seek to lay claim to the funds.

A trust device may operate in circumstances where funds are delivered to a company for a specified purpose, the funds are held on trust by the company until the specified purpose is achieved. A case example which illustrates the potential validity of a trust device is *Re Kayford* [1975] 1 WLR 279. Here a mail order company took the commendable step of attempting to protect customers' funds by establishing a special trust fund into which advance payment for goods was to be deposited. The mail order company went into liquidation. The question which the court had to decide was whether this purported trust fund had the effect of protecting the company's customers' interests or whether such funds should be included as part of the assets available for distribution amongst the general body of the company's creditors? Megarry J found in favour of upholding the validity of the trust device. The learned judge stated that:

> 'Different considerations may perhaps arise in relation to trade creditors but here I am concerned with members of the public, some of whom can ill afford to exchange their money for a claim to a dividend in the liquidation.' (at p 282)

Suggested further reading

Registration of charges
McCormack [1990] LMCLQ 520
Ferran and Mayo [1991] JBL 152

Retention of title clauses
McCormack (1995) *Reservation of Title*. London: Sweet & Maxwell

16

DIRECTORS AND THE MANAGEMENT
OF A COMPANY

INTRODUCTION

*This chapter is the first of six chapters to examine the legal characteristics,
powers and responsibilities associated with the management of a company.
The management functions of a company are predominantly conferred on
company directors and other officers, though shareholders are afforded some
limited powers. This particular chapter concerns itself with an analysis of the
different types of company officer, the constitution and characteristics of a
company's board of directors, issues relating to directors' remuneration,
directors' service contracts and general matters of corporate governance.*

COMPANY DIRECTORS

The Companies Act 1985 provides little guidance in relation to identifying
the managerial characteristics associated with the office of a director. Section
741(1) of the Companies Act 1985 provides the only negligible reference to
the identity of the office. The section states that the term 'director' includes:

'Any person occupying the position of director, by whatever name called.'

Appointment

Shareholders, who are entitled to attend and vote at general meetings, are
responsible for the appointment of company directors. Unless a company's
articles provide otherwise, a director will be appointed by the passing of an
ordinary resolution. Section 282 of the Companies Act 1985 provides that a
public company registered on or after the 1 November 1929 must have at
least two directors, whereas a private company, whenever registered, need
only have one director. A director is not required to be a natural person,
therefore one company may be the director of another company.

Following a director's appointment, details of the director's name, nation-
ality, occupation and address, together with details of any other directorships
held or directorships held within the preceding five years, must be entered
into a register which is kept at the company's registered office; the register is
open to public inspection. A previously held directorship does not have to be
declared in a situation where the company in which the director held office

no longer exists, or where it was part of the group of companies in which the director now holds office (ss 288–289, CA 1985). The Registrar of Companies must also be notified of the details of persons appointed to directorships; such details are entered in a register which is also open to public inspection (s 288(2), CA 1985).

Qualifications

Unlike a company secretary (discussed below), a person appointed to a directorship does not require any formal qualifications; it is even possible for an infant to be appointed to a directorship; see e.g. *Marquis of Bute's case* [1892] 2 Ch 100. However, in some companies the articles may require a person to hold a specified number of shares before taking up a directorship. Where the articles of a company do require a share qualification, s 291 of the Companies Act 1985 states that unless the articles provide otherwise, the share qualification must be taken up within two months of the director's appointment.

Retirement

Once appointed, a director will hold office for a period to be determined by the company's articles. Where, for example, a company adopts articles prescribed by Table A of the Companies (Table A–F) Regulations 1985 ('Table A articles'), Table A, Art 73 states that a company's first director(s) must retire at the first annual general meeting of the company or seek re-election. At subsequent annual general meetings one-third of the directors must retire or seek re-election. The one-third requirement is determined by a director's length of service, i.e. the one-third of directors to retire at any given annual general meeting will, at the time of the meeting, be those directors who held their directorship for the longest period of time. Although Art 73 fails to distinguish between the retirement of non-executive directors and executive directors who hold service contracts, it is to be observed that Art 84 does provide that a managing director and a director holding any other executive office shall not be subject to retirement by rotation. Accordingly, Art 73 will have no application where executive directors are appointed under service contracts in circumstances where the period of the appointment exceeds the rotational requirements.

Except in a situation where a director holds office in a public company or in a company which is a subsidiary of a public company, there is no compulsory retirement age for a director. Where the compulsory age requirement is applicable, a director must retire at the age of 70, unless he continues to hold office with the approval of the company's general meeting (s 293(1), CA 1985).

TYPES OF DIRECTORS

The executive director

An executive director will normally be a full-time officer of the company, who will be employed by the company to perform specific tasks. A company which adopts Table A articles may, subject to the provisions of the Companies Act 1985, appoint one or more of their number to the office of managing director or to any other executive office (Table A, Art 84). The most obvious example of an executive office is the post of managing director/chief executive. A managing director is normally appointed to oversee the day-to-day running of a company. The terms of an executive director's service contract (discussed below) and the specific powers delegated to the office held, are determined by the collective board of directors.

The non-executive director

The post of non-executive director is one which does not carry any contractual managerial responsibilities, a non-executive director is not a salaried employee of the company. Nevertheless, a non-executive director will be entitled, if the general meeting of the company so determines, to directors' remuneration and payments in respect to business expenses (discussed below). A person appointed to hold office as a non-executive director will often be chosen to hold office because of an expertise or public recognition in some particular field.

Although non-executive directors are not expected to regularly attend board meetings, it is important that they should keep in touch with corporate matters, i.e. a non-executive director may, for example, be personally liable for a breach of corporate duty (discussed in Chapter 20). A non-executive director, once appointed, will hold office for a period determined by the company's articles (see Table A, Art 73).

The *de facto* director

In addition to a formally appointed director (a *de jure* director), a person may also, in accordance with s 741 of the Companies Act 1985, be deemed to act as a *de facto* director, in so far as the identification of a company director is not necessarily dependent upon a formal appointment to office. Therefore, a person may be deemed to be a *de facto* director where that person performs managerial tasks properly associated with the office of a director. The tasks performed by that person must exceed those of a mere employee; they must extend to an authority in matters related to the administration of the company's affairs.

The courts have struggled to define the nature and degree of control which is necessary to identify a person as a *de facto* director. Unfortunately, where formal guidelines have been formulated, they have not always been of a uniform nature. Basically, two tests to determine the character of a *de facto* director have been advanced: the 'equal footing test' and 'the holding out test'. The former test was put forward in *Re Richborough Furniture* [1996] 1 BCLC 507. Here Timothy Lloyd QC, sitting as a deputy High Court judge, considered that a *de facto* director would be identifiable, where there was –

> '... clear evidence that he had been either the sole person directing the affairs of the company (or acting with others all equally lacking in a valid appointment ...) or, if there were others who were true directors, that he was acting on an equal footing with the others in directing the affairs of the company.' (at p 524)

By contrast, in *Re Hydrodam (Corby) Ltd* [1994] 2 BCLC Millet J defined a *de facto* director in the following way:

> 'A *de facto* director is a person who assumes to act as a director. He is held out as a director by the company, and claims and purports to be a director, although never actually or validly appointed as such. To establish that a person was a *de facto* director of a company it is necessary to plead and prove that he undertook functions in relation to the company which could properly be discharged only by a director. It is not sufficient to show that he was concerned in the management of the company's affairs or undertook tasks in relation to its business which can properly be performed by a manager below board level.' (at p 183)

In comparing the respective definitions, it is to be observed that in *Re Richborough Furniture* the determination of a *de facto* director is, prima facie, in terms of the evidence required to substantiate that finding, more restrictive than the definition applied in *Re Hydrodam (Corby) Ltd*. In accordance with a literal interpretation of the definition advanced in *Re Richborough Furniture*, a person could fail to be defined as a *de facto* director where, despite performing functions akin to those of a company director, such functions were at a less substantive level than the management activities of either a person exercising a dominant influence over the affairs of a company or, alternatively, the management activities of the company's formally appointed directors.

However, it is to be observed that following the decisions of Judge Cooke in *Secretary of State for Trade and Industry v Elms* (16 January 1997, unreported) and Jacob J in *Secretary of State v Tjolle* [1998] BCLC 333, the equal footing test has been subject to some modification/clarification. In *Secretary of State v Tjolle* Jacob J quoted with approval the following passage taken from the judgment of Judge Cooke in *Secretary of State for Trade and Industry v Elms*:

> 'At the forefront of the test I think I have to go on to consider by way of further analysis what Lloyd J meant by "on an equal footing". As to one, it seems to me clear that this cannot be limited simply to statutory functions and to my mind it would mean and include any one or more of the following: directing others, putting it very compendiously, committing the company to major

obligations, and thirdly, (really I think what we are concerned with here) taking part in an equally based collective decision process at board level, i.e. at the level of a director in effect with a foot in the board room. As to Lloyd J's test, I think it is very much on the lines of that third test to which I have just referred. It is not I think in any way a question of equality of power but equality of ability to participate in the notional board room. Is he somebody who is simply advising and, as it were, withdrawing having advised, or somebody who joins the other directors, *de facto* or *de jure*, in decisions which affect the future of the company?'

Indeed, given the above explanation of the 'equal footing test', it is now possible in many respects to marry that explanation with the definition of a *de facto* director as advanced in *Re Hydrodam (Corby) Ltd*. Under the revised 'equal footing test' and under the 'holding out test', a person will act as a *de facto* director if his contribution to the management of a company is concerned with matters which portray to the outside world an obvious relationship with the functions one would normally expect to be undertaken by a director of a company. Although, in relation to the test advanced by Millet J, the concept of 'holding out' implies that a person will only act as a *de facto* director following a representation from the company to confirm him in that capacity, the said representation may simply be intimated from the company's acquiescence in the performance of a person's managerial functions. Clearly, in any given case the decision as to whether a person acted as a *de facto* director will ultimately be a question of fact. It is to be observed that in *Re Kaytech International plc. Portier* v *Secretary of State for Trade and Industry* [1999] BCC 390, the first case in which the Court of Appeal was asked to consider the meaning of the term '*de facto*' director, the court approved a statement (at p 402) taken from the judgment of Jacob J in *Secretary of State* v *Tjolle*, namely:

'... it may be difficult to postulate any one decisive test. I think what is involved is very much a question of degree. The court takes into account all the relevant factors. Those factors include at least whether or not there was a holding out by the company of the individual as a director, whether the individual used the title, whether the individual had proper information (e.g. management accounts) on which to base decisions, and whether the individual has to make major decisions and so on. Taking all these factors into account, one asks "was this individual part of the corporate governing structure?", answering it as a kind of jury question.'

The shadow director

Section 741(2) of the Companies Act 1985 defines a shadow director as:

'A person in accordance with whose directions or instructions the directors of a company are accustomed to act ... a person is not deemed a shadow director by reason only that the directors act on advice given by him in a professional capacity.'

Accordingly, a person will act as a shadow director where he is responsible for engineering and directing corporate activity through a 'puppet' board of directors. In contrast to a *de facto* director, a shadow director will not be held out as a director of the company, see the judgment of Millet J in *Re Hydrodam (Corby) Ltd* (1994) BCC 161 at p 162. The shadow director will, in effect, instruct the company's *de jure* and *de facto* directors in relation to the management of the company's affairs. The shadow director will be obeyed in those instructions.

The need to attach responsibility to a person who engineers and directs corporate activity through a 'puppet' board of directors is necessary because it prevents such a person from evading duties designed to prevent the mismanagement of corporate affairs. Equity also recognises the potential liability of a shadow director in that persons who are knowingly party to a breach of a fiduciary duty may be liable to the company as constructive trustees; see e.g. *Selangor United Rubber Estates Ltd* v *Cradock (No 3)* [1968] 1 WLR 1555 (discussed further in Chapter 17).

Although s 741(2) of the Companies Act 1985 would appear to expressly exempt a person from being construed as a shadow director when acting in a professional capacity, the exemption is limited and will not cover a situation where, for example, a professional offers advice beyond the reasonable scope of the advice one would normally expect from a person occupying a similar professional status. For example, in *Re Tasbian Ltd (No 3)* [1992] BCC 358 an accountant, Mr Nixon (N), was employed by a finance company, Castle Finance Ltd (C), to act as financial consultant to C's subsidiary and client, Tasbian Ltd (T). The Court of Appeal, in upholding the first instance decision of Vinelott J, held that to justify a finding that N acted as a shadow director of T, it was necessary to establish that N exercised a degree of control over the company's affairs which went beyond the influence one would expect from an accountant offering financial advice to a company. In concluding that there was sufficient evidence to establish a finding that N had acted as a shadow director of T, Balcombe LJ stated:

> 'Mr Nixon decided which cheques drawn by the company could and which could not be submitted to the bank. This meant that he was concerned with which of the company's creditors were paid and in which order, and to that extent it would appear – I say no more than that, that he was able to control the company's affairs.' (at p 364)

The court's finding was strengthened by the fact that N had manipulated the management functions of the company's appointed directors. (See also *Re a Company (No. 005009 of 1987)* (1988) 4 BCC 424 in which Knox J refused to hold, on a preliminary point of law, that a company's bank was incapable of acting as the company's shadow director.)

The distinction between a *de facto* and a shadow director

The distinction between a *de facto* director and a shadow director has received little attention in the reported cases. Moreover, in some cases the distinction has appeared quite irrelevant. For example, in *Re Tasbian (No 3)* [1993] BCLC 297 the Court of Appeal, affirming the decision of Vinelott J ([1991] BCLC 792), made no attempt in analysing the facts of the case to distinguish between a person's involvement in the management of a company as a *de facto* or shadow director. Instead, the court was quite satisfied to conclude that the evidence of the case was sufficient to establish that the person acted as either a *de facto* director or a shadow director.

Yet, clearly, the evidence required to establish that a person acted as a *de facto* director will be less substantive than that which would justify a person being labelled a shadow director. Whereas a shadow director is defined in terms of a person exerting a dominant and controlling influence over the company's affairs, the identification of a person having acted in the capacity of a *de facto* director is less stringent, i.e. in respect of the degree of control which he will be expected to exert over a company's affairs.

However, it must be observed that although the definitions attributed to a *de facto* and shadow director are in theory quite separate, in practice, their distinguishing characteristics may not be so well defined. A shadow director may occasionally experience a need to step from the shadow to resolve corporate issues, thereby identifying himself as active in the conduct of the company's external affairs. When stepping from the shadow, his conduct will be more akin to that of a *de facto* director. Accordingly, a person may occasionally act in a dual capacity as both a shadow and *de facto* director.

The company chairman

The company chairman is an appointed director of the company with responsibilities of a supervisory nature. The chairman presides over meetings of the board of directors. Table A, Arts 42–43 also provide that the chairman of the board, or in his absence some other director, is to preside over general meetings of the company. Although a company chairman will normally have no special powers, it is to be observed that where a vote at a meeting of the board or general meeting is tied, he may be entitled to a second or casting vote (Table A, Art 88 so provides).

The alternate director

Where a director is to be absent from board meetings, he may appoint a person to act in his place, the said person is termed an alternate director. The authority to appoint an alternate director must be provided for in a company's articles. Companies which adopt Table A, Arts 65–69 provide for such an authority. The said articles of Table A provide that an alternate director may attend and vote at all the board meetings or committee meetings at which the duly appointed director would have been eligible to attend and vote. The person appointed to act as an alternate director may be an existing director of the company or any other person. The appointment of an alternate director must be approved by the board of directors. Although an alternate director acts as a director's replacement, an alternate director is not to be regarded as an agent for the absent director, accordingly, the alternate director may act and vote according to his own conscience. As such, an alternate director is responsible for his own acts.

THE COMPANY SECRETARY

In accordance with s 283(1) of the Companies Act 1985, every company must have a company secretary. Table A, Art 99 states that the company secretary is to be appointed by the company's directors on such terms as they may decide and that the power to remove the secretary is to be vested in the directors. A company must keep details at its registered office (similar to those kept for directors) of its company secretary (s 290, CA 1985). It must also send the relevant details of its secretary to the Registrar of Companies who must be notified of any change in the person appointed as company secretary (s 288(2), CA 1985).

A sole director of a company is not permitted to act as the company's secretary (s 283(2), CA 1985). However, in companies where there is more than one director, a director may be authorised by the board to act in the place of a formally appointed secretary; the director may so act providing a task which requires the act of both the secretary and director is not performed by one person acting as both the director and secretary (s 284, CA 1985). A company may itself act as the secretary of another company providing in doing so it does not side-step the requirements of s 283(4). The rather confusingly drafted requirements of s 283(4) may be summarised by the following example.

Company A cannot appoint company B as its secretary where the sole director of both A and B is the same person. In addition, A cannot appoint a person as its secretary where that person is the sole director of B in a situation where B is also the sole director of A (s 283(4), CA 1985).

In relation to a public company, the secretary must be a suitably qualified person, either by having what the directors of the company consider to be the necessary experience to perform the secretary's functions or by having professionally recognised qualifications (s 286, CA 1985).

Although a secretary's responsibilities are primarily of an administrative, as opposed to a managerial nature, the role of a company secretary is nevertheless vital to the proper functioning of the corporate entity. The specific responsibilities of a company's secretary will depend upon the size and nature of the company in which office is held. However, tasks common to all secretaries will include maintaining the company's registers, sending relevant details to the Registrar of Companies, preparing share certificates, making arrangements for board meetings, drafting the minutes of such meetings, keeping the company's documentation in order, and keeping abreast of the relevant companies legislation in so far as it affects the running and administration of the company. As a company secretary's responsibilities are geared to the administration of the company's affairs, the post may carry with it an authority to bind the company in contracts which are specifically concerned with functions within the ambit of a particular secretary's actual or ostensible authority; see e.g. *Panorama Developments Ltd* v *Fidelis Furnishing Fabrics Ltd* [1971] 2 QB 711.

It is to be noted that the role and authority of the company secretary is, in today's corporate world, of marked contrast to the nineteenth and early part of the twentieth century, at which time the company secretary was regarded as a 'somewhat humble character'. Indeed, in *Barnett Hoares* v *South London Tramways* (1877) 18 QB 815, a company's secretary was described as 'a mere servant', a person who was supposed to do what he was told and who had no authority to represent the company and upon whom third parties should not rely.

THE AUDITOR

A company, unless dormant or exempted by the Companies Act 1985 (Audit Exemption) Regulations 1994 (SI 1994/1935), is obliged by the legislation to appoint an auditor to undertake certain statutory prescribed tasks. The 1994 Regulations exempt the statutory audit requirement for small private companies with a turnover below £90 000 and balance sheet total which is under £1.4m (see s 249A, CA 1985) and partially exempt small companies with a turnover between £90 000 and £350 000 and balance sheet total not exceeding £1.4m. It should be noted that a proposal to abolish the partial exemptions in favour of a complete exception for all qualifying small companies was recommended in a Department of Trade and Industry consultation document issued in 1997, entitled 'Small Companies Audit Exception'.

An auditor, once appointed, holds office (s 384, CA 1985), but the nature of an auditor's office cannot be equated with the office held by a director or company secretary. An auditor is not part of a company's general management team, the auditor is an independent contractor. In accordance with the Eighth EC Company Law Directive, the Companies Act 1989 provides stringent requirements for the appointment of auditors. (Note that ss 24–54, CA 1989 – provisions dealing with an auditor's appointment – are unique in that they do not amend or introduce new provisions into the CA 1985.) The 1989 Act requires that for a person to be appointed as an auditor that person must be a suitably qualified member of a supervisory body, eligible for appointment under the rules of that body; the body must be recognised by the Secretary of State. The Secretary of State, in accordance with s 35, CA 1989, is obliged to establish a register of individuals and firms eligible for appointment.

As previously noted, an auditor is an independent contractor and as such, s 27 of the Companies Act 1989 expressly prohibits officers and employees of a company from being appointed as the company's auditor. Somewhat surprisingly, there is, however, no statutory prohibition against a member of a company being appointed as the company's auditor (other than where the member is an officer or employee), even in a situation where the member holds a substantial number of shares and therefore wields great influence over the affairs of the company.

Subject to a private company's ability to elect otherwise (discussed in Chapter 18), a company must appoint its auditor at its annual general meeting (AGM) (s 384(1), CA 1985). Once appointed, an auditor's task is primarily to advise the shareholding body in respect of the financial affairs of the company. Section 390A(1) of the Companies Act 1985 provides that an auditor's remuneration is to be determined by the shareholders in general meeting or in such a manner as the company in general meeting shall determine. In theory, s 390A, by removing the board of directors' influence over the determination of the monetary consideration payable to the company's auditor, dispels any charge that a company's board may influence the auditor in terms of dissuading him from pursing a thorough investigation of the company's financial affairs. However, in practice, it is permissible by the terms of s 390A(1) for the general meeting to delegate, by ordinary resolution, the determination of the auditor's remuneration award to the company's board.

Notwithstanding any agreement between a company and an auditor, the general meeting may remove the auditor by ordinary resolution (s 391(1), CA 1985). Nevertheless, dismissal will not preclude the auditor from seeking recompense for a breach of any service contract. Special notice (those proposing the motion to dismiss must give at least 28 days' notice to the company before the meeting at which the motion to remove is to be heard) is required for a resolution to remove an auditor where the removal would take place prior to the expiration of the auditor's term of office. Before calling the meeting to consider the auditor's removal, the auditor may make written representations to the company for distribution to the company's members (s 391A, CA 1985). Where an auditor resigns office, he is entitled to require the company to convene an extraordinary general meeting for the purpose of receiving and considering an explanation of circumstances which the auditor considers relevant to his decision to resign (s 392, CA 1985).

THE BOARD OF DIRECTORS

A company's board of directors is comprised of the individually appointed *de jure* directors of the company. The board is the ultimate decision-making body and determines the delegation of powers throughout the company; it is considered to be the primary organ of the company. The scope of a board's management powers is determined by the company's articles. Subject to specific powers which are conferred on the general meeting, articles akin to the format of Table A, Art 70 will confer the general management powers of a company to the company's board. Table A, Art 70 provides:

'Subject to the provisions of the Act, the memorandum and the articles and to any directions given by special resolution, the business of the company shall be managed by the directors who may exercise all the powers of the company. No alteration of the memorandum or articles and no such direction shall invalidate any prior act of the directors which would have been valid if that alteration had not been made or that direction had not been given. The powers given by this regulation shall not be limited by any special power given to the directors by the articles and a meeting of directors at which a quorum is present may exercise all powers exercisable by the directors.'

Although the power structure of a company is firmly rooted in the board of directors, at the time of the birth of the registered company, a company's board of directors was viewed as subservient to the general meeting. The gradual decline in the influence of the general meeting (discussed further in Chapter 19) may be attributed to a number of factors. Clearly, in the case of larger companies, apathy and disinterest in shareholder meetings has resulted in a fall in its perception as the company's theoretical and practical power base, and in respect of small companies, directors of the company are often the company's majority shareholders, therefore rendering the independence and significance of the general meeting somewhat illusory.

While the collective board may be regarded as an organ of the company, it should be stressed that save in a situation where the board delegates all its powers to an individual director, an individual director is not to be regarded as a distinct organ of the company. The terms of a director's management functions are delegated to the extent that an individual director cannot *prima facie* bind the company in situations outside the limits imposed upon the director's individual authority. Nevertheless, the board can as an organ of the company pursue and authorise any corporate act. Indeed, as a result of the Companies Act 1989, the board may even bind the company in a situation where the corporate act is outside the company's own contractual capacity, i.e. as determined by the company's constitution (see Chapter 8).

Board meetings

The regulation of board meetings is determined by the company's articles. Where Table A, Arts 88–89 are adopted, the calling and regulation of board meetings will be decided upon by the directors. Table A, Arts 88–89 provide that any director may call a board meeting. A board meeting must, unless the directors decide otherwise, ordinarily have a quorum of two directors. Resolutions of the directors should, unless otherwise provided for by the articles, be passed at properly convened board meetings. In terms of voting on motions put before the board, each member of the board is entitled to one vote. A resolution is passed by a simple majority of directors. However, it is to be noted that in accordance with Table A, Art 94 a director is prohibited from voting on a matter in which he has an interest or duty which is material and which conflicts or may conflict with the interests of the company (discussed further in Chapter 17). Where there is an equality of votes the resolution will be lost, see e.g. *Re Hackney Pavilion Ltd* [1924] 1 Ch 276. To avoid the possibility of a deadlock situation it is quite common for a company's articles to provide for the company's chairman to have a casting vote in the case of a tied vote (Table A, Art 88).

Where all the directors of a company informally agree on the outcome of a motion, it would appear that the informal agreement of the board will be valid without the need to formally pass a resolution at a board meeting, see e.g. *Re Bonelli's Telegraph Co* (1871) LR 12 Eq 246. Table A, Art 93 provides that the informal agreement must be in writing and signed by all the company's directors. (By analogy, see the discussion on informal resolutions of the general meeting, see Chapter 18.)

Table A, Art 88 seeks to regulate the notice requirements for board meetings. Except for directors absent from the UK, notice of board meetings must be given to all the members of the board. It should be noted that in accordance with the decision of Carnwath J in *Hood Sailmakers Ltd v Axford* [1997]1 BCLC 721, a resolution passed by a single director in the absence of a co-director, who was abroad and therefore not entitled to notice of the meeting at which the resolution was passed will, nevertheless, be invalid where it impugns the quorum requirement as provided by Table A, Art 99. This decision would appear logical in so far as it would be unjust for a director to have the capacity to evade the quorum requirements by simply waiting for his fellow director(s) to be absent from the UK. However, as occurred in *Hood Sailmakers Ltd v Axford*, a company may nevertheless be estopped from denying the validity of the resolution in a situation where it acted on the terms of the resolution and where it would have been unconscionable to subsequently deny its validity.

Although Art 88 does not specify what amounts to an appropriate period of notice, should the court be called upon to determine the validity of a notice period it is likely that it will be influenced by whether it was reasonable to expect a director to attend a particular meeting, given the period of notice in question. For example, in *Bentley-Stevens v Jones* [1974] 1 WLR 638 Plowman J was of the opinion that a letter sent to a director on a Sunday, convening a meeting of the board for the morning of the next day (Monday), was inadequate notice. The director in question had been away on a weekend holiday and did not discover the letter until the Monday evening by which time the board meeting had taken place. However, despite the fact that the notice was inadequate, Plowman J concluded that the director's absence would not have altered the outcome of the board meeting and therefore the motion passed at the meeting was not overturned. Accordingly, the learned judge refused to invalidate the meeting. Plowman J quoted with approval from the judgment of Lindley LJ in *Browne v La Trinidad* (1887) 37 Ch D 1. Lindley LJ stated:

> 'I think it is most important that the court should hold fast to the rule upon which it has always acted, not to interfere for the purpose of forcing companies to conduct their business according to the strictest rules, where the irregularity complained of can be set right at a moment.' (at p 17)

Where a board meeting is called and a director's non-attendance would not affect the outcome of any vote taken at the meeting, it would appear logical that the court should not set aside the meeting on the basis of it having been called at short notice. However, in some situations this apparent logic may be misplaced especially where, for example, an individual director, had he attended the meeting, may have been able to influence other members of the board to vote in a manner which would have reversed the outcome of the final vote.

Delegation of the board's powers to individual directors

It is commonplace for a company's articles to empower its board to appoint committees of one or more of the directors to exercise powers normally reserved to the board. For example, Table A, Art 72 states:

'The directors may delegate any of their powers to any committee consisting of one or more directors. They may also delegate to any managing director or any director holding any other executive office such of their powers as they consider desirable to be exercised by him. Any such delegation may be made subject to any conditions the directors may impose, and either collaterally with or to the exclusion of their own powers and may be revoked or altered. Subject to any such conditions, the proceedings of a committee with two or more members shall be governed by the articles regulating the proceedings of directors so far as they are capable of applying.'

The necessity for a board to delegate its powers arises from the practical difficulties which arise from the day-to-day management of a corporate enterprise. A company would cease to function if all senior managerial decisions could only be justified on the basis of a resolution of the company's board.

DIRECTORS' REMUNERATION

A director's remuneration is a payment received by a director for services provided to the company in which he holds office. The method of remuneration may be in cash or other financial type incentives such as share options. It should be noted that a director is not entitled, as of right, to any remuneration other than in a situation where the director holds a service contract under which a level of remuneration is included as a contractual term of the contract. Where a company adopts Table A, Art 83, directors are entitled to receive such remuneration as the company by ordinary resolution determines. As the power to grant remuneration is vested in the general meeting, the board has no authority to delegate this power to individual directors or a committee of directors.

However, where a company has not elected to adopt Table A, Art 83 its articles may provide that remuneration awards are to be determined by the board. For example, in *Guinness* v *Saunders* [1990] 2 AC 663 Guinness' (G) articles provided that G's board could determine directors' remuneration up to £100 000, anything in excess of that amount was to be determined by the general meeting. G's articles further provided that the board was responsible for fixing any special remuneration payable to a director who served on a committee. A committee of three directors with full authority from the Guinness board was appointed to facilitate a takeover bid. Mr Ward (W), a member of the committee, undertook successful negotiations which resulted in the takeover of the target company. W was paid, in accordance with the committee's instructions, remuneration to the sum of 0.2 per cent of the estimated value of the takeover; he was paid a total of £5.2m! The validity of this payment was later challenged by G on the ground that the committee had no authority to authorise the remuneration award. (The payment was also challenged in that it infringed s 317 of the Companies Act 1985 (non-declaration of a director's interest in a contract, discussed in Chapter 17).) In addition to the relevant articles of G as mentioned above, G's articles also contained an article similar in format to Table A, Art 72 (see above) and one which provided that the board was to be defined as, 'The directors of the company for the time being ... or any committee authorised to act on its behalf'.

In determining the case, the House of Lords found in G's favour. Lord Templeman regarded the company's articles to be incompatible with a finding that a committee could be regarded as 'the board'. His lordship found that the intention behind the wording of the article which provided that the board was responsible for fixing the remuneration of a director who served on a special committee would have been meaningless if a committee itself had the capacity to award remuneration to its own members, i.e. a committee of directors could not be regarded as the board. His lordship remarked:

> 'It cannot have been intended that any committee should be able to grant special remuneration to any director ... The board must compare the work of an individual director with ordinary duties of a director. The board must decide whether special remuneration shall be paid in addition to or in substitution for the annual remuneration determined by the board ... These decisions could only be made by the board surveying the work and remuneration of each and every director.' (at p 687)

Nevertheless, despite the common-sense wisdom of Lord Templeman's words, it is submitted that a literal construction of G's articles inferred that the committee of three directors were indeed capable of awarding one of their number special remuneration. The articles clearly permitted a duly appointed committee to undertake the functions of the board, functions which included the power to award remuneration. Indeed, although the interpretation afforded to the relevant articles by Lord Templeman may appear to be one which was born of a practical logic, the interpretation may nevertheless be criticised on the premise that it was based upon an assumption of the meaning of the company's articles rather than the interpretation to be attributed to the literal wording of the articles.

Service contracts

The majority of company directors appointed to executive posts hold service contracts. The remuneration for the services of such directors may often be negotiable on an annual basis. The terms of a director's service contract will be determined in accordance with the company's articles. Where a company adopts articles in the form of Table A, Art 84, the remuneration for the services of executive directors will be determined by the board of directors. In accordance with Table A, Art 94, a director is prohibited from voting on the terms of his own service contract. Table A, Art 95 further provides that a director cannot be counted as part of the quorum for the meeting at which his service contract is to be considered. Other than where s 319 of the Companies Act 1985 is applicable (discussed below), the terms of a director's service contract do not require the approval of the general meeting, although s 318 of the Companies Act 1985 states that a director's service contract must be made available for inspection by the general meeting. Although the terms of a director's service contract are normally decided upon at a formal board meeting, in *Runciman* v *Walter Runciman plc* [1992] BCLC 1084 it was held that providing the members of a company's board unanimously agree to the terms of a service contract then an informal agreement will suffice to effect a valid service contract without the need to call a board meeting. (The *Runciman* case is discussed further in Chapter 17 in relation to s 317, CA 1985.)

In accordance with s 318 of the Companies Act 1985, the terms of a director's service contract must be made available for inspection by the company's membership. However, where a director's service contract or director's contract for services or consultancy is for a period in excess of five years and contains a term under which the company cannot terminate the director's employment by notice, or can only do so in specified circumstances, the contract must be approved by general meeting (s 319, CA 1985). However, it is to be noted that following the decision of the Court of Appeal in *Atlas Wright (Europe) Ltd* v *Wright* [1999] BCC 163, the formal approval of the general meeting may be waived in a situation where there was an implied approval of the service contract by the entire body of shareholders.

Section 319(2) further provides that where there is more than six months of a director's service period to run and the company enters into a new service agreement with the director, then the period of the former service contract which is yet to expire should be added to the new period of the service contract for the purpose of calculating whether the new service contract is one which should be approved by the general meeting. For example, if a director has a service contract for a period of four years and after three years the company decides to renew the service agreement for a further period of five years, the new service contract would require the approval of the general meeting, i.e. the one year left on the original service contract would be added to the new service contract to give a total of six years. Sections 318 and 319 also apply to shadow directors, although a contract of services supplied by a parent company to its subsidiary does not have to be approved in accordance with s 319 if the only reason for treating the parent company as the subsidiary's shadow director is based on the fact that the subsidiary's directors are accustomed to act in accordance with the holding company's directions.

THE REMOVAL OF DIRECTORS

It is commonplace for a company's articles to contain conditions which relate to circumstances whereby directors may be removed from office. For example, Table A, Art 81 provides that a director will cease to hold office if he resigns, is prohibited by law from holding office, becomes bankrupt, is committed to a mental hospital or is absent from board meetings without due excuse for a period of six months. While outside the ambit of Table A, it is also commonplace to find that the articles of public companies often provide that a director may be removed by a simple resolution of the board.

In accordance with s 303(1) of the Companies Act 1985, and notwithstanding any contrary provision in a company's articles or an agreement between a company and any director, a director may be removed from office by the passing of an ordinary resolution (but note the possibility of a weighted voting clause (see below) or a clause prohibiting dismissal within a membership agreement, discussed in Chapter 7). Section 303(5) of the Companies Act 1985 provides that the power of the general meeting to dismiss a director will not, however, deprive the director of a claim to compensation or damages for a breach of service contract; see e.g. *Southern Foundries Ltd* v *Shirlaw* [1940] AC 701 (discussed in Chapter 7). Special notice (28 days) must be given to the company of the intention to introduce a motion calling for the dismissal of a director (s 303(2), CA 1985). A director must be given a copy of the form of motion together with the opportunity to present a defence, a copy of which may, if required, be distributed to members (s 304, CA 1985). One exception to a director's right to present a defence is in a situation where the court finds that the rights conferred by s 304 are being abused to secure needless publicity for a defamatory matter.

Although a company's articles are not permitted to preclude the implementation of s 303, it is nevertheless possible to include within the articles a device commonly known as a 'weighted voting clause'. This device seeks to confer weighted voting rights on a director in a situation where a motion for his removal is proposed. The weighted voting clause affects voting rights and does not theoretically operate to fetter s 303. Nevertheless, where a director is able to take the benefit of a weighted voting clause, the practical effect of the increased voting rights clearly frustrates the intention behind s 303. The concept of the weighted voting clause was approved by the House of Lords in *Bushell* v *Faith* [1970] 1 All ER 53 (the facts of this case are discussed in Chapter 7). In giving its approval to the weighted voting clause, the House of Lords emphasised that such a clause was solely concerned with the allocation of a company's voting rights and because Parliament had never sought to fetter the right of a company to issue a share with special rights or restrictions, it was certainly, in the opinion of their lordships, not a matter in which the judiciary should interfere.

Although a weighted voting clause is concerned with voting rights as opposed to the creation of a direct assault on the ability of a company to exercise its statutory power pursuant to s 303, the practical effect of a weighted voting clause is one which fetters the power of removal embodied in s 303. If a director with the benefit of a weighted voting clause does not wish to be dismissed there seems little a company's membership can do to execute his removal, other than to offer to purchase the director's shares; a purchase which would undoubtedly result in an inflated price tag being attached to the shares. Lord Morris of Borth-y-Gest, in a dissenting judgment in the *Bushell* case, opined that the acceptance of a weighted voting clause made a mockery of the law in that it nullified the exercise of the statutory power to remove a director. It is difficult to disagree with such logic.

It is interesting to note that *Bushell v Faith* would have been reversed by legislation had the Companies Bill of 1973 been passed and not lost as a result of the political instability of that time. In today's corporate world weighted voting clauses are commonly used by private companies although they are prohibited in the case of listed companies by Stock Exchange rules. The continued acceptance and validity of weighted voting clauses is indicative of the view that statutory powers, whilst workable in theory, can, in specified circumstances, be manipulated to an extent whereby they are of little practical worth.

CORPORATE GOVERNANCE AND PROPOSALS FOR THE REFORM OF MANAGEMENT STRUCTURES

The Cadbury Committee Report

In 1991, the Cadbury Committee was set up by the Financial Reporting Council, the London Stock Exchange and the accountancy professions to report on financial aspects of corporate governance. The report, issued in December 1992, recommended a code of practice which was to be complied with by the boards of listed companies as a condition of continued listing. The code was monitored by the Stock Exchange and a monitoring sub-committee of the Cadbury Committee (set up in May 1991). The code, which came into force for accounting periods ending after June 1993, recognised the importance of the following practices:

- the appointment of independent non-executive directors to the boards of listed companies;
- appointments to the post of executive director to be vetted by a nomination committee, the appointees of which were to be principally taken from the ranks of a company's non-executive directors;
- the roles of chief executive and chairman should, where possible, not be held by the same person so as to promote the independent nature of the board;

- service contracts in excess of three years should not be made to executive directors unless approved by the general meeting;
- executive directors' salaries should be determined by means of a remuneration committee to be made up wholly or principally from non-executive directors;
- the creation of an audit committee to oversee the company's financial matters, the constitution of which should have a majority of non-executive directors.

The code required all listed companies to include a statement in its annual report acknowledging compliance with the code's terms or justifying instances of non-compliance. Although the code had no statutory force and compliance with its terms could not be regarded as an absolute prerequisite for listing, it was generally adhered to, especially in the case of large plc's and particularly its requirement for the further appointment of non-executive directors. Indeed, by 1999, non-executive directors comprised half the board of listed companies.

The Greenbury Committee Report

The Greenbury Report, which was concerned with an investigation into directors' remuneration, was published in July 1995. The report followed the highly publicised criticism of the levels of remuneration awarded to directors of public limited companies and more especially the remuneration awarded to directors of the previously nationalised utility industries. The criticism appeared justified, given that the UK's economic policy in the 1990s had, in its desire to eliminate inflation, been geared to the promotion of a policy of minimal salary increases within both the public and private sectors. Indeed, the massive salary awards and other incentives such as the issue of discounted share options, pensionable annual bonuses and compensation payments to departing directors, proved something of a political embarrassment.

The Greenbury Report contained a new code of best practice for directors of plc's and was specifically targeted at directors of listed companies. The report recommended that all listed companies should comply with its terms and that the nature and extent of that compliance should be reported annually to shareholders. The report's findings echoed many of the proposals advanced in the Cadbury Report. In addition to the proposals contained in the Cadbury Report, the Greenbury Report recommended:

- the compilation (by a remuneration committee) of an annual report which should form part of the annual accounts and which should be put before the company's shareholders. The annual report would include a statement that full consideration had been given to the best practice provisions of the Greenbury Report (see below). Where there was non-compliance with such provisions, the report had to explain the reasons why that had been the case.

Examples of the best practice provisions

- The interests of both shareholders and directors should be considered by the remuneration committee in their determination of the levels of directors' remuneration;
- share options should never be issued to directors at a discount and annual bonuses should not be pensionable;
- the notice periods for service contracts of executive directors should be no more than one year;
- shareholders should approve long-term incentive schemes.

As from October 1995, the recommendations of the Greenbury Report, other than those concerned with rules relating to long-term incentive schemes, options and pension entitlements, were incorporated into the Stock Exchange's listing rules, taking effect from 31 December 1995. As such, compliance with many of the recommendations of the report are to be regarded as a prerequisite for a company's listing on the Stock Exchange.

The Hampel Committee Report

The Hampel Committee Report on Corporate Governance was published on 28 January 1998. The Hampel Report sought to progress and where necessary add to the recommendations of the reports of the Cadbury Committee and Greenbury Committee. The remit of the Hampel Committee was to review the role of both executive and non-executive directors, consider matters relating to directors' remuneration, and to consider the role of both shareholders and auditors in corporate governance issues. As with the reports of the Cadbury and Greenbury Committees, the Hampel Report was primarily, though not exclusively, concerned with public companies. The conclusions of the Hampel Report, in respect of management structures, were as follows:

- both executive and non-executive directors should be subject to the same corporate duties. However, directors should be provided with more information and instruction in relation to such duties;
- although the report fell short of recommending that executive directors should have some form of recognised qualification, the report considered that persons who held an executive directorship should have the necessary experience to be capable of understanding the nature and extent of the interests of the company in which they held office;
- the majority of non-executive directors in companies of all sizes should be independent and make up at least one-third of the board;
- an individual should not ordinarily occupy the role of chairman and chief executive;
- all companies should have nomination committees for the purpose of recommending new board appointments. All directors should be obliged to seek re-election at least every three years;

- executive director's remuneration should not be excessive and should be based upon recommendations from remuneration committees which should be comprised of non-executive directors. Remuneration should be related to performance and a general statement on remuneration policy should be included in the annual report;
- directors' contracts should not exceed one year.

The Hampel Report has further sought to generate a set of principles and a general code of good practice for public companies, embracing Cadbury, Greenbury and its own work, with the ultimate purpose of incorporation into the Listing Rules. Indeed on 25 June 1998, the London Stock Exchange published a Code of Best Practice, 'The Combined Code' which is, in effect, based upon the Hampel Report. This code became mandatory for all listed companies for financial years ending on or after 31 December 1998. However, it must be noted that the Combined Code, as with the Cadbury and Greenbury Reports, does not have the force of law, i.e. it remains a code of best practice.

The EC Fifth Draft Directive

The EC Fifth Draft Directive sets out what, if implemented, would be a radical reformation of the board structure for UK companies. Taking its model from the German system, the draft Directive makes provision for employee participation in management functions within certain public companies, i.e. those which alone or with subsidiaries employ 1000 or more persons. The participation envisaged by the draft Directive would be by way of directors appointed from the workforce, a works council or a system established by collective agreement. The Fifth Draft Directive is discussed in detail in Chapter 5.

Suggested further reading
Corporate governance
Parkinson (1993) *Corporate Power and Responsibility*. Oxford: Clarendon
Finch [1992] JBL 581
Dine (1994) 15 Co Law 73
Griffiths [1995] LMCLQ 372
Dignam (1998) 19 Co Law 140 (The Hampel Report)

17

THE DUTIES OF THE MANAGEMENT
OF A COMPANY

INTRODUCTION

The board of directors, together with persons expressly or impliedly autho-
rised to act on the board's behalf, represent the brain: the nerve centre of the
corporate body. Against this backcloth of corporate power, fiduciary, com-
mon law and statutory duties have evolved in order to eradicate abuses of
power. It is the purpose of this chapter to identify and analyse the scope of
such duties. The penalties which arise as a consequence of a director's breach
of duty will also be examined, as will proposals to reform the law relating to
the duties and responsibilities of directors. For issues relating to the reform
of this topic, see the Appendix at p. 373.

THE NATURE OF THE DUTY

A company director owes duties to the company in which he holds office and
accordingly will not ordinarily owe duties to individual shareholders or creditors of the company, see e.g. *Percival* v *Wright* [1902] 2 Ch 421 (discussed
further in Chapter 13). However, it would be very misleading to consider
that 'the company' should be interpreted solely in terms of a commercial
entity. A corporate entity, while possessing a legal identity of its own, is in
reality a lifeless figurehead. Typically, corporate activity will be determined
by the concerns and constraints of human self-interest. Directors of companies will aim to maximise the profit potential of a company, a director's
inability to do so may often result in his dismissal. The general body of
shareholders will, for the most part, seek a return on their investment.
Likewise, creditors will inject capital into a company in the belief that a
profit can be made from doing so. Company employees will seek to protect
and better their salaries and conditions of employment.

Accordingly, a company may be viewed as a collection of individuals whose
participation in the corporate entity is most typically for the promotion of their
own individual self-interests. The view that a company can have a separate
and distinct interest in a given project, an interest which is independent of
the interests of its human constituents and players, is in reality somewhat of
a myth. As such, management duties may, in appropriate cases, be owed
specifically to the general body of shareholders, company creditors and company employees. Indeed, in interpreting the term 'the company', the company
should be viewed as comprising the interests of the company as a whole.

The interests of the shareholding body

The term 'the interests of the company as a whole' is quite frequently interpreted by the courts as equating to 'the interests of the general body of shareholders'. For example, in *Gething* v *Kilner* [1972] 1 WLR 337, it was held that in the course of competing takeover bids, the directors of a company would be in breach of a fiduciary duty where they failed to inform the shareholding body of the nature of the relevant bids; the directors in giving such information were obliged to provide information which was not of a misleading nature. Indeed, in the case of *Heron International* v *Lord Grade* [1983] BCLC 244 the Court of Appeal went one step further by suggesting that when considering competing bids, the directors of a company were under a duty to ensure that they did not exercise their powers to prevent shareholders obtaining the best possible price available for their shares.

Although directors do not owe fiduciary duties to individual shareholders, it is conceivable that where a company is dominated by a single shareholder, say, with 90 per cent voting control, the collective body of shareholders may well be interpreted as the majority shareholder's interest. By way of an analogy, in the New Zealand case of *Coleman* v *Myers* [1977] 2 NZLR 225 it was held that in a domestic type company, fiduciary duties could be owed by the directors of a company to those shareholders (or shareholder) who had been responsible for their appointment.

A creditor's interest

Although a director may owe duties to the general body of shareholders, the scope of a director's duty does not ordinarily extend to a consideration of the interests of a company's creditors; see e.g. *Multinational Gas & Petrochemical Co* v *Multinational Gas & Petrochemical Services Ltd* [1983] Ch 258. This view can be supported on the basis that a company's objective will normally be to maximise profits in order to pay dividends to its shareholders. Therefore, the interests of the shareholding body outweigh considerations relating to the payment of company creditors.

Nevertheless, in a situation where a company continues trading after having reached a state of insolvency (a state of insolvency is defined by s 123 of the IA 1986 as applicable to a situation where a company's liabilities exceed its assets), it is apparent that the interests of creditors will begin to outweigh those of the general body of shareholders, apparent in the sense that once a company becomes insolvent there is a substantial risk that it may be unable to discharge its debts. Accordingly, following a company's slide into an insolvent state it is logical to surmise that the interests of creditors will become paramount, to the extent that the company's directors will owe a duty to creditors in respect of the maintenance of corporate assets. This so-called 'insolvency qualification' in respect of the determination of directors' duties owes a great deal of its development to the Australian High Court's decision in *Walker* v *Wimbourne* [1976] 137 CLR 1. The English courts' acceptance of the insolvency qualification is much more of a recent phenomena. One of the earliest cases to discuss the possibility of the company's interest being construed in terms of creditor interests was the Court of Appeal's decision in *Re Horsley & Weight Ltd* [1982] Ch 442. Subsequent case law has confirmed that creditor interests may displace those of the general body of shareholders in circumstances where a company has declined into a state of insolvency. For example, in *Brady v Brady* [1988] BCLC 20 Nourse LJ expressed the following opinion:

'Where the company is insolvent, or doubly solvent the interests of the company are in reality the interests of the existing creditors alone.' (at p 40)

(While the House of Lords overturned the Court of Appeal's decision in *Brady* [1989] AC 755, the comments of Nourse LJ were not criticised or disapproved of.)

The Court of Appeal's decision in *West Mercia Safetywear Ltd v Dodd* [1988] BCLC 250 reaffirmed Nourse LJ's reasoning in the *Brady* case. In this case a holding company was owed some £30 000 by its subsidiary company. Both the holding company and its subsidiary were in an insolvent state. D, a director of both the holding company and its subsidiary, had personally guaranteed the repayment of debts owed to the parent company's bank. D was responsible for authorising the payment of £4000 from the account of the subsidiary in order to pay part of the subsidiary's debt to the holding company. Upon the subsidiary company's liquidation, the liquidator sought to recover the £4000 from D on the ground that the payment constituted a breach of duty to the subsidiary company. The Court of Appeal, in reversing the first instance judgment of Ward J, held that because the subsidiary company was insolvent, the interests of the company's creditors should have been paramount. Accordingly, D acted in breach of his fiduciary duties in not considering the interests of the creditors of the subsidiary company. D was made personally liable to account for the £4000.

In respect of the judicial acceptance of the insolvency qualification, the interests of the company as a whole will comprise the interests of creditors. The director's duty to consider the interests of creditors should not however be viewed as an independent duty, the creditor's interests are but a constituent part of a specific group of interests which are captured under the corporate umbrella, albeit that they will take centre stage when a company trades in an insolvent state.

The interests of company employees

As a result of s 309(1) of the Companies Act 1985, the matters to which the directors of a company should have regard include the interests of their employees. This duty is not directly enforceable by employees, in the sense that the enforcement of this duty would be dependent upon a resolution supported by a majority of the company's shareholders, or most probably, if the company becomes insolvent, the support of company creditors. Accordingly, the duty can properly be considered to be of a negative character. Whilst the enforceability of this duty is dependent upon the support of the other constituent parts of the 'company as a whole', it is nevertheless an improvement upon the position prior to the implementation of s 309(1). Prior to s 309(1), the majority shareholders of a company had an ability to prevent the interests of employees being taken into account in that a consideration of employee interests would ordinarily have been *ultra vires*, i.e. a matter outside the objects of a company; see e.g. *Parke* v *Daily News Ltd* [1962] Ch 927.

FIDUCIARY DUTIES

Directors and other company officers owe fiduciary duties to the company in which they hold office. In practical terms, the exact scope of an individual director's duties will depend upon the responsibility he is afforded in the corporate structure and the manner in which the company's business is organised. The most common analogy of the fiduciary duties owed by a director to a company is that of a trust or agency relationship. In relation to a trust relationship, in *Re Lands Allotment Co* [1884] 1 Ch 616 Lindley LJ opined:

> 'Although directors are not properly speaking trustees, yet they have always been considered and treated as trustees of money which comes to their hands or which is actually under their control; and ever since joint stock companies were invented, directors have been held liable to make good moneys which they have misapplied upon the same footings as if they were trustees'. (at p 631)

The basis for a comparison between directors duties and the duties arising from a trustee–beneficiary relationship can be traced back to the early part of the nineteenth century. Prior to the passing of the Joint Stock Companies Act of 1844, unincorporated companies vested the property of the company in trustee directors (see Chapter 1). However, in today's corporate world the analogy between trustees and directors seems less likely. Although directors may still be regarded as occupying the status of a trustee in situations where they are responsible for the misapplication of corporate funds, a more apt analogy of the relationship between a director and company is that of agency. As agents, the directors stand in a fiduciary relationship to the principal: the company.

THE SPECIFIC FIDUCIARY DUTIES

The duty to act *bona fide* in the interests of the company

A director must conduct the business affairs of a company for the benefit of the company as a whole and not for some other collateral purpose, see e.g. *Re Smith & Fawcett Ltd* [1942] Ch 304. The test to determine whether a director acted in breach of the *bona fide* duty is a subjective one, i.e. the court must consider whether the director believed that he was acting for the benefit of the company as a whole. The case of *Re W & M Roith Ltd* [1967] 1 WLR 432, provides an excellent example of a factual situation which gave rise to a breach of the *bona fide* duty. Here, a director, who was in very poor health, entered into a new service agreement with the company, an agreement which included amongst its terms a provision for a generous pension to be paid to his widow in the event of his death. The director, who failed to disclose his poor health, died shortly after entering into the agreement. His widow claimed the benefit of the pension. As the deceased director's service agreement had been entered into with the object of enabling his wife to make a claim upon the company's assets (in the form of the pension payments) in excess of an amount that might otherwise have been considered appropriate by the company had it been aware of the seriousness of the undisclosed illness, the court held that the director had acted contrary to the interests of the company as a whole. The director's sole intention was to benefit his wife, irrespective of the interests of the company.

The duty to act for a proper purpose

Although a director may honestly believe that in entering into a transaction he is acting in the best interests of the company as a whole, he will nevertheless be held to be in breach of his fiduciary duty if the purpose of the transaction was outside or an abuse of the director's allocated powers, even though the transaction may not have been outside the contractual capacity of the company; see e.g. *Hogg v Cramphorn* [1967] Ch 254. The duty to act for a proper purpose applies to the exercise of any of a director's powers. In *Bishopsgate Investment Management Ltd* [1993] BCC 140, Hoffmann LJ described the duty thus:

> 'If a director chooses to participate in the management of a company and exercises powers on its behalf, he owes a duty to act bona fide in the interests of the company. He must exercise the power solely for the purpose for which it was conferred. To exercise the power for another purpose is a breach of his fiduciary duty.' (at p 140)

A leading case on the application and interpretation of the proper purpose duty is the Privy Council's decision in *Howard Smith Ltd v Ampol Petroleum Ltd* [1974] AC 821. The facts of this case were as follows. Ampol (A) controlled 54 per cent of the issued share capital in a company (X) and unsuccessfully submitted a bid for X's remaining shares. Howard Smith Ltd (H) then submitted a rival bid for the remaining shares but that bid was also rejected (Ampol, X's majority shareholder rejected the bid). X's board of directors favoured H's offer and to overcome the problem of A's majority control in X, the board allotted unissued shares to H. The purpose of the allotment was to provide needy capital as well as relegating A to the position of a minority shareholder, i.e. A's shareholding in X would have fallen below the 50 per cent mark.

A objected to the allotment of the new share issue on the ground that it had not been for a proper purpose. X's directors argued that the allotment had been in the best interests of the company as a whole, i.e. that they had not been motivated by self interest but had genuinely believed that the company's best interests would be served if H was in a position to secure majority control in X. The Privy Council, in giving judgment in favour of A, held that X's power to allot shares had not been used for a proper purpose. Lord Wilberforce opined that in order to decide whether the allotment was for a proper purpose the court should first consider the *bona fide* intentions of the directors. However, even if the directors honestly believed that they acted for the benefit of the company, the *bona fide* test could not be viewed in isolation. The court then had to consider, in an objective sense, whether the underlying reason for the allotment had been made for a proper purpose.

In applying the objective test, the Privy Council concluded that although X would have benefited from the capital raised from the sale of shares to H, the dominant purpose behind the share allotment had nevertheless been an improper one, namely the allotment had, as its primary purpose, the aim of manipulation of voting control in favour of H. Lord Wilberforce stated:

> 'Just as it is established that directors, within their management powers, may take decisions against the wishes of the majority shareholders, and indeed that the majority of shareholders cannot control them in the exercise of these powers while they remain in office, ... so it must be unconstitutional for directors to use their fiduciary powers over the shares in the company purely for the purpose of destroying an existing majority, or creating a new majority which did not previously exist. To do so is to interfere with that element of the company's constitution which is separate from and set against their powers.' (at p 837)

The reasoning of the Privy Council in that a court must seek out the dominant purpose behind a power use to determine if the proper purpose duty has been infringed, is one which has been subsequently applied by the courts. For example, in *Mutual Life Insurance Co v The Rank Organisation Ltd* [1985] BCLC 11 a company decided to issue further shares, a proportion of which were to be made available to its existing shareholders. However, the company resolved not to make the offer of the issue available to shareholders situated in the USA and Canada. Although the company's decision may *prima facie* have suggested some form of discrimination, Goulding J held that the dominant purpose behind this share allocation did not seek to discriminate against the shareholders situated in the USA and Canada. The learned judge held that the company's decision was based upon the practical commercial reality of avoiding the considerable expense involved in complying with the share issue procedures in the USA and Canada. The decision not to offer shares to members in those countries was a legitimate exercise of the board of directors' discretion to consider the best interests of the company as a whole.

Although the Privy Council's reasoning in the *Ampol* case is now firmly established as dictating the policy of deciding between any potential conflict between the *bona fide* duty and the proper purpose duty, the outcome of a limited number of subsequent cases may appear to contradict the reasoning in *Ampol*. For example, in *Re a Company (No 005136 of 1986)* [1987] BCLC 82 Hoffmann J expressed the view that a company as a separate legal entity was unconcerned with the identity of its shareholders. Such an opinion may appear to suggest that directors of a company have no duty to consider whether the effect of an allotment of shares would result in a change in the identity of a company's majority shareholder. By contrast, in the Scottish case of *Dawson International plc v Coats Patrons plc* (1988) SLT 854 Lord Cullen took the opposite view, namely that in cases involving a takeover bid the directors of a company could be justified in considering the identity of the majority shareholder in deciding whether or not it was in the best interests of a company to permit the takeover to go ahead: see also the Commonwealth decisions (pre-*Ampol*) of *Harlowe's Nominees Ltd* v *Woodside Oil Co* [1968] 121 CLR and *Teck Corporation Ltd* v *Millar* [1973] 2 WWR 385. Whilst the respective judgments of Hoffmann J and Lord Cullen are in conflict with each other, both would appear to be in conflict with the Privy Council's decision in the *Ampol* case.

However, the approach of construing the proper purpose rule to be the dominant element in the determination of whether a corporate act was in the best interests of a company is generally followed by the English courts. A more recent decision of the Court of Appeal which is emphatic as to the dominance of the proper purpose rule over deliberations concerning the benefit of the company concept, is the case of *Lee Panavision Ltd* v *Lee Lighting Ltd* [1992] BCLC 22. In this case, Panavision Ltd (P) was given an option to purchase the share capital of Lee Lighting Ltd (L). During the period of time in which the option had to run, P had been given a proxy over the voting shares of L and had been given the right to appoint the directors of L. P decided not to exercise the option to purchase the share capital but a majority of the directors of L (appointees of P), acting under the instructions of P, and aware of the fact they would be removed from office if the option period came to an end, voted in favour of extending the management agreement with P. Such a vote was against the wishes of L's majority shareholder. A dominant reason why P wished to carry on managing L was to ensure L paid sums due under a loan agreement made in favour of one of P's associated companies.

While the Court of Appeal considered that it was for the directors of L to decide if it was in the best interests of L to continue the management agreement with P, the court nevertheless considered that in determining that issue, the directors should have taken into account the views of the general body of shareholders as opposed to the artificial interests of the company as a commercial entity. The Court of Appeal held that it was unconstitutional for the directors, knowing that the general body of shareholders were proposing to end the management agreement with L, to commit the management powers of L to P, thus removing the powers of L's future board of directors. The purpose behind the vote, to retain P's domination over the management functions of L, was clearly one which had been taken for an improper purpose, namely to secure L's payment of a debt to P's associated company.

THE CONFLICT OF INTEREST RULE

The conflict of interest rule is, as a rule of equity, closely related to the fiduciary duties owed by a director of a company. However, it should be noted that a breach of the conflict of interest rule will not always result in a breach of a fiduciary duty.

The conflict of interest rule may be stated as a rule which prohibits a company director from using a corporate opportunity for his own personal use. This principle of equity, equally applicable to a trustee–beneficiary relationship, is often referred to as the fair dealing rule. Except in circumstances where a company's articles provide for a relaxation of this equitable principle (discussed below), a transaction which involves a conflict of interest will, unlike a breach of a fiduciary duty, be set aside without enquiry as to whether any harm was inflicted on the company. In *Aberdeen Railway Co v Blaikie Bros* (1854) 1 Macq 461, Lord Cranworth proposed that this rule involved –

> '... a rule of universal application that no one, having ... duties to discharge, shall be allowed to enter into engagements in which he has, or can have, a personal interest conflicting, or which may possibly conflict, with the interests of those whom he is bound to protect.' (at p 471)

In *Boardman & Anor v Phipps* [1967] AC 46 Lord Upjohn suggested that Lord Cranworth's remarks relating to the 'possibility of conflict' should be construed to mean:

> '... the reasonable man looking at the relevant facts and circumstances of the particular case would think that there was a real sensible possibility of conflict.' (at p 124)

Accordingly, while the effect of the conflict of interest rule is strict, the nature of the conflict giving rise to its application must involve more than a trivial interest, i.e. there must be a real sensible possibility of conflict. Prior to *Boardman & Anor v Phipps*, in *Boulting v ACTAT* [1963] 2 QB 606 Lord Upjohn had remarked that the conflict of interest rule should be applied in the following manner:

> '... a broad rule like this must be applied with common sense and with an appreciation of the sort of circumstances in which over the last 200 years and more it has been applied and thrived. It must be applied realistically to a state of affairs which discloses a real conflict of duty and interest and not some theoretical or rhetorical contract.' (at p 637)

Application of the conflict of interest rule

Corporate opportunity/secret profits

A director of a company will be in breach of the conflict of interest rule where, by virtue of his fiduciary position, he uses to his own advantage, information which came into his hands whilst holding office (information in which the company had an interest); see the judgment of Lord Blanesburgh in *Bell* v *Lever Bros Ltd* [1932] AC 161, especially at p 194. The prohibition against a director benefiting from a corporate opportunity is operative for the duration of a director's term of office but may also be enforced against an ex-director in circumstances where the ex-director exploited information which came to his attention during the period in which he held office. For example, in *Industrial Development Consultants Ltd* v *Cooley* [1972] 1 WLR 443 a director was approached by a third party who wished to employ him in a personal capacity without involving the director's company. As a result of this offer, the director retired from the company on the grounds of ill-health. Shortly after his retirement the ex-director took up the offer from the third party. The court found that the director had improperly taken advantage of the third party's employment offer, in that the opportunity was one which came to his notice in his capacity as a director of the company. As such, the director was made liable to account for the profit made as a consequence of entering into the contract. By contrast to the *Cooley* case, it is interesting to note the more recent decision of Blackburne J in *Framlington Group plc* v *Anderson* [1995] BCC 611. Here the conflict of interest rule was deemed to be inapplicable in a situation which *prima facie* appeared similar to the one found in *Cooley*. The facts of the *Framlington* case were as follows. Two directors (A and B) of a holding company (F) were appointed to the board of F's wholly owned subsidiary (S). S was subsequently sold by F to R. The directors of S i.e. A, B and a third director (C) were subsequently employed by R to continue the management of S's business. During the negotiations for the sale of S to P it had been understood by all parties that A, B and C would subsequently be employed by P to manage S's business. However, unknown to F, in consideration of A, B and C's continued employment with S, R had paid the three directors a considerable sum (in the form of shares in R), a sum which was related to the value of the business transferred from F to R. It was alleged by F that the three directors had obtained a secret profit as a result of the sale of S.

The *Cooley* case was distinguished on the basis that in *Framlington* the directors who were accused of acting in breach of the conflict of interest rule had never sought to divert to themselves a business opportunity which had belonged to the company. The said business opportunity was made available to the company (i.e. the sale of S) and indeed was exploited by the company. Although the directors impliedly benefited from the opportunity, they did so without prejudice to the company's own interests.

It should also be noted that an ex-director of a company will not have misused a corporate opportunity where he merely obtains an advantage by reason of a past association with a company. In order to abuse a corporate opportunity the director must exploit information which came into his possession whilst holding office; see e.g. *Cranleigh Precision Engineering Ltd* v *Bryant* [1964] 3 All ER 289 and *Island Export Finance Ltd* v *Umunna* [1986] BCLC 460.

The conflict of interest rule is strict in the sense that it fails to distinguish between on the one hand, directors who have purposely set out to exploit a corporate opportunity (an intentional abuse of the rule), and on the other hand, directors who have personally profited from a corporate opportunity in a situation where the company was, at the time of the opportunity, unable or unwilling to act upon the opportunity (an unintentional abuse of the rule). An example of an intentional exploitation of a corporate opportunity is to be found in *Cook* v *Deeks* [1916] 1 AC 554. In this case directors, aware that a lucrative contract was to be made available to the company in which they held office, resigned their directorships and formed another company. The newly formed company was awarded the lucrative contract. In such circumstances it was patently obvious that the directors had resigned from office with the intention of exploiting the corporate information which had been obtained from their former company.

A case example of an unintentional exploitation of a corporate opportunity is to be found in *Regal (Hastings) Ltd* v *Gulliver* [1942] 1 All ER 378, [1967] 2 AC 134. The case involved a company (R) which was the owner of a cinema. The directors of R wished to obtain two more cinemas with a view to eventually selling the company as a going concern. R formed a subsidiary company (A) for the purpose of obtaining a leasing agreement for the two other cinemas in question. In order to secure the leasing agreement the subsidiary company was required to raise £5000. However, R was unable to meet this requirement as a result of which R's directors injected their own personal funds (£3000) to finance the balance between R's contribution and the total amount required. The directors subsequently sold their shares in both A and R, making a substantial profit in the process. The new controllers of R sought to recover the profit which the directors had made from the sale of the shares in A in so far as it was alleged that the directors had made the profit as a result of their exploitation of a corporate opportunity.

The House of Lords unanimously held that the directors were liable to account for the profits made from the sale of the shares. Lord Russell commenting on the conflict of interest rule declared that:

> 'The rule of equity which insists on those, who by use of a fiduciary position make a profit, being liable to account for that profit, in no way depends on fraud or absence of bona fides; or upon such questions or considerations as whether the profit would or should otherwise have gone to the plaintiff, or whether the profiteer was under a duty to obtain the source of the profit for the plaintiff, or whether he took a risk or acted as he did for the benefit of the plaintiff, or whether the plaintiff has in fact been damaged or benefited by his action. The liability arises from the mere fact of a profit having, in the stated circumstances, been made. The profiteer, however honest and well intentioned, cannot escape the risk of being called to account.' (at pp 144–5)

The strict application of the conflict of interest rule is most probably derived from the judiciary's fear that a relaxation in its severity would result in a director being more inclined to disregard the company's interests in favour of the consideration of personal interests. Nevertheless, it is to be noted that a more liberal and just interpretation of the rule would seem to be indicated by its interpretation in some Commonwealth jurisdictions. For example, in Canada the construction of the rule is such as to only impose liability in circumstances which suggest that the director in question acted in bad faith. For example, in *Peso Silver Mines Ltd* v *Cropper* (1966) 58 DLR (2d) 1 a company's (P) board of directors failed to act upon the advice of the company's geologist in respect of the purchase of certain prospecting claims. The geologist left the employment of the company and formed his own company (X) which purchased the said prospecting claims. One of P's directors became a shareholder in X and made substantial profits following the success of the prospecting claims. P brought an action against the said director claiming that he should account to P for the profits made as a result of information relating to the claims which he had initially received as a director of P. P's action failed. The court held that the relevant information concerning the potential success of the claims had never been withheld from P, the director had acted in good faith and had not attempted to exploit his position as a director of P.

Competing directorships

Although there is no specific statutory provision or common law principle which prohibits a person from holding a directorship in two or more competing companies (see e.g. *London & Mashonaland Exploration Co Ltd* v *New Mashonaland Exploration Co Ltd* [1891] WN 165), the test to determine the existence of a conflict of interest could in theory be indicative of a positive finding of conflict in such cases. Another potential situation where a conflict of interest may arise is where a director is appointed with the support of a holding company to the board of the holding company's subsidiary. In such circumstances the loyalty of the director towards the subsidiary company's interests may be called into question and it is not inconceivable that despite owing his duties to the subsidiary company, the director may nevertheless be influenced by the holding company to pursue policies which may be beneficial to the holding company but detrimental to its subsidiary; see e.g. *Scottish Co-Op Wholesale Society Ltd* v *Meyer* [1959] AC 324 (discussed in Chapter 2).

Disclosure in contracts in which a director has an interest

Unless otherwise provided for by the terms of a company's articles, for example, where Table A, Art 85 is adopted (see below), a contract to which the company is a party and in which a director has a conflicting interest may be avoided by the company; see e.g. *Hely Hutchinson* v *Brayhead Ltd* [1968] 1 QB 549. In such circumstances, the director must reimburse the company for any benefit gained or loss sustained as a result of entering into the contract. A dishonest agreement between a company's directors to impede the exercise of the company's right to recover any benefit gained as a result of a director entering into a transaction involving a conflict of interest, will constitute a conspiracy to defraud; see *Adams* v *R* [1995] BCC 376 (Privy Council).

Where a director has an interest in a contract to which the company is a party, s 317 of the Companies Act 1985 requires the director to disclose the interest to a meeting of the full board of directors, disclosure to a committee of directors will not suffice. To comply with s 317, a director is not required to provide specific details of the nature of his interest, all that is required is a general notice of the interest. A director who fails to notify a meeting of the board of directors of such an interest is liable to be fined in accordance with s 317(7). As a breach of s 317 constitutes a criminal and not a civil wrong, the non-disclosure of an interest in contravention of s 317 would not in itself invalidate the contract in which the director has an interest. However, the contract will become voidable on the basis of the actual conflict of interest, i.e. its ultimate validity will then depend upon a resolution of the general meeting; see the comments of Lord Goff in *Guinness plc* v *Saunders* [1990] 2 AC 663 and Knox J in *Cowan de Groot Properties Ltd* v *Eagle Trust plc* [1991] BCLC 1045.

However, it would appear from the decision of the Court of Appeal in *Lee Panavision Ltd* v *Lee Lighting Ltd* [1992] BCLC 22 that disclosure for the purpose of complying with s 317 may be given informally. In this case the Court of Appeal held that there was no breach of s 317 in circumstances where the interest in question had been informally made known to the members of the board, although the said interest had never been declared at a formal board meeting.

The Court of Appeal's decision in *Lee Panavision* was subsequently applied and possibly extended by the decision of Simon Brown J in *Runciman* v *Walter Runciman plc* [1992] BCLC 1084. Here, Simon Brown J held that disclosure may be implied from circumstances which suggested that all the directors were aware of the interest, albeit that the interest had not been declared on a formal or informal basis. The facts of the *Runciman* case were as follows. The plaintiff (P), the former chairman of the defendant company (R) had been dismissed from office following a hostile takeover of R. P claimed damages for unfair dismissal and R sought to reduce the damages payable to P for his unfair dismissal (R conceded that P had been unfairly dismissed). R sought to reduce the damages payable on the basis that P's service contract had, as with the other service contracts of executive directors of the company, been invalidly extended, i.e. no board approval. Secondly, R contended that P had failed to disclose his personal interest with respect to the extension of his own service contract and as such the contract was voidable, i.e. as a breach of s 317. Thirdly, R contended that the decision to extend the service contract had not been made in the interests of the company.

In relation to R's first contention, P contended that, as a matter of practice, he had the executive authority (albeit ostensible in nature) to formulate the nature of salary increases for the company's executive directors, provided that such increases were approved by two non-executive directors of the company. However, R argued that P's authority was inappropriate, in so far as it conflicted with the company's articles which provided that the office of an executive director was held on such terms as the company's directors determined. The company's articles defined directors as the body or quorum of directors present at a meeting of the directors. Nevertheless, although in the present case the directors (as defined in the articles) had not been involved in the decision-making process, in respect of both the level of salary to be paid to executive directors and the length of service contracts, Simon Brown J held that if all the executive directors had impliedly agreed to the decisions taken by P (and the two non-executive directors) in the exercise of the alleged ostensible authority, it was immaterial that such an agreement had not been approved at a board meeting.

In relation to the second contention, R argued that for P to have complied with the company's articles in relation to disclosure of an interest (the relevant article was similar to Table A, Art 85), P would have been required to disclose, at a board meeting, the nature of his interest in respect of the variations to his own service contract. Compliance with the relevant article would have also meant compliance with s 317. R argued that P's failure to disclose the interest rendered the variations in his own service contract to be invalid, i.e. unless ratified by the general meeting. Although Simon Brown J accepted that there had been a technical breach of s 317, as clearly there had been no disclosure of P's interest to a meeting of the board, the learned judge held that the circumstances of the case were such as to render the breach ineffectual in that it seemed a nonsense that a director should have to declare an interest in his own service contract in circumstances where it was blatantly obvious to anyone involved in the management of the company that such an interest existed.

R's third contention was rejected on the basis that the purpose of extending the executive service contracts was to prevent the executive directors from being 'head hunted', a decision which the court regarded as beneficial to the interests of the company.

In accordance with the liberal but justifiable decisions in *Lee Panavision Ltd* v *Lee Lighting Ltd* and *Runciman* v *Walter Runciman plc*, it is difficult to justify the logic of the decision in *Neptune* (*Vehicle Washing Equipment*) *Ltd* v *Fitzgerald* [1995] BCC 474. Here Lightman J, in giving summary judgment, ruled, amongst other matters, that a sole director of a company was subject to s 317. The decision is surprising in the sense that it seems improbable that a sole director would seek to even consider declaring an interest to a meeting of the board in circumstances where the board is in effect comprised of but himself. Indeed, how is it possible for a sole director to have a meeting with himself? However, Lightman J thought it was indeed possible and explained his decision in the following manner:

'The sole director may hold a meeting attended by himself alone or he may hold a meeting attended by someone else, normally the company secretary. When holding the meeting on his own, he must still make the declaration to himself and have the statutory pause for thought, though it may be that the declaration does not have to be out loud, and he must record that he made the declaration in the minutes. The court may well find it difficult to accept that the declaration has been made if it is not recorded. If the meeting is attended by anyone else, the declaration must be made out loud and in the hearing of those attending, and again should be recorded. In this case, if it is proved that the declaration was made, the fact that the minutes do not record the making of the declaration will not preclude proof of its making. In either situation the language of the section must be given full effect: there must be a declaration of interest.' (at p 481)

It is respectfully suggested that the learned judge's strained explanation was one born of a technical desire to apply the wording of s 317 to a situation which, in all reality, should not fall within the ambit of the provision. It is interesting to note that at the trial of the proceedings (following the preliminary hearing), A G Steinfield QC, sitting as a deputy judge of the Chancery Division [1995] BCC 1000, concluded that as there was no appeal against the judgment of Lightman J in respect of the s 317 issue, he was bound to follow that judgment. Nevertheless, A G Steinfield QC, commenting on the interpretation afforded to s 317 by Lightman J, stated:

'Accordingly it is a ruling which I am bound to follow and apply even if I had doubts as to its correctness.' (at p 1003)

THE WAIVER OF THE CONFLICT OF INTEREST RULE

A company may waive the conflict of interest rule by including within its articles a provision which corresponds to the form adopted by Table A, Art 85. Article 85 is drafted in the following manner:

'Subject to the provisions of the Companies Act, and provided that he has disclosed to the directors the nature and extent of any material interest, a director notwithstanding his office –

(a) may be a party to, or otherwise interested in, any transaction or arrangement with the company or in which the company is otherwise interested;
(b) may be a director or other officer of, or employed by, or party to any transaction or arrangement with, or otherwise interested in, any body corporate promoted by the company or in which the company is otherwise interested; and
(c) shall not, by reason of his office, be accountable to the company for any benefit which he derives from any such office or employment or from any such transaction or arrangement or from any interest in any such body corporate and no such transaction or arrangement shall be liable to be avoided on the ground of any such interest or benefit.'

The relationship between Art 85 and section 317 of the Companies Act 1985

Although both s 317 and Table A, Art 85 are concerned with disclosure requirements, it is important to observe that the extent of the disclosure required to comply with s 317 is not as extensive as that under Table A, Art 85; disclosure under Art 85 must be of a specific nature whereas disclosure under s 317 may only be of a general nature. It is unclear whether an informal type of disclosure to the board will, as under s 317, suffice for the purpose of complying with Art 85; see e.g. *Gwembe Valley Development* v *Koshy* [1998] 2 BCLC 613.

While the ability to rescind a contract in accordance with non-compliance of s 317 may be waived by an ordinary resolution of the general meeting, it is almost certain that the provision would be impliedly waived in a situation where a director complied with the disclosure provisions in respect of Table A, Art 85. However, it should be noted that in accordance with s 317(9) nothing contained within s 317 prejudices the operation of any rule of law restricting directors from having an interest in contracts with the company, i.e. compliance with s 317 will **NOT NECESSARILY** waive the conflict of interest rule.

Where a director fails to disclose an interest in a particular contract, but the failure to disclose does not result in a breach of duty to the company, the company cannot waive its right to rescind the contract and at the same time compel the director to account for any profit obtained under the contract; see e.g. *Burland* v *Earle* [1902] AC 83.

The relationship between Art 85 and section 310 of the Companies Act 1985

At first sight, Table A, Art 85 may appear to conflict with s 310 of the CA 1985, in so far as s 310 precludes a company from including a provision within its articles or in any contract with a director, which purports to exempt a director from liability in respect of a breach of duty. The potential discrepancy between s 310 and Table A, Art 85 was considered by Vinelott J in *Movitex Ltd* v *Bulfield and Ors* [1986] 2 BCC 99, 403. Vinelott J concluded that the conflict of interest rule was an overriding rule of equity, a distinct rule of equity, a breach of which would not necessarily cause harm to a company or result in a breach of duty. Therefore, according to Vinelott J, a company's articles could relax the application of the equitable rule without bringing itself into conflict with s 310. Vinelott J stated:

> 'The true principle is that if a director places himself in a position in which his duty to the company conflicts with his personal interest or duty to another, the court will intervene to set aside the transaction without inquiring whether there was any breach of the director's duty to the company. That is an overriding principle of equity. The shareholders in formulating the articles can exclude or modify the application of the principle. In doing so they do not exempt the director from the consequences of a breach of duty owed to the company.' (at pp 99, 423)

It should be noted that as a result of an amendment made to s 310 (inserted by s 137(1), CA 1989), a new s 310(3)(a) of the Companies Act 1985 permits a company to purchase and maintain insurance for company directors in respect of a liability which might arise as a result of a breach of duty.

THE COMMON LAW DUTY OF CARE

A director of a company will, by the very nature of business and commercial reality, occasionally be called upon to enter into business transactions which carry a potential element of risk. A commercial gamble may be necessary to secure economic stability or growth. Accordingly, although a director will be expected to exhibit a reasonable degree of care in the performance of his duties, it is clear that the standard and extent of care will be far less onerous than, for example, a trustee. The standard of care which will be required of a director is not measured in terms of a professional standard applicable to directors as a class, but is in part dependent upon the abilities and qualifications of the particular director in question. Mere errors of judgment or acts of imprudence will not necessarily constitute a breach of duty, although directors qualified in a particular business-related area will be expected to exhibit a reasonable standard of skill appropriate to that area of expertise.

Although one might presume that the standard of care to be expected from executive directors would be of a higher standard than for non-executive directors, the presumption may be displaced where, for example, non-executive directors are entrusted with business matters in which they have personal expertise. For example, in *Dorchester Finance Co Ltd* v *Stebbing* [1989] BCLC 498 a company successfully brought an action against two non-executive directors for a breach of their duty of care. One of the said directors was a chartered accountant while the other had considerable accounting experience. The company's action was commenced as a result of the two directors having been in the practice of signing blank cheques relating to the company's bank account. As experienced accountants, the directors should have known better; their actions amounted to a breach of their duty of care to the company.

In order to comply with the duty of care, a director must pay diligent attention to the business affairs of the company in which he holds office. Clearly the duty of a director to participate in the management of a company will depend on the manner in which the particular company's business is organised and the part the director is reasonably expected to play. A director's non-performance of an act which it is his duty to perform may result in a breach of his duty of care. For example, in *Re Duomatic* [1969] 2 Ch 365, a director who failed to seek specialist help or guidance (in this case from the general body of shareholders), when it was reasonable in the circumstances for him to do so, was found to be in breach of his duty of care.

Historically, the judicial interpretation of the nature of the duty of care expected of a director was based upon the judgment of Romer J in *Re City Equitable Fire Insurance Co Ltd* [1925] Ch 407. Romer J identified the characteristics of the duty in the following way:

- a director need not exhibit in the performance of his duties a greater skill than may be expected from a person of his knowledge and experience;
- a director is not bound to give continuous attention to the affairs of a company. A director's duties are of an intermittent nature to be formed at

periodical board meetings. A director is not bound to attend all board meetings although he should do so whenever possible (see e.g. *Re Cardiff Savings Bank (Marquis of Bute's case)* [1892] 2 Ch 100);

- in respect of duties which are left to some other official in the company, a director is, in the absence of suspicious circumstances, justified in trusting that official to perform the delegated responsibilities in an honest manner. For example, in *Dovey v Cory* [1901] AC 477 a director was not negligent in approving irregular accounting records which had been drawn up by the company's chairman and general manager.

However, the characteristics put forward by Romer J have now been subjected to a significant shift towards a more stricter approach to the construction of the duty. In the light of cases such as *Lister v Romford Ice & Cold Storage Ltd* [1957] AC 555, *Norman v Theodore Goddard* [1991] BCLC 1028 and *Re D'Jan of London Ltd* [1993] BCC 646, the first characteristic of the duty of care advanced by Romer J has been modified to include objective considerations. The characteristic may now be said to comprise a standard whereby, a director need not exhibit in the performance of his duties any greater degree of skill than could be expected from a reasonable diligent person, the diligent person being imputed with the general knowledge, skill and experience that may reasonably be expected of the holder of the position in question. The test is therefore comparable to the one used to determine wrongful trading under s 214 of the Insolvency Act 1986 (discussed in Chapter 21).

In relation to the second characteristic put forward by Romer J, this clearly does not apply in the case of executive directors although in part it may still be applicable to non-executive directors. The third characteristic is still probably applicable although a director who relies upon another official in the company to perform delegated tasks may be negligent in circumstances where he allows an official to assume exclusive control over a part of the company's business without any form of supervision.

THE CONSEQUENCES OF A BREACH OF DUTY/CONFLICT OF INTEREST

Where a director is discovered to be contemplating pursuing a transaction which, if completed, would amount to a breach of duty or a breach of the conflict of interest rule, the company may apply for an injunction to restrain the commission of the breach. In circumstances where a breach of duty or a breach of the conflict of interest has actually occurred, the director in breach may be liable to account for any profit made or loss sustained as a result of his transgression. However, save in a situation where a breach of duty or a breach of the conflict of interest rule results in a fraud on the minority (discussed in Chapter 22), the company may legitimately excuse the breach by the passing of an ordinary resolution. A director who is in breach of duty or who is in breach of the conflict of interest rule will be permitted to vote at the general meeting at which the motion to excuse the breach is considered.

Relief available from the court

In accordance with s 727 of the Companies Act 1985, a director who is found to be in breach of duty or in breach of the conflict of interest rule may be partly or wholly relieved of his liability; see e.g. *Selangor United Rubber Estates Ltd* v *Cradock and Ors (No 3)* [1968] 1 WLR 1555. Section 727 may only be relied upon where proceedings are brought against a director by the company; see e.g. *Commissioners of Customs & Excise* v *Hedon Alpha Ltd* [1981] QB 818. A director may apply for relief in the course of proceedings (see e.g. *Re Kirby's Coaches Ltd* [1991] BCC 130) or he may make an anticipatory application under s 727(2).

The ability of a director to successfully bring himself within the ambit of the s 727 defence will depend upon his capacity to convince the court that the instigation of the course of conduct which resulted in a breach was not intended to cause prejudice to the interests of the company as a whole. The director must establish that he acted honestly in pursing a course of conduct; clearly the conduct must not have been undertaken with a view to benefiting the director's own interests or the interests of some other third party. Nevertheless, notwithstanding that a director may have genuinely believed his actions to have been in the best interests of the company as a whole, he will not succeed in establishing the s 727 defence where, in relation to all the circumstances of a case, his conduct was viewed to have been of an unreasonable nature.

Following the decision of Hoffmann LJ in *Re D'Jan of London* [1993] BCC 646, s 727 may even prove to be an appropriate defence to a negligent breach of duty. In *Re D'Jan of London* Hoffmann LJ held that, although objectively, the respondent's conduct was unreasonable, thereby justifying the court in finding that he was liable for the negligent breach of duty, such conduct could, for the purposes of s 727, still be viewed to be both honest and reasonable. This decision was reached on the basis that s 727 lent itself to a subjective consideration of the director's conduct and notwithstanding that the director's negligent conduct could not be ignored, the director's error of judgement was, in this particular case, of a type which could happen to any busy man. However, it is suggested that the ability to apply the s 727 defence to a case involving a negligent breach of duty must be viewed with some caution, in so far as the s 727 defence should not be construed by an entirely subjective standard, i.e. it should only apply in circumstances where the director acted in both an honest *and reasonable way* (emphasis added). Indeed Hoffmann LJ, conceded that:

> 'It may seem odd that a person found to have been guilty of negligence which involves failing to take reasonable care, can ever satisfy a court that he acted reasonably.' (at p 649)

FETTERING THE FUTURE EXERCISE OF A DIRECTOR'S DISCRETION

A director will exercise corporate powers in a fiduciary capacity and as such it may be assumed that he may not, by a contractual agreement or otherwise, fetter the future exercise of such powers. However, commercial reality dictates that it may occasionally be necessary for directors to bind the company to a certain course of future conduct. The Australian High Court recognised this need in *Thornby* v *Goldberg* [1964] 112 CLR 597, where Kitto J stated:

> 'There are many kinds of transactions in which the proper time for the exercise of the directors' discretion is the time of the negotiation of a contract and not the time at which the contract is to be performed ... If at the former time they are bona fide of opinion that it is in the interests of the company that the transaction should be entered into and carried into effect I see no reason in law why they should not bind themselves.' (at p 605–6)

Prior to the Court of Appeal's consideration of the matter in *Fulham Football Club Ltd* v *Cabra Estates plc* [1992] BCC 863, the extent by which the rule against the fetter on a future exercise of a director's discretion would be enforced, was somewhat unclear. However, support for the view that a director was unable to bind a company to a future course of conduct where subsequently, it became apparent that the conduct in question was contrary to the company's interests, may be found in the High Court decisions of *Rackham* v *Peek Foods Ltd* [1990] BCLC 895 and *John Crowther Group plc* v *Carpets International plc* [1990] BCLC 460. Both the aforementioned cases were concerned with agreements which sought to bind company directors to recommend share acquisition agreements to the shareholders of their respective companies. In both cases the share acquisition agreements were subsequently found to be contrary to the interests of the shareholding body and as such were not enforced.

The case of *Fulham Football Club Ltd* v *Cabra Estates plc* involved an undertaking by the plaintiffs, four directors of Fulham football club (F), to the effect that they would support, in preference to a plan proposed by the local authority, a planning application by the ground's owners (Cabra Estates plc (C)) for the future development of 'Craven Cottage' (the football club's ground). At the time of giving the undertaking, which was given in return for substantial financial support by C to the football club, the directors believed that their decision had been taken in the best interests of the company. In accordance with the terms of the agreement, F supported C's proposals at a public enquiry.

However, subsequent events resulted in the directors and shareholders of F changing their minds on the pretext that the agreement with C could no longer be construed as beneficial to F. The plaintiffs sought a declaration from the court that they were not bound by the agreement in that to honour the undertakings would have been inconsistent with their fiduciary duties to F. At first instance, Chadwick J found in favour of the plaintiffs on the basis that whilst it was permissible for F's directors to bind F to a future course of conduct, the terms of the agreement only extended to the first public enquiry, i.e. F had fulfilled its obligation at that enquiry. The Court of Appeal, which was in complete agreement with the principles enunciated in *Thornby* v *Goldberg* (1964) 112 CLR 597, allowed C's appeal. Therefore, F was bound by the terms of its agreement with C, an agreement which had not been restricted to the first public enquiry. In so far as F had obtained a substantial benefit at the time of entering into the agreement, it was permissible for the directors to have acted to bind the company to the agreed future course of conduct.

It is submitted that the decision of the Court of Appeal in *Fulham*, in respect of allowing company directors to bind the company to some future course of conduct, irrespective of whether that conduct was subsequently found to be detrimental to the company's interests, must be viewed with some caution; it should not be seen as setting an absolute and irreversible precedent. However, in considering the particular facts of the *Fulham* case, i.e. the length of time the agreement was in force before it was challenged (over two years), the substantial financial consideration which F received on entering into the agreement, and the fact that the agreement was, at the time of its conception, supported by the company's directors and shareholding body, the decision of the Court of Appeal may, in the light of such circumstances, be regarded as just.

THE CONSTRUCTIVE TRUSTEE

Where corporate property is transferred to a third party as a result of a breach of trust (breach of fiduciary duty), the company may be able to recover the property in question or the value of the property. Where the third party is liable for the return of property or its value, the third party is deemed to be a constructive trustee. A person (or of course a corporate entity) may become a constructive trustee where the person 'received and became charged with some part of the trust property' (knowing receipt) or secondly, where the person 'assisted with knowledge in a dishonest and fraudulent design' (knowing assistance). Under the second head it is therefore possible for a third party who is a stranger to the trust, having never had possession of the trust property, to be made liable as a constructive trustee, i.e. in the sense of being an accessory to the breach of trust. The criteria to establish a third party's responsibility and liability as a constructive trustee, takes its roots from the *dictum* of Lord Selborne LC in *Barnes* v *Addy* (1874) LR 9 Ch App 244. Lord Selborne opined that the liability of third parties may exist:

> '... if they are found ... actually participating in any fraudulent conduct of the trustee to the injury of the *cestui que trust*. But ... strangers are not to be made constructive trustees merely because they act as the agents of trustees in transactions within their legal powers, transactions, perhaps of which a Court of Equity may disapprove, unless those agents receive and become chargeable

with some part of the trust property, or unless they assist with knowledge in a dishonest and fraudulent design on the part of trustees.'

The interpretation of the nature of the conduct and state of mind necessary to establish a person's liability as a constructive trustee has, however, been marred by a degree of uncertainty in terms of the judicial terminology applied to the manner in which a person's knowledge may be regarded as sufficient to establish that person's conduct as the conduct of a constructive trustee. According to the decision of Ungoed-Thomas J in *Selangor United Rubber Estates Ltd v Cradock and Ors (No 3)* [1968] 1 WLR 1555, knowing assistance may be established where the circumstances of a case indicated that a person who had no actual or obvious knowledge of the illegality of the transaction that person was nevertheless in a position to have been reasonably suspicious of the situation and as such should have acted upon those suspicions. Therefore, this decision would seem to suggest that a person's recklessness or perhaps negligence in not acting upon the suspicious circumstances of a transaction may suffice to satisfy the requirement of 'knowing assistance'. This interpretation was followed in part in *Lipkin Gorman v Karpnale Ltd* [1989] 1 WLR 402 and *Baden Delvaux & Lecuit v Société Générale pour Favoriser le Développement du Commerce et de l'Industrie en France SA* [1983] BCLC 325, affirmed by the Court of Appeal [1985] BCLC 258.

Subsequent cases which have been concerned with the interpretation of factors which justify a person as having acted with knowing assistance have sought to adopt a reformulated test with an emphasis upon a need to prove the dishonesty element of a third party's assistance in a breach of trust; see e.g. *Re Montague's Settlement Trusts* [1987] Ch 264 and *Polly Peck International v Nadir (No 2)* [1992] 4 All ER 769.

Indeed, the more recent decision of the Privy Council in *Royal Brunei Airlines Sdn Bhd v Tan Kok Ming* [1995] BCC 899 has echoed the importance to be placed upon the dishonesty element in relation to establishing a third party's participation as a constructive trustee. However, the Privy Council stressed that dishonesty should not be interpreted as indicative of a person's subjective understanding of a situation. Accordingly, dishonesty is to measured against the standard of honesty one would reasonably expect a person to display in the circumstances of a given case, taking into account the personal attributes of that person such as his experience and intelligence. As such, conduct may be perceived as dishonest where the type of conduct was objectively perceived to be of a commercially unacceptable nature; see e.g. *Cowan de Groot Properties Ltd v Eagle Trust plc* [1992] 4 All ER 700.

While the two tests to establish 'knowledge', i.e. the reasonable suspicion test as advanced in *Selangor* and the dishonesty test championed by the Privy Council in *Royal Brunei Airlines*, may appear prima facie somewhat contradictory, in reality, the distinction between the two tests is a very fine one. As both tests adopt an objective standard to determine a person's potential liability as a constructive trustee, conduct which is construed to be of a suspicious nature in a commercial setting would, it is suggested, in most cases also give rise to a finding that the conduct was objectively dishonest.

OTHER STATUTORY DUTIES AND OBLIGATIONS

Companies legislation has made considerable inroads into regulating the activities of directors. In addition to the statutory provisions dealt with in an earlier part of this chapter, companies legislation purports to regulate the activities of directors in a number of other ways.

Substantial property transactions

According to s 320 of the Companies Act 1985, a company is prohibited from entering into an arrangement whereby a director or connected person acquires, or is to acquire, one or more non-cash assets of the requisite value from the company (the requisite value is currently set at £100 000 or 10 per cent of the company's net assets; transactions of less than £2000 are not included). In addition, the section prohibits an arrangement whereby the company acquires or is to acquire one or more non-cash assets of the requisite value from a director or connected person. A connected person is defined by s 346(2) of the Companies Act 1985 and includes amongst others, the director's spouse, child or step-child and a company with which the director is associated, i.e. if the director and the persons connected with him, hold at least one-fifth of the associated company's share capital, or are entitled to exercise or control the exercise of more than one-fifth of the voting power at any general meeting of that body.

In *Re Duckwari plc* [1997] 2 BCLC 713 the Court of Appeal was called upon to determine whether s 320 was applicable in respect of the following facts. C was a director and shareholder of a company, 'O'. O agreed to purchase freehold property for £495 000 and paid a deposit of £49 500. However, on completion, the property was conveyed to another company, 'D', of which C was also a director. D paid the balance of the purchase price and reimbursed O for the deposit. However, as a result of a decline in the market value of the property, D sought to avoid the transaction on the premise that it contravened s 320. O was connected with C for the purposes of s 320(1)(b). The contravention was alleged in the sense that D acquired from O, the benefit of the contract to purchase the property and the value of that asset was at least £49 500, the value of the deposit which was subsequently reimbursed. At first instance the contravention was established.

On appeal, O and C argued that the transaction did not involve the acquisition of an asset by D from O, but rather there had been a novation of the purchase contract. The Court of Appeal dismissed the appeal, finding that there had been no novation; the asset acquired by D was a single asset which could be described as either the benefit of the purchase contract or O's beneficial interest in the property. They were both non-cash assets within the meaning of s 739 of the Companies Act 1985, worth at least £49 500. (See also *Lander v Premier Pict Petroleum Ltd & Anor* [1998] BCC 248.)

An arrangement of the type covered by s 320 may nevertheless be made where it is disclosed to the general meeting and to the board of directors in accordance with s 317. The general meeting must approve the arrangement although the interested director is entitled to vote on the matter. It should be noted that a shareholder agreement (as opposed to a resolution of the general meeting) which seeks to validate an arrangement will not ordinarily amount to shareholder approval under s 320, save perhaps, in a situation where the agreement represents the unanimous consent of the membership and where it specifically includes all the necessary details of the terms of the proposed arrangement; see e.g. *Demite Ltd v Protec Health Ltd and Ors* [1998] BCC 638.

Where an arrangement which involves a substantial property transaction with a director or connected person is not approved by the general meeting, the transaction will become voidable at the company's option (s 322, CA 1985). A company will lose its right to avoid the transaction where restitution of the subject matter is no longer possible or where the company is indemnified by any other person for the loss or damage which it has suffered, or where rights to the property have been acquired by a *bona fide* third party for value without actual notice of the contravention of s 320. Regardless of whether the transaction is or can be avoided, the director or connected person in breach of s 320 and any other director who authorised the transaction, will be liable to account to the company for any profit or loss sustained as a result of the breach of the provision (the loss sustained may be measured in relation to any depreciation in value of the asset which was acquired in contravention of s 320; see *Re Duckwari plc (No 2)* [1998] 2 BCLC 315 and *Re Duckwari plc (No 3)* [1999] 1 BCLC 168). However, where the breach of s 320 was committed by a connected person, the director to whom the person is connected will not be liable if he can prove that he took all reasonable steps to secure the company's compliance with s 320. The connected person and any authorising director may also be able to escape liability if they can prove that at the time of the transaction they were unaware of the fact that they were contravening s 320.

Exceptions to section 320

(1) Group transactions
An exception to s 320 is provided by s 321(2). This provision permits the acquisition or transfer of assets by holding companies from, or to their wholly owned subsidiaries or, by wholly owned subsidiaries from or to other wholly owned subsidiaries within the group.

(2) Winding up
Section 321(2)(b) provides an exception to s 320 in the case of an arrangement entered into by a company which is being wound up, i.e. provided that it is not a members' voluntary winding up petition. In a members' voluntary

winding up, the members will retain an interest in the disposal of the company's assets. It should be noted that the operation of s 320 will not be excluded in relation to a sale made by a company through a receiver as its agent; see e.g. *Demite Ltd* v *Protec Health Ltd and Ors* [1998] BCC 638.

(3) Members

Section 321(3) provides a further exception to s 320, namely, in a situation where a person is to acquire an asset from a company in which he is a member, i.e. if the arrangement is made with that person in his character as a member and not in some other capacity.

Contracts for loans and guarantees

In order to curb any potential abuse by directors of the use of corporate funds, statutory rules seek to regulate a company's ability to loan funds to its directors and connected persons (connected persons are defined in s 346(2), see above). The theme of the legislation is to prohibit all such loans (and also guarantees of directors' debts) but then to allow certain exceptions to the general prohibitions (ss 332–338, CA 1985).

The general prohibition applies where a company makes a loan to a director, shadow director, connected person or a director of its holding company. In addition to this general prohibition, certain other prohibitive rules apply to 'relevant' companies. A 'relevant' company is defined as a public company but can include a private company in a situation where the private company is part of a group of companies to which a public company belongs.

Exceptions to section 330

The following statutory provisions allow transactions which are rendered permissible as exceptions to s 330 (although note the further prohibitions made in respect of relevant companies, discussed below).

(1) Section 333, CA 1985

A loan or quasi-loan made by a relevant company to another member of the group of companies to which it belongs, or the provision of a guarantee or security in connection with a loan or quasi-loan made by any person to another member of the group. A quasi-loan is defined by s 331(3) as an arrangement under which a company meets some financial obligation of a director, a connected person, or its holding company, for example, the payment of a credit card. The obligation is met on the understanding that it will be reimbursed at some later date.

(2) Section 336, CA 1985

A loan made by a subsidiary to its holding company or the provision of a guarantee or of security in connection with a loan or quasi-loan made to the subsidiary's holding company.

(3) Section 336(6), CA 1985

A credit transaction by a company whereby the company acts as a creditor for its holding company or where it enters into a guarantee or provides security in connection with a credit transaction made by any other person for the benefit of the holding company.

(4) Section 337, CA 1985

Funds made available to a director for the purpose of company business to facilitate the performance of the director's duties. The general meeting must approve the purpose and amount of expenditure incurred.

(5) Section 338, CA 1985

Moneylending companies enjoy wide exceptions. Any loan, quasi-loan or guarantee made by a moneylending company is permissible providing it is made within the ordinary course of business on terms which the company might reasonably have afforded to an unconnected person of the same financial standing. A loan made to one of the company's directors or a director of the company's holding company to enable the director to purchase or improve his main residence is permissible, providing the loan is made on such terms as would normally be made available to an employee of the company. Such payments must not exceed £100 000.

Prohibitions for relevant companies

(a) Quasi-loans

Quasi-loans are prohibited in the case of a relevant company unless the quasi-loan is to be reimbursed within two months and the total amount outstanding on all quasi-loans made by the company does not exceed £5000. The prohibition in relation to quasi-loans also applies to guarantees entered into by a company in respect of a quasi-loan made by a third party for the benefit of a director, connected person or holding company (s 332, CA 1985).

(b) Credit transactions

Any credit transaction entered into by a relevant company for the benefit of a director, connected person or holding company is prohibited, as is a guarantee given by the company in respect of a credit transaction between a director, connected person or holding company and third party. The only exception to this prohibition is in respect of a credit transaction which does not exceed £10 000, i.e. provided that the credit transaction is entered into in the ordinary course of a company's business upon terms which the company would have been prepared to extend to any unconnected person of the same financial standing (s 335(2), CA 1985).

(c) Funds for company business

Any arrangement made by a relevant company with a director for the provision of funds for the purpose of enabling the director to perform his duties must be approved by the general meeting and must not exceed £20 000 (s 337, CA 1985).

(d) Moneylending companies

A moneylending company which is a relevant company (unless it is a banking company) may not enter into any loan, quasi-loan or guarantee if the aggregate of the relevant amount exceeds £100 000 (s 338(4), CA 1985).

Civil penalties for a breach of s 330

A breach of s 330 will render the transaction in question voidable. Where a company does not avoid the transaction, a director and/or connected person to whom voidable payments were made (and any director who authorised such payments) will be liable to account for any loss incurred by the company as a consequence of the breach. However, an authorising director or a director to whom a person was connected may escape liability where it is proved that at the time of the transaction he was not aware of the relevant circumstances constituting the contravention of s 330 (s 341, CA 1985).

Criminal sanctions

Criminal sanctions only apply in the case of relevant companies. The company and any director who, with knowledge or reasonable cause was aware of a breach of s 330, authorised or permitted it to occur, and any other person who, with knowledge or with reasonable cause to know of the contravention, procured the transaction or arrangement, will be guilty of an offence and as such liable on conviction to be imprisoned, fined, or both. A relevant company may escape liability if it can prove that at the time the transaction or arrangement was entered into, it did not know, i.e. the company's directing mind did not know, of the relevant circumstances which gave rise to the contravention (s 342, CA 1985).

THE LAW COMMISSION'S PROPOSALS FOR REFORMING DIRECTORS' DUTIES AND REGULATING CONFLICTS OF INTEREST

In 1998, the Law Commission issued a consultation paper (No 153) entitled 'Company Directors: Regulating Conflicts of Interest and Formulating a Statement of Duties'. The consultation paper considered (amongst other matters) the possibility of a statutory codification of directors' duties and considered a number of options in which this could be achieved, for example, a comprehensive codification, a partial codification, a statutory statement for guidance purposes only, and a non-binding statement on the principal duties in the general law to be used in certain prescribed forms. However, as the consultation paper points out, codification would be likely to be difficult and may not work, indeed it is likely to result in a loss of flexibility. Accordingly, it is likely that the way forward in this matter will be either to have a Schedule attached to the Companies Act, for the purpose of guidance in establishing examples and explanations of directors' duties or, alternatively, guidance in the form of a document which would not form part of companies legislation but which would nevertheless be issued to company directors.

In relation to a director's duty of care, the consultation paper provides for a draft s 309A, to be inserted into the Companies Act 1985, a provision which would give statutory force to a test based upon a reasonable person having both the knowledge and experience that could reasonably be expected of a diligent person acting in the same position as the director. The test would also consider the director's own knowledge and experience. In effect, the provision would be akin to s 214 of the Insolvency Act 1986. It should be noted that the consultation paper did not seek to consider directors' duties in respect of the Insolvency Act 1986; this, it is suggested, is an unfortunate omission.

In respect of the conflict of interest rule, the consultation paper considers potential proposals to amend s 317. For example, it suggests the possibility of amending s 317 to the extent that only material interests should need to be disclosed. This appears to make much sense and would accord with the wording of Art 85, albeit that the term 'material interest', in the context of s 317, may be too vague and as such may be open to many variable interpretations. The consultation paper also considers the benefits of exempting companies with a single director from the ambit of s 317. This proposal, which in effect would overturn the decision in *Neptune Ltd v Fitzgerald* [1995] BCC 474, would make much sense. However, the consultation paper's suggestion that sole directors of companies should, in instances of a conflict of interest, seek the approval of the general meeting would, in the majority of cases involving such companies, be somewhat nonsensical, in that a sole director will, in all probability, also command a majority of the company's shares.

The consultation paper further favours the removal of the criminal sanction attached to s 317, the sanction to be replaced by a civil penalty. This proposal would, in addition to the addition of the term 'material interest' be such as to duplicate the effect of Table A, Art 85. In addition to the removal of the criminal sanction for s 317, the consultation paper also favours the removal of criminal sanctions in respect of other parts of Part X of the Companies Act 1985 and a general simplification in the wording of provisions contained in this part of the Companies Act.

Suggested further reading

Fiduciary duties/conflict of interest
Sealy [1967] CLJ 83
Xeuberg [1988] MLR 156
Sealy [1991] 12 Co Law 175

Grantham [1991] JBL 1
Lowry (1997) 48 NILQ 211

Management duties/problems in respect of corporate groups
Yeung [1997] LMCLQ 209

Duty of care
Finch [1992] MLR 179

Constructive trustee
Birks (1989) LMCLQ 296
Loughlan (1989) 9 OJLS 260

18

THE COMPANY IN GENERAL MEETING

INTRODUCTION

This chapter considers the powers and procedures of the general meeting. Historically, the general meeting was perceived as the ultimate source of corporate power. Today its position of power has declined in relation to its influence over the management of corporate affairs. Nevertheless, it is still, in the exercise of its inherent powers, to be properly regarded as an essential organ of the body corporate. The chapter commences by analysing the classification and requirements relating to general meetings. The chapter then moves on to consider the various types of formal resolutions which may be passed at a general meeting. In addition, it includes an analysis of informal types of resolutions. For issues relating to the reform of this topic, see the Appendix at p. 373.

THE ANNUAL GENERAL MEETING

Except in a situation where a private company has resolved to dispense with the holding of an annual general meeting (discussed below), s 366(1) of the Companies Act 1985 provides that a company must hold a general meeting once every calendar year, and no more than 15 months must elapse between each annual general meeting (AGM) (s 366(3), CA 1985). Where an AGM is not held within the prescribed period of time, the Secretary of State may, on an application from a member of the company, order a meeting to be held. In addition, the company and its officers may be fined in respect of a contravention of the statutory requirement (s 367, CA 1985).

Although the matters dealt with at a company's AGM are dependent upon the business raised by the board or individual members of the company, certain procedural tasks must be addressed at an AGM. The procedural tasks include: the appointment of an auditor and adoption of accounts, the receipt of the directors' report, the election of directors and, in appropriate circumstances, the determination of directors' remuneration.

Notice to members of motions to be presented at the AGM

Section 376 of the Companies Act 1985 provides that members holding not less than one-twentieth of the total voting rights or 100 members holding shares on which an average sum per member of not less than £100 has been paid up, may require (at the expense of the requisitionists) the company to give notice of and statements relating to motions which they intend to present at the company's next AGM. A requisition of this type must be deposited at the company's registered office at least six weeks prior to the intended date of the AGM (s 377, CA 1985). In relation to other members of the company, the company should give notice of the general effect of any intended motion (in relation to which s 376 is applicable) which is to be moved at the AGM (s 376(4), CA 1985).

Proposed reform

In 1997, the Hampel Report suggested the following reforms in relation to the conduct of AGMs:

- the report took the view that institutional investors had a responsibility to their clients to use the votes held at AGM's to the benefit of their investors. Accordingly, the report recommended that institutional investors should, in appropriate circumstances, seek to vote the shares under their control;
- companies should cease the practice of placing unrelated proposals into a single resolution. As such, shareholders should be permitted to vote separately on separate issues;
- the AGM should contain a resolution on the annual report and accounts;
- in addition, the report approved the aims of a DTI consultative document entitled 'Shareholder Communications and the Annual General Meeting' (published 16 April 1996). The DTI document report was *inter alia* concerned with the statutory rules under which shareholders are permitted to table resolutions for discussion at their company's AGM. The DTI document recommended that s 376 of the Companies Act 1985 should be amended to allow companies to circulate members' resolutions which were limited in length and supported by a sufficient number of shareholders.

THE EXTRAORDINARY GENERAL MEETING

A general meeting, other than an AGM, is called an extraordinary general meeting (EGM). A public company must call an EGM in circumstances where its net assets have fallen to one-half or less of its called-up capital (s 142(1), CA 1985). In other respects, an EGM may be convened, by both public and private companies, at the will of the company's board of directors. Alternatively, the board may be required to convene an EGM where requisitioned to do so by holders of not less than 10 per cent of the company's paid-up share capital, i.e. share capital which carries voting rights (s 368(1) and (2), CA 1985). In the case of a company not having a share capital, one-tenth of the members holding voting rights may requisition an

EGM. In accordance with s 368, the membership's statutory right to require the board to convene an EGM exists 'irrespective of anything contained within the articles'. It should be noted that the aforementioned term fails to distinguish between articles that prescribe a higher percentage of members required to requisition an EGM and articles which prescribe a percentage requirement lower than the 10 per cent figure stipulated by s 368(1). Where the articles of a company allow its membership a more accessible means of requisitioning EGMs, i.e. a lower percentage requirement than stipulated in s 368(1) it would, contrary to a literal interpretation of s 368, seem illogical not to give effect to the lower and less restrictive percentage requirement.

Where a company's articles are silent as to the required percentage requirement of members needed to requisition an EGM, s 370(3) of the Companies Act 1985 provides that an EGM may be called by two or more members holding not less than one-tenth of the issued share capital (i.e. this complies with the percentage figure in s 368) or where a company has no share capital, not less than 5 per cent of the company's members (this represents a lower figure than prescribed by s 368).

If the directors of a company are requisitioned to call a meeting they should, within 21 days of receiving the requisition, give the membership notice of the meeting; see e.g. *Re Windward Islands (Enterprises Ltd)* (1988) 4 BCC 158. The meeting must be called no more than 28 days after the notice to convene the meeting is sent out (s 368(8), CA 1985, introduced by Sch 19(9), CA 1989). Where, after receiving the requisition, the directors fail to give notice of the meeting within the 21-day period, the requisitionists or any of them representing more than one-half of the total voting rights of all of them, may convene the meeting, provided that the meeting is held before the end of three months from the date on which it was convened (s 368(4), CA 1985).

THE COURT'S DISCRETION TO CALL MEETINGS

In accordance with s 371 of the Companies Act 1985, if it is impracticable to call or conduct a meeting of a company by a manner prescribed by either the Companies Act or the company's articles, the court may, on an application from a director or a member of the company entitled to attend and vote at the meeting, order a meeting to be called, held and conducted in a manner prescribed by the court. The substance of the provision now contained in s 371 dates back to 1862. Earlier examples of its application include *Re Consolidated Mines Ltd* [1914] 1 Ch 883 and *Re El Sombrero Ltd* [1958] Ch 900. A more recent example of the application of the provision is to be found in *Re Opera Photographic* [1989] 5 BCC 601. Here Morrit J directed that a meeting should be held for the purpose of passing a resolution to dismiss one of the two members of the company from his directorship. The meeting was called despite the fact that it would be inquorate, the director against which dismissal was sought having refused to attend, i.e. the quorum requirement of two members present at the meeting could not be satisfied (see s 370(4),

CA 1985 discussed below). In allowing the meeting to proceed, Morrit J prevented the quorum requirement from being used as a device to curb the implementation of a statutory power, i.e. the ability of the general meeting to pass an ordinary resolution to remove a director from office.

However, it should be noted that, in accordance with the decision of the Court of Appeal in *Ross* v *Telford* [1997] BCC 945, s 371 is not to be viewed as an appropriate vehicle for resolving a deadlock between two equal shareholders or for overriding the class rights of a shareholder. Accordingly, in a dispute between shareholders the provision can only be invoked in a situation where a minority shareholder purports to employ quorum tactics to prevent a majority shareholder from exercising the voting rights attached to his shares. Section 371 is a procedural provision which was not designed to affect substantive voting rights or to shift the balance of power between share-holders in a case where they have agreed that power shall be shared equally and where the potential deadlock is something which must be taken to have been agreed on with the consent and for the protection of each of them. For other recent examples of the application of s 371, see *Re Sticky Fingers Restaurant Ltd* [1992] BCLC 84, *Re Whitchurch Insurance Consultants Ltd* [1994] BCC 51 and *Re British Union for the Abolition of Vivisection* [1995] 2 BCLC 1.

FORMAL REQUIREMENTS

The quorum requirement

Section 370 (4) of the Companies Act 1985 states that unless a company's articles provide otherwise, two members must be present in person at a general meeting to satisfy the quorum requirement (see Table A, Arts 40 and 41 which stipulate a requirement of two members). In the case of single member companies, s 370A of the Companies Act 1985 provides that one member present in person or by proxy shall constitute a quorum. Where at a general meeting the quorum requirement is not satisfied, the meeting will be null and void other than in a situation where the court exercises its power under s 371 (see above).

The notice requirement

Notice of the intention to call a general meeting of a company must, unless the articles provide otherwise, be given to every member of the company, irrespective of whether or not the member has the right to attend and vote at the meeting (s 370(2), CA 1985). (Note that the rights attached to a particular type of share will determine the voting rights of a member.) Notice of general meetings must also be given to the company's auditor; the auditor is given a right to attend general meetings (s 387(1), CA 1985). Section 376 of the Companies Act 1985 provides that members holding not less than one-twentieth of the total voting rights or 100 members holding shares on which an average sum per member of not less than £100 has been paid up, may require (at the expense of the requisitionists) the company to give statements relating to motions which they intend to present at a general meeting. A requisition of this type must be deposited at the company's registered office at least six weeks prior to the intended date of the AGM (s 377, CA 1985). In relation to other members of the company, the company should give notice of the general effect of any intended motion (in relation to which s 376 is applicable) which is to be moved at the AGM (s 376(4), CA 1985).

In respect of an AGM or a meeting at which a motion to pass a special resolution is proposed, a company must give not less than 21 days' notice in writing. In all other cases, other than for an adjourned meeting, 14 days' written notice must be given (seven days in the case of unlimited companies). A provision in a company's articles which seeks to shorten the prescribed notice time will be void unless, in respect of an AGM, all the members of a company entitled to attend and vote at the meeting agree to a shorter period of notice (s 369(1), CA 1985). In the case of a meeting other than an AGM, the notice period may be shortened where a majority of the membership, holding not less than 95 per cent in nominal value of shares carrying a right to attend and vote at the meeting, agree to a shorter period of notice (s 369(3), CA 1985). (Note that private companies may elect to reduce the 95 per cent requirement, discussed below.)

Although the accidental omission by a company in failing to give notice to a member would not normally invalidate a meeting (see Table A, Art 39), a deliberate act or omission on the part of a company would invalidate a meeting where its effect was to prevent a member from receiving proper and adequate notice of the meeting; see e.g. *Royal Mutual Benefit Building Society* v *Sharman* [1963] 1 WLR 581.

Circulars

When giving notice of a general meeting it is quite common for a company to issue circulars. The usual purpose of a circular is to inform the membership of the views of the company's board. Although it is possible for dissentient members to issue circulars, i.e. to explain an opposing view to the one taken by the board, the expense of issuing circulars may prove prohibitive, especially in companies with a large membership.

As a company's board is authorised to represent the company's interests, then provided that the information contained in a notice or circular is designed to benefit the company as a whole, the expense of issuing circulars may be met from the company's funds. Nevertheless, the board of directors must not issue information for the purpose of personal gain or advantage, nor must the purpose for the circular be to paint a false and misleading picture of a company's affairs. Where, in giving notice or issuing a circular a company misrepresents a state of affairs, then, in respect of a meeting for which a misleading notice (and/or circular) was issued and at which a resolution favoured by those responsible for the notice was passed, the resolution may be set aside. The misrepresentation may take the form of an omission to provide accurate information. For example, in *Kaye* v *Croydon Tramways Co* [1898] 1 Ch 358 a purchase agreement was made between Croydon Tramways Co (C) and the British Electric Traction Co Ltd (B) for the sale of C's business. The agreement also provided that B would pay compensation to C's directors for loss of office. The notice of the meeting convened to consider B's offer failed to mention the offer of compensation made to the directors. It was held that the notice, by failing to refer to the compensation offer, did not fairly disclose the purpose of the meeting. Accordingly, the general meeting's approval of the sale transaction was set aside. (See also *Baillie* v *Oriental Telephone & Electric Co Ltd* [1915] 1 Ch 503.)

Motions (resolutions) which require special notice

Where a provision of the Companies Act 1985 expressly stipulates that a company must be given special notice of an intention to pass a resolution, s 379(1) of the Companies Act 1985 requires the proposers of the motion to give at least 28 days' notice to the company before the meeting at which the resolution is to be moved. On receiving special notice, a company must give its membership at least 21 days' notice prior to the date upon which the meeting is to be held (s 379(2), CA 1985). Providing at least 21 days' notice is given to the membership, a company may nevertheless call the meeting at a date prior to the date on which the 28 days' special notice would have expired (s 379(3), CA 1985). Special notice is required for a resolution to remove a director (s 303, CA 1985), a resolution to remove an auditor (s 388, CA 1985) and one which seeks to elect a director of a public company (or a director of the subsidiary of a public company) in circumstances where the director is aged 70 or over (s 293, CA 1985).

TYPES OF RESOLUTION

The ordinary resolution

An ordinary resolution is one which is passed by a simple majority of members entitled to attend and vote at a company meeting. Unless a contrary intention appears in the companies legislation or within a company's articles, resolutions passed by a company in general meeting are to be effected by an ordinary resolution.

The special resolution

In some instances, companies legislation or a company's articles may specify that a resolution may only be passed by a 75 per cent majority of those members entitled to attend and vote at a company meeting, i.e. by special resolution. Where a motion is proposed which, if passed, would take the form of a special resolution, the membership of the company must be given at least 21 clear days' notice of the intended motion (s 378(2), CA 1985).

Nevertheless, where 95 per cent of the holders of a company's share capital agree (or in the case of a company not having a share capital members holding not less than 95 per cent of the voting rights agree), a special resolution may be passed at a meeting of which less than 21 days' notice has been given (s 378(3), CA 1985). (Note that a private company may elect to reduce the 95 per cent requirement – see below.)

The extraordinary resolution

As with a special resolution, an extraordinary resolution must be passed by a 75 per cent majority of those members entitled to attend and vote at a company meeting (s 378(1), CA 1985). Notice specifying an intention to propose a motion to pass an extraordinary resolution must be given not less than 14 days prior to the meeting at which the motion is to be heard. Examples of instances whereby the companies legislation requires an extraordinary resolution to be passed include, a resolution to commence a voluntary winding up of a company (s 84(1), IA 1986) and a resolution of a class of members where the company proposes to vary the rights of the class in accordance with the variation procedure (s 125(2)(b), CA 1985).

In accordance with s 380 of the Companies Act 1985, a company is obliged to deliver copies of all special and extraordinary resolutions passed in general meeting to the Registrar of Companies.

The elective resolution

Section 379A of the Companies Act 1985 (introduced by ss 115 and 116, CA 1989) provides that the members of a private company may elect by resolution in general meeting or by a written resolution (s 381A(1)), to dispense with certain resolution requirements prescribed by the Companies Act 1985. An elective resolution may only be implemented if all the members of the company entitled to attend and vote at the meeting, vote in favour of it. An elective resolution, once passed, may be revoked by ordinary resolution. As enacted by s 379A(2), an elective resolution was not effective unless at least 21 days' notice in writing had been given in respect of the date of the motion to consider the passing of the elective resolution. However, as from 19 June 1996, as a result of s 379A(2A) of the Companies Act 1985 (inserted by the Deregulation (Resolutions of Private Companies) Order 1996 (SI 1996/1471), the procedure for passing elective resolutions has been simplified with the effect that a private company may now pass an elective resolution on short notice (before the 21-day period has expired) provided that all the members of the company entitled to vote at the meeting would have voted in favour of the resolution.

A private company may pass an elective resolution in respect of the following matters:

- to disapply s 80(4) and (5), in respect of the giving or renewal of directors' authority to allot shares in the company for a maximum period of five years. Where s 80(4) and (5) of the Companies Act 1985 are not applicable, the directors' authority to allot shares will be governed by s 80A of the Companies Act 1985. Section 80A provides that an authority to allot shares must state the maximum amount of relevant securities to be allotted and whether the authority is given for a fixed or indefinite period. The authority may be revoked or varied by the passing of an ordinary resolution. Where the elective resolution ceases to have effect, for example, if it is revoked by the general meeting, then an authority to allot shares then in force will be extinguished in a situation where it had already been in operation for five or more years. Where however, the authority had operated for a period of less than five years, it will in such circumstances continue to run from the date when it was first granted, for a maximum of five years (s 80A(7), CA 1985);

- to dispense with the holding of an AGM (s 366A, CA 1985). It should be noted that in accordance with s 366A(3) of the Companies Act 1985, any member of a company which has elected to dispense with the holding of an AGM may, by notice to the company, not later than three months before the end of the year in which an AGM was scheduled to take place, require the holding of an AGM in that year. Where a member of a company asserts his right under s 366A(3), then s 366(1) and (4) of the Companies Act 1985 will apply in respect to the calling of the meeting and the consequences attached to a default;

- to reduce the number of members required to sanction a company meeting at short notice or effect notice of a motion to pass a special resolution from 95 per cent to a number not below 90 per cent (ss 369(4) and 378(3), CA 1985). The percentage of members required may be specified in the elective resolution or subsequently determined by the company in general meeting;

- to dispense with the laying of accounts and reports before general meetings (s 252(1), CA 1985);

- to elect to exempt the annual appointment of auditors (s 386(1), CA 1985).

In introducing a system of elective resolutions, the Companies Act 1989 has undoubtedly made some progress in easing the regulatory burden of legislation which is placed upon private companies. The 1989 Act has moved towards creating some form of distinction between the applicability of companies legislation in respect of private and public companies. It should be noted that under s 117, CA 1989, the Secretary of State has the power to make regulations enabling private companies to pass elective resolutions dispensing with further requirements of the companies legislation.

THE INFORMAL RESOLUTION

At common law, a motion to pass a resolution may be approved, without a formal resolution of the general meeting, providing the resolution carries the unanimous support of those members who are entitled to attend and vote, had the motion been put before a general meeting; see e.g. *Parker & Cooper Ltd* v *Reading* [1926] Ch 975. The articles of companies frequently reiterate the common law position. For example, Table A, Art 53 provides as follows:

'A resolution in writing executed by or on behalf of each member who would have been entitled to vote upon it if it had been proposed at a general meeting at which he was present shall be as effectual as if it had been passed at a general meeting duly convened and held and may consist of several instruments in the like form each executed by or on behalf of one or more members.'

However, it would appear unclear whether notice of an intention to pass an informal agreement must, as with a formal resolution, be sent to all members of the company. Section 370(2) only provides for notice requirements in respect of the calling of general meetings, i.e. the section makes no mention of any notice requirement in relation to the passing of a resolution other than at a formal general meeting. Auditors of companies would also appear to be denied the right to any notice requirement in respect to the passing of an informal agreement.

An informal agreement may be as valid as if a resolution in general meeting had been passed, notwithstanding whether the informal agreement seeks to approve a matter which would normally require a vote from either a simple or a 75 per cent majority of voting members. For example, in *Cane* v *Jones* [1980] 1 WLR 1451 the court approved an alteration to a company's articles by the unanimous but informal agreement of the company's voting members (s 9, CA 1985 requires an alteration to a company's articles to be effected by a special resolution, i.e. 75 per cent majority vote).

While Table A, Art 53 requires an informal resolution to be in writing, the common law makes no such demand. For example, in *Re Duomatic* [1969] 2 Ch 365 an informal agreement to authorise directors' remuneration (a matter which would normally require an ordinary resolution of the general meeting) was upheld, despite the fact that the agreement was not in writing. Buckley J stated:

'... I proceed upon the basis that where it can be shown that all shareholders who have a right to attend and vote at a general meeting of the company assent to some matter which a general meeting of the company could carry into effect, that assent is as binding as a resolution in general meeting would be.'

Although the members of a company who have adopted articles to include Table A, Art 53, would by agreeing to an unwritten type of informal resolution commit a technical breach of s 14 of the Companies Act 1985 (discussed in Chapter 7), the breach would nevertheless be of a procedural nature and could be corrected by the company in general meeting (all the members entitled to vote having agreed to the informal resolution). Therefore, it would be highly unlikely that a court would invalidate an informal unwritten resolution on the basis that it constituted a breach of the articles. In *Re Bailey, Hay & Co Ltd* [1971] 3 All ER 693, *Re Home Treat Ltd* [1991] BCC 165 and *Atlas Wright (Europe) Ltd* v *Wright and Anor* [1999] BCC 163 the flexibility of the common law approach was emphasised by the validation of informal resolutions in situations where there had been no written confirmation of the resolution. Indeed, in *Re Home Treat Ltd*, Harman J went one stage further by suggesting that:

> '... acquiescence by shareholders with knowledge of the matter is as good as actual consent.' (at p 168)

It should be also noted that it may be possible for a shareholder agreement to constitute an implied form of informal resolution in circumstances where, the subject matter of the resolution is specifically dealt with by the terms of the shareholders' agreement and where the agreement comprises the entire membership of the company. However, the terms of a shareholder agreement will not be equated with a resolution where the agreement is absent of some material matter, so specified by the nature of the resolution; see e.g. *Demite Ltd* v *Proctec Health Ltd* [1998] BCC 638.

Statutory provisions which require a formal resolution

Where, in relation to a procedural requirement, a statutory provision is drafted so as to expressly require that a resolution is to be formally passed by the general meeting of the company (see e.g. s 303, CA 1985 – removal of director), an informal resolution would, in such a case, be ineffective, and if relied upon would be liable to be set aside. The courts adopt a strict approach to the formal requirements laid down by statutory provisions. For example, in *Re R W Peak (King's Lynn) Ltd* [1998] BCC 596 Lindsay J held that a requirement for a special resolution, in respect of sanctioning a company's purchase of its own shares (see s 143, CA 1985), could not be overridden by an informal resolution.

Nevertheless, on occasions this strict approach has been relaxed. For example, in *Re Home Treat Ltd* [1991] BCC 165 Harman J held that an informal resolution could validly alter a company's objects clause in conjunction with s 4 of the Companies Act 1985. His lordship so found, despite the fact that s 5 of the Companies Act 1985 permits the holders of not less than 15 per cent in nominal value of the company's issued share capital or any class of it, or holders of not less than 15 per cent of the company's debentures, a right to object to the court in respect of the alteration. The right to challenge the alteration continuing for up to a period of 21 days after the special resolution securing the change in objects had been passed. In upholding the validity of the informal resolution, Harman J effectively ignored the procedural requirement of s 5, i.e. a special resolution had never been passed and as such there was no date from which the 21-day period could run. However, whilst ignoring the procedural requirement, the learned judge acknowledged the purpose behind s 5, namely to safeguard shareholder and creditor interests. He considered such interests prior to his decision to validate the informal resolution.

Further, it is to be observed that in contrast to the strict approach adopted in *Re R W Peak (King's Lynn) Ltd*, the decision of Nourse J in *Re Barry Artist Ltd* [1985] BCLC 283 provides a a more flexible, albeit reluctant acceptance of the fact that the members of a company may be capable of unanimously passing an informal written resolution, instead of the statutory prescribed special resolution to effect a reduction of the company's capital in accordance with s 66(1), CA 1948 (now s 135, CA 1985). The court's reluctance to the acceptance of an informal resolution was born of the fact that the provision states that the court must exercise its discretion in respect of whether or not to approve a special resolution passed in general meeting for the purpose of reducing a company's share capital. In *Re Barry Artist* there had never been a formal resolution of which to approve or disapprove, i.e. no formal special resolution had been passed. However, the acceptance of the informal resolution was a logical and common-sense means by which the technical requirements of the provision could be abandoned, i.e. the court was still able to exercise its discretion in respect of whether to sanction the reduction of capital (in this instance the reduction was approved). However, as stated, the court's decision was taken with some aversion. Nourse J commented:

> 'My strong inclination has been to adjourn this petition so that a meeting can be held and a special resolution passed, but it has been represented to me that the company has a good reason, into which I need not go, for having the reduction confirmed before the end of this term. In the circumstances, although with great reluctance, I am prepared to accede to the petition today. I would not be prepared to do so in any similar case in the future.' (at pp 284–5)

THE STANDING OF INFORMAL WRITTEN RESOLUTIONS FOLLOWING THE COMPANIES ACT 1989

Section 381A of the Companies Act 1985 (introduced by s 113(1), CA 1989) provides that in relation to private companies, the passing of a resolution in general meeting or at a separate meeting of a specific class of shareholders may be conducted by means of a written resolution. The written resolution takes effect as if agreed by the company in general meeting or by a meeting of the relevant class of members of the company (s 382A, CA 1985). However, unlike a resolution passed by the general meeting, no formal notice requirements are attached to the passing of a written resolution.

A written resolution may be passed by the written assent of those members of the company who, as of the date of the resolution, would have been entitled to attend and vote at a general meeting of the company. Section 381A may be invoked to pass any form of resolution whether ordinary, special, extraordinary or elective. A written resolution is passed when signed by or on behalf of the last voting member of the company to sign.

Section 381A is drafted in a similar but more extensive manner than Table A, Art 53 (discussed above). Indeed, any previous purpose served by Art 53 (in so far as s 381A is more extensive in its scope) would at first sight appear to have been extinguished, other than where a company wished to preserve Art 53 as a more stringent method of passing an informal resolution. For example, unlike Table A, Art 53, s 381A would appear to be applicable even in a situation where a statutory provision is prohibitive of a company passing a resolution otherwise than in general meeting. For instance, the doubts expressed by Nourse J in *Re Barry Artist* appear to have been removed in respect of a private company's ability to pass a written resolution to invoke a reduction of the company's capital. (However, in accordance with s 135, CA 1985, the reduction in capital would still need to be affirmed by the court.)

Section 381A is nevertheless, subject to an exception in the form of Sch 15A, Companies Act 1985 (introduced by s 114, CA 1989). This schedule provides that a written resolution cannot be employed to pass a resolution under s 303 of the Companies Act 1985 (to remove a director) or under s 391 of the Companies Act 1985 (to remove an auditor).

As originally enacted s 381B(1) required a copy of any proposed written resolution to be sent to the company's auditors. Where the resolution concerned the auditors in their capacity as auditors they had an opportunity, within seven days of receiving a copy of the resolution, to give notice to the company to compel it to have the resolution considered by the general meeting or, where appropriate, by a separate meeting of a class of shareholders. A written resolution would not take effect until either the auditors notified the company that the resolution did not concern them or, alternatively, after seven days in a situation where the auditors had failed to notify the company of their intention to seek a general meeting. However, proposals were laid before Parliament in October 1995 with the purpose of simplifying the procedure for written resolutions. The effect of the resulting legislation (SI 1996/1471) is to eradicate the need for proposed resolutions to be sent to a company's auditors.

In respect of some private companies, the removal of the need to call a general meeting to pass a resolution may ease administrative burdens. However, as the majority of private companies are very small concerns, the management of which may often comprise the entire membership of the company, the burden of calling a general meeting may often be no less than organising the implementation of a written resolution, albeit that the written resolution will no longer invoke the administrative burden of having to be sent to the company's auditors. It is interesting to note that in *Re Barry Artist Ltd* [1985] BCLC 283 Nourse J, commenting on a comparison between the convenience of a written resolution and a resolution passed at a general meeting of a small private company, stated:

> 'The practical advantages of procuring all four members to sign one document, as opposed to inviting them to sign consents to short notice of the meeting and the necessary proxy forms and then getting two of them to attend a meeting in the company's offices, must have been marginal, to say the least.' (at p 284)

It is to be noted that s 381C(2) provides that ss 381A and 381B have no effect on any enactment or rule of law as to things done otherwise than by passing a resolution or cases in which a resolution is treated as being passed. However, the 1989 Act, in giving its statutory blessing to written resolutions has created an acceptable class of informal resolution. Indeed, under the common law, the informal unwritten type of unanimous consent agreement and the more radical consent by acquiescence may, in the future, be given a less than sympathetic hearing by the courts.

In accordance with s 380 of the Companies Act 1985, a company is obliged to deliver copies of all elective resolutions and resolutions and agreements of its members which, had they been agreed otherwise than in an informal manner, would only have been effective if passed as special or extraordinary resolutions.

VOTING PROCEDURE

At general meetings the standard procedure for casting votes in favour or against proposed motions is by the members present at the meeting to vote by a show of hands. In effect this means that if, for example, a motion is required to be carried by a special resolution and only 100 members out of a total membership of 1000 turned up to the meeting at which the motion was proposed, then the resolution would be carried by just 75 members voting in its favour. Indeed, it is quite a common feature at meetings of companies with a large membership for resolutions to be passed by but a small percentage of the total membership, albeit that the resolutions are passed in compliance with the prescribed majority of votes.

Irrespective of the numbers of shares held by a member, a member may, in a vote by the show of hands, only cast one vote. However, unlike a vote decided by the show of hands, a poll vote entitles members to cast votes in proportion to the number of voting shares held, i.e. if a member holds 50 shares he would be entitled to cast 50 votes. A poll vote may, if demanded, be taken instead of, or after, a vote by a show of hands. Section 373(1) of the Companies Act 1985 provides that any provision contained within a company's articles which seeks to exclude the right to demand a poll on any matter other than the election of a chairman or, the adjournment of a meeting, will be void (Table A, Art 51 does, by implication, allow for a poll to be taken on the election of a chairman or the adjournment of a meeting). Section 373(1) further provides that any provision contained within a company's articles will be void where it prohibits a poll from being demanded by not less than five members (Table A, Art 46 allows a poll to be demanded by two members or, by a member(s) representing not less than one-tenth of the total voting rights of all the members having the right to vote at the meeting or, member(s) holding shares conferring the right to vote on which an aggregate sum has been paid representing not less in total, than the sum of one-tenth of the company's existing paid up capital on shares conferring the right to vote). Table A, Art 46 further provides that a poll may be demanded by the chairman of the meeting. (Further regulations pertinent to procedural aspects of poll votes are contained in Table A, Arts 48–53.)

Proxies

A proxy is a person appointed by a member of a company to represent the member's voting interests at a general meeting. Section 372(1) of the Companies Act 1985 provides that any member of a company who is entitled to attend and vote at a general meeting may appoint a proxy; the proxy need not himself be a member of the company. Where a proxy is appointed by a member of a private company the proxy may speak at the meeting on the member's behalf. However, a member of a private company cannot appoint more than one proxy to attend a meeting unless the company's articles provide otherwise (s 372(2), CA 1985). It should be noted that Table A, Art 59 does provide otherwise.

A member who appoints a proxy has no statutory right to demand that the proxy vote be counted on a vote conducted by a show of hands. Nevertheless, a person acting as a proxy may, if permitted by the terms of the company's articles (see above), demand that a poll vote be taken on any motion put before the meeting. The legitimacy of the demand will be determined as if made by the member upon whose behalf the proxy acts (s 373(2), CA 1985). As a member's agent, a proxy should vote in accordance with the wishes of his principal, nevertheless, where a proxy acts contrary to his principal's instructions, the votes cast will not normally be discounted unless they were considered crucial to the final outcome of the vote; see e.g. *Oliver v Dalgleish* [1963] 3 All ER 330.

Adjournments

In certain circumstances, the necessity may arise for the chairman of a general meeting to adjourn a meeting. In such a case unfinished matters of business will be postponed to a new date. Table A, Art 45 states as follows:

> 'The chairman may, with the consent of a meeting at which a quorum is present (and shall if so directed by the meeting) adjourn the meeting from time to time and from place to place, but no business shall be transacted at an adjourned meeting other than business which might properly have been transacted at the meeting. When a meeting is adjourned for fourteen days or more, at least seven clear days notice shall be given specifying the time and place of the adjourned meeting and the general nature of the business to be transacted. Otherwise it shall not be necessary to give such notice.'

In exercising the power to adjourn a meeting the chairman must act *bona fide* in the best interests of the company. The decision to adjourn must have been a reasonable one to take in the light of all the relevant circumstances. A meeting must not be adjourned as a means to prevent, delay or handicap the will of the company in general meeting. An example of a chairman's decision to adjourn a meeting which attracted judicial disapproval is to be found in *Byng* v *London Life Association Ltd* [1990] Ch 170. In this case the Court of Appeal considered it impracticable for a chairman to adjourn a meeting for a period of two hours, the meeting having been adjourned to a venue located in a part of London different from the one where the original meeting had taken place (the original meeting was adjourned because the meeting hall was too small). The haste at which the adjourned meeting was rearranged meant that many of the members who attended the original meeting were unable to attend the rescheduled meeting. As a result of the adjournment, a special resolution, which had the support of the board but which had attracted opposition from a faction of the membership, was passed; had the original meeting not been adjourned, the outcome of the vote may have been different. The fact that the meeting was rescheduled at such short notice and at a different venue gave rise to a finding that in the circumstances of the case the chairman's decision had been unreasonable. The vote to secure the resolution was declared invalid.

Minutes

Every company must keep minutes of the proceedings of its general meetings and meetings of its directors. The minutes must be entered into books kept especially for the purpose of recording minutes. Minutes purporting to be signed by the chairman of a meeting or the chairman of the next succeeding meeting are evidence of the fact that the proceedings of the meeting were conducted in a manner as recorded in the minute book (s 382(1), CA 1985). Provided that minutes have been kept and duly signed, then, unless the contrary is proved, a meeting will be regarded as having been duly held and convened and all resolutions passed at the meeting will be deemed to have been validly approved (s 382(4), CA 1985).

Class meetings

A class meeting is held when it is necessary for a class of shareholders to decide a matter which affects their particular class of share. For example, a class meeting of shareholders holding share type X would be held in accordance with s 125 of the Companies Act 1985 in a situation where the company wished to vary the rights of holders of share type X (see Chapter 10). Meetings of a particular class of shareholder are regulated in accordance with the terms of a company's articles. The procedure for conducting class meetings is, on the whole, comparable to the procedure which governs general meetings (s 125(6), CA 1985). The standard quorum required at a class meeting is two persons holding or representing by proxy at least one-third in nominal value of the issued share capital of the class in question (s 125(6)(a), CA 1985).

Suggested further reading

Baxter [1976] JBL 323
Prentice [1977] 40 MLR 587
Xuereb (1985) 6 Co Law 199
Xuereb (1986) 7 Co Law 53
Xuereb (1987) 8 Co Law 16
Baker (1991) 12 Co Law 64
Jaffey (1996) 16 LS 27
Grantham (1998) 55 CLJ 554

19

THE DIVISION OF A COMPANY'S POWERS BETWEEN THE BOARD AND GENERAL MEETING

INTRODUCTION

This chapter seeks to examine the relationship between the board of directors and the general meeting in respect of the policy and decision-making process of a company. The chapter undertakes a brief historical analysis of the division of powers between the two primary organs of the company before moving on to consider the determination and exercise of corporate powers in more modern times. Although earlier chapters of this book have dealt with the individual characteristics and legal responsibilities of both directors and the general meeting, the purpose here is to consider the relationship between the two organs of the company in terms of their respective influence, determination, control and implementation of corporate powers.

THE HISTORICAL DEVELOPMENT OF THE DIVISION OF CORPORATE POWERS

The registered company was born out of the unincorporated partnership businesses of the nineteenth century (see Chapter 1). Therefore, in many respects, it is not surprising that the power structure of the registered company was originally determined in a manner comparable with principles derived from partnership law. As such, the early statutory regulation of the division of corporate powers was ordained in favour of the collective will of a company's membership, i.e. the company in general meeting. A company's board of directors was not, as it now is, considered to be an organ of the company, but was merely appointed to carry out the will of the general meeting. Accordingly, conflicts between the board and general meeting were ordinarily resolved to the latter's advantage. Section 90 of the Companies Clauses Consolidated Act 1845 provided *inter alia* that the exercise of the board's general powers of management should be –

> '... *subject also to the control and regulation of any general meeting specifically convened for the purpose,* but not so as to render invalid any act done by the directors prior to any resolution passed by such general meeting.' (emphasis added)

In *Isle of Wight Rly Co v Tahourdin* (1883) 25 Ch D 320 Cotton LJ emphasised the ultimate dominance of the general meeting. He stated:

> '... If a shareholder complains of the conduct of the directors while they keep within their powers, the court says to him, "If you want to alter the management of the affairs of the company go to the general meeting, and if they agree with you they will pass a resolution obliging the directors to alter their course of proceeding".' (at p 329)

The ability of the general meeting to supervise and if necessary determine corporate policy persisted throughout the nineteenth century. However, the growth and expansion of the corporate form was, with time, to inevitably result in the general meeting's decline in matters of dictating corporate policy. In many companies expansion brought growth both in terms of wealth and membership numbers. Many shareholders invested in companies for potential profit and not for the right to participate in management decisions. In expanding companies the partnership principles on which the corporate form had been founded no longer ruled supreme; membership interest, attendance, and participation at general meetings all declined. This decline was and still is today particularly prevalent in larger companies where commercial reality dictates that the administration of corporate policy demands a consolidation of corporate powers into a centralised body (the board of directors).

THE ARTICLES OF ASSOCIATION AND THE DETERMINATION OF CORPORATE POWER

The decline in the importance of the general meeting as the principal corporate power base has historically been reflected in the reduction in powers afforded to the general meeting by the articles of association. The articles were, and still are considered to this day, to be the dominant factor in determining the division of powers between the board and general meeting. In *Automatic Self-Cleansing Filter Syndicate Co v Cuninghame* [1906] 2 Ch 34 the Court of Appeal recognised that, subject to certain powers reserved to the general meeting by statute, a company's articles were decisive as to the extent of powers to be exercised by both the board and general meeting, i.e. an acceptance of the contractual effect of the articles in accordance with what is now s 14 of the Companies Act 1985. The facts of the *Cuninghame* case were as follows. A dispute arose between the directors and a group of shareholders of a company over the extent of the general meeting's power to substitute the views of the company's board with their own. The general meeting passed an ordinary resolution instructing the company's board of directors to sell the company's undertaking; the directors disapproved of the proposed sale. Article 96 of the company's articles was drafted so as to enable the directors of the company to exercise all corporate powers other than those powers which were expressly reserved to the company in general meeting; subject to such regulations as, from time to time, were made by the general meeting by extraordinary resolution. The company's articles specifically provided that a decision to sell company property was one to be taken by the board of directors.

The Court of Appeal, in upholding the decision of Warrington J, found that Art 96 provided the shareholders with no right to insist that the company's undertaking be sold in accordance with the resolution which had been passed at general meeting. In giving effect to the terms of the company's articles, the court held that an alteration of directors' powers, in accordance with Art 96, could only take place by the passing of an extraordinary resolution.

Following the decision of the Court of Appeal in *Cuninghame*, the determination of the division of corporate powers has continued to be determined by the construction of the terms of a company's articles. However, prior to the adoption of the current Table A, Art 70 (discussed below), the construction of the standard form Table A articles was the source of much controversy. For example, the 1948 Companies Act Table A, Art 80 (previous Table A articles dealing with a division of powers were written in a similar vein to Art 80) provided that:

> 'The business of the company shall be managed by the directors, and [they] may exercise all such powers of the company as are not by the Companies [legislation] or by these regulations, required to be exercised by the company in general meeting, subject, nevertheless ... to such regulations being not inconsistent with the aforesaid regulations or provisions, as may be prescribed by the company in general meeting; but no regulation made by the company in general meeting shall invalidate any prior act of the directors which would have been valid if that regulation had not been made.'

(It should be noted that a company incorporated prior to the implementation of the Companies Act 1985, which adopted Table A articles will still (unless the articles have been altered) have articles based upon the 1948 Table A articles.)

Prima facie, the wording of Art 80 was ambiguous. It permitted conflicts appertaining to the division of corporate powers to be resolved by the general meeting, in so far as it provided that the company's directors were to manage the company but subject to any contrary regulations passed by the company in general meeting. Indeed, to some extent, the first-instance decision of Neville J in *Marshall's Valve Gear Co Ltd v Manning, Wardle & Co Ltd* [1909] 1 Ch 267 was supportive of the view that the general meeting had ultimate authority over the board in a situation of conflict. In *Marshall's* case the court permitted a majority shareholder to commence litigation in the name of the company despite the refusal of a majority of the board to sanction the litigation. The relevant article of the company which determined the division of powers between the board and general meeting was drafted in a similar vein to 1948 Table A, Art 80.

Neville J's interpretation of the Art 80 type of provision suggested that the general meeting's power to interfere with management powers of the board, powers contained in the company's articles, was one untouched by the statutory prescribed method for the alteration of articles, i.e. by special resolution.

Accordingly, in a situation of conflict between the general meeting and the board the court's ruling in *Marshall* was indicative of the view that the Art 80 type of provision provided the general meeting with a power, by ordinary resolution, to effect a temporary change to the board's powers, as opposed to a permanent change in those powers, in so far as to effect a permanent change the company would have had to alter its articles.

Nevertheless, it is suggested that a contrary explanation of the court's finding in *Marshall's* case may be found in the fact that the litigation in question was concerned with a matter in which a majority of the directors had a personal interest. As such, it could be contended (though this explanation was not alluded to by Neville J) that the personal-interest factor raised a presumption that the board, in declining to commence litigation, had acted otherwise than in the best interests of the company. It would therefore have followed, in accordance with principles related to the rule in *Foss v Harbottle* (1843) 2 Hare 461 (discussed in Chapter 22), that it was possible for the majority shareholder (providing the resolution to litigate was sanctioned by the company in general meeting) to commence litigation in the name of the company without the need to seek the approval of the board.

Indeed, in subsequent cases which have dealt with the interpretation of Art 80, the courts have been unwilling to accept that the general meeting have the right to interfere in the board's management powers by passing an ordinary resolution to effect an alteration in the board's corporate policy; see e.g. *Quinn & Axtens v Salmon* [1909] 1 Ch 311, *John Shaw & Sons (Salford) Ltd v Shaw* [1935] 2 KB 113 and *Scott v Scott* [1943] 1 All ER 582.

A more recent example is provided by *Breckland Group Holdings Ltd v London and Suffolk Properties* [1989] BCLC 100. Here a company, (C), had two corporate members: company A (the majority shareholder) and company B. The board of C included two directors appointed by A and one director appointed by B. The corporate members agreed by a formal shareholders' agreement that should C wish to commence any form of litigation the matter would first require the approval of one director from both A and B. In contravention of this agreement, C commenced litigation with the support of A (the majority shareholder). B moved to restrain the action from being commenced in C's name. In denying that A, as the majority shareholder, had a right to overturn the powers properly vested in the board of C, the court refused to accept that had a general meeting of C been convened to 'rubber stamp' A's decision to commence litigation, the general meeting's authorisation would have been capable of overturning the powers properly vested in the board. The court restrained proceedings until a properly held board meeting could decide the matter, i.e. whether or not C should commence litigation.

An interesting, although collateral point arising from this case was whether or not the final decision of the board had to be taken in accordance with the terms of the shareholder agreement. In his judgment Harman J did not expressly adjudicate on this matter, but his lordship did appear to presume that the shareholder agreement would have been binding. If so, had the majority of the board voted in favour of litigation (company A through its nominees held a majority of the directorships in the company), the decision of the majority would have been overridden by the terms of the shareholder agreement. In effect, the shareholder agreement would have restricted the powers of the board, despite the fact that in a strict sense, the board, as an organ of the company, was not a party to it. Although the articles of a company bind the membership and the company in a form of contractual agreement, it is surely wrong to assume that the board, acting as an organ of the company, should be bound by the terms of a shareholder agreement. Although individual members of the board can, as members of the company, be bound by such an agreement, they should not be so bound when acting in a capacity other than as members of the company. (Shareholder agreements are discussed further in Chapter 11.)

While the courts, in construing 1948 Table A, Art 80 have, with the exception of *Marshall's* case, positively denied that Art 80 is permissive of the general meeting's right by ordinary resolution to regulate the management of a company in instances of conflict with the board of directors, it should be noted that where a company's board has been unable to carry out its management functions, for example, where directors have been unable to reach a decision because of deadlock or lack of a competent quorum, the courts have been willing to permit the general meeting to act for them; see e.g. *Barron v Potter* [1914] 1 Ch 895 and *Foster v Foster* [1916] 1 Ch 352.

A compelling reason for denying the general meeting the power, by ordinary resolution, to regulate the management of a company is that to do so would be allow it to alter the powers afforded to directors (as contained in the articles) other than in a manner normally associated with an ability to alter a company's articles, i.e. by a special resolution (s 9, CA 1985). As Greer LJ stated in *John Shaw & Sons (Salford) Ltd v Shaw* [1935] 2 KB 113:

> 'If the powers of management are vested in the directors, they and they alone can exercise these powers. The only way in which the general body of the shareholders can control the exercise of the powers vested by the articles in the directors is by altering their articles.' (at p 134)

Indeed, it may even be possible to contend that Art 80 merely endorses the statutory requirement that an alteration of the board's powers must take place by means of a special resolution. Article 80 provides that where there is inconsistency between the views of the general meeting and the board, in order for the views of the general meeting to prevail, regulations to remove the board's powers must be prescribed. If in construing Art 80 the term 'regulations' is simply interpreted to mean 'articles' (this interpretation is quite possible in that Table A articles are, in the context of companies legislation, referred to as 'Table A Regulations'), then an alteration of the regulations (articles) may only be effected by means of a special resolution.

1985 Table A, Art 70

In respect of the current 1985 Table A articles, Art 70 provides that the general meeting is afforded a power to effect a temporary change in directors' powers, albeit that the temporary change of power must be exercised by special resolution. Article 70 states:

> 'Subject to the provisions of the Act and the memorandum and the articles and to any directions given by special resolution the business of the company shall be managed by the directors who may exercise all the powers of the company. No alteration of the memorandum or articles and no such direction shall invalidate any prior act of the directors which would have been valid if that alteration had not been given.'

Therefore, Table A, Art 70 empowers the general meeting, by direction, to regulate management affairs properly vested in the directors without the need to formally adopt a resolution to alter the articles. By specifying the need for a special resolution, Table A, Art 70 removes the controversy which had previously surrounded the general meeting's capacity to regulate management powers by the passing of an ordinary resolution.

POWERS OF MANAGEMENT SPECIFICALLY RESERVED TO THE GENERAL MEETING

The articles of most companies are drafted in line with the standard Table A articles so as to confer powers of management on the board of directors. Nevertheless, the articles of a company will normally reserve limited powers of management to the general meeting. For example, Table A provides that the election of directors (Art 78), the remuneration of directors (Art 82) and the declaration of dividends up to an amount recommended by the directors (Art 102) are powers to be reserved to the general meeting.

The Companies Act 1985 also reserves certain exclusive powers of management to the general meeting. The powers reserved are few, but are nevertheless quite substantive, being concerned with the constitutional functioning of the company. For example, a company must, in order to alter its principal constitutional documents, i.e. the memorandum (s 4, CA 1985) and the articles (s 9, CA 1985) seek a special resolution of the general meeting. Also, a company, if permitted to do so by its articles, may only alter its share capital clause contained within the memorandum, by an ordinary resolution of the general meeting (s 121, CA 1985).

In addition to the aforementioned powers of management, the general meeting also has the right, by ordinary resolution, to remove any director from office. This power is of some significance because where members of a company disagree with their board's management policy they may, if they command sufficient support, either threaten the directors with dismissal or, if that tactic fails, actually enforce s 303 of the Companies Act 1985, i.e. remove the directors from office. The power of the general meeting in respect of s 303 is in theory a very important one. However, in practice, its importance may be overestimated, especially in a situation where a director is able to directly or indirectly control a bare majority of the membership. Nevertheless, in the hands of an effective and independent membership possessing sufficient support, s 303 provides an indirect means to challenge the management policy of the directors in a manner which exceeds the powers given to the general meeting by the articles of association.

THE DUTY OF THE GENERAL MEETING TO ACT FOR THE BENEFIT OF THE COMPANY AS A WHOLE

In exercising its limited powers of management, the general meeting is under a similar obligation to company directors in so far as the general meeting must also apply its powers for the benefit of the company as a whole. In any given situation, the test to determine whether the general meeting acted for the benefit of the company as whole may, by analogy with the duties owed to a company by its directors, be said to be dominated by an objective consideration of whether the general meeting's powers were exercised for a proper purpose. However, the interpretation of the test is one which has at times been clouded in some confusion. The confusion over the 'benefit of the company' test as applied to the exercise of corporate powers by the general meeting was most evident in the case of *Clemens* v *Clemens Bros Ltd* [1976] 2 All ER 268.

The facts of the *Clemens* case were as follows. The company, Clemens Bros Ltd (C), was a small domestic concern. Its share capital was divided between Miss Clemens (M) and her niece (N). M held 55 per cent of the shares and N the remaining 45 per cent. M was one of five directors; the other four directors were not shareholders in the company. The board of directors proposed a new share issue, the substance of the issue was to create an employee share scheme and also to allow the four non-shareholding directors to hold a small minority of the company's shares. The effect of the new share issue would have been to reduce M's shareholding interest in C to below 50 per cent, N's holding would have been reduced to below 25 per cent.

M exercised her voting control to pass the new share issue. N objected on the premise that as a result of the new share issue, the income which she derived from dividend payments would be reduced. In addition, and perhaps of more importance in terms of the outcome of the case, N's proposed new holding of less than 25 per cent would have resulted in the loss of her negative control in C, i.e. she would have been unable to prevent (had she so wished) the passing of a special resolution. The loss of N's negative control was an advantage to M because prior to the new share issue N and M had a very poor working relationship.

Foster J, in finding in favour of N's minority action, held that M's majority voting control could not be exercised without reference to whether such votes had been exercised for the benefit of the company as a whole. His lordship took the view that M's motive in assenting to the resolution was primarily aimed at removing N's voting influence in the company and not by a desire to benefit the company's employees and four non-voting directors. Therefore, his lordship concluded that M had not acted for the benefit of the company as a whole but for her own selfish interests.

Although the actual outcome of the case may be defended, it is nevertheless impossible to decipher the precise principle of law on which the interpretation of the test applied to the 'benefit of the company as a whole' was reached. Foster J was content to leave the reasoning for his decision wrapped up in a number of principles, or, as he put it:

> 'I think that one thing which emerges from the case to which I have referred is that in such a case as the present Miss Clemens is not entitled to exercise her majority vote in whatever way she pleases. The difficulty is in finding a principle, and obviously expressions such as "bona fide for the benefit of the company as a whole", "fraud on a minority" and "oppressive" do not assist in formulating a principle.' (at p 282)

The decision taken in *Clemens* in relation to the interpretation of 'the benefit of the company as a whole' is difficult to rationalise in terms of anything other than having been decided on purely equitable considerations. However, was justice really served? Was Miss Clemens' act a purely selfish one? If one objectively considers the effect of the new share issue, it is to be observed that M would have lost her majority control in the company. In addition, M's income from dividend payments would also have been reduced. Indeed, the contention that M acted for her own selfish interests may have been somewhat overstated.

In addition to considering the interests of minority shareholders, a power reserved to the general meeting must not be used where its effect would be to defraud or seriously prejudice creditors (by analogy, directors of a company, in considering the interests of the company as a whole, may be obliged to consider the interests of creditors). A case example which illustrates that the general meeting's use of its powers must take account of the interests of creditors, in so far as corporate creditors may fall within the interests expressed within the concept of the company as a whole, is the case of *Re Halt Garage* [1982] 3 All ER 1016. Here the court was called upon to determine the question of whether a company's membership, comprised of a husband and wife team, both of whom also held directorships in the company, had, in authorising remuneration payments to themselves as directors, awarded payments which were in reality gratuitous distributions out of capital dressed up as remuneration. The company, which had been put into liquidation, sought through its liquidator the return of remuneration payments over a period of three years.

In determining whether the shareholders had authorised remuneration payments in a manner consistent with a proper exercise of that power, Oliver J formulated the following test:

> '... I think that in circumstances such as exist in this case where payments are made under the authority of a general meeting acting pursuant to an express

power, the matter falls to be tested by reference to the genuineness and honesty of the transaction rather than reference to some abstract standard of benefit ... As it seems to me, the submission of counsel for the respondents involves the notion that where there is a purported exercise of an express power by a general meeting the court is a slave to whatever form of words the members may have chosen to use in the resolution which they may pass. I do not think that can be so. I agree with counsel for the liquidator that it cannot be right that shareholder directors acting in unison can draw any sum they like out of the company's capital and leave the liquidator and the company's creditors without remedy in the absence of proof of intent to defraud because they choose to dignify the drawing with a particular description ... the court is not, in my judgement, precluded from examining the true nature of the payments merely because the members choose to call them remuneration.' (at p 1043)

In applying the above test to the facts of the case, Oliver J concluded that while there was no evidence of the husband's level of takings being excessive or unreasonable the level of takings paid to the wife, had been unreasonably high. The wife had ceased to be active in the company during the period over which the complaint related. Although the company's articles included a power to award remuneration for the mere assumption of the office of director, Oliver J was of the opinion that the awards made to the wife were so out of proportion to any possible value attributable to her holding office that the court was justified in not treating them as genuine payments of remuneration but, rather, as dressed-up dividends out of capital. Accordingly it was held that the payments to the wife had been invalidly authorised by the general meeting.

The general meeting's ability to ratify an irregular act of the directors

Where a company director commits a breach of duty or exceeds his authority in exercising a management power, the irregular act will, in most instances, be voidable. The general meeting may ratify the irregular act, usually by an ordinary resolution. An irregular act will be capable of ratification if the general meeting acts for the benefit of the company as a whole, i.e. without instigating a fraud on minority shareholders. (Fraud on the minority is discussed in Chapter 22.)

Where an irregular act of the directors is liable to cause damage to creditor interests, any purported ratification of the act by the general meeting may be set aside in circumstances which indicate that the general meeting acted without honestly considering the question of whether it was fair and proper to ratify the act; see e.g. the *obiter* comments of Cumming-Bruce and Templeman LJJ in *Re Horsley & Weight Ltd* [1982] 3 All ER 1045. (By analogy see *Re Halt Garage* (above), a case concerned with the exercise of a general meeting's power to award directors' remuneration.)

Although directors are not permitted to exercise powers which, are by the terms of a company's articles, vested in the general meeting, should such a usurpation of a power occur, the general meeting may nevertheless ratify the abuse of power by ordinary resolution, regardless of the fact that had the power been properly exercised by the general meeting its exercise would have required a special resolution; see e.g. *Grant* v *United Kingdom Switchback Railways Co* (1888) 40 Ch D 135. While, in such a case, the general meeting's power to ratify by ordinary resolution would appear to be contradictory to the terms of the company's articles, in reality the power affects the approval of an unauthorised act as opposed to an unconstitutional attempt to alter the terms of the company's articles, i.e. ratification does not confer future powers on the directors, whereas an alteration of the articles would of course have a permanent effect. Where, however, an ordinary resolution of the general meeting purports to ratify an irregular act which would have contravened the terms of a company's articles, then in such a case, the general meeting's attempted ratification would be invalid. For example, in *Boschoek Proprietary Co Ltd* v *Fuke* [1906] 1 Ch 148 the directors of a company appointed a managing director at a level of remuneration in excess of the amount specified in the company's articles and also in contravention of a share qualification clause. The appointment was purportedly ratified by the general meeting. The court, in finding that the appointment was invalid concluded that the general meeting could not of itself have appointed or ratified the terms of the appointment in contravention of the terms of the articles. The articles, until altered, bound the membership in the same manner as they bound the board of directors.

FUTURE REFORM

The EC Draft Fifth Directive

Under Art 12 of the Draft Fifth Directive (for a general discussion on the Draft Fifth Directive see Chapter 5), it is proposed that the management board of a company should first seek the approval of the supervisory board (or equivalent representatives under a one-tier system) prior to a management board's decision in relation to the following matters:

- the closure or reallocation of the company;
- major cut-backs or expansions in the company;
- major changes in the organisation of the company; or
- the company's establishment or termination of long-term co-operation agreements with other enterprises.

The draft Directive also makes provision for the supervisory board to have the power to dismiss members of the management board. As previously discussed (see Chapter 5), it is to be observed that the membership of the supervisory body is (whichever method of appointing the body is adopted) to comprise a significant proportion of members appointed in accordance with the wishes of the general meeting. It is apparent that should the draft Directive be implemented in its present form, the general meeting will gain a more authoritative role in some of the major managerial decisions of companies.

Suggested further reading

Goldberg (1970) 33 MLR 177
Sullivan (1977) 93 LQR 569
Mackenzie (1983) 4 Co Law 99

20

A DIRECTOR'S PERSONAL LIABILITY TO CONTRIBUTE TOWARDS THE DEBTS AND LIABILITIES OF THE COMPANY

INTRODUCTION

Although the separate legal identity of a limited liability company (discussed in Chapter 2) ordinarily divorces the company's interests and responsibilities from its membership and management, a member/director of a company may nevertheless be deemed to be responsible for the repayment of a corporate debt in circumstances where the member/director gave a personal undertaking to repay the said debt. Further, the corporate veil may, in accordance with an appropriate statutory provision, be disturbed, with the effect that a director may be made personally liable to discharge a particular liability of the company or, alternatively, be made liable to contribute towards the company's assets. Where a statutory provision seeks to disturb the corporate veil, its effect will not normally deny the existence of the corporate entity but will primarily be aimed at penalising company directors for some form of corporate malpractice.

THE LIABILITY OF A DIRECTOR FOR PERSONAL UNDERTAKINGS

Although the corporate veil will, in circumstances where a director acted in accordance with his designated authority, usually shield the director from the incursion of personal liability, a director's immunity from the imposition of personal liability will not be safeguarded where he undertook a collateral and personal obligation on behalf of the company, notwithstanding that the undertaking was instigated to benefit the company. For example, in circumstances where the assets of a company are insufficient to secure corporate liabilities, a director may be obliged to enter into a contractual obligation to personally guarantee the repayment of the company's debts.

A binding contractual agreement to guarantee a corporate debt may also be found in the guise of a letter of comfort. A letter of comfort may take the form of a personal assurance from a director of a company whereby he personally promises that a corporate debt will be met. Where, in reliance on the terms of the letter, its recipient alters his position in respect of a right to enforce the debt, that reliance may amount to consideration, thereby in law substantiating the creditor's right to enforce the director's promise that the debt will be met; see e.g. *Edwards v Skyways* [1964] 1 All ER 494.

A director of a company will also be personally liable on any contract which he entered into on behalf of the company at a time prior to the company's incorporation (discussed in Chapter 3). Although a pre-incorporation contract may be for the future benefit of a company, until the company is incorporated, it can have no legal existence and therefore cannot be bound by contracts made in its name or on its behalf. Even after its incorporation, a company cannot expressly or by conduct retrospectively ratify or adopt a contract made in its name or on its behalf.

A DIRECTOR'S LIABILITY UNDER SPECIFIC PROVISIONS OF THE COMPANIES ACT 1985

Section 117 of the CA 1985

When applicable, this provision disturbs the corporate veil by imposing a liability on the directors of a public company. The section provides that if the directors of a public company enter into a transaction prior to receiving a trading certificate from the Companies Registrar (the certificate confirms that the Registrar is satisfied that the nominal value of the company's allotted share capital is not less than the authorised minimum of £50 000), the directors concerned may be held personally liable for the transaction if the company fails to meet its liability within 21 days from being called to do so.

Section 349(4) of the CA 1985

An officer of a company or other authorised person acting on behalf of a company may incur personal liability in accordance with s 349(4) of the Companies Act 1985. This section is of some practical importance and is not restricted to public companies. The section provides that where an officer of a company or a person acting on the company's behalf signs or authorises the signature of any bill of exchange, promissory note, endorsement, cheque or order for money or goods without reference on the document concerned to the company's correct and full name, then, unless the company agrees to discharge the liability, the officer or authorised person in question may be made personally liable for the amount specified on the document. The section also imposes criminal liability in the form of a fine. Section 349(4) imposes a strict form of liability.

The historical roots of s 349(4) may be traced back to s 31 of the Joint Stock Companies Act 1856, a provision which sought to counter the potential danger which followed on from the birth of the registered company and the benefits of limited liability, i.e. with the creation of the limited company, it became increasingly important for a third party in advancing credit or goods to be aware that if the business was an incorporated concern then any monetary obligation owed by the business could be put at risk, should the limited company fall into a state of insolvency. However, the protection afforded by s 349(4) is more extensive than merely imposing personal liability for omitting to include the limited liability status of the company, in so far as the provision is drafted in such a way that any error in the representation of the linguistic characteristics of a company's name may give rise to the implementation of the section; see e.g. *Atkin & Co v Wardle* (1889) 61 LT 23. Indeed, s 349(4) and its earlier statutory reincarnations have been exposed to a strict and arbitrary application. Accordingly, even small variations in the representation of a company's name have proved fatal to an officer of a company in his attempt to escape the rigours of the provision. The judicial obedience to an austere construction of the statutory provision is such that an officer of a company, having incorrectly represented the company's name on an instrument, may not seek, in an attempt to avoid the liability imposed by the provision, reliance on the fact that the instrument did not in any way cause its recipient any confusion in respect to the company's true identity.

Judicial support for a more flexible and less onerous interpretation of s 349(4) has found little favour, albeit that the provision has given way to some imaginative attempts to curtail its application. For example, in *Durham Fancy Goods Ltd v Michael Jackson (Fancy Goods) Ltd* [1968] 2 QB 839 Donaldson J avoided applying the section by advancing the equitable remedies of promissory estoppel and rectification to case facts which, with respect, did not justify the attention of either of the equitable doctrines. A more recent example of a flexible approach to the construction of the section is to be found in *Jenice Ltd v Dan* [1993] BCLC 1349. Here the plaintiffs commenced actions under s 349(4) in respect of five cheques which had been signed by a director of Primekeen Ltd, but which incorrectly represented the company's name as PRIM-KEEN Ltd, i.e. the representation of the company's name omitted the letter 'E' so that the first part of the company's name read 'PRIM' instead of 'PRIME'.

According to Titheridge QC (sitting as a deputy High Court judge), common sense dictated that the spelling error's effect caused no confusion in relation to the identity of the company, thus precluding a finding that the company's name had been identified other than in accordance with s 349(4). Somewhat surprisingly, the learned deputy judge opined that his common-sense approach was not inconsistent or overshadowed by any binding precedent which obliged him to find in favour of the plaintiffs. Although Titheridge QC accepted that s 349(4) should, in accordance with accepted judicial practice, be construed strictly, he nevertheless found that the degree and extent of the error in the case before him did not prevent the company's name, as identified in the cheque, from meeting the primary requirement of s 349(4), namely, that the company's name was properly mentioned on the cheque.

Despite an apparent common-sense logic which flows from the conclusions drawn by Titheridge QC, the belief that an omission of one letter or the misplacing of two letters in the name of a company should not give rise to a successful action under s 349(4), in circumstances where the error was incapable of causing confusion, is clearly inconsistent with the accepted judicial interpretation of the section. Indeed, the most recent Court of Appeal decisions on the interpretation of the section – *Blum* v *OCP Reparation* [1988] BCLC 170 and *Lindholst & Co* v *Fowler* [1988] BCLC 166 – indicate that it is extraneous to consider whether an error in the company's name was liable to cause confusion.

A DIRECTOR'S LIABILITY UNDER SPECIFIC PROVISIONS OF THE INSOLVENCY ACT 1986

One of the most serious attempts to safeguard the interests of corporate creditors is provided by the statutory obligations placed upon directors and officers of a company in respect of their potential personal liability for the debts and liabilities of the company, following the company's slide into a state of insolvency. In accordance with the statutory provisions discussed below, a company may be viewed to be insolvent in a situation where its liabilities exceed its assets (see s 123(2), IA 1986). In calculating liabilities, contingent and prospective liabilities are taken into account. Directors and other officers of the company may be made personally liable to contribute towards the company's liabilities and debts under the following statutory provisions.

Section 212 of the Insolvency Act 1986 (misfeasance proceedings)

Where a company is in liquidation, s 212 of the Insolvency Act 1986 allows the court, on the application of the official receiver, liquidator or any creditor or contributory (member), to examine the conduct of any promoter or officer of the company, liquidator, administrator or administrative receiver of the company in respect of an alleged misfeasance, i.e. the misapplication of moneys or property belonging to the company, or company creditors. Following the examination, the court may order that the person responsible for any misapplication of corporate funds should:

(a) repay, restore or account for the money or property or any part of it with interest, at such rate as the court thinks just; or
(b) contribute such a sum to the company's assets by way of compensation in respect of the misfeasance or breach of fiduciary or other duty as the court thinks just.

Section 212 is a procedural device and provides a summary remedy whereby persons who were involved in the management of a company may be held accountable for any breach of duty or other act of misfeasance. Accordingly, proceedings under s 212 may only be pursued where, prior to a company's liquidation, the misconduct which formed the subject matter of the misfeasance claim, was capable of being made the subject of an action by the company. Further, as a prerequisite to successfully pursuing a misfeasance claim, the applicant must establish that the breach of duty or other act of misfeasance resulted in a pecuniary loss to the company. Pecuniary loss, however, is defined in wide terms so that an action under s 212 may still be sustained even in a situation where the company suffered no accountable financial loss, for example, in a situation where a director exploited his position to obtain a secret profit; see e.g. *Regal (Hastings) Ltd* v *Gulliver* [1942] 1 All ER 378, [1967] 2 AC 134 (this case is discussed further in Chapter 17).

Under s 212, misfeasance proceedings may be commenced in circumstances where a director is in breach of any of his corporate duties. In accordance with the decision of Hoffmann LJ in *Re D'Jan of London Ltd* [1993] BCC 646, the term 'any duty' is indicative of the provision's applicability to both a breach of fiduciary duty and a breach of a director's duty of care (directors' duties are discussed in Chapter 17).

A potential difficulty in implementing s 212 may arise in circumstances where, prior to a company's liquidation, a breach of duty or other act of misfeasance was ratified by the company's general meeting. Other than where the director's wrongful act results in a fraud on the company (discussed in Chapter 21), ratification will ordinarily excuse the delinquent director from the incursion of any personal liability incurred as a consequence of the wrongful act. However, in circumstances where the ratification of the breach of duty or other act of misfeasance occurred at a time when the company was insolvent, that is, at a time when creditor interests were paramount, the effectiveness of ratification may be questioned. Where a company is insolvent, the interests of the company's creditors will effectively override the interests of its shareholders in so far as the latter's financial interest in the company will be superseded by the former's expectation of participating in the liquidation of the company's assets. The effectiveness of ratification will be particularly dubious in a situation where the alleged wrong occurred at a time when the company's liquidation was an inescapable certainty; see *West Mercia Safetywear Ltd* v *Dodd* [1988] BCLC 250.

Section 213 of the Insolvency Act 1986 (fraudulent trading)

Section 213 of the Insolvency Act 1986 purports to impose a civil liability for acts of fraudulent trading. Fraudulent trading is also a criminal offence; the offence is governed by s 458 of the Companies Act 1985. The constituent elements of both provisions are virtually identical, indeed the distinction between the civil law and criminal law provisions are primarily of a procedural nature.

In accordance with s 213, if in the course of a winding up of a company it appears to the liquidator that the company carried on business with the intent to defraud its creditors or creditors of any other person, or for any fraudulent purpose, the liquidator may apply to the court for an order that those responsible should, where they were knowing parties to the carrying on of the business, be liable to make such contributions to the company's assets as the court sees fit.

Fraudulent trading will be established in a situation where a person, fully aware that the company had no reasonable prospect of being able to pay its debts, nevertheless allowed the company to carry on its business. The carrying on of business may include a single transaction designed to defraud a single creditor; see e.g. *Re Gerald Cooper Chemicals Ltd* [1978] Ch 262. Although s 213 is primarily aimed at protecting the interests of corporate creditors, it may also cover a fraudulent act committed against persons other than creditors of a company, for example, a customer of the company; see e.g. *Re Cyona Distributors Ltd* [1967] Ch 889.

In determining whether a company was privy to an act of fraudulent trading, the court will assess the nature and degree of the alleged fraudulent conduct in respect of the company's present and potential capacity to repay its debts. In *Re William C Leitch Bros Ltd* [1932] 2 Ch 71 Maugham J stated:

> '**If a company continues to carry on business and to incur debts at a time when there is to the knowledge of the directors no reasonable prospect of the creditors ever receiving payment of those debts, it is, in general, a proper inference that the company is carrying on business with intent to defraud.**' (at p 77)

For a person to incur liability for fraudulent trading, it must first be established that he was knowingly a party to the carrying on of the company's business. The courts have construed this requirement as indicative of a person's active involvement in the commission of an act of fraudulent trading. Although fraudulent trading may be committed by any person who was actively involved in the commission of the fraud (see e.g. *Re Gerald Cooper Chemicals Ltd* [1978] Ch 262), in practice, liability will ordinary fall on a person who is construed to have been actively involved in the management of a company's affairs. It must be established that the person knowingly participated in the carrying on of a company's business with an intention to defraud creditors of the company or creditors of any other person, or for any fraudulent purpose.

In seeking to prove that a person intended to commit the fraudulent act, it is unnecessary to establish that, as a consequence of the fraud, the object of the fraudulent trading suffered any actual economic loss. The essential requirement of the provision is, quite simply, to establish that there was an intention to perpetrate the fraudulent act, an intention which must be established by proving that the person was dishonest; dishonesty is an essential constituent of establishing any type of fraudulent conduct; see e.g. the comments of the House of Lords in *Welham* v *DPP* [1961] AC 103.

In accordance with s 213 of the Insolvency Act 1986, a person's dishonesty will be ascertained on the basis of whether, at the time of the incursion of a corporate debt, he was aware that the debt would not be met on the date it was due or shortly after that date; see e.g. *Re Patrick Lyon Ltd* [1933] 1 Ch 786. In determining whether a person's participation in the fraudulent trading activities of a company was of a dishonest nature, the courts will employ a subjective test to determine the state of mind of the respondent at the time of the alleged fraudulent trading. Although a person's culpability for fraudulent trading will be dependent upon whether he formed an intention to commit the fraudulent act, the definition of an intention to defraud has been stretched to the point whereby, in reality, it resembles a test based upon recklessness, albeit that recklessness will be measured in a subjective as opposed to an objective sense; see e.g. *R v Grantham* [1984] QB 675.

Where a person is found to be liable for fraudulent trading under s 213, that person may be made to make such contributions (if any) to the company's assets as the court thinks proper. Notwithstanding that the fraudulent trading activities of a company may have predominantly caused damage to an individual creditor, any contribution which the court orders to be paid will be allocated to discharge the collective debts of the company's unsecured creditors.

Section 214 of the Insolvency Act (wrongful trading)

The difficulties encountered in establishing 'an intent to defraud', for the purposes of establishing a case of fraudulent trading, led the Cork Committee 1982 (Cmnd 8558) to recommend the introduction of a new provision under which civil liability would arise in a much broader context. The recommendations of the Cork Committee were enacted, in part, in the form of s 214, IA 1986.

As with the fraudulent trading provision, s 214 only applies where a company is in liquidation, however, unlike s 213, s 214 only purports to impose liability on company directors (or shadow directors). In accordance with s 214, a director of a company in insolvent liquidation may incur a personal responsibility for the repayment of corporate debts in circumstances where the director allowed the company to continue to trade, at a date up to the commencement of the company's winding up, when he knew or ought to have concluded that there was no reasonable prospect of the company being able to avoid insolvent liquidation. Any contribution is paid to the company's unsecured creditors. Section 214 therefore seeks to prevent an abuse of the corporate form and also aims to protect the interests of unsecured creditors.

In determining whether a director ought to have been aware that there was no reasonable prospect of the company avoiding liquidation, s 214(4) provides that:

> '... the facts which a director of a company ought to know or ascertain, the conclusions which he ought to reach and the steps which he ought to take are those which would be known or ascertained, or reached or taken, by a reasonably diligent person having both –
>
> (a) the general knowledge, skill and experience that may reasonably be expected of a person carrying out the same functions as those which were carried out by that director in relation to the company, and *O*
>
> (b) the general knowledge, skill and experience of the director.' *S*

For a court to reach the conclusion that a director ought to have been aware that there was no reasonable prospect of the company avoiding liquidation, the liquidator must establish that the director's expectation of the company's ability to halt its decline into liquidation was unreasonable. Accordingly, a director's expectation of the company's future survival, based solely upon business instinct and which is speculative in its nature, will be viewed with much caution, whereas an expectation based upon factual evidence, indicative of a possible reversal in the company's fortunes, will be more apt in convincing the court that the company had a reasonable prospect of avoiding liquidation.

In the first reported case in which s 214 was considered, namely, *Re Produce Marketing Consortium Ltd* [1989] 5 BCC 569, Knox J construed s 214(4) in the following manner:

> 'The facts which the [directors] ought to have known or ascertained and the conclusions that they ought to have reached are not limited to those which they themselves, showing reasonable diligence and having the general knowledge, skill and experience which they respectfully had, would have known, ascertained or reached, but also those that a person with the general knowledge skill and experience of someone carrying out their functions would have known, ascertained or reached.' (at p 593)

This interpretation confirms the importance of considering both the subjective and objective elements of the section. However, although s 214(4)(b) creates a flexible standard against which a director's awareness of a company's pending liquidation should be measured, it does not permit a purely subjective consideration of whether an individual director (at whatever level of skill or experience) was himself, justified in believing (albeit mistakenly) that the company would have a reasonable prospect of avoiding liquidation. The particular level of skill, knowledge and experience attributable to any given director must, in effect, always be viewed through the eyes of and in accordance with the expectations of the reasonably diligent person. However, in some circumstances, the subjective nature of s 214(4)(b) may be permissive of different levels of competency against which the standards of company directors may be gauged. For example, in *Re Produce Marketing Consortium Ltd* Knox J, commenting on the effect of s 214(4)(b), stated that:

> '... the general knowledge, skill and experience postulated will be much less extensive in a small company in a modest way of business, with simple accounting procedures and equipment, than it will be in a large company with sophisticated procedures.' (at pp 594–5)

Liability under s 214 may be avoided in circumstances where the s 214(3) defence is satisfied. The defence will be established where the court is convinced that the director, on first becoming aware that there was no reasonable prospect of the company avoiding liquidation, took every step with a view to minimising the potential loss to the company's creditors. In pleading the defence, a director will be assessed by applying the reasonable diligent person test provided by s 214(4). Therefore, to satisfy the s 214(3) defence, the court must be persuaded that a reasonable diligent person, imputed with the director's own skill, experience and knowledge, following his realisation that there was no reasonable prospect of the company avoiding liquidation and in seeking to minimise the loss to corporate creditors, would have been unable to take any further steps other than those that had actually been taken by the respondent director.

In the absence of any detailed judicial pronouncements on the scope and the requirements for establishing the s 214(3) defence, its potential application remains uncertain. However, for a director to convince the court that he took every step to safeguard the interests of creditors, it is patently obvious that he will ordinarily be required to establish that his participation in the company's affairs was, as from the date upon which he realised that there was no reasonable prospect of the company avoiding liquidation, both active and geared to the protection of the interests of corporate creditors. The taking of all possible steps may include, for example, seeking professional legal and accounting advice, meetings with creditors to rearrange payment facilities and regular board meetings and minutes to establish the management's efforts to minimise losses to creditors.

Although evidence which supports a director's claim to have taken every step to safeguard creditors' interests will be more readily found from the director's continued and active participation in the affairs of the company, in exceptional cases, it may be possible to establish that a director's resignation from office was the final and only step available for the director to take, for example, in circumstances where the resignation followed a prolonged but unsuccessful attempt on the part of the director to convince the board of its folly in pursuing a course of action.

Where the court finds that a director was a party to wrongful trading, the court may order the director to contribute towards the assets of the company (as under s 213). The extent of a director's liability under s 214 will be calculated according to the effect that the director's conduct had on the company's losses as from the date that the director should have reasonably concluded that the company had no reasonable prospect of avoiding entering an insolvent state; see e.g. *Re Purpoint Ltd* [1990] BCC 121.

While the objective of introducing s 214 was to produce a stricter regime, in terms of policing and correcting abuses of managerial malpractice, the reality of the matter is that s 214 has not lived up to such expectations. One of the main reasons for the relative failure of the provision has been in relation to the financing of the action. As it is extremely doubtful whether the costs involved in the pursuit of a s 214 action can be regarded as liquidation expenses and therefore, in accordance with s 115 of the Insolvency Act 1986, be financed in priority to the claims of a company's preferential creditors and holders of floating charges (in accordance with priority rules, see Chapter 14) then, other than where the totality of a company's assets are abundant, a liquidator may have insufficient funds to pursue the action. See e.g. *Re M C Bacon Ltd (No 2)* [1991] Ch 127, confirmed by Knox J in *Re Ayala Holdings (No 2)* [1996] 1 BCLC 467 and, more recently by the Court of

Appeal, *Re Oasis Merchandising Services Ltd* [1997] BCC 282; however, note the *obiter* comments of the Court of Appeal in *Katz v Mcnally* [1997] BCC 784, where the validity of the assertions advanced in *Re M C Bacon Ltd (No 2)* were challenged.

A further reason for the relative failure of the s 214 provision has been that it is only operative at a time when a company is in liquidation. Accordingly, the liquidator in seeking to commence an action under s 214 has the sometimes problematic task of having to establish that, prior to the liquidation of the company the offending director(s) was aware or should have been aware that there was no reasonable prospect of the company avoiding liquidation. In some cases the liquidator's task may be straightforward in the light of overwhelming evidence indicative of the director's folly in permitting the company to trade, but in other cases the evidence may only be marginal and less obvious in so far as the liquidator's assessment of the situation necessarily requires the retrospective consideration of commercial decisions taken prior to the company's liquidation, decisions which, when taken, may have been speculative but driven by a desire and the perceived possibility of preventing the company from entering into liquidation.

A further problem, and one associated with the time lapse of the conduct giving rise to the s 214 action, is that a liquidator in seeking to commence an action under s 214 is required to assess the relevant dates as to when the wrongful trading was alleged to have occurred. The liquidator must select the relevant dates in his pleadings and a failure to select dates when the wrongful trading could be established will be detrimental to the liquidator's case. For example, in *Re Sherbourne Associates Ltd* [1995] BCC 40 His Honour Jack QC, sitting as a High Court judge, dismissed an action under s 214 on the basis that although it was probable that the dates chosen by the liquidator were dates indicative of a period of the company's insolvent state, it was however by no means conclusive that by such dates the liquidation of the company had become inevitable. As such, there was a reasonable prospect, to which the directors had addressed their minds, that the company could still be saved at the time of the dates pleaded by the liquidator. The judge concluded that it was not until three months after the dates chosen by the liquidator that a reasonable assumption could have been made as to the inevitability of the company's liquidation. In so concluding, he refused to allow the liquidator to substitute new dates for the ones pleaded on the premise that this would have prejudiced the preparation of the respondent's defence.

It should be noted that the limitation period for a s 214 claim is six years under s 9(1) of the Limitation Act 1980; the period begins to run as from the date the company enters into liquidation. Once a liquidator commences an action under s 214, it must be prosecuted without inexcusable delay; see e.g. *Re Farmizer (Products) Ltd* [1995] BCC 926.

As the test for wrongful trading is primarily an objective one, it is probable that a director who incurs liability under s 214 will be unable to seek the protection of s 727 of the Companies Act 1985 (discussed in Chapter 17) in so far as s 727 only allows relief from liability in a situation where it is reasonable to give relief; see e.g. *Re DKG Contractors Ltd* [1990] BCC 903. Finally, it should be noted that the court, upon finding that a director is liable in accordance with ss 213 or 214 of the Insolvency Act 1986 may, in accordance with s 10 of the Company Directors Disqualification Act 1986, impose a disqualification order against the director for a period up to a maximum of 15 years; see e.g. *Re Brian D Pierson (Contractors) Ltd* [1999] BCC 26. (Disqualification orders are discussed in Chapter 21.)

Sections 216 and 217 of the Insolvency Act 1986 (the phoenix syndrome)

Sections 216 and 217 of the Insolvency Act 1986, following in part the recommendations of the Cork Committee (Cmnd 8558), seek to limit the ease in which a person, trading through the medium of a company, may liquidate the company, form a new company and then carry on trading much as before, leaving in his wake unpaid creditors of the liquidated company. Such a scenario is commonly referred to as the 'phoenix syndrome'. However, ss 216 and 217 do not completely eradicate the phoenix syndrome in so far that the provisions are only applicable in a situation where the successor company adopts a name which is the same as or very similar to the liquidated company.

Section 216 prohibits a director or shadow director of a company which is in liquidation (the section applies to a director who had held office up to 12 months before the company's liquidation) from being involved, for the next five years as from the date of the company's liquidation, in the management of another company which adopts the name or a name closely associated with the insolvent company. A breach of the provision is a criminal offence (s 216(4)).

Although s 216 may be viewed as an offence of strict liability (see *R v Cole, Lees & Birch* [1998] BCC 87), it must be observed that there are important exceptions which preclude the provision's operation. The said exceptions are contained in s 216(3). Potentially, the most far-reaching exception is the courts' discretionary power to grant leave to a person to be associated with the management of a company which has adopted a prohibited name; see e.g. *Re Bonus Breaks Ltd* [1991] BCC 546, *Penrose v Official Receiver* [1996] 1 BCLC 389 and *Re Lightning Electrical Contractors* [1996] BCC 950.

In accordance with s 217, IA 1986, a person who is guilty under s 216 is also personally liable for the debts of the company. However, it should be noted that liability under s 217 is not dependent upon an actual conviction under s 216, albeit that the constituent elements of s 216 must be met before liability can be invoked under s 217. In circumstances where a person is deemed to be liable under s 217, the said person will be jointly and severally liable with the company and any other person who may be also deemed liable, i.e. liability will be in respect of the debts of the successor company which adopted the name of the insolvent company. A person will be personally liable to discharge the debts of a corporate creditor under s 217, irrespective of the fact that the creditor was aware and possibly aided and abetted the commission of the criminal offence under s 216; see the decision of the Court of Appeal in *Thorne* v *Silverleaf* [1994] BCC 109.

Suggested further reading

Griffin (1999) *Personal Liability and Disqualification of Directors.* Oxford: Hart Publishing

Section 349, CA 1985
Griffin [1997] JBL 438

Section 212, IA 1986
Oditah [1992] LMCLQ 207

Section 214, IA 1986
Oditah [1990] LMCLQ 205
Prentice (1990) 10 OJLS 265
Doyle (1992) 13 Co Law 96
Griffin (1999) 4 SLPQ 193

Section 216, IA 1986
Wilson (1996) 47 NILQ 344

21

THE DISQUALIFICATION OF COMPANY DIRECTORS

INTRODUCTION

The disqualification process, which is governed by the Company Directors Disqualification Act 1986 (CDDA 1986), comprises the imposition of what may tentatively be described as a quasi-penal provision. During a period of disqualification, the liberty attached to a director's capacity to participate in the activities of a limited company is temporarily removed, with the ultimate objective of protecting the public interest. The purpose of this chapter is to consider and analyse the circumstances in which the courts may impose disqualification orders.

AN OVERVIEW OF THE DISQUALIFICATION PROCESS

The reported cases confirm that examples of corporate mismanagement giving rise to the imposition of a disqualification order will be most evident following the collapse of a corporate enterprise. Accordingly, while many of the provisions of the CDDA 1986 may be implemented against a person involved in the management of a solvent company, the majority of disqualification proceedings will be commenced against persons who were involved in the management of insolvent companies. In all but a minority of cases, a person against whom a disqualification order is to be instigated will have acted as a company director, though other than for ss 6 and 8 of the CDDA 1986, a disqualification order may be imposed against a person whose management activities are not necessarily defined as those of a company director.

The CDDA 1986 aims to protect the general public from the activities of delinquent persons who are or who have been involved in the management of a company. Section 1(1) of the CDDA 1986 provides that in accordance with the circumstances specified in the Act, a court may, and under s 6 shall, make a disqualification order against a person with the effect that the person shall not without the leave of the court –

(a) be a director of a company; or
(b) be a liquidator or administrator of a company; or
(c) be a receiver or manager of a company's property; or
(d) in any way, whether directly or indirectly, be concerned or take part in the promotion, formation or management of a company.

A disqualification period takes effect from the date of the order, and while the period of disqualification is operative, s 1(1) will, following the judgment of the Court of Appeal in *Re Cannonquest, Official Receiver v Hannan* [1997] BCC 644, have the effect of disqualifying a person from acting in all the capacities indicated by s 1(1)(a)–(d). The effect of a disqualification order is to prevent a person from being a director, liquidator, administrator, receiver or manager of a company's property or in any other way from being involved, whether directly or indirectly, in the promotion, formation or management of a company. Under s 33 of the CDDA 1986, a breach of a disqualification order carries a maximum penalty of two years' imprisonment and a fine. A director in breach of the order will also be made jointly and severally liable (with the company and any other person) for the debts of the company incurred during the period in which the director acted in breach of the order (s 15, CDDA 1986). It is to be noted that the definition of a director for the purposes of the CDDA 1986 is, as in the Companies Act 1985, scantily alluded to. Section 22(4), CDDA 1986 states that a director is any person occupying the position of director, by whatever name called (an exact copy of s 741, CA 1985).

Disqualification orders which may be imposed at the courts' discretion

Under ss 2 to 5 of the CDDA 1986, the courts are given a discretion as to whether to impose a disqualification order. Section 2 provides that a court may make a disqualification order in circumstances where a person has been convicted of an indictable offence connected with the promotion, formation, management or liquidation of a company, or with the receivership or management of a company's property. The maximum period of disqualification is five years where the order is made by a court of summary jurisdiction and 15 years in any other case.

In accordance with s 3, a disqualification order may be made where a director has persistently breached provisions of companies legislation which require any return, account or other document to be filed with, delivered, or sent, or notice of any matter to be given to the Registrar of Companies; see e.g. *Re Civica Investments Ltd and Ors* [1983] BCLC 456. In disqualifying a person under s 3, the relevant court may make an order for a maximum period of five years.

The imposition of a disqualification order under s 4 will occur where, during the winding up of a company, evidence is placed before the court which establishes that a person involved in the management activities of the company, acted in a fraudulent manner in the conduct of the company's affairs. For the purpose of a s 4 order, a person will be adjudged to have acted in a fraudulent manner where he appears to have been guilty of:

(a) fraudulent trading, under s 458 of the Companies Act 1985, irrespective of whether that person has been convicted of that offence; or

(b) where he has otherwise been guilty while an officer, liquidator, receiver of the company or manager of the company's property of any fraud connected with the management of the company or any breach of duty to the company.

Under s 4, a person may be disqualified up to a maximum period of 15 years.

The circumstances giving rise to a court's ability to impose a disqualification order under s 5 of the CDDA 1986 are identical to those which give rise to disqualification under s 3 of the CDDA 1986, namely, a disqualification order may be made against a person who persistently breached those provisions of companies legislation which require any return, account or other document to be filed with, delivered or sent, or notice of any matter to be given to the Registrar of Companies. As with s 3, the maximum period of disqualification under s 5 is five years. The difference between s 3 and s 5 is that under the former provision, the imposition of a disqualification order may be made by a court which has a jurisdiction to wind up a company, whereas under s 5, the ability to impose a disqualification order is restricted to the court of summary conviction at which a person was found guilty of an offence which went to establish a finding of a persistent breach of companies legislation, i.e. in relation to the return, filing, etc. of relevant documents.

Disqualification following a DTI investigation

Section 8 CDDA 1986 provides that a person may be disqualified as a director following a DTI investigation (see Chapter 24) on the ground that the person is unfit to be concerned in the management of a company and that the disqualification order would be in the public interest; see e.g. *Re Samuel Sherman plc* [1991] BCC 699. The maximum period of disqualification under s 8 is 15 years.

Disqualification for fraudulent/wrongful trading

Where a court finds a person liable under s 213 of the Insolvency Act 1986 for fraudulent trading or under s 214 of the Insolvency Act 1986 for wrongful trading (ss 213 and 214, IA 1986, discussed further in Chapter 20), the court, under s 10 of the CDDA 1986, may of its own volition make a disqualification order against that person. The maximum period for an order under s 10 is 15 years; see e.g. *Re Brian D Pierson (Contractors) Ltd* [1999] BCC 26.

MANDATORY DISQUALIFICATION UNDER SECTION 6 OF THE CDDA 1986

Section 6(1) of the CDDA 1986 provides that it is the duty of the court to make a disqualification order against any person in a case where:

(a) that person is or has been a director of a company which has at any time become insolvent (whether while the person was a director or subsequently); and

(b) that person's conduct as a director of the company (either taken alone or taken together with the person's conduct as a director of another company or companies) makes the person unfit to be concerned in the management of a company.

Under s 6(4) of the CDDA 1986, the minimum period of disqualification following a contravention of s 6(1) is two years. The maximum period for disqualification under s 6 is 15 years.

In accordance with s 7(1) of the CDDA 1986, the justification for commencing disqualification proceedings under s 6 is to protect the public interest from the unfit conduct of delinquent directors.

An insolvent company

An insolvent company is defined in broad terms by s 6(2) of the CDDA 1986 as either:

(a) a company which goes into liquidation at a time when its assets are insufficient for the payment of its debts and other liabilities and the expenses of the winding up;

(b) where an administration order is made in relation to a company; or

(c) where an administrative receiver is appointed to the company.

Commencement of proceedings

Section 7(1) of the CDDA 1986 specifies that, if it appears to the Secretary of State to be expedient in the public interest that a disqualification order under s 6 should be made against any person, an application for the making of such an order against that person may be made –

(a) by the Secretary of State; or

(b) if the Secretary of State so directs in the case of a person who is or has been a director of a company which is being wound up by the court in England and Wales, by the Official Receiver.

Accordingly, in respect of s 7(1)(b), where a director is subject to disqualification proceedings and the company in which he held office has already been wound up, the application should be made by the Secretary of State.

The standard of proof

As a contravention of s 6 does not invoke a penal sanction, the civil standard of proof will be employed to determine whether the evidence of a case justifies the imposition of a disqualification order. Therefore, for the purposes of s 6, a director's unfitness must be established 'on a balance of probabilities'. However, as allegations made in the course of disqualification proceedings may involve very serious insinuations of misconduct, the courts have been reluctant to apply a standard of proof based upon evidence which is indicative but not sufficiently conclusive of a director's culpability. Indeed, some case examples have specifically alluded to the standard of proof applicable to s 6 in language compatible to, and on occasions, positively affirmative of, a standard which is appropriate to criminal proceedings. For example, in *Re Swift 736 Ltd* [1993] BCLC 1 Hoffmann J construed s 6 as a penal provision and as such found that a court in assessing the evidence of a case should afford a director the benefit of any reasonable doubt in its perception of the evidence of the case.

Conduct of an unfit nature

To establish a director's culpability in respect of s 6 of the CDDA 1986, it is necessary to prove that the director's conduct in the management of a company or of companies is such as to make him unfit to be concerned in the future management of a company. At first sight, s 6 suggests that a director's capacity to act in the future management of a company is the essential yardstick by which a court should determine whether or not to impose a disqualification order. However, following a finding of a director's unfit conduct, the imposition of a disqualification order is mandatory under s 6 and accordingly the section would appear to restrict the court's consideration of whether a director possessed a potential to reform his past misconduct. Indeed, the Court of Appeal in *Secretary of State v Gray* [1995] 1 BCLC 276 made it clear that under s 6 the courts were obliged to make a disqualification order in circumstances where it was established that a director's past conduct was of an unfit nature, a conclusion which was not to be interfered with by considering a director's potential to reform his past indiscretions. Although it was conceded in the case that extenuating circumstances may affect the court's consideration of whether a director's past conduct had reached an appropriate standard of unfitness to justify disqualification, it was stressed that any decision to impose a disqualification order should not be influenced by considering a director's capacity to reform his past activities.

For the purposes of s 6, the court, in assessing whether a director is unfit to act in the management of a company, should, in accordance with s 9 of the CDDA 1986, have particular regard to the matters set out in both Part 1 and Part 2 of Sch 1 to the CDDA 1986. However, as s 9 directs the court to have *particular regard* to the matters contained in Sch 1, as opposed to confining the court to the matters mentioned in Sch 1, conduct giving rise to a finding of unfitness may still be found in circumstances which are not directly governed by the Schedule.

The matters mentioned in Part 1 of Sch 1 require the court to consider whether a director, against which a disqualification order is sought, was responsible for:

1 any misfeasance or breach of any fiduciary or other duty in relation to the company;

2 any misapplication or retention by the director of, or any conduct by the director giving rise to an obligation to account for, any money or property of the company;

3 the extent of a director's responsibility for the company entering into any transaction liable to be set aside under Part XVI of the Insolvency Act (provisions against debt avoidance);

4 the extent of a director's responsibility for any failure by the company to comply with any of the following provisions of the CA 1985, namely:

(a) s 221 (companies to keep accounting records);

(b) s 222 (where and for how long records are to be kept);

(c) s 228 (register of directors and secretaries);

(d) s 352 (obligation to keep and enter up register of members);

(e) s 353 (location of register of members);

(f) s 363 (duty of company to make annual returns); and

(h) ss 399 and 415 (company's duty to register charges which it creates);

(It should be noted that former paragraph (g) – time for completion of annual returns (s 365) was removed from the above headings of relevant matters by s 139(4), CA 1989.)

5 the extent of the director's responsibility for any failure by the directors of the company to comply with:

(a) s 226 or s 227 (duty to prepare annual accounts); or

(b) s 233 (approval and signature of accounts).

The matters mentioned in Part 2 of Sch 1 (where a company has become insolvent) are as follows:

6 the extent of the director's responsibility for the causes of the company becoming insolvent;

7 the extent of the director's responsibility for any failure by the company to supply any goods or services which have been paid for (in whole or in part);

8 the extent of the director's responsibility for the company entering into any transaction or giving any preference, being a transaction or preference –

(a) liable to be set aside under s 127 or ss 238–240 of the Insolvency Act 1986; or

(b) open to challenge under s 242 or 243 of the Insolvency Act 1986 (or any rule of law in Scotland);

9 the extent of the director's responsibility for any failure by the directors of the company to comply with s 98 of the Insolvency Act 1986 (duty to call creditors' meeting in creditors' voluntary winding up);

10 any failure by the director to comply with any obligation imposed on

him by or under any of the following provisions of the Insolvency Act 1986 –

(a) s 22 (company's statement of affairs in administration);
(b) s 47 (statement of affairs to administrative receiver);
(c) s 66 (statement of affairs in Scottish receivership);
(d) s 99 (directors' duty to attend meeting, statement of affairs in creditors' voluntary winding up);
(e) s 131 (statement of affairs in winding up by the court);
(f) s 234 (duty of anyone with company property to deliver it up);
(g) s 235 (duty to co-operate with liquidator, etc.).

In considering the matters mentioned in Sch 1, the court must, on a balance of probabilities, be satisfied that the nature of a director's conduct was sufficiently serious to justify his disqualification. The need to establish that a director's conduct was of a type which constituted a serious failure to have regard to a matter or matters mentioned in Sch 1 or other matters related to a director's involvement in the managerial activities of a company may be explained on the premise that the effect of a disqualification order may dramatically infringe upon the commercial liberty of a director in relation to his ability to pursue employment in the management of a company. Indeed, although disqualification proceedings are governed by the civil law, the courts have adopted a tendency to afford the respondent the benefit of any reasonable doubt in the course of the proceedings.

Accordingly, the courts have expressed an unwillingness to impose disqualification orders in situations whereby the fault element attached to a director's act or omission was attributable to business practices of an improper but nevertheless naive and imprudent standard. Indeed, in the majority of cases, the courts have emphasised that to justify the imposition of a disqualification order, a director's misconduct will need to be established at a level which is harmful to the public interest whereby it conveys a clear exploitation of the privileges attributable to the limited-liability status of a company. In the majority, if not all cases, such exploitation will be exhibited by evidence of a wanton disregard and abuse of creditor interests, a director's recklessness or gross negligence in the management of a company or an obvious and serious (if not persistent) failure to comply with provisions of companies legislation.

In *Re Sevenoaks Stationers (Retail) Ltd* [1991] Ch 164, the first case in which the Court of Appeal was asked to consider the appropriateness of a disqualification order under s 6, the court emphasised that a disqualification order should only be made where there was conclusive proof of conduct which established that a director's actions amounted to commercially culpable behaviour of a type viewed as constituting a threat to the commercial community. The ability of a court to label a particular course of business malpractice as conduct constituting commercially culpable behaviour will obviously depend upon the individual circumstances and facts of a given case. Indeed, in *Re Sevenoaks Stationers (Retail) Ltd* the Court of Appeal observed that the true question to be tried in s 6 proceedings was a question of fact. Cases in which a s 6 order have been imposed include the following examples of unfit conduct:

- a persistent failure to comply with a statutory provision(s) (see e.g. *Secretary of State* v *Arif* [1996] BCC 586);
- a serious breach of duty. In relation to disqualification proceedings under s 6, the courts will be particularly concerned with the effect of a breach of a director's duty, where its effect is to prevent the repayment of corporate debts. Therefore, a director's breach of fiduciary duty may be equated with unfit conduct where it causes a company to fall into an insolvent state or where the breach exasperates a company's already insolvent position (see e.g. *Secretary of State* v *Lubrani* [1997] 2 BCLC 115);
- reckless/negligent conduct which exceeds mere business folly. Although conduct which is attributable to an act of mere commercial misjudgement or business folly will normally be discarded in the calculation of the appropriate standard by which a director's conduct may be properly construed to be of an unfit nature, such folly may be considered particularly relevant in circumstances where the consequences of the commercial misjudgement was of a reckless nature or where it exhibited the hallmarks of gross commercial incompetence (see e.g. *Re GSAR Realisations Ltd* [1993] BCLC 409, *Re Continental Assurance Co Ltd* [1997] BCLC 48 and *Re Barings plc* [1999] 1 BCLC 433, especially at pp 482–95).

Conduct falling outside the ambit of section 6

Where a court perceives a director's imprudent conduct to have been undertaken without any form of malice or serious neglect, then such conduct will not justify the application of s 6. However, other than where a director of an insolvent company honestly and reasonably believed that the company was capable of trading itself out of its financial difficulties, a director's continued involvement in the affairs of the insolvent company will provide *prima facie* evidence of his unfit conduct. However, it is to be observed, following the decision of Chadwick J in *Secretary of State* v *Gash* [1997] 1 BCLC 341, that a director of an insolvent company who continues to hold office, despite realising the folly of existing corporate policy, may escape any charge of having acted in an unfit manner if it can be established that he objected to and took no part in or had no responsibility for the deployment of the ill-fated policy.

Determining the length of a disqualification order

Where, under s 6, the court finds a director to be unfit to be concerned in the future management of a company, it will be obliged to impose a disqualification order. In accordance with s 6(4) of the CDDA 1986, the length of a disqualification order must be for a minimum of two years, the maximum period of disqualification being 15 years. In determining the length of a disqualification period, the court must be mindful of the seriousness and extent of a director's misconduct and will also take into account the director's position within the management structure of the company. For example, where a director holds a senior executive position, or otherwise has capacity to dictate a company's operations, it may ordinarily be presumed, in accordance with his position of responsibility, that the extent of his culpability (and the duration of any disqualification order) will be more pronounced than for officers of the company who exerted less influence in the management of the company's affairs. Where a director's misconduct involves dishonest conduct, it is more logical to assume that the disqualification period will of a greater duration than had the misconduct been of a reckless or negligent manner.

In *Re Sevenoaks Stationers (Retail) Ltd* the Court of Appeal, in an attempt to alleviate the potential for inconsistency in setting disqualification periods, gave the following guidelines:

1   the top bracket of disqualification for periods of over ten years should be reserved for particularly serious cases. Disqualification in this bracket could include those cases where a director who had previously been disqualified was the subject of a further disqualification order;
2   the middle bracket of disqualification for a period between six to ten years should apply in serious cases but cases which did not merit the attention of the top bracket of disqualification;
3   the minimum bracket of two to five years should be applied in cases where a director was found to be unfit to be concerned in the management of a company, but it was nevertheless established that the misconduct was not of a particularly serious nature.

However, notwithstanding that some form of guidance in relation to appropriate disqualification periods would be beneficial to the lower courts, in reality, the Court of Appeal's guidelines are of little assistance. In effect, they amount to little more than common-sense generalisations. Indeed, at best they may be regarded as but a reminder to the lower courts for the need to adopt a greater degree of consistency in the imposition of disqualification periods.

An application for leave to act (section 17 of the CDDA 1986)

Although a court is obliged to make a disqualification order under s 6 where a director's conduct in the management of a company was of an unfit nature, in some circumstances the court may be reluctant to fetter the future management activities of the director, especially where a director is successfully involved in the management of another company. In such a case the imposition of a disqualification order may adversely affect the interests of the successful company, causing prejudice to the company's employees and creditors. Accordingly, in such cases, the imposition of a disqualification order may cause more harm than good.

A possible solution to the mandatory effect of a disqualification order is to be found in s 17 of the CDDA 1986. S 17(1) provides:

> As regards the court to which application must be made for leave under a disqualification order, the following applies –
>
> (a) where the application is for leave to promote or form a company, it is any court with jurisdiction to wind up companies, and
>
> (b) where the application is for leave to be a liquidator, administrator or director of, or otherwise to take part in the management of a company, or to be a receiver or manager of a company's property, it is any court having jurisdiction to wind up that company.

The practical effect of a grant of leave is the creation of a modified type of disqualification order, whereby a director is disqualified following a finding of his unfitness to act in the management of a company, but is nevertheless allowed to continue in the management of another company (or companies), as specified by the terms of the order. The director is in effect given a 'second chance' in respect of the specified company on the premise that his involvement in the management of that company is considered to be in the public interest. While the adoption of a modified order may be considered justifiable in the sense that it protects the interests of the employees and creditors of the specified company, in reality, the nature of the order would appear to permit a director with a dubious past history in the management of a company or companies to, in part, escape the consequences of his past indiscretions. Accordingly, the adoption of the modified order must be applied with caution and when considering whether to grant leave the court must ponder the likelihood of a director re-offending; see e.g. the comments of Hoffmann LJ in *Re Grayan* [1995] BCC 554, at p 574.

Disqualification proceedings by way of summary procedure (the *Carecraft* procedure)

In circumstances where facts relating to a director's conduct are not disputed and where both the Secretary of State and the respondent are willing to allow the case to be dealt with on the understanding that a disqualification order is to be made for a period falling within one of the brackets specified in *Re Sevenoaks Stationers (Retail) Ltd*, then disqualification proceedings may be dealt with by a summary form of procedure. This procedure was first sanctioned by Ferris J in *Re Carecraft Construction Co Ltd* [1994] 1 WLR 172. Following the Practice Direction No 2 of 1995, whenever a *Carecraft* application is made, the applicant must:

(a) except in simple cases where the circumstances do not merit it or when the court otherwise directs, submit a written statement containing in respect of each respondent any material facts which (for the purposes of the application) are either agreed or not opposed (by either party); and

(b) specify in the written statement or, a separate document, the period of disqualification which the parties will invite the court to make or the bracket (i.e. 2–5 years, 6–10 years, 11–15 years) into which they will submit that the case falls.

In *Secretary of State* v *Rogers* [1996] 2 BCLC 513 the summary procedure was approved by the Court of Appeal because, where applicable, it would inevitably save the court and the parties involved in the proceedings, the time and expense that would have otherwise been incurred had the application proceeded to a full trial. Nevertheless, the court was reluctant to remove a judge's discretion to overturn the findings of an agreement entered into between a director and the Secretary of State in respect of the agreed facts of a case and an agreed disqualification period. Whilst the Court of Appeal considered it unlikely that a judge would ever wish to interfere with such an agreement, it felt that it would be inappropriate to sanction a judge, on the basis of a pre-trial agreement, to always be obliged to concur with the findings of the agreement.

Disqualification by way of a formal undertaking?
The advantage of a procedure whereby a director is capable of being precluded from taking part in the future management of a company without the necessity of the court having to impose a disqualification order would, in the light of an ever expanding number of pending disqualification cases, ease the pressure upon the courts and as such advance the *Carecraft* procedure in a most logical way. However, notwithstanding that a system which sanctioned disqualification by means of a formal undertaking would undoubtedly ease the pressure on both the Insolvency Service and the judicial system, the acceptance of such a procedure may be open to criticism on the basis that it would be contrary to the public interest to have matters relating to the accountability of unfit company directors dealt with in a manner absent of judicial scrutiny. Although the *Carecraft* procedure is in itself little more than a judicial 'rubber stamping' of an agreement reached between the Secretary of State and the respondent director, it does at least maintain the role of the court as the guardian of justice and the protector of the public interest. Indeed, it is possible (albeit unlikely) for a court to overturn the terms of a *Carecraft* agreement.

Despite the above criticisms, the introduction of a statutory procedure to permit the use of formal undertakings could, if used in well-defined circumstances, be of great advantage in those cases where the public interest would not be served by having a formal court hearing. Indeed, it does appear logical to conclude that the Insolvency Service, the judiciary and the courts' time would be more efficiently taken up in relation to the prosecution of cases in which there was a real dispute between the parties. Accordingly, an obvious example of where the use of formal undertakings would be beneficial would be in relation to cases where a director, having admitted that he was a party to commercially culpable behaviour, agreed to a life-long abstention from acting in any of the capacities prescribed by s 1(1) of the CDDA 1986.

Notwithstanding that the formal undertaking procedure is, as yet, devoid of any statutory recognition, the courts have in at least three reported cases already stayed disqualification proceedings following a respondent's undertaking to refrain from acting in the future management of a company. In these cases the judicial acceptance of a formal undertaking was justified because the ill health and age of the directors in question warranted a conclusion that it was highly improbable that they would ever again act in the management of a company. However, it is important to note that the actions were stayed and not dismissed, that is, it remained open to the Secretary of State to apply for the stay to be lifted if, for example, it was subsequently discovered that the terms of the undertaking had been broken; see e.g. *Secretary of State for Trade and Industry* v *Cleland* [1997] BCC 473.

However, it is to be noted that following the decision of the Court of Appeal in *Secretary of State* v *Davies* [1998] BCC 11, the validity of a judicial procedure which recognises formal undertakings as an alternative option to the imposition of a disqualification order will only be permitted in a situation where a director is willing to agree to make a full admission to the effect that his misconduct was of a commercially culpable nature.

Suggested further reading

Griffin (1999) *Personal Liability and Disqualification of Company Directors.* Oxford: Hart Publishing
Dine (1988) Co Law 213
Hicks (1988) JBL 27
Finch (1990) 53 MLR 385
Dine (1991) Co Law 6
Milman (1992) 43 NILQ 1
Dine [1994] JBL 325

22

THE MINORITY SHAREHOLDER AND THE PROTECTION OF THE COMPANY'S INTERESTS

INTRODUCTION

This chapter commences by examining the types of action available to an aggrieved minority shareholder under the common law. However, the primary purpose of this chapter is to concentrate on the availability of a minority shareholder action, the purpose of which is to protect the interests of the company as a whole. Accordingly, the principal part of the chapter seeks to examine the ability of a minority shareholder(s) to redress a wrong committed against the company. The availability of such an action seeks to override a fundamental principle of company law which dictates that an action to correct a corporate wrong should only be pursued in a situation where the general meeting approves the action. The personal remedies of an aggrieved minority shareholder are primarily governed by statute; such remedies are dealt with in Chapter 23.

THE TYPES OF ACTION AVAILABLE TO THE MINORITY SHAREHOLDER

The personal action

A personal action may be commenced where a shareholder's legal rights of membership have been infringed by the company. The action will be commenced by an individual shareholder against the company. A typical example of a personal action would be where a shareholder sought to enforce the terms of the company's contractual obligations, as governed by s 14 of the Companies Act 1985 (see Chapter 7). Mere procedural irregularities will not normally substantiate a personal action, but the right to challenge a resolution which was passed otherwise than in accordance with a prescribed majority, for example, where an ordinary resolution was passed to authorise an act which required a special resolution, will provide grounds for a cause of action; see e.g. *Edwards v Halliwell* [1950] 2 All ER 1064.

To justify an action for a procedural irregularity, the irregularity must ordinarily be of a type whereby the majority shareholders in purporting to approve the irregularity seek to obtain an unfair and discriminatory advantage over the minority. The type and degree of discrimination required is akin to the discriminatory effect needed to substantiate an action based upon a fraud on the minority (see below).

The representative action

Where an individual shareholder's legal rights have been infringed, the infringement may also affect other shareholders in the company. In this situation the appropriate action will be a representative one. The action will be commenced by a shareholder on behalf of himself and other aggrieved shareholders and will be instigated against the company. Any judgment obtained as a result of a representative action will bind all the parties which are made subject to it. The company may defend a representative action by showing that the plaintiff took part or acquiesced in the act which was the subject matter of the complaint; see e.g. *Nurcombe v Nurcombe* [1985] 1 WLR 370.

The derivative action

In instances whereby a director or other officer of the company acts without due authority or in breach of his duties and as such commits a wrong against the company, the wrongful act will be voidable. The act may be avoided by the general meeting passing an ordinary resolution. Where the act is not avoided, the director or officer concerned may, in accordance with agency principles, be made liable to account to the company for any profit made or loss sustained as a result of entering into the transaction in question. However, it should be noted that any decision to pursue litigation to, for example, recover corporate property which was lost as a consequence of a wrongful act, will normally be a decision which is vested in the board of directors (Table A, Art 70); see e.g. *Breckland Group v London & Suffolk Properties* [1989] BCLC 100. Accordingly, in theory it would be possible for the general meeting to sanction litigation, but for the pursuit of the action to be refused by the board of directors. However, such a scenario would be most unlikely given that the general meeting could ordinarily, by passing an ordinary resolution, remove any dissenting members of the board.

Where a wrong is committed against the company, the company will be the proper plaintiff to instigate proceedings. An action which is brought in the company's name without the support of the general meeting will ordinarily be struck out by the court and will render the applicant and his solicitor personally liable to pay the costs of the litigation. Accordingly, if an individual shareholder (or a group of shareholders) wish to pursue an action on behalf of the company without the support of the general meeting, the action must be in the derivative form. To so proceed, the shareholder(s) must convince the court that the wrong against which the complaint is made was a wrong perpetrated by persons in control of the company's affairs, i.e. those representing a majority of the general meeting. The wrong must be of a serious nature: 'a fraud on the company'. A shareholder must bring the action on behalf of himself and all other shareholders (save for any shareholders who were party to the alleged wrongdoing). The alleged wrongdoers and the company will be made defendants to the action. The company is made a defendant so as to enable it to take the benefit of any court order. In commencing a derivative action, the court has a discretion to order that a plaintiff's costs be paid by the company, even where the plaintiff's action proves to be unsuccessful; see e.g. *Wallersteiner* v *Moir (No 2)* [1975] QB 373. It is important to note that an order for costs may only be made where the plaintiff sues in the derivative form; see e.g. *Re Sherborne Park Residents Co Ltd* [1987] BCLC 82.

THE RULE IN *FOSS* v *HARBOTTLE*

In situations where a wrong was allegedly committed against a company, the protection of minority interests is regulated by the rule taken from the judgment of Wigram V-C in the case of *Foss* v *Harbottle* (1843) 2 Hare 461. The rule is prohibitive of the availability of minority actions, for as Wigram V-C made clear in his judgment, every individual shareholder must realise that on becoming a member of a company, majority rule will, as in all other walks of society, prevail. The rule born of *Foss* v *Harbottle* can be stated in the following way:

> An individual shareholder has no absolute right to seek redress for a wrong purportedly committed against the company in which he is a member. The company in such an instance is the proper plaintiff to instigate such an action. Whether the company proceeds with the action will depend upon the will of the general meeting and its board of directors. Only in exceptional circumstances will the court interfere with a decision taken by the company to sanction the alleged wrongful act.

Justifications for the rule in *Foss* v *Harbottle*

The internal management principle
The internal management principle may be defined as confirming a company's right to decide for itself, in accordance with the wishes of its general meeting and management structure, corporate strategy in respect of decisions appertaining to alleged acts of a wrongful character; see e.g. *Carlen* v *Drury* (1812) 1 Ves & B 154 and, more recently, *Breckland Group Holdings* v *London & Suffolk Properties Ltd* [1989] BCLC 100.

The proper plaintiff principle
To allow a minority shareholder to commence an action on behalf of a company whenever the company has suffered some alleged wrong would be to open the floodgates to many future actions. As such, if a company is allegedly wronged, the company should be viewed as the proper plaintiff to the action, it must, if it so decides, pursue the action in its own name; see e.g. the judgment of Mellish LJ in *MacDougall* v *Gardiner* (1875) 1 Ch 13. Where a minority shareholder purports to commence an action on behalf of

the company, it is a normal procedure of the court to postpone proceedings until the general meeting is convened to determine whether to authorise proceedings to be commenced in the company's name; see e.g. *Danish Mercantile Co Ltd* v *Beaumont* [1951] Ch 680.

The ratifiability principle

Where a minority shareholder alleges that the company's directors have acted in a wrongful manner, an action arising from such an allegation may not be pursued in a situation where the wrong in question was capable of being ratified by the general meeting, i.e. the general meeting of the company must be given the opportunity to confirm, and if it so decides, validate the act which forms the subject matter of the complaint.

In voting to ratify a wrongful act, a shareholder may generally vote in a manner beneficial to his own interests; see e.g. *North West Transportation Co Ltd* v *Beatty* [1887] 12 App Cas 289, *Peters American Delicacy Co* v *Heath* (1939) 61 CLR 457 and *Mills* v *Mills* (1938) 60 CLR 150. However, it should be noted that the acceptance of allowing a member to vote in accordance with his self-interests may be overturned if what is considered to be beneficial to an individual shareholder is nevertheless construed to be detrimental to the interests of the company as a whole (discussed below).

The irregularity principle

If it is clear that had the correct corporate procedure been adhered to a mere informality or minor irregularity in the course of the internal management of a company would not have taken place, then an action challenging the effect of such an irregularity will not be permitted. For example, in *Browne* v *La Trinidad* (1887) 37 Ch D 1 a meeting of directors was called and as a result of the meeting it was decided that an extraordinary general meeting of the company should be held to consider a motion to remove one of the directors, a Mr Browne (B). The resolution was subsequently passed whereupon B claimed that the resolution had been invalidly passed in so far as he had received inadequate notice of the directors' meeting. The Court of Appeal held that the irregularity (the inadequate notice) was not a significant factor in respect of the vote to oust B from his directorship. The resolution was upheld.

However, where the effect of an irregularity may potentially alter the outcome of a vote, the court will intervene to render the vote invalid; see e.g. *Pender* v *Lushington* (1877) 6 Ch D 70 (discussed further in Chapter 7).

EXCEPTIONS TO THE RULE IN *FOSS* v *HARBOTTLE*

The underlying theme for the protection of minority interests is set against a backcloth which vests the guardianship of a company's interests in the hands of the board of directors and majority shareholders. To protect and correct any abuse of this guardianship, the courts must in appropriate circumstances depart from the concept of majority rule. However, a court will be reluctant to overturn the wishes of the majority and will only do so where the actions of those in control of the company were inspired by motives other than to promote the best interests of the company as a whole.

The courts' ability to override the rule of majority control is itself derived from the case of *Foss* v *Harbottle*. In giving the judgment of the court, Wigram V-C stated:

> 'If a case should arise of injury to a corporation by some of its members, for which no adequate remedy remained, except that of a suit by individual corporators in their private characters, and of asking in such a character the protection of those rights to which in their corporate character they were entitled, I cannot but think that the claims of justice would be found superior to any difficulties arising out of technical rules respecting the mode in which corporators are required to sue.' (at p 492)

Although Wigram V-C spoke of the 'claims of justice', the determination of whether a minority shareholder may proceed on the basis of justice must be viewed as a double-edged sword in that justice is not solely to be measured in terms of the rights of the minority, but is also to be determined by observing the corresponding rights of the majority. Accordingly, those in control of the company's affairs are generally presumed, as guardians of the company's affairs, to have acted in the best interests of the company as a whole. The presumption is rebuttable, but the controllers of a company may often be able to justify their actions on the premise that the wrong in question was not significant enough to merit expensive litigation or that, if the wrong had been litigated, it would have caused a lapse of confidence in the corporate body and possible panic amongst its investors and creditors; see *Prudential Assurance Co Ltd* v *Newman Industries Ltd (No 2)* [1982] Ch 204.

To convince the court that a corporate wrong should be righted, an aggrieved minority shareholder must show that those in control of the company failed to act in the best interests of the company as a whole. Although judicial obscurity masks the exact meaning of the term 'the best interests of the company as a whole', it is clear that a shareholder will not be permitted to commence a derivative action in circumstances where, irrespective of corporate irregularities, the complaint was primarily inspired by an ulterior purpose devoid of any connection to the alleged wrongdoing; see e.g. *Barrett* v *Duckett* [1995] 1 BCLC 243.

The Court of Appeal's decision in *Barrett* v *Duckett* is also indicative of the view that a derivative action should not be available where the complainant had the option of pursuing an alternative remedy. In *Barrett* the alternative remedy in question was the liquidation of the company. As such, the Court of Appeal took the view that a derivative action is one which should only be pursued as a last resort. Indeed, if one considers the progressive and extensive remedies afforded to shareholders by s 459 of the Companies Act 1985 (discussed in Chapter 23), it would appear that the need for a court to sanction a derivative action without recourse to s 459 will be unlikely, save perhaps in a situation where the underlying motive for pursuing the derivative action is one which seeks to benefit the company as a distinct commercial entity as opposed to one which purports to directly or indirectly benefit the personal interests of a minority shareholder(s).

Fraud against the company (fraud on the minority)

A corporate act which has not been pursued *bona fide* in the best interests of the company as a whole may be simply defined as a corporate act which results in a fraud on the company. Therefore, a minority shareholder of a company may pursue a derivative action in circumstances where the company has been the victim of a fraud. However, it should be stressed from the outset that the case law pertinent to this area is indicative of the view that a fraud extends beyond more than just the common law concept of fraud, exemplified by cases such as *Derry v Peek* (1889) 14 App Cas 337. Indeed, the term 'fraud on the minority' may cover a breach of director's duty (see *Knight v Frost* [1999] 1 BCLC 364) and, as discussed below, may extend to apply to intentional acts of discrimination or even unintentional abuses of corporate power. Indeed it may be an improbable task to attempt to provide a precise definition of which 'wrongs' may or may not be judicially perceived as constituting 'frauds'.

A derivative action may proceed even if, at the time the fraud was discovered, the plaintiff is no longer a member of the company against which the fraud was perpetrated. Where an individual acquires shares from a member who was a party to a fraud or a member who voted against any action to redress a fraudulent act, it would appear that the wrong in question cannot be pursued by the subsequent holder of the shares; see e.g. *Ffooks v South Western Railway Co* (1853) 1 Sm & G 142.

The fraud exception to the rule in *Foss v Harbottle* is commonly referred to as 'fraud on the minority shareholder', despite the fact that the wrong will invariably be committed against the company. In allowing a minority shareholder to commence an action on behalf of the company, i.e. to commence a derivative action, the court will have to distinguish the necessity of adhering to one or more of the four justifications for the rule in *Foss v Harbottle* (discussed above). An accepted instance, triggering one of the fraud on the minority exceptions (see below) will render any ratification of the alleged wrong ineffective, save perhaps, where an independent board of directors or a majority of the independent part of the minority (those not involved in the wrongdoing) resolve to rescind from proceeding with an action; see e.g. *Atwool v Merryweather* (1868) LR 5 Eq, *Rights and Issues Investment Trust v Stylo Shoes* [1956] Ch 250 and, more recently, *Smith v Croft (No 2 and No 3)* [1987] BCLC 206 and [1987] BCLC 355.

Accepted instances of a fraud on the minority

An intentional misappropriation of corporate assets

This heading is akin to the common law concept of fraud and involves instances whereby those in control of a company have acted in a dishonest manner by appropriating to themselves corporate property or other assets; see e.g. *Cook v Deeks* [1916] 1 AC 554.

A negligent misappropriation of corporate assets

In considering this heading it must be stressed that not every negligent act which results in the loss of a corporate asset may be termed a fraud on the minority; see e.g. *Pavlides v Jensen* [1956] Ch 565. However, where those in control of a company benefit at the company's expense from self-serving negligence, a minority shareholder may in such an instance be capable of intervening on behalf of the company to right the wrong. For example, in the case of *Daniels v Daniels* [1978] Ch 406, a company's board of directors negligently sold a corporate asset to one of their number at a gross undervaluation. Four years later, the asset was resold and a substantial profit made. The validity of the transaction was successfully challenged. Templeman J opined that a minority shareholder would be capable of commencing an action on behalf of the company in circumstances where directors of a company used their powers in a manner which benefited themselves or one of their number at the expense of the company, irrespective of whether the power had been used intentionally, unintentionally, fraudulently or negligently.

Unfair advantage

The classification of a fraud on the minority based upon facts which establish that the controlling body of a company obtained some unfair advantage at the expense of the company and its minority shareholders is a controversial classification, in so far as the scope of this definition of fraud closely resembles one which is touched with the notion that justice may have a primary role to play in determining a minority shareholder's ability to pursue a derivative action. Nevertheless, case examples do exist to justify the inclusion of a classification based upon unfair advantage; see e.g. *Alexander v Automatic Telephone Co* [1900] 2 Ch 56 and *Estmanco v Greater London Council* [1982] 1 All ER 437.

In the latter case, a minority shareholder of a company formed by the Greater London Council (GLC) to manage a block of flats, sued the GLC on behalf of the company to enforce an agreement entered into by the tenants of the flats. The agreement provided that the block of flats in question (comprising 60 flats) would be sold privately and that each purchaser would acquire one share in the company; the shares of the individual purchasers were not to carry voting rights until all the flats had been sold. After 12 of the flats had been sold, the political constitution of the GLC changed and as a result of this change the Council altered its policy of selling off the flats:

instead of being sold privately, the flats were to be rented to needy council tenants. As the GLC retained 48 of the flats (a figure representing the total number of flats unsold), the GLC was able to prevent the company from taking any action to challenge the policy change, i.e. the purchasers of the 12 flats were in the minority and in any case had no voting rights.

Megarry V-C held that the circumstances of the case were such that the Council (in effect the majority shareholders) had acted otherwise than in the best interests of the company as a whole. The Council had gained an unfair advantage by preventing the company from challenging its decision to alter its policy in respect of the sale of the council flats.

Although it is arguable that the decision in *Estmanco* v *Greater London Council* is supportive of a claim that the justice of a case may form the basis for a valid exception to the rule in *Foss* v *Harbottle*, it is submitted that the facts of the *Estmanco* case were such as to indicate that the GLC's decision to depart from its agreement with the flat owners, i.e. a type of shareholder agreement, was clearly detrimental to the interests of the company as a whole because the GLC's decision was intended to end the very existence of the company.

LIMITING THE INTERPRETATION OF FRAUD

Although the justice of a case may not in itself be regarded as a standard exception to the rule in *Foss* v *Harbottle*, justice does, however, provide the foundation stone upon which all acceptable forms of the exception to the rule in *Foss* v *Harbottle* have been built. Indeed, in at least one case the justice criteria prevailed as the overwhelming factor in the court's decision to afford relief to the claims of a minority shareholder, albeit that the case in question, *Clemens* v *Clemens Bros Ltd* [1976] 2 All ER 268 (discussed in Chapter 19) was not pursued in the derivative form.

Nevertheless, the availability of an exception to the rule in *Foss* v *Harbottle* based primarily on issues of justice, was one which was strongly refuted by the Court of Appeal in *Prudential Assurance Co Ltd* v *Newman Industries (No 2)* [1982] Ch 204. The facts of the case were as follows. The plaintiff, a large industrial investor, held 3 per cent of the share capital in Newman Ind Ltd (N). The plaintiff alleged that two of the directors in N had dishonestly purchased the assets of another company in which they held a majority of the shares, and in doing so had defrauded N of some £400 000. The plaintiff maintained that the two directors had misled the general body of shareholders into approving the transaction by issuing tricky and misleading circulars which failed to properly set out the actual amount which had been paid by N to purchase the assets of the other company. The plaintiff commenced both a personal and derivative action against the two directors concerned. At first instance, Vinelott J, in allowing the derivative action, implied that an exception to the rule in *Foss* v *Harbottle* could be made out where justice so demanded.

In respect of an exception to the rule in *Foss* v *Harbottle* based upon the justice of the case, the Court of Appeal disagreed with Vinelott J, in so far as the court was not convinced that the justice of any case could ever be advanced as a practical test to determine the merits of a derivative action. However, in delivering a joint judgment, Cumming-Bruce, Templeman and Brightman LJJ considered that on the facts of the appeal it was unnecessary for the court to attempt to define the exact scope of the exceptions to the rule in *Foss* v *Harbottle* in so far as N, following the High Court proceedings, had agreed to accept the benefit of any order made in the company's favour, i.e. it was no longer necessary for the Court of Appeal to determine the derivative action.

The controlling interest

In addition to establishing a fraud on the minority, in order for a minority shareholder to proceed with a derivative action, he must show that the company was unable to bring an action in its own name, i.e. those persons accused of the alleged wrongdoing were in control of the company and were unwilling to proceed with an action; see e.g. *Birch* v *Sullivan* [1957] 1 WLR 1247.

Where the ratification of a wrongful act rests on a decision of the general body of shareholders, it is somewhat unclear whether the alleged wrongdoers' control of a company can be interpreted to mean majority voting control in terms of an arithmetic ability (50+ per cent of the voting shares) to secure the passing of an ordinary resolution or, whether, *de facto* control would be sufficient? For example, in large public companies where many shareholders fail to attend meetings, an alleged wrongdoer holding, for example, 30 per cent of the share capital, may be able to secure the passing of an ordinary resolution to prevent the company pursuing an action, i.e. the alleged wrongdoer may exert *de facto* control.

Although *obiter* comments exist to support the view that if an alleged wrongdoer has *de facto* control, then such control should be sufficient to establish majority control (see e.g. *Pavlides* v *Jensen* [1956] Ch 565 and Vinelott J in *Prudential Assurance* v *Newman Industries Ltd* [1981] Ch 257), it is to be observed that the Court of Appeal in *Prudential Assurance* v *Newman Industries Ltd* (*No 2*) ([1982] Ch 204) strongly opposed such reasoning (in *Prudential* the alleged wrongdoers did not hold a majority of the voting shares in the company).

The principal objection of allowing an action to proceed where a person or persons hold *de facto* control is the inability to precisely define the exact meaning of *de facto* control, i.e. it is impossible to predict how many shareholders will attend any given company meeting; *de facto* control may arise where one shareholder holds just 20 per cent of the voting shares, or 30 per cent, 40 per cent, 45 per cent, indeed any figure up to the figure required to pass an ordinary resolution.

The preliminary hearing

In *Prudential Assurance* v *Newman Industries Ltd* (*No 2*) [1982] Ch 204 the Court of Appeal took the view that in order to determine whether a potentially long and expensive trial was deemed necessary, a preliminary hearing should be held to assess the merits of any case brought as an exception to the rule in *Foss* v *Harbottle*. The Court of Appeal stated that the preliminary hearing should determine whether the wrong against which an action was based, was one which was capable of ratification and whether the supposed wrongdoers were, in fact, in control of the company. Whilst the Court of Appeal's reasoning was theoretically sound, it is suggested that in many cases it will be impossible to determine a prospective plaintiff's standing to commence an action without a full investigation into whether or not the purported action is of a type which can be identified as a fraud on the minority; a view endorsed by the Australian courts; see e.g. the decision of the Supreme Court of Western Australia in *Eromanga Hydrocarbons* v *Australis Mining* (1989) 14 ACLR 486.

A PERSONAL OR DERIVATIVE ACTION?

Occasionally, and quite often justifiably, the courts have found great difficulty in distinguishing between an action which seeks to redress a wrong to the company (derivative in character) and an action which is of a personal nature. Indeed, in circumstances where, for example, the wrongful act directly conflicts with the terms of a company's constitution, thereby affecting both the personal rights of the membership and the rights of the company, an action may be brought either in the derivative form or as a personal action. An example of this 'dual' type of action would be one which sought to restrain a company from entering into an activity which was *ultra vires* (see e.g. *Simpson* v *Westminster Palace Hotel* (1860) 8 HLC 712) or where a company purported to pass a resolution by a simple majority vote instead of a prescribed special resolution (see *Edwards* v *Halliwell* [1950] 2 All ER 1064).

Indeed, much confusion as to whether an action should be of a personal or derivative nature has occurred in those cases in which a shareholder suffers an indirect loss as a result of a wrong having been committed against the company, namely in a situation where the value of shares depreciate as a result of a breach of directors' duty. For example, an allotment of shares for an improper purpose would appear to constitute a wrong committed against the company. Accordingly, in such circumstances it would seem unlikely that an individual or group of shareholders would have the capacity to commence a personal (or representative) action where, for example, the general meeting of the company refused to sanction an action to be taken in the company's name. Certainly, the Court of Appeal in *Prudential Assurance Co Ltd* v *Newman Industries Ltd* (*No 2*) [1982] Ch 204 was of the view that where a shareholder suffered an indirect loss as a result of a wrong committed against a company, a personal (representative action) would not be sustainable on the basis of a shareholder's indirect loss – a view which was confirmed by the Privy Council in *Lee* v *Chou Wen Hsien* [1984] 1 WLR 1202. Other cases which may be used to support the view advanced in *Prudential* include *Bamford* v *Bamford* [1970] Ch 212 and *Devlin* v *Slough Estates Ltd* [1983] BCLC 497.

However, in *Re a Company (No 005136 of 1986)* [1987] BCLC 82 Hoffmann J opined that a personal or representative action could be commenced as a result of, for example, an improper allotment of shares, in circumstances where the allotment constituted an unlawful exercise of a director's corporate powers, i.e. the unlawful exercise of powers could constitute an abuse of the company's contractual obligations towards its shareholders. Support for the view advanced by Hoffmann J can be found in *Alexander* v *Automatic Telephone Co* [1900] 2 Ch 56, *Hogg* v *Cramphorn Ltd* [1967] Ch 254 and *Heron International Ltd* v *Lord Grade* [1983] BCLC 244.

A more recent case in which the availability of a personal action was considered in circumstances resulting in an indirect loss to shareholders was the decision of the Court of Appeal in *George Fischer (Great Britain) Ltd* v *Multi Construction Ltd* [1995] BCC 310. Here a holding company, Fischer (F), which conducted its business through wholly owned subsidiaries, sought to recoup the losses incurred by its subsidiaries as a consequence of a third party defaulting on a contract entered into for the benefit of three of F's subsidiary companies. F sued as the sole shareholder of the subsidiaries; the subsidiaries could not pursue an action in their own right as they were not a party to the contract, i.e. no privity of contract. F therefore pursued a personal action for the indirect losses which it sustained as a result of the losses incurred by its subsidiaries. The nature of the indirect losses caused by the breach of contract were alleged to comprise a fall in the value of F's holding in the subsidiaries and the loss in profits sustained by F as a consequence of a fall in the profits of the subsidiary companies.

In allowing F, suing *qua* shareholder, to recover the indirect losses, the Court of Appeal recognised the availability of a personal action in circumstances where the alleged wrong was one which had been primarily committed against the company (F's subsidiaries) and not the company's shareholders (F). However, the *Fischer* case should not be viewed as opening the floodgates to personal actions involving wrongs which are in essence committed against the company. Clearly, the facts of the case were not those which are normally associated with cases in which a potential conflict between the pursuit of a derivative or personal action would arise, i.e. in *Fischer* the alleged wrong had not been committed as a result of any internal malpractice. Further, the wrong was incapable of being corrected by the subsidiary companies, i.e. the wrong in question resulted from a breach of contract to which the subsidiary companies were not privy.

The reluctance of the courts to permit a personal action in a situation where the wrong in question resulted in a corporate loss was recently emphasised by the Court of Appeal in *Stein* v *Blake* [1998] 1 BCLC 573. The case involved a group of companies (the old companies) in which D held 50 per cent of the group's shares (he was also sole director of those companies). P held the remaining 50 per cent of the shares. D purchased the assets of the old companies and transferred them to another group of companies under his control. The old companies were subsequently placed into liquidation. P contended that the transactions were in breach of D's duty to the group of companies, in so far as D had acquired the assets at an undervaluation. P alleged that his personal rights had been indirectly infringed as a result of D's actions. P commenced a personal action; he would have been unable to commence a derivative action in so far as the old companies had been put into liquidation. D successfully applied to have the action struck out. The Court of Appeal held that P's loss was in reality a corporate loss. P's loss was not independent or distinct from the corporate loss. It is to be observed that as the old companies were in liquidation, the liquidator (acting on behalf of the old companies) would have been the only person able to instigate proceedings (misfeasance proceedings) in respect of the alleged misappropriation of corporate assets. In giving the leading judgment of the court, Millet LJ observed that:

> 'Directors owe fiduciary duties to their company to preserve and defend its assets and to the shareholders to advise them properly so that they are not induced or compelled to part with their shares at an undervalue. No doubt other fiduciary duties are also owed both to the company and to its shareholders. Shareholders may suffer loss in the event of a breach of either duty, but in the first case the loss consists of a diminution of the value of their shares, is fully reflected in the loss sustained by the company, and is fully compensated by restitution to the company. In the second case the company suffers no loss. Its assets are unaffected ... All that is pleaded in the present case is wrongdoing to the company and loss suffered by the company. The only loss alleged to have been suffered by the plaintiff is reflected in the loss sustained by the company.' (at p 579)

PROPOSALS FOR FUTURE REFORM

The statutory derivative action

The difficulty in establishing a derivative action based upon the exceptions to the rule in *Foss* v *Harbottle* has led some commentators to call for the introduction of a statutory derivative action. This call was recently echoed in the Law Commission Report 'Shareholder Remedies' (1997 Law Com No 246), discussed below. Indeed, statutory derivative actions are already available in a number of Commonwealth jurisdictions. For example, in Canada (the action was introduced by s 232 of the Canada Business Corporation Act 1974) a complainant may apply to the court to commence a statutory derivative action where the complainant, in seeking to enforce the action, acted in good faith, and the action was construed to be in the best interests of the company. The term 'complainant' is defined to include past and present shareholders, creditors and any other party who is considered, at the court's discretion, to have been a proper person to bring an action. The definition of a 'proper person' includes persons who have a direct financial interest in how the company is being managed. Therefore, in appropriate circumstances the term 'proper person' may be permissive of the right of employees and creditors of the company to apply to the court.

Although the court may take into account, in determining whether to allow the derivative action to proceed, any ratification of the alleged wrong by the company's general meeting, ratification will not be regarded as conclusive in relation to the court's decision to allow or refuse the derivative action. In determining whether an application should proceed by way of a derivative action the court will also consider the constitution of a company's board of directors. Where, for example, a decision of the board concluded that an action should not be pursued on behalf of the company, then in circumstances where the board was divorced from the interests of the alleged wrongdoers, i.e. independent, the court will attach importance and weight to the independently constituted board. It should be noted that a statutory derivative action based upon the Canadian system would allow actions to be commenced in the name of and on behalf of the company irrespective of whether fraud or an intentional abuse of corporate power had taken place. Therefore, reckless or negligent abuses of corporate power would fall within the ambit of a potential action. Indeed, the discretion of the court in its determination of whether to permit an action to proceed would, following the Canadian model, be very wide.

The Law Commission's proposals

In theory, the principal advantage of introducing a statutory derivative action in the UK would be to provide a more accessible route by which a minority shareholder could challenge the ordinance of a corporate wrong. To this end the Law Commission have proposed the introduction of a statutory derivative action to totally replace the existing derivative action based upon the exceptions to the rule in *Foss* v *Harbottle*. The Commission's Report recommends that the new procedure should only be available in the case of an existing member of a company in circumstances where the cause of action arises –

> '... as a result of an actual or threatened act or omission involving (a) negligence, default, breach of duty or breach of trust by a director of the company, or (b) a director putting himself in a position where his personal interests conflict with his duties to the company. The cause of action may be against the director or another person (or both). We also recommend that, for these purposes, director should include a shadow director.' (para 6.49)

In relation to the manner in which a derivative action should proceed, the report recommends the introduction of a case management conference for all derivative actions, although in an appropriate case, it suggests that it may be possible for a respondent to apply to strike out the claim at the outset. On the application for leave, the report recommends that the court should have the power to either: grant leave to continue the claim for such period and on such terms as it thinks fit, refuse leave and dismiss the claim, strike out the claim, or adjourn the proceedings relating to the application and give such directions as it thinks fit. Where the claimant does not apply for leave to continue the action at the case management conference (or at such earlier time as the court directs), the Commission recommends that the defendant should be able to apply to strike out the claim. In considering the issue of leave, the report provides that the court should take into account all the relevant circumstances without limit. However, the Commission advances five specific matters which it considers that the court should take into account, namely: the applicant's good faith; the interests of the company; that the wrong has been, or may be, approved in general meeting; the views of an independent organ; and the availability of alternative remedies.

With regard to the general meeting's ability to ratify a wrongful act, the Law Commission's proposals are, to say the least, somewhat confusing. While the report seeks to completely abrogate the existing common law derivative action, it nevertheless provides that the ratification of a wrongful act should be able to be impugned in cases involving fraud, but in all other cases, the Commission recommends that effective ratification should continue to be a complete bar to the continuation of a derivative action. Although the report does not define the concept of fraud, neither does it attempt to limit its definition in a way which would preclude the existing examples of a 'fraud on the minority'. Accordingly, it is probable that the examples of fraud, as expounded in cases involving the common law derivative action, will remain capable, if ratified, of being impugned, i.e. a shareholder's ability to commence a derivative action will still exist, irrespective of the ratification of a wrongful (fraudulent) act. Yet in such cases it is to be noted that the report recommends that the court should take account of the fact that the company in general meeting has resolved not to pursue the cause of action. Further, the report recommends that the rules on derivative actions should provide that the court has a power to adjourn a hearing to enable a meeting of shareholders to be convened for the purpose of considering a resolution affecting the claim.

Although the advantage of a statutory derivative action would *prima facie* increase the ability of a complainant's right to seek redress for abuses of corporate power, it is nevertheless questionable whether the shift towards the protection of minority interests, by the adoption of a statutory derivative action, is in truth necessary in the light of the protection already provided by s 459 of the Companies Act 1985 (discussed in Chapter 23). Although s 459 is presently almost exclusively used as a means to pursue a personal and not a derivative action, s 459 is permissive of an action which affects members generally. An action affecting the company as whole may therefore be actionable under s 459. Indeed, under s 461 of the Companies Act 1985, specific reference is made to a remedy which is of a derivative character, i.e. s 461(c) provides that the court may authorise civil proceedings to be brought in the name and on behalf of the company by such person or persons and on such terms as the court may direct.

Suggested further reading

Wedderburn (1957) CLJ 194 and (1958) CLJ 93
Prentice (1976) 92 LQR 502
Joffe (1977) 40 MLR 71
Smith [1978] 41 MLR 147
Boyle (1980) 1 Co Law 3
Burridge [1981] MLR 40
Sullivan [1985] CLJ 236
Drury (1986) 45 CLJ 219
Baxter (1987) 38 NILQ 6
Sterling (1987) 50 MLR 468
Prentice (1988) 104 LQR

23

THE STATUTORY PROTECTION
OF A MINORITY SHAREHOLDER

INTRODUCTION

*The purpose of this chapter is to consider the impact of statutory interven-
tion in relation to the protection of minority shareholders. The expansive
and sometimes problematic nature of the case law which has developed from
the statutory provisions will be explored in depth. The focal point of the
chapter is a discussion of the unfair prejudice remedy represented by s 459 of
the Companies Act 1985. The chapter also examines s 122(1)(g) of the
Insolvency Act 1986, a provision which permits a shareholder to apply to
have a company wound up in circumstances where the court considers that
remedy to be just and equitable.*

THE DEVELOPMENT OF A STATUTORY REMEDY FOR
OPPRESSIVE CONDUCT

In 1945, the Cohen Committee (Cmd 6659) considered it essential that legislation should be introduced to protect the interests of minority shareholders.
The reason why legislative intervention was deemed essential was largely
because of an absence in the availability of remedies for aggrieved minority
shareholders together with the many failures and restrictions of the derivative action. Although in appropriate circumstances, a minority shareholder
had a right to seek a winding up order against the company, this alternative
was rather a drastic measure of the last resort (discussed below).

In response to the Cohen Committee recommendations, statutory intervention was introduced into the Companies Act 1948 by s 210. This section
provided a remedy against conduct which was considered oppressive to the
interests of a part of the membership. Unfortunately, s 210 did not establish
itself as a practical remedy for the minority shareholder. The failings of s 210
may be briefly summarised as follows. In order to succeed under s 210, a
petitioner had to establish that the facts of his case justified the court in
ordering that the company should be wound up on just and equitable
grounds. Once that requirement was established, the petitioner had to convince the court that a s 210 remedy was more apt as an alternative to the
winding up order; see e.g. *Re Bellador Silk Ltd* [1965] 1 All ER 667.
Secondly, the judicial interpretation of s 210 proved to be of an inflexible
nature in relation to the term 'oppressive conduct'. In *Scottish Co-operative*

Wholesale Society v *Meyer* [1959] AC 324 Lord Simmonds defined the term to mean 'burdensome, harsh and wrongful'. Such an austere definition was a paramount factor in limiting the successful application of the section to only two actions, namely, *Scottish Co-operative Wholesale Society* v *Meyer* and *Re H Harmer Ltd* [1959] 1 WLR 62. Further difficulties with the s 210 remedy included a need to establish that the oppressive conduct was of a continuous nature up to the time of the petition and further that the conduct affected the petitioning member, *qua* member, and not in some outside capacity; see e.g. *Ebrahimi* v *Westbourne Galleries Ltd* [1973] AC 360 (discussed below).

THE UNFAIR PREJUDICE REMEDY

The difficulties associated with the s 210 remedy were to a large extent removed by s 75 of the Companies Act 1980. In accordance with the recommendations of the Jenkins Committee 1962, the phrase 'oppressive conduct' was replaced with a more flexible requirement based upon the petitioner's need to substantiate an action for 'unfairly prejudicial conduct'. In addition, the requirements under s 210 for a petitioner to establish grounds for a winding up order and that a continuous course of oppression had occurred up to the time of the petition, were removed by the new legislation. With the passing of the Companies Act 1985, s 75 of the Companies Act 1980 became (without any change in its wording) s 459 of the 1985 Act. With the implementation of Sch 19, para 11 of the Companies Act 1989, the wording of s 459 was slightly, although significantly altered, in order to confirm that an action under s 459 extended to a situation whereby unfairly prejudicial conduct affected members generally; prior to the implementation of the 1989 Act, an action under s 459 had been limited to one whereby the unfairly prejudicial conduct affected but a part of the membership. Therefore, s 459(1) now provides as follows:

> 'A member of a company may apply to the court by petition for an order ... on the ground that the company's affairs are being or have been conducted in a manner which is unfairly prejudicial to the interests of its *members generally* or some part of its members (including himself) or that any actual or proposed act or omission on the part of the company (including an act or omission on its behalf) is or would be prejudicial.' (*1989 Act amendment*)

The effect of the 1989 Act amendment

Prior to the amendment to s 459 by the Companies Act 1989, the interpretation of unfairly prejudicial conduct was often dominated by the fact that unfairly prejudicial conduct had to affect but a part of the membership; see e.g. *Re Carrington Viyella plc* (1983) 1 BCC 98, 951 and *Re a Company* (*No 00370*) *of 1987* [1988] 1 WLR 1068, where Harman J remarked:

> 'It may be regrettable but, in my view, the statute providing a statutory remedy, although in wide terms in part, does contain the essential provision that

the conduct complained of must be conduct unfairly prejudicial to a part of the members, and that cannot possibly mean unfairly prejudicial to all the members ... I am of the opinion that no s 459 petition could be based on conduct that has had an equal effect on all the shareholders and was not intended to be discriminatory between shareholders.' (at pp 1074–5)

Harman's J interpretation of s 459 supported the view that the section was inapplicable where the conduct in question was applied without any intention to discriminate against the legal rights of a part of the membership. Unfortunately, this interpretation failed to consider the consequences of a prejudicial act upon variable membership interests. In *Re Sam Weller* [1990] BCLC 80 Peter Gibson J strongly opposed the idea that a member's interest should be viewed without recall to the variable nature of shareholding interests. His lordship firmly believed that where corporate conduct had a prejudicial effect on the legal rights of the entire membership then such a scenario would not in itself present an obstacle to an action on behalf of a part of the membership. In support of his proposition, Peter Gibson J cited with approval the decision of the House of Lords in *Scottish Co-operative Wholesale Society v Meyer* [1959] AC 324. Although the *Meyer* case was commenced under s 210 of the Companies Act 1948, the wording of s 210 mirrored that of s 459 in so far as the conduct in question had to affect a part of the membership. The House of Lords held that conduct which touched the whole of the membership in an oppressive manner could nevertheless substantiate an action by a part of the membership. The House fully endorsed the decisions of the Court of Session (Scotland) from which the *Meyer* appeal originated ((1954) SLT 273). The Lord President of the Inner House of the Court of Session expressed the following opinion (at p 277), an opinion quoted by Peter Gibson J in *Re Sam Weller*:

'... a point is taken with regard to the statutory requirement that the oppression must affect "some part of the members", the suggestion being that s 210 is not available in any case where all the members, as distinguished from a part, are in the same boat ... I have come to think that this is to give too narrow a meaning to this remedial position and to place on the words "some part" an emphasis which they were not intended to bear ... When the section inquires whether the affairs of the company are being conducted in a manner oppressive to some part of the members, including the complainer, that question can still be answered in the affirmative even if, *qua* member of the company, the oppressor has suffered the same or even a greater prejudice.' (at p 86)

As a result of the Companies Act 1989, a petition under s 459 may now be commenced irrespective of whether the unfairly prejudicial conduct affects a part of the membership or the members generally. As such, the difficulties encountered by the interpretation of the term 'part of the membership' have *prima facie* been resolved.

However, although the phrase 'members generally' may have been intended to impart a meaning which can be equated with the whole or the entire membership, it is arguable that the word 'generally' falls short of such an objective. If conduct affects interests generally, it is arguable that it may only affect a majority of interests, in which case is not a majority of the membership merely a part, albeit a large part of the total membership? In Commonwealth countries where the oppression/unfair prejudice remedy is employed, it has become commonplace to state that the corporate conduct may affect either a part or the whole of the membership. Accordingly the use of the word 'whole' would surely have been a more emphatic alternative to the use of the word 'generally'. For example, s 320(1)(a)(i) of the Australian Companies Code provides:

> **'A member who believes that the affairs of the company are being conducted in a manner that is oppressive or unfairly prejudicial to, or unfairly discriminatory against, a member or members, or in a manner that is contrary to the interests of the members as a whole ...'**

However, it is difficult to appreciate how corporate conduct may be perceived as affecting the totality of membership interests in an unfairly prejudicial manner. Whilst conduct may have a prejudicial effect on the entire membership of a company, it is unlikely that every membership interest will be affected in an unfairly prejudicial manner. Membership interests are of course of a variable nature. For example, is it logical to suppose that those in control of a company would ever instigate conduct which would have the effect of unfairly prejudicing their own interests? While it is possible to imagine a situation where those in control of a company might, through their negligence, conduct the affairs of a company to the prejudice of all membership interests, it is nevertheless unlikely that the company's affairs would, in respect of those responsible for the misconduct, be considered to have been conducted in an unfair manner, i.e. those responsible for the misconduct could surely not complain of an unfairly prejudicial act which was of their own making.

DEFINING THE CONCEPT OF UNFAIRLY PREJUDICIAL CONDUCT

The court employs an objective test to determine whether a particular type of conduct may or may not be classed as unfairly prejudicial. The objective test was also used to ascertain oppressive conduct under s 210 of the Companies Act 1948. The test to determine unfairly prejudicial conduct may be tentatively expressed in the following manner: 'Would a reasonable bystander regard the conduct, which forms the subject matter of the complaint, as constituting conduct which affected the petitioner's membership interests in an unfairly prejudicial manner?'

According to Hoffmann LJ in *Re Saul D Harrison & Sons plc* [1994] BCC 475 at p 488, the starting point in any case under s 459 will be to ask whether the conduct of which the shareholder complains was conduct of a type which transgressed the terms of the company's articles, for it is the articles in which the contractual terms which govern the relationship between the shareholders and the company are to be found. However, as Hoffmann LJ pointed out (at p 489), there will be cases in which a company's articles do not fully reflect the understandings upon which the shareholders are associated, so that conduct which apparently complies with the terms of a company's articles may still found a petition under s 459.

While it is impossible to give a precise definition as to what type of conduct may fall to be defined as unfairly prejudicial, the term 'unfairly prejudicial' does in some respects appear synonymous with conduct which may be described as 'unjust and inequitable' (by analogy, see the discussion of the just and equitable winding up order, discussed below). It should also be noted that while s 459 provides a primary function in offering statutory protection to minority shareholders, the section does not in itself preclude the possibility of a majority shareholder commencing an action for unfairly prejudicial conduct; see e.g. *Re Baltic Real Estate Ltd* [1992] BCC 629 and, more recently, *Re Legal Costs Negotiators Ltd* [1999] BCC 547.

Prejudicial conduct

Prejudicial conduct is damaging conduct which is caused in a commercial as opposed to an emotional sense; see e.g. the judgment of Harman J in *Re Unisoft Group Ltd (No 3)* [1994] 2 BCLC 609 at p 611. Accordingly, the most obvious example of a membership interest being subjected to prejudice in the commercial sense is where the conduct of a company's affairs depreciates the monetary value of a member's shareholding interest.

Unfair conduct

The ability to label conduct as being 'unfair' will obviously depend upon the nature and extent of the effect of the conduct and in many cases will also be influenced by the underlying motive behind the pursuit of the particular conduct in question. Certainly it is clear that in cases where the motive for and the effect of prejudicial conduct creates a discriminatory imbalance in relation to the rights and/or interests of a member or the members generally, that such conduct will amount to conduct of an unfair nature. However, by contrast, other than where an alleged instance of commercial misjudgement is of a type which amounts to negligence of a degree to substantiate a breach of a director's duty of care, or results in self-serving negligence, it is doubtful whether such a misjudgement will ever amount to unfair conduct. For example, in *Re Elgindata Ltd* [1991] BCLC 959, a case in which a petitioner claimed that his membership interest had been subjected to unfairly prejudicial conduct as a result of the company's negligent mismanagement, Warner J opined:

'... it is not for this court to resolve such disagreements on a petition under s 459. Not only is a judge ill qualified to do so, but there can be no unfairness to the petitioner in those in control of the company's affairs taking a different view from theirs on such matters ... a shareholder acquires shares in a company knowing that their value will depend in some measure on the competence of the management. He takes the risk that the management may not prove to be of the highest quality. Short of a breach by a director of his duty of skill and care ... there is prima facie no unfairness to a shareholder ...'
(at p 994)

(See also *Re Blackwood Hodge plc* [1997] 2 BCLC 650.)

However, in accordance with the decision of Arden J in *Re Macro (Ipswich) Ltd* [1994] 2 BCLC 354, it would appear that the learned judge, while not purporting to challenge the accepted view that members of the judiciary should not ordinarily involve themselves in determining the commercial value of management decisions, nevertheless sought to extend the scope of an action under s 459 in respect of an action based upon negligent conduct. Briefly, the facts of the case were as follows. Mr Thompson (T), the majority shareholder and sole director of two independent companies (companies linked however, in the sense that the share capital of both was divided between two families), failed to adequately supervise the management of properties owned by the two companies. The supervision of the said properties was under the control of an estate agency controlled by T. As a result of the mismanagement of the properties, the value of the shareholding interests depreciated. In concluding that the minority shareholder's interest had been unfairly prejudiced, Arden J held that a s 459 action was sustainable in circumstances where the mismanagement of a company was related to the administration of a company's affairs, i.e. as opposed to an instance or instances of commercial misjudgement involving, for example, the purchase or sale of corporate assets. It is also interesting to note that Arden J (in referring to the recommendations of the Cadbury Committee Report, despite the fact that the report was concerned with public and not private companies) regarded the absence of any independent director on the boards of the two companies as unfairly prejudicial to the interests of minority shareholders. Indeed, it is submitted that this innovative suggestion relating to the deficiencies of the actual board structure of a private company may be taken up in future cases where, for example, despite the absence of a petitioner's legitimate expectation to participate in the management of a company, a court is of the opinion that the interests of shareholders were unfairly prejudiced by the existence of a situation in which the control of corporate affairs had been vested in the hands of a dominant and inflexible master.

Nevertheless, it should be noted following the decision of Jonathan Parker J in *Re Astec (BSR) plc* [1999] BCC 59, that it is unlikely whether a public company's non-compliance with corporate governance issues, such as those raised in the Cadbury Report, will ever be capable of giving rise to a successful action under s 459. Although the learned judge held that the shareholders of a public company would rightly expect that rules relating to corporate governance issues should be complied with, he nevertheless opined that such an expectation could not give rise to an equitable constraint on the exercise of legal rights so contained within the company's constitution. Jonathan Parker J justified his belief on the premise that for the legal rights of the membership to be subject to equitable constraints it would be essential to establish a personal relationship (of mutual trust and understanding) as between the petitioner and the company, a relationship which may be apt to describe the internal workings of a private company but one which would be misplaced in the context of a public company.

Conduct of a company's affairs

As a company's management functions are primarily vested in its board of directors, it is to be expected that the board or individual directors who have been authorised to act by the board, will normally be responsible for the conduct of the company's affairs. However, this may not always be the case. For example, in *Nicholas* v *Soundcraft Electronics Ltd* [1993] BCLC 360 the Court of Appeal found that in a holding company/subsidiary relationship, the holding company could be held responsible for conducting the affairs of its subsidiary. The case concerned an allegation by a minority shareholder of the subsidiary to the effect that, the holding company's policy of withholding payments due to its subsidiary amounted to unfairly prejudicial conduct. While the Court of Appeal concluded that the holding company had conducted the affairs of its subsidiary in a prejudicial way, the court nevertheless held that by withholding funds from its subsidiary, the holding company had acted for the greater good of the group, i.e. to secure the survival of the holding company without which the subsidiary company would have perished. As such, it was not possible to argue that the holding company had conducted the affairs of its subsidiary in an unfair manner; see also *Scottish Co-op Wholesale Society* v *Meyer* [1959] AC 324 (discussed in Chapter 2).

Although, in appropriate circumstances, a s 459 action may be successfully commenced in the context of a holding company–subsidiary relationship, i.e. where the unfairly prejudicial conduct of the subsidiary's affairs was instigated as a consequence of its holding company's *de facto* control, it is nevertheless improbable whether a majority shareholder of a company could, *qua* shareholder, ever be found to have conducted the company's affairs, other than where he controlled the constitution of the company's board; see e.g. *Re Astec (BSR) plc* [1999] BCC 59. However, where the subject matter of an allegation under s 459 is founded on conduct emanating from a resolution of the general meeting, it is not inconceivable that a majority shareholder, in sanctioning the conduct in question, could, in such a case, be deemed to have had a prime responsibility for the conduct of the company's affairs.

Effect of the conduct

To substantiate a finding of unfairly prejudicial conduct, a petitioner must produce evidence to confirm that those responsible for the management of the company's affairs commenced a course of conduct which produced more than a trivial prejudicial effect on the petitioner's membership interest; see e.g. *Re Saul D Harrison & Sons plc* [1994] BCC 475. Where the evidence which purports to support a s 459 petition is considered to be inadequate, the alleged wrongdoers may apply to the court to strike out the petition. For example, in *Re a Company, ex parte Burr* [1992] BCLC 724 a petition under s 459 was dismissed on the premise that the alleged misconduct, namely, the decision of a company's board of directors to continue to trade the business for the purpose of protecting the directors' own interests, could not be corroborated by documentary evidence. In dismissing the petition Vinelott J remarked thus:

> 'In my judgment, the petitioner has not adduced any evidence which, if accepted at trial would support the allegations in the petition and justify the relief sought. The petitioner's case in substance is that something might be revealed on discovery in the course of cross examination of the directors that could be relied on as justifying the petition. That is not a proper ground for presenting a petition. The damaging effect which the presentation of the petition may have on the business of the company, even if it is not advertised, has often been the subject of judicial comment. A petition should not be presented unless it can be supported by evidence which, if accepted at the trial, would found a claim for relief.' (at p 736)

(See also *Re a Company (No 008699 of 1985)* [1986] BCLC 382.)

The definition of a member for the purposes of s 459

The definition of 'a member of a company' is provided by s 22 of the Companies Act 1985. Section 22(1) states:

> 'The subscribers of a company's memorandum are deemed to have agreed to become members of the company, and on its registration shall be entered as such on its register of members.'

Section 22(2) provides that:

> 'Every other person who agrees to become a member of a company, and whose name is entered in its register of members, is a member of the company.'

A mere promise to transfer shares to a third party is not sufficient to enable the third party to claim that he has agreed to become a member; see e.g. *Re a Company (No 003160 of 1986)* [1986] BCLC 391. However, in *Re Nuneaton Borough AFC Ltd* [1989] BCLC 454 it was held that the phrase 'agrees to become a member' would be satisfied where a person claiming to be a member of a company had actually assented to become a member, even if such an assent was not confirmed by the signing of a contractual document.

A matter of some doubt exists in relation to the ability of a past member of a company to petition under s 459. On a literal construction of the section, it would appear that a past member would not have the capacity to present a petition, i.e. it is impossible to construe a past member as 'a member of the company'. However, in *Re a Company (No 005287 of 1985)* [1986] 1 WLR 281 Hoffmann J suggested that there should be no such bar to a past member petitioning under s 459. It is suggested (despite the literal interpretation of s 459 and despite the contrary recommendations of the Law Commission, discussed below) that where the instigation of the conduct which forms the subject matter of a complaint under s 459 occurred at a time when the petitioner was a member of the company, an action under s 459 should be possible, irrespective of the fact that any malpractice surrounding the instigation of the conduct was only discovered after the petitioner ceased to be a member. Surely, it would be unreasonable and inequitable to deny a past shareholder the right to seek redress where, for example, the resulting effect of the conduct had an active influence on either the shareholder's decision to dispose of his shareholding interest or the value of the interest at the time of its disposal.

It should however be noted that s 459(2) does provide a remedy to non-members of a company in circumstances where shares have been transferred or transmitted by operation of law, for example, in the case of personal representatives or trustees in bankruptcy; see e.g. *Re Quickdome Ltd* [1988] BCLC 370.

While it may be doubtful as to whether a past member can pursue an action under s 459, there seems little doubt that a past member of a company may be held responsible for the unfairly prejudicial conduct of a company's affairs in a situation where the conduct was instigated by the past member prior to the disposal of his shareholding interest: so held in *Re a Company (No 005287 of 1985)* [1986] 1 WLR 281. Indeed, as the scope of the remedies available to a petitioner under s 459 are very wide (discussed below), it would seem to follow that in a situation where a party was likely to be affected by any order made by the court, a court could deem that the said party be made a respondent to the petition notwithstanding that the party in question had not been involved in the conduct giving rise to the petition; see e.g. the decision of Lindsay J in *Re Little Olympian Each Ways Ltd* [1994] 2 BCLC 420, also the decision of Vinelott J in *Re a Company (No 007281 of 1986)* [1987] BCLC 593.

The definition of membership interests (legitimate expectations) for the purposes of section 459

To substantiate an action under s 459, the offending corporate act must affect a membership interest or, as in *Re Kenyon Swansea Ltd* [1987] BCLC 514, there must be evidence to establish the likelihood of a threatened act, i.e. an act which, if it was to be implemented, would constitute unfairly prejudicial conduct. Where a petition is sought to restrain a threatened act, there must be positive as opposed to speculative evidence of a future intention to instigate the conduct in question. However, such an action may be sustainable even in circumstances where the immediate threat of employing the conduct had momentarily passed.

Although the phrase 'membership interests' includes those membership rights which are protected by companies legislation and the rights attached to the memorandum and articles, the distinction between membership rights and membership interests is obscure and, as one might therefore expect, the judicial interpretation of the term 'interests' has been somewhat vague. In *Re Carrington Viyella plc* [1983] 1 BCC 98, 951, Vinelott J opined that a membership interest was in reality no more than a membership right. On the other hand, in *Re a Company (No 008699 of 1985)* [1986] BCLC 382 Hoffmann J considered that a membership interest encompassed a wider concept than a membership right and that coupled with the word 'unfair' s 459 allowed the court to consider the legitimate expectations of the membership of a company. For example, Hoffmann J believed that in a small domestic type company a legitimate expectation could exist in a situation where a person became a shareholder on the premise that he would be allowed to participate in the management of the company (under s 14 of the CA 1985 no such expectation would be enforceable in so far as it would amount to the enforcement of an outsider right). Hoffmann's J view was echoed by the decision of the Privy Council in *Tay Bok Choon v Tahansan Sdn Bhd* [1987] 3 BCC 132 and the judgment of Mummery J in *Re a Company (No 00314 of 1989)* [1991] BCLC 154. Indeed, it is now firmly established that a member of a private company may have a legitimate expectation to participate in the management of the company in circumstances where the member's legitimate expectation was related to some form of express or implied understanding which confirmed his right to participate in the management of the company; see e.g. *R & H Electrical Ltd v Haden Bill Electrical Ltd* [1995] BCC 958 and *Quinlan v Essex Hinge Co Ltd* [1996] 2 BCLC 417.

Nevertheless, it is interesting to observe that, in accordance with the decision of Rattee J in *Re Leeds United Holdings Ltd* [1996] 2 BCLC 545, it would appear essential for a petitioner in seeking to establish a legitimate expectation to ensure that the exception is related to the conduct of a company's affairs as opposed to, for example, personal rights afforded to the petitioner by the terms of a shareholder agreement. The case in question concerned the restructuring of Leeds United football club into a public limited company. In anticipation of the reconstruction, the three shareholder/directors of the club (G, S and F) entered into a shareholders' agreement; the agreement had been intended to incorporate pre-emption proposals, but such proposals were never formalised. A new company, Leeds United Holdings plc ('the company'), was incorporated for the purpose of acquiring the club. The bulk of the company's shares were held by three companies, each in turn individually owned or partly controlled by G, S and F. G, S and F were appointed as directors of the new company; a fourth director was subsequently appointed. G later complained that S and F were making decisions concerning the running of the club and the company without consulting him.

Subsequently, the new company was made the subject matter of two competing bids. G favoured one bid while S and F favoured the other. G was outvoted. G then presented a petition under s 459 in which it was alleged that the company was a quasi-partnership company consisting of G, S and F and that the relationship of mutual trust and confidence between them had irretrievably broken down. It was further contended that G had legitimate expectations which had been breached, including the failure to implement the pre-emption rights mentioned in the restructuring.

Rattee J held that the petition should be struck out. The learned judge opined that even if G's evidence was accepted as to his understanding of a shareholders' agreement containing pre-emption rights, such an agreement would not give rise to a legitimate expectation that the respondents would not deal with those shares without the petitioner's consent. An expectation that a shareholder would not sell his shares without the consent of other shareholders did not relate in any way to conduct of the company's affairs and could not be protected under s 459. In reality G's real grievance was that the board of the company had recommended one bid rather than the other. The learned judge commented:

> 'In my judgment, the legitimate expectation which the court has held in other cases can give rise to a claim for relief under s 459 must, having regard to the purpose of the section as expressed in s 459(1), be a legitimate expectation relating to the conduct of the company's affairs, the most obvious and common example being an expectation of being allowed to participate in decisions as to such conduct. An expectation that a shareholder will not sell his shares without the consent of some other or other shareholders does not relate in any way to the conduct of the company's affairs and, therefore, cannot, in my judgment, fall to be protected by the court under s 459.' (at pp 559–60)

In *Re J E Cade & Son Ltd* [1991] BCC 360 Warner J equated the concept of a membership interest with the interpretation afforded to the use of 'interests' so used in determining an action brought under the just and equitable winding up provision, i.e. s 122(1)(g) of the Insolvency Act 1986 (this provision is discussed below). However, Warner J believed that the determination of a membership interest was to be strictly confined to obligations which were related to strict legal rights, for example, the terms of a company's constitution, a director's service contract or an express shareholder agreement. In other words, although Warner J accepted that equitable considerations should be examined when determining the scope of a membership interest, he nevertheless believed that pure outsider interests unconnected to the strict legal rights of membership could not, for the purposes of s 459 (and s 122(1)(g), IA 1986), found appropriate grounds upon which relief could be sought. Warner J was of the opinion that there could be:

> '... no such third tier of rights and obligations. The court, exercising its jurisdiction to wind up a company on the just and equitable ground or jurisdiction conferred by s 459 ... has a very wide discretion, but it does not sit under a palm tree.' (at p 372)

However, notwithstanding that Warner's J interpretation of the concept of a membership interest has been widely approved in subsequent cases, it is suggested that the said interpretation is too restrictive. Although it is accepted that proper boundaries must be drawn to limit the concept of membership interests – otherwise a membership interest might fall to be defined in terms of a member's personal interest: an interest quite unrelated to the functioning of a company – to suggest that a membership interest must be in some way linked to a strict legal right is perhaps to endanger the very essence of the distinction between a membership interest and membership right. Some support for this view is to be found in the words of Sir Donald Nicholls V–C in *Re Tottenham Hotspur plc* [1994] 1 BCLC 655, namely:

> '**In deciding whether and how to exercise its wide powers under s 459, the court will have regard not only to the company's constitution but also to equitable considerations arising from expectations created by the dealings between members. The court will do what is just and equitable in all the circumstances.**' (at p 659)

Notwithstanding the potentially restrictive nature of the interpretation afforded to the definition of 'legitimate expectations' by Warner J in *Re J E Cade*, it would now appear to be settled, that the said interpretation is to be regarded as the acceptable norm in construing actions under s 459. This view is confirmed by *O'Neill v Phillips* [1999] 2 BCLC 1, the first appeal under s 459 to have reached the House of Lords. The facts of the case were as follows.

P controlled a company involved in the construction industry, owning the company's entire share capital and acting as its sole director. A company employee (R) proved himself to be invaluable to the company and was rewarded with a gift of a 25 per cent holding of the company's shares, and a directorship in the company. O was also credited with half of the company's profits (some of which he left in the company). O acted as the company's *de facto* managing director and his personal involvement and commitment to the company was such that he guaranteed the company's bank overdraft, secured by a charge on his house. As a result of O's involvement in the company, P gave R an informal promise (though no formal agreement was ever signed) to the effect that if certain targets were met, R would be given a 50 per cent holding in the company (50 per cent voting rights).

Although with O at its helm the company initially prospered, a decline in the growth of the construction industry led to a gradual decline in the company's fortunes, to the extent that P became extremely concerned about the company's performance and O's involvement in the management of its affairs. P's concern was such that he returned to head the management of the company. Subsequently, O was informed that he would no longer be paid 50 per cent of the profits and that he would only be paid his salary and dividends in respect of his 25 per cent holding in the company. After leaving the employment of the company, O petitioned under s 459 on the basis that his legitimate expectations of membership had been unfairly prejudiced. He claimed he had a legitimate expectation of acquiring a 50 per cent holding in the company and an expectation of continuing to receive 50 per cent of the profits. O further claimed that P's actions and treatment of him had, in effect, forced him to leave the employment of the company.

At first instance (heard by Judge Paul Baker QC), O failed in his action, in so far as P had never entered into any formal agreement with O in respect of the alleged share issue nor had there been any formal promise to pay P 50 per cent of the company's profits, i.e. there was no legal right to which any legitimate expectation could attach. In reversing this decision, the Court of Appeal (heard as *Re a Company No 00709 of 1992 – Re Pectel Ltd* [1997] 2 BCLC 739) held that, notwithstanding the absence of any formal agreement, O did have a legitimate expectation of receiving 50 per cent of the profits and 50 per cent of the shares, i.e. when the targets were met. Nourse LJ stated:

> 'I am, with respect to the judge, unable to accept his assessment of the position. On 29 January 1985, less than two years after he had started to work for the company, Mr O'Neill became both a member and a director of it. It is true that he did not subscribe for his shares and did not bring any capital into the company. But that is immaterial. From the end of January 1985, or at any rate from May of that year when the understanding as to an equal sharing of profits was come to, the company represented an association continued on the basis of a personal relationship involving mutual confidence between Mr Phillips and Mr O'Neill, with an understanding that Mr O'Neill should participate in the conduct of the business and restrictions on share transfers. All three typical elements of a quasi-partnership were present. At all times thereafter Mr O'Neill had a legitimate expectation that he would receive 50 per cent of the profits. By the beginning of 1991 he had a legitimate expectation, subject to meeting the £500 000 and £1 000 000 targets respectively, that he would receive 50 per cent of its voting shares.' (at p 769)

In overturning the decision of the Court of Appeal, Lord Hoffmann, giving the leading judgment of the House, stated:

> 'In the case of s 459, the background has the following two features. First, a company is an association of persons for an economic purpose, usually entered into with legal advice and some degree of formality. The terms of the association are contained in the articles of association and sometimes in collateral agreements between the shareholders. Thus the manner in which the affairs of the company may be conducted is closely regulated by rules to which the shareholders have agreed. Secondly, company law has developed seamlessly from the law of partnership, which was treated by equity, like the Roman *societas*, as a contract of good faith. One of the traditional roles of equity, as a separate jurisdiction, was to restrain the exercise of strict legal rights in certain relationships in which it considered that this would be contrary to good faith. These principles have, with appropriate modification, been carried over into company law.
>
> The first of these two features leads to the conclusion that a member of a company will not ordinarily be entitled to complain of unfairness unless there has been some breach of the terms on which he agreed that the affairs of the

company should be conducted. But the second leads to the conclusion that there will be cases in which equitable considerations make it unfair for those conducting the affairs of the company to rely upon their strict legal powers. Thus unfairness may consist in a breach of the rules or in using the rules in a manner which equity would regard as contrary to good faith ... In my view, a balance has to be struck between the breadth of the discretion given to the court and the principle of legal certainty. The way in which such equitable principles operate is tolerably well settled and in my view it would be wrong to abandon them in favour of some wholly indefinite notion of fairness. In *Re Saul D Harrison & Sons plc*, I used the term "legitimate expectation", borrowed from public law, as a label for the "correlative right" to which a relationship between company members may give rise in a case when, on equitable principles, it would be regarded as unfair for a majority to exercise a power conferred upon them by the articles to the prejudice of another member ... It was probably a mistake to use this term, as it usually is when one introduces a new label to describe a concept which is already sufficiently defined in other terms. The concept of a legitimate expectation should not be allowed to lead a life of its own, capable of giving rise to equitable restraints in circumstances to which the traditional equitable principles have no application.' (at pp 7–11)

More specifically, in relation to the facts of the case, Lord Hoffmann concluded:

'... I think that the Court of Appeal may have been misled by the expression "legitimate expectation". The real question is whether in fairness or equity [O] had a right to the shares. On this point, one runs up against what seems to me the insuperable obstacle of the judge's finding that [P] never agreed to give them. He made no promise on the point. From which it seems to me to follow that there is no basis, consistent with established principles of equity, for a court to hold that [P] was behaving unfairly in withdrawing from the negotiation. This would not be restraining the exercise of legal rights. It would be imposing upon [P] an obligation to which he never agreed. Where, as here, parties enter into negotiations with a view to a transfer of shares on professional advice and subject to a condition that they are not to be bound until a formal document has been executed, I do not think it is possible to say that an obligation has arisen in fairness or equity at an earlier stage. The same reasoning applies to the sharing of profits. The judge found as a fact that [P] made no unconditional promise about the sharing of profits. He had said informally that he would share the profits equally while [O] managed the company and he himself did not have to be involved in day-to-day business. He deliberately retained control of the company and with it, as the judge said, the right to redraw [O's] responsibilities. This he did without objection in August 1991. The consequence was that he came back to running the business and [O] was no longer managing director. He had made no promise to share the profits equally in such circumstances and it was therefore not inequitable or unfair for him to refuse to carry on doing so.' (at pp 12–13)

In respect of a public company, it is to be noted from *Re Blue Arrow plc* [1987] BCLC 585 and *Re a Company (No 003096 of 1987)* [1988] 4 BCC 80 that there can be no legitimate expectation appertaining to a member's participation in management. Indeed, if a contrary view was taken the management control of a public company could be artificially protected, a notion which would be contradictory to the ability of future shareholders to assert their wishes in respect of determining the persons best suited to participate in the management of the company. Further, in *Re Astec (BSR) plc* [1999] BCC 59 Jonathan Palmer J opined that it would be a misconception to assume that any form of legitimate expectation could be properly attached to the shares of a public company. The learned judge stated:

> 'In my judgment, as the authorities stand today, the concept of "legitimate expectation" as explained by Hoffmann LJ in *Saul D Harrison* can have no place in the context of public listed companies. Moreover, its introduction in that context would, as it seems to me, in all probability prove to be a recipe for chaos. If the market in a company's shares is to have any credibility, members of the public dealing in that market must it seems to me be entitled to proceed on the footing that the constitution of the company is as it appears in the company's public documents, unaffected by any extraneous equitable considerations and constraints.'

However, notwithstanding the logic of the above statement, it is to be observed that while the rights of shareholders of a public company may not ordinarily be viewed as comprising equitable considerations, i.e. legitimate expectations, it may nevertheless be conceivable, albeit unlikely, for a legitimate expectation to be found where, for example, a public company is the subject of an action in which shareholder interests are not solely dominated or motivated by commercial considerations. The source of this suggestion is to be found within the judgment of Sir Donald Nicholls in *Re Tottenham Hotspur* [1994] BCLC 655.

The interests of the company as a whole?

Where a company's affairs have been conducted in the best interests of the company as a whole, is it nevertheless possible that such conduct could still give rise to a minority action for unfairly prejudicial conduct? Is an individual member's interest independent from an interest which serves the greater good of a company? If affirmative answers are given to such questions, logic would seem to dictate that the notion of majority rule is but a theoretical myth, even where the majority purport to act to benefit the company as a whole.

Yet, in *Re D R Chemicals Ltd* [1989] 5 BCC 39 Peter Gibson J appeared to suggest that an individual member's interest was quite independent from the interests of the company as a whole. The learned judge observed:

> 'I do not doubt that if the objective bystander observes unfairly prejudicial conduct by a respondent the fact that the respondent had a proper motive will not prevent the conduct from falling within the section.' (at p 46)

However, notwithstanding the above comment, is it correct to assert that fairness, in relation to a course of conduct, should be measured only in terms of an individual shareholder's interests without further consideration of any potential benefits to the company as a whole? For example, a company may make a rights issue at a fair and reasonable price so as to inject more capital into the company. A member may nevertheless complain that because of his poor financial position he cannot afford to participate in the issue. His interest in the company would be diluted if other members subscribed for shares, his legitimate expectations in relation to his membership interest would be prejudiced. Yet, if the shares were issued for a proper purpose and the issue was objectively determined to benefit the company as a whole, surely it would be a radical and improper distortion of the balance of corporate power, as between shareholders and the management of the company, to allow the prejudiced member to claim unfair prejudice and succeed in an action under s 459. (See *Nicholas* v *Soundcraft Electronics Ltd* [1993] BCLC 360, discussed above.) Naturally, in the above example the position would be quite different matter if a company was aware of a member's inability to take up shares, and such knowledge was a factor in the company's decision to issue shares. In such a case the conduct would be unfairly prejudicial in so far as the share issue would not have been for a proper purpose; see e.g., *Re Cumana Ltd* [1986] BCLC 430.

A company's involvement in a section 459 action

As is the norm, a dispute which gives rise to a s 459 action is essentially one as between different sections of the shareholders. As such, the court may prevent the management of a company from causing the company's money to be spent on financing the defence of the action; see e.g. *Re Milgate Developments Ltd* [1991] BCC 24, *Re a Company (No 004502 of 1988) ex parte Johnson* [1991] BCC 234 and *Corbett* v *Corbett* [1998] BCC 93. Accordingly, although a company will necessarily be included in a s 459 petition, the inclusion will often be as a nominal respondent to the action.

However, according to the judgment of Lindsay J in *Re a Company (No 1126 of 1992)* [1994] 2 BCLC 146, a presumption that a company should not be responsible for financing the defence of a s 459 petition involving a dispute between the majority and minority shareholders of the company may not be viewed as an absolute rule and accordingly may be subject to an exception where, for example, the defence of the action is viewed to be beneficial to the company as a whole. According to Lindsay J, the onus of establishing that the defence would benefit the company should fall upon the board of directors. Where the court is of the opinion that corporate funds were improperly used to finance the defence, the board, in such an instance, may be made personally liable to account to the company.

THE AVAILABLE REMEDIES TO AN ACTION UNDER SECTION 459

Where a petitioner succeeds in convincing the court that a company's affairs have been conducted in a manner which is unfairly prejudicial to the interests of a part of the membership or the membership generally, the court may make an order under s 461 of the Companies Act 1985. However, it should be noted that even where a petitioner establishes unfairly prejudicial conduct, the court may nevertheless decide that an order under s 461 would be inappropriate. The court may also come to the conclusion that a more convenient alternative remedy is available. For example, in *Re Full Cup International Trading Ltd* [1995] BCC 682 Ferris J (a decision which was later to be approved by the Court of Appeal) considered that the petitioner's interest would be better served if the company in question was subjected to a winding up order.

The courts have a very wide discretion in determining the nature of the relief under s 461(1) and may make an order as it thinks fit. A list of some examples of the type of orders which are available is given in s 461(2). The section provides that without prejudice to the generality of subsection (1), the court's order may:

(a) regulate the conduct of the company's affairs in the future;
(b) require the company to refrain from doing or continuing an act complained of by the petitioner or to do an act which the petitioner has complained it has omitted to do;
(c) authorise civil proceedings to be brought in the name and on behalf of the company by such person or persons and on such terms as the court may direct;
(d) provide for the purchase of the shares of any members of the company by other members or by the company itself and, in the case of a purchase by the company itself, authorise the reduction of the company's capital.

Section 461(3) and (4) further provides that the court has the power to restrain the company from making any alterations to the company's memorandum and articles or conversely that the court may make any alterations to the company's memorandum or articles as it sees fit.

The most common type of order which is sought is the one provided for by example (d), namely, the purchase of the petitioner's shares. In such cases the valuation of shares will be of paramount importance. The underlying theme in determining the value of shares is that of fairness. As such, the actual moment in time at which the valuation is to be calculated is apt to vary from case to case, i.e. the fairness of a particular valuation procedure will depend upon the individual circumstances of a case. Accordingly, depending upon the circumstances of a case, the valuation of shares may be based upon the value of the shares at a time prior to the petition, at the date of the petition or the actual date of the hearing.

In *Re London School of Electronics Ltd* [1986] Ch 211 it was suggested that the valuation procedure should normally take place at the time of the hearing (see e.g. *Re D R Chemicals Ltd* [1989] 5 BCC 39). However, this presumption is rebuttable. Indeed, in *Re London School of Electronics Ltd* it was decided that the valuation procedure should be as of the date of the petition, in so far as the company's fortunes had improved in the period between the petition and the hearing. It was considered unfair to allow the petitioner to gain any benefit from the company's improved position because the company had prospered following the petitioner's exclusion from its management. As stated, much will depend upon the individual circumstances of the case. For example, in *Scottish Co-operative Society* v *Meyer* [1959] AC 324 (heard under s 210, CA 1948), the House of Lords also valued the company's shares prior to the date of the hearing on the basis that the time of valuation should be at a moment in time prior to any effect that the offending conduct might have had on the value of the shares.

Indeed, circumstances may justify the valuation procedure being commenced at a time prior to the actual date of the petition. In *Re Cumana Ltd* [1986] BCLC 430 Lawton LJ put forward an example of a situation which would warrant the court in valuing shares prior to the commencement of the petition, namely:

> 'If, for example, there is before the court evidence that the majority shareholder deliberately took steps to depreciate the value of shares in anticipation of a petition being presented, it would be permissible to value the shares at a date before such action was taken.' (at p 436)

In accordance with the case of *Re Castleburn* [1989] 5 BCC 652, it would appear that where the articles of association provide a mechanism for a fair and independent valuation of shares, the court should not ordinarily interfere with the independent valuation procedure, unless the mechanism for the valuation is not properly adhered to or, where it is considered to be unjust. An example of where the court did depart from the valuation procedure within a company's articles is to be found in *Re Abbey Leisure* [1990] BCC 60 (discussed further below); also see *Re a Company (No 00330 of 1991) ex parte Holden* [1991] BCLC 597).

In determining the value of shares, the court will normally discount the value of a minority holding. However, for the purposes of s 461, no universal rule exists whereby a minority holding must be valued at a discount. Once again, the determining factor for the valuation process will be a desire to achieve justice between the parties to the petition. In cases where the petitioner's interest is affected in such an extreme and oppressive manner, the court's desire to achieve justice may involve it awarding an implied form of compensation, i.e. by its refusal to discount the value of a minority holding; see e.g. *Re Bird Precision Bellow* [1986] 1 Ch 658 and *Quinlan* v *Essex Hinge Co Ltd* [1996] 2 BCLC 417.

In the majority of cases involving a share purchase order, the order will be to the effect that the majority purchase the petitioner's shares. Nevertheless, it is possible for the court to order that the minority shareholder be permitted to purchase the majority's holding; see e.g. *Re Brenfield Squash Racquets*

Club [1996] 2 BCLC 184 and *Re Nuneaton Borough AFC Ltd (No 2)* [1991] BCC 44 (discussed below). However, it should be noted that in *Re Ringtower Holdings plc* [1989] 5 BCC 82 Peter Gibson J opined that an order for the purchase of the shares of the majority was an inappropriate one to make where the majority opposed the sale and the minority held less than 5 per cent of the company's share capital.

A decision which highlights the power of the courts to exercise their discretion in the making of an order under s 461 is provided by the case of *Re Nuneaton Borough AFC Ltd (No 2)* [1991] BCC 44. The peculiar facts of the case resulted in a decision to allow a minority shareholder (P) to purchase a controlling interest in the company (from R). However, as R had given substantial loans to the company, Harman J declared that it would be inequitable to force R to surrender his majority control without being able to recoup the money loaned to the company. Accordingly, his lordship ordered that as a condition of the purchase of R's shares, P should be required to repay the amount of the loan on behalf of the company. This decision is extreme in that the minority shareholder, in whose favour the s 459 petition was decided, was ultimately to be made responsible for the company's debts. It is respectfully submitted that where, as in this case, a creditor is unable to enforce a loan agreement against a company, the court, in exercising its very wide powers under s 461, should not readily overturn the principle that a company in its guise as a separate legal entity is accountable for its own debts.

As to the other s 461 orders, an excellent example of the type of situation which would invoke an order under s 461(a) is provided by the case of *Re Harmer Ltd* [1959] 1 WLR 62. This case (decided under s 210, CA 1948) involved a domestic company, the voting control of which was in the hands of the company's founder (H). H also held the post of 'governing director' (akin to the post of managing director). H, whilst retaining voting control of the company, had nevertheless gifted a greater proportion of the company's shares to his sons who also held directorships in the company. H (who was 88 years old) imposed his will against the wishes of the other members of the company and was apt to ignore the wishes of the board by, for example, entering into contracts without the board's approval. As a result of H's attitude, the company's business suffered. The sons pursued an action under s 210 of the Companies Act 1948. The Court of Appeal, in approving the decision of Roxburgh J, ordered that H should be stripped of his control in the company. This was achieved by removing H's executive powers. H was made a president of the company for life, a title given in recognition of H's past services to the company, but one which carried no power or authority in relation to the management of the company's affairs.

An example of a s 461(b) type of order would be where a minority shareholder of a company sought to prevent the company from engaging in an act which, if instigated, would constitute conduct which was unfairly prejudicial to the interests of the shareholders. An example of a case illustration of this type of order is to be found in *Re Kenyon Swansea Ltd* [1987] 3 BCC 259.

As yet, it would appear that there is no reported case to illustrate a conclusive example of the court's application of a s 461(c) order. Section 461(c) is, in effect, a statutory alternative to the derivative action (discussed in Chapter 22). Under s 461(c), the court has a power to order civil proceedings to be brought in the name and on behalf of the company. In not having to overcome the hurdles imposed by the procedural requirements of the rule in *Foss* v *Harbottle*, i.e. establishing a fraud on the minority, a s 461(c) order may be established where a petitioner establishes that the company's affairs have been conducted in a manner which was unfairly prejudicial to the interests of the company as a whole. It is suggested that s 461(c) may not, as yet, have been invoked because of the previous requirement of s 459 that the offending conduct had to affect a part of the membership as opposed to the whole of the membership. Another possible reason for the non-application of this type of order may be related to the potential inability of a petitioner to obtain a *Wallersteiner*-type order for costs. However, it should be noted that in *Re a Company (No 005136 of 1986)* [1987] BCLC 82 (sub nom *Re Sherbourne Park Residents Co Ltd*), Hoffmann J suggested that where a derivative action was brought by way of a s 459 petition, the petitioner would be entitled to an indemnity from the company for his costs, as under *Wallersteiner* v *Moir (No 2)* [1975] QB 373.

It should be stressed that under s 461, the court may make any order it sees fit and as such is not bound to prescribe an order of the type represented by s 461(a)–(d). For example, in *Wilton Davies* v *Kirk* [1997] BCC 770 the court concluded that as a result of an irretrievable breakdown in the relationship between the company's shareholders, either the plaintiff or respondent should purchase the shares of the other. However, in order to preserve the assets of the company during the interim period, the court, exercising its jurisdiction under s 37 of the Supreme Court Act 1981, and in accordance with the petitioner's application, ordered that a receiver be appointed so as to oversee the company's affairs.

The relationship between section 459 and the rule in *Foss* v *Harbottle*

It should first be pointed out that while the theoretical remnants of the exceptions to the rule in *Foss* v *Harbottle* remain, in practice, the extent by which s 459 actions now dominate the law relating to the protection of minority shareholders, reflect and will continue to give effect to a rapid decline in actions brought on the basis of the fraud on the minority exception. Although actions brought under s 459 are to a large measure dominated by personal claims pursued against those responsible for the conduct of a company's affairs, a strict adherence to the distinction between personal actions and those actions seeking to right a corporate wrong (the rule and exceptions to *Foss* v *Harbottle*) have not been observed by the interpretation of s 459. Matters which, in accordance with the rule in *Foss* v *Harbottle*, should only be commenced by the company (other than where a fraud on the minority was established) are now capable of being commenced under s 459. For example, an action may be commenced on the premise that a company's board of directors acted for an improper purpose where the act resulted in a diminution in the value of the company's shares. In such a case the offending conduct should strictly be viewed as a corporate wrong, yet where it affects the value of a member's shareholding interest, such a wrong may also constitute unfairly prejudicial conduct. Additionally, although a minority shareholder would, in commencing a s 459 action, ordinarily be concerned with a personal remedy, i.e. a remedy other than one which seeks to redress a wrong to the company, it is nevertheless possible that an underlying motive for the action may be one which seeks to protect the company's interests. Indeed, it would be possible under s 461 for a remedy to be couched in terms which would give effect to both a petitioner's interests and the interests of the company as a whole.

FUTURE REFORM

In its consultation paper entitled, 'Shareholder Remedies' (1997 Law Com, No 246) the Law Commission advanced proposals aimed at improving the efficiency of actions under s 459. The final recommendations of the Commission may be summarised as follows.

The length and cost of proceedings

The problems of excessive length and cost of many proceedings brought under s 459 should be dealt with primarily by active case management by the courts. In this respect, the Commission recommends that greater use be made of the power to direct that preliminary issues be heard, or that some issues be tried, before others. Further, the Commission recommends that the courts be given the power to dismiss any claim or part of a claim or defence thereto which, in the opinion of the court, has no realistic prospect of success at full trial. In respect of costs, the Commission recommends that the court should have a greater flexibility in its ability to make costs orders so as to reflect the manner in which the successful party conducted the proceedings and the outcome of individual issues.

A presumption of unfairly prejudicial conduct

In the case of a private company limited by shares, the Commission recommends a presumption of unfairly prejudicial conduct in a situation where, immediately prior to a petitioner's exclusion from management, the petitioner:

(a) held 10 per cent or more of the company's voting shares; and
(b) all or substantially all of the company's members were directors.

The Commission considers that the presumption should be rebuttable; the burden of establishing that it should not apply would be on the respondent.

Accordingly, it would be open to the respondent to show, for example, that the petitioner had no legitimate expectation of being able to continue to participate in the management of the company, or that the removal was justified by the petitioner's conduct.

It is to be observed that the Commission recommends that the presumption should be based on 'structural' factors (for example, the percentage holding of the petitioner) rather than the expectations of the parties. However, the Commission noted that if a case did not satisfy the conditions for the presumption to arise, it would not necessarily be precluded from being heard under s 459.

The Commission believes the above recommendations to be advantageous in so far as they would provide some degree of certainty in respect of the outcome of proceedings relating to the exclusion of a director. Further, the Commission considers that the implementation of the recommendations would result in cases being dealt with more quickly following the issue of proceedings.

Limitation period

The Commission recommends the creation of a limitation period in respect of claims under the section. This recommendation was advanced on the premise that on many occasions allegations made in s 459 proceedings involve conduct which spans a time period going back over a number of years. Accordingly, investigations into such cases increase the length and cost of the cases.

Winding up as an available remedy

The Commission recommends that winding up should be added to the available remedies under s 461, in so far as the Commission considers that while s 459 proceedings are very wide, they do not include the power to order the company to be wound up. Accordingly, the Commission considers that it is desirable to have a single remedy (incorporating winding up) which would give the court the maximum flexibility to deal with the matters before it. However, in an attempt to prevent claims for a winding up order from being used as a means of 'blackmail', the Commission recommends that a petitioner should seek the court's leave to apply for winding up under ss 459–461. On an application for leave, the court would then, for example, determine whether the petitioner was seeking to exert unjustified pressure on the respondents by claiming winding up. It is to be observed that the Commission stressed that winding up should still remain a remedy of last resort and that s 122(1)(g) of the Insolvency Act 1986 should remain as a distinct provision.

Exit rights

The Commission recommends that a draft regulation be included in Table A so as to encourage parties to resolve areas of potential dispute at the outset of their difficulties, thereby avoiding the need to commence legal proceedings. Accordingly, the Commission recommends the introduction of exit rights, to be conferred by ordinary resolution. In respect of the authorising resolution, the Commission recommends that every shareholder who is to have or is to be subject to exit rights must be named in the resolution and must consent to it, and that the resolution must set out the events which will trigger the operation of the exit rights. In circumstances where an exit right is operative, the Commission recommends that the shareholder entitled to the right may require other shareholders named in the resolution to buy his shares at a 'fair price'; those shares must be shares he held when the resolution was passed or shares acquired in right of them. In relation to determining the 'fair price', the resolution must provide a mechanism for its calculation.

THE JUST AND EQUITABLE WINDING UP PROVISION

Section 122(1)(g) of the Insolvency Act 1986 is often referred to as a remedy of the last resort, in so far as a company against which a s 122(1)(g) order is invoked will be wound up, i.e. its existence will end. Under s 122(1)(g), a company may be wound up on the premise that its liquidation would provide a just and equitable remedy. Prior to the implementation of the unfair prejudice remedy, the just and equitable winding up provision was often seen as the only alternative to the problematic remedies afforded to minority shareholders by the common law.

Section 124 of the Insolvency Act 1986 allows any contributory to petition for the equitable winding up order, provided that the proposed petitioner's shares were either originally allotted to him or held by him and registered in his name for at least six months during the 18 months before the presentation of a petition. A contributory is defined by s 79 of the 1986 Act as 'every person liable to contribute to the assets of the company in the event of it being wound up'. Although the Insolvency Act 1986 fails to mention the availability of an action under s 122(1)(g) to members of a company whose shares have been fully paid up, the courts have allowed such petitions. However, in all cases, the courts will require the member concerned to have a tangible interest in the winding up of the company.

Tangible interest

For a member of a company to establish a tangible interest, the member must show that the company is solvent. However, even where a company is solvent a winding up order may still be refused if, after paying its creditors, the company would have no available surplus assets for distribution amongst its membership; see e.g. *Re Expanded Plugs Ltd* [1966] 1 WLR 514.

Further, a petitioner must not, in commencing an action under s 122(1)(g), seek to have the company wound up for a collateral purpose. Therefore, a member must not seek a winding up order where, for example, the purpose of the order is to benefit a competing company in which the petitioning member has an interest.

The *qua* member requirement

A member must petition in his capacity as a member, i.e. *qua* member and not in some other capacity. For example, in *Re J E Cade & Son Ltd* [1991] BCC 360 a petitioner (P) claimed relief under s 459 (discussed above) and in the alternative sought a winding up order on the just and equitable ground. The facts of the case were as follows. P granted a licence to his brother (R), to occupy and farm land which was in P's ownership. The licence was in fact granted to a company in which R was the majority shareholder; P held a minority shareholding in the company. The licence was granted for a five-year period and on terms which included an option for R to purchase the farm and P's shares in the company at any time during the five-year period. P contended that an underlying feature of the agreement was that if the option was not exercised the farm would be sold. After the end of the five-year period the option had not been exercised. The company refused to give up its occupation of the farm. P commenced actions under ss 459 and 122(1)(g). Warner J refused to grant relief under both heads of the petition. The learned judge held that although a court could give effect to equitable considerations, such considerations only arose where a petitioner pursued his interests as a member of the company. According to Warner J, the petitioner had pursued his interests as the owner of the freehold.

Just and equitable considerations

In *Re J E Cade & Son Ltd* [1991] BCC 360 Warner J took the view that to satisfy the requirements of ss 459 and 122(1)(g), a petitioner's claim had to be based upon an interest which was linked to a legal right of membership. Although Warner J did not believe that a petitioner's claim had to be necessarily based upon the strict legal rights of membership, he nevertheless contended that a shareholder's interest in a company was not subject to expectations which were founded on a general concept of fairness, i.e. expectations which were unrelated to the legal rights of membership. For the purpose of interpreting the scope of a membership interest, the learned judge maintained that the interpretation was the same under both provisions.

As was previously suggested in the context of s 459, Warner J's interpretation of a membership interest would appear to be too narrow. It is asserted that whilst the term 'membership interest' does indeed have the same meaning for both ss 459 and 122(1)(g), that meaning must surely go beyond the interpretation ascribed to it by Warner J. Indeed, in the leading case on the interpretation of the just and equitable winding up provision, namely, the House of Lords' decision in *Ebrahimi* v *Westbourne Galleries* [1973] AC 360, Lord Wilberforce said, regarding the interpretation of the words 'just and equitable':

> 'If there is any respect in which some of the cases may be open to criticism it is that the courts may sometimes have been too timorous in giving them full force.' (at p 379)

The facts of *Ebrahimi* were as follows. A partnership business was incorporated with a share capital which was split equally between two shareholders (E and N). Both E and N became directors of the company. Subsequently, N's son became a director and one-fifth of both E and N's shares were transferred to him. The company prospered until there was a serious and irreconcilable difference of opinion as between E and N; E alleged that N had made secret profits at the expense of the company. An extraordinary general meeting was called by N at which E was removed from his directorship; the votes of N and his son being sufficient to pass the required ordinary resolution to enforce E's dismissal. As a result of being dismissed from office, E lost his right to claim directors' remuneration and as the company was not in the practice of declaring dividends (the company's profits were distributed via directors' remuneration), E, whilst holding two-fifths of the share capital, was in effect deprived of any return on his shareholding investment.

In reversing the decision of the Court of Appeal, the House of Lords held that E was entitled to a winding up order on the just and equitable ground. In delivering the leading judgment of the House, Lord Wilberforce stressed that the court should not be restricted to the enforcement of strict legal rights in a situation where it was established that there was a special underlying obligation between the membership of the company. In such circumstances, the court, if of the opinion that it was just and equitable to enforce such an obligation, could do so to the extent that where the obligation had been broken, a company could be dissolved. Lord Wilberforce suggested that the circumstances in which a court could depart from adhering to the strict legal rights of the membership might arise where one or more of the following elements were present:

(a) where a company was formed or continued on the basis of a personal relationship which involved mutual confidence;
(b) if there was an agreement or understanding that all or some of the members of the company would be responsible for the management of the company;
(c) where there was a restriction on the transfer of a member's interest in a company with the consequence that a member who had lost confidence in the running of the company's affairs or had been removed from management would be unable to dispose of his shares.

In the majority of cases where the just and equitable provision has been applied, the category of company made subject to a winding up order has been the quasi-partnership or domestic type of company. For a petition for the just and equitable winding up of a company to succeed, it will be necessary to establish what Lord Wilberforce described as an 'underlying obligation or agreement between the shareholding parties'. In the decided cases this obligation has arisen as a result of either:

(a) an implied agreement on the part of the shareholders to conduct the company's business in a certain manner (see e.g. *Re Crown Bank Ltd* (1890) 44 Ch D 634 and *Loch v John Blackwood Ltd* [1924] AC 783);
(b) an implied understanding as to a shareholder's right to participate in the management of the company (see e.g. *Re A & BC Chewing Gum Ltd* (1975) 1 WLR 579, *Re R A Noble Clothing Ltd* [1983] BCLC 273 and *Re Zinotty Properties Ltd* [1984] 1 WLR 1249);
(c) an implied duty on the part of the directors to consider the distribution and proper payment of dividends to the company's shareholders (see e.g. *Re a Company (No 00370 of 1987)* [1988] 1 WLR 1068).

A comparison between section 459 and section 122(1)(g)

Unfairly prejudicial conduct and conduct which is of a type to justify a court in concluding that a company should be wound up on the just and equitable ground may, in many cases, be indistinguishable. However, it should be noted that in *Jesner v Jarrad Properties Ltd* [1992] BCC 807 the Court of Session (Inner House) held that conduct, though not unfairly prejudicial, could in a quasi-partnership type of company still result in a breakdown of mutual confidence so as to substantiate an action under s 122(1)(g).

Prior to the amendment made to s 459 by the Companies Act 1989, it may have been possible (albeit unlikely) to contend that whereas s 122(1)(g) was applicable to a situation where the oppressive conduct in question affected the membership as a whole, that was not the position with a s 459 action. However, as a result of the Companies Act 1989, such an argument can no longer be maintained. In which case, it would appear that there will be few cases in which a petitioner will be granted a winding up order on the just and equitable ground, instead of being obliged to seek a remedy under s 459, in so far as s 125(2) of the Insolvency Act 1986 provides that a winding up order may be struck out if the court is of the opinion that it was unreasonable for the petitioner not to have pursued an alternative course of action where another form of remedy was available. The alternative course of action will normally be under s 459, though it could quite simply be founded on an unreasonable refusal by the petitioner to refuse an offer from other members to purchase his shares at a price comparable to the one he would have received had the company been wound up; see generally *Re Copeland & Craddock Ltd* [1997] BCC 294.

In order to prevent a petitioner under s 459 from using the threat of winding up as an alternative, but improper device, i.e. so as to pursuade the respondents to the action under s 459 to settle his claim, Practice Direction No 1 of 1990 ([1990] 1 WLR) stipulates that s 122(1)(g) should not ordinarily be pleaded as an alternative to an action under s 459. The direction provides that ss 459 and 122(1)(g) should not ordinarily be pleaded together, and that an action under s 122(1)(g) should only be sought as an alternative to an action under s 459 in circumstances where it is established that the relief under s 122(1)(g) would be preferred, or where it is considered that it may be the only form of relief available; see *Re Copeland & Craddock Ltd* [1997] BCC 294.

An example of where a just and equitable winding up order would be a more appropriate remedy is in a situation where a petitioner contends that a company was formed to defraud the investing public. In such circumstances, where the petitioner's claim is proved, it would be improper to allow the company to continue in existence. An equitable winding up order would also be a more appropriate type of remedy in circumstances similar to those which arose in *Re Abbey Leisure* [1990] BCC 60. In this case, the petitioner based his action on the fact that there had been an understanding between the shareholders of the company that its formation was for the sole purpose of acquiring, refurbishing and managing a night club. The night club in question was acquired but subsequently sold. The petitioner argued that as the principal purpose in forming the company had failed, i.e. the night club had been sold, the company should be wound up. The Court of Appeal in determining whether to grant the winding up order had to consider whether the petitioner had been unreasonable in not seeking some other form of remedy, i.e. under s 459. The respondents contended that the petitioner should have petitioned under s 459 and as such obtained an order under s 461 for the purchase of his shares at a fair price. The valuation procedure to ascertain the fair price was, in accordance with the company's articles, to be determined by an independent valuer.

The Court of Appeal, in reversing the first instance judgment of Hoffmann J, held that the winding up order was, in the circumstances of the case, the most appropriate remedy. Relying to a large extent on Lord Wilberforce's comments in *Ebrahimi*, the court was of the opinion that the strict legal rights of the petitioner, represented by the valuation procedure contained within the company's articles, should be made subject to equitable considerations. In so far as the petitioner would gain a greater financial benefit in having the company wound up, rather than if he sold his shares in accordance with the valuation procedure, the court concluded that the just and equitable provision could be employed to override the strict legal rights contained within the company's articles. Accordingly, the circumstances of the case vindicated the application of the just and equitable winding up order.

Suggested further reading

Section 459
Instone [1986] NLJ 973

Prentice (1988) 8 OJLS 55
Bouchier [1991] JBL 132
Griffin (1992) 13 Co Law 83
Griffin (1993) 14 Co Law 64
Lowry [1995] LMCLQ 337

The statutory derivative action
Giggs and Lowry [1994] JBL 463

Section 122(1)(g)
Prentice (1973) 89 LQR 107
Chesterman (1973) 36 MLR 129

24

DEPARTMENT OF TRADE AND INDUSTRY INVESTIGATIONS

INTRODUCTION

The protection of minority interests is further enhanced by the availability of Department of Trade and Industry (DTI) investigations. The aim of this chapter is to briefly outline the powers and procedures associated with the conduct of such investigations. Whilst the powers of the DTI will be seen to be far ranging, it should be pointed out, from the outset of this chapter, that the DTI has thus far been restricted in its ability to police the affairs of corporations by shortages of staff and the constraints placed upon it by government, i.e. in relation to its levels of funding.

THE NEED FOR DTI INVESTIGATIONS

In the case of a public company or large private company, the size and scale of business activity may be such so as to preclude a minority shareholder from obtaining evidence of a suspected abuse of corporate power by the company's management. To police the activities of such companies and to gather evidence of any suspected corporate abuse, the Secretary of State for the Department of Trade and Industry may, in certain defined circumstances, appoint inspectors to investigate a company's affairs. Inspectors may also be appointed in circumstances where, despite a company having the full support of its shareholders, its pursuit of certain corporate activities is considered contrary to the public interest.

Inspections under section 447, Companies Act 1985

The majority of company investigations are commenced under s 447 of the Companies Act 1985 (as amended by s 63, CA 1989). This section authorises a type of preliminary investigation; the s 447 investigation is limited to the inspection of documents. As a consequence of the Companies Act 1989, the term 'document' is defined to include recorded material, for example, a computer disk is now included within the general definition of a document. Where a s 447 type of investigation produces evidence of some corporate misconduct, a full investigation into the company's affairs may then be ordered. It is a criminal offence to fail to produce documents which are legitimately requested by an inspector, unless the person concerned can prove that the documents in question were not in his possession or under his control. Any present or past officer or employee of the company may be requested to provide an explanation for the contents of documents which have been requested for inspection. It is also an offence for a person to give a false or reckless statement in respect of the contents of a document. Where the Secretary of State believes that certain documents are being kept in undisclosed premises, he may apply to a magistrate for a search warrant (s 448(1) and (2), CA 1985).

Investigations under section 431, Companies Act 1985

The Secretary of State may at his discretion order a s 431 investigation where:

(a) the investigation is demanded by a company;
(b) in the case of a company with a share capital, where shareholders holding at least 200 shares in the company or holding 10 per cent of the issued share capital apply for an investigation;
(c) in the case of a company not having a share capital, where not less than 20 per cent of the company's members apply for an investigation.

Shareholders must establish a reasonable cause for an investigation to proceed; shareholders who apply for an investigation may, where it is undertaken, be liable for its cost and the Secretary of State may ask the applicants to give a security of up to £5000. The investigation will normally be conducted by two inspectors, one of whom is normally a senior accountant, and the other a Queen's Counsel or senior solicitor.

Investigations under section 432 Companies Act 1985

The Secretary of State must appoint inspectors where the court declares that a company's affairs should be investigated (s 432(1)). Further, in accordance with s 432(2), the Secretary of State may at his discretion order an investigation where grounds exist to substantiate a finding of at least one of the following matters:

(a) the company's affairs are, or have been conducted with an intent to defraud creditors, or the company's affairs have been conducted for some other fraudulent or unlawful purpose, or in a manner which is, or which might result in unfairly prejudicial conduct to any part of its members; or
(b) any actual or proposed act or omission of the company (including an act or omission on its behalf) is or would be prejudicial, or that the company was formed for any fraudulent or unlawful purpose; or
(c) persons connected with the company's formation or management have been guilty of fraud, misfeasance or other misconduct towards the company or its members; or

(d) shareholders have not been given all the information with respect to the management of a company's affairs which they might reasonably have expected to have been given.

In relation to the negligent conduct of a company's affairs, such conduct should not normally give the Secretary of State a right to order an investigation; see e.g. *SBA Properties Ltd v Cradock* [1967] 1 WLR 716. However, as the Secretary of State is not obliged to disclose why an investigation was ordered (see e.g. *Norwest Holst Ltd v Secretary of State for Trade* [1978] Ch 201), it is not inconceivable that the negligent conduct of a company's affairs may be the catalyst for the instigation of an investigation. It should be noted that the Secretary of State may exercise his power to instigate an investigation even where a company is in the process of being voluntarily wound up (s 432(3), CA 1985).

SPECIFIC TYPES OF INVESTIGATION

Ownership or control

In accordance with ss 442–445 of the Companies Act 1985, an inspector has the power to investigate the ownership of shares and debentures and may impose certain restrictions upon the internal structure of a company in relation to its securities, for example, the restrictions upon the rights of certain shareholders to vote and/or receive dividend payments (discussed further in Chapter 10).

Share dealings

An inspector may investigate dealings in a company's securities (s 446, CA 1985).

Related companies

An inspector appointed to investigate a company may also investigate the company's related companies, i.e. the company's holding company or subsidiary companies. A related company may be investigated whether it is incorporated in the UK or overseas (s 433, CA 1985).

COMPANY DOCUMENTS

In accordance with s 434 of the Companies Act 1985, where inspectors are appointed under ss 431 or 432, it is the duty of the officers and agents of the company under investigation and other officers and agents of any other related companies privy to the investigation to produce corporate documents which are requested by the inspectors. Persons requested to attend before the inspectors must do so and such persons must offer any other form of assistance which is required of them by the inspectors.

In accordance with s 434(2), an inspector may require a director of a company under investigation to produce any document in his custody where that document is considered relevant to the investigation and may order a director to comply with matters specified in s 434(1). An inspector may for the purposes of the investigation examine any person on oath. An answer given by a person to a question put to him may be used in evidence against that person; see e.g. *London & County Securities Ltd* v *Nicholson* [1980] 3 All ER 861 (s 434(5), CA 1985). Any person who withholds information to an inspector may be reported to the court and may be punished for contempt of court.

Inspectors may examine documents relating to bank accounts into or out of which money has been paid, where such money is suspected of being connected with alleged corporate misconduct. An inspector may also require documents relating to corporate finances where such finances should have been disclosed in the company's accounts but, for whatever reason, were not so disclosed.

THE REPORT OF AN INVESTIGATION

A copy of the report of an investigation is admissible in any legal proceedings as evidence of the opinion of the inspectors in respect of any matter contained within the report (s 441, CA 1985). It is not, however, save under s 8 of the Company Directors Disqualification Act 1986, admissible as evidence of fact; see e.g. *Savings and Investment Bank Ltd* v *Gasco Investments* [1984] 1 All ER 296.

As a result of the implementation of s 55 of the Companies Act 1989, incorporated into the Companies Act 1985 as s 432(2A), the Secretary of State has the power to appoint inspectors on the understanding that their report is not to be published, i.e. made available to the general public. This new section may be seen as an extension of s 437 of the Companies Act 1985 which deems that a report does not have to be published unless the Secretary of State thinks fit. The implementation of the Secretary of State's power in s 432(2A) removes the danger of criticism and controversy as to a decision not to publish under s 437. A positive and welcomed consequence of the power not to publish a report is that non-publication reduces the time taken to complete investigations. Nevertheless, on the negative side, a report's non-disclosure may be criticised as overprotective in respect of the non-divulgence of suspected corporate malpractice.

THE CONSEQUENCES OF AN INVESTIGATION

If, as a result of an investigation, the Secretary of State believes that it is in the public interest to dissolve a company, he may present a winding up petition on the just and equitable ground. Alternatively, he may order that civil proceedings be taken on behalf of and in the company's name (s 438, CA 1985) or bring proceedings under s 460 of the Companies Act 1985 on the

ground that the company's affairs have been conducted in an unfairly prejudicial manner against a part of the membership. (It should be noted that the
power to commence proceedings on the basis of unfairly prejudicial conduct
does not, unlike s 459, CA 1985 expressly extend to a situation whereby the
company's affairs were conducted in a manner which was unfairly prejudicial
to members generally.) The Secretary of State may also apply to the court for
a disqualification order to be made against a company director(s) under s 8
of the Company Directors Disqualification Act 1986, see e.g. *Re
Aldermanbury Trust plc* [1993] BCC 598. In appropriate circumstances,
criminal proceedings may also be commenced against any individual.

During the course of an investigation, a person called to answer the questions of the inspectors is obliged to answer all questions. There exists no
privilege against self-incrimination and the evidence given may be used in
subsequent proceedings; see e.g. *R v Lord Spens* [1992] 1 WLR 148. A person of whom the inspectors have put questions is not allowed to attend or be
represented when another witness is giving evidence, nor is he allowed to see
a transcript of that evidence or challenge it. There is no right of appeal
against the inspectors' findings; see e.g. *Re Pergamon Press Ltd* [1971]
Ch 388.

THE SERIOUS FRAUD OFFICE

Following the recommendations of the Roskill Report 1986, the Serious
Fraud Office (SFO) was set up under the Criminal Justice Act 1987 (CJA).
The purpose of its creation was to investigate any suspected offence involving serious or complex fraud. The SFO is made up of lawyers, accountants
and police. Section 1(3) of the CJA empowers the SFO to investigate any suspected offence which it has reasonable grounds to believe involves serious or
complex fraud. The powers of officers of the Serious Fraud Office are similar
to those of the DTI inspectors, save that their powers are not limited to companies and extend to the investigation of any person. Under s 2 of the CJA,
the SFO may compel a person to answer questions and provide information
and documents that might be used to subsequently convict that individual. A
person may be compelled to provide information even after he has been
charged with an offence, so held by the House of Lords in *R v Director of
Serious Fraud Office, ex parte Smith* [1993] AC 1. It is a criminal offence,
without reasonable excuse, to refuse to provide the requisite information.
(Note the conflict with Art 6(1) of the European Convention on Human
Rights, in so far as the European Court of Human Rights has held that Art 6,
which protects the fairness of a criminal trial, includes the right of a defendant to remain silent and not to contribute anything to incriminate himself;
see *Saunders v UK* [1998] 1 BCLC 362. Section 3, CJA expressly overturns
any duty of confidence imposed by or under any statute (other than the
Taxes Management Act 1970). However, the CJA does expressly preserve
two specific duties of confidence, namely, legal professional privilege and
banking confidence. A recent application of s 3, CJA can be found in *Re*

Arrows Ltd (No 4) [1994] BCC 641, where the House of Lords held that a court had no discretion to prevent the SFO from obtaining and using in evidence the transcripts of a respondent's private examination under s 236, IA 1986.

Suggested further reading

Lidbetter (1999) *Company Investigations and Public Law*, Hart Publishing, Oxford
Fraser (1971) 34 MLR 260
Instone [1978] JBL 121
Chaikin (1982) 3 Co Law 115

Serious Fraud Office
Frommel (1994) 15 Co Law 227
Sarker (1995) 16 Co Law 56, 212

APPENDIX

FUTURE REFORM – COMPANY FORMATION AND CAPITAL MAINTENANCE (SEE CHAPTERS 3, 4, 7, 8, 9 AND 12)

In October 1999, the DTI (the company law steering group) issued a consultation document entitled "Modern Company Law for a Competitive Economy – Company Formation and Capital Maintenance." In respect of issues related to company formation and matters concerning a company's constitution, the document favoured the following reforms:

- The memorandum and articles should no longer represent the constitution of new companies. Instead, constitutional issues should be contained in one distinct document; the document would broadly correspond to the current format of company articles (the contents of the new document could also be altered in a manner akin to altering a company's articles, i.e. by special resolution). On the formation of a company this new document would be presented for registration in conjunction with a new style registration form. The latter would contain information held on the public register, much of which is currently included within a company's memorandum.

- Any type of company (private or public) should be capable of being formed by a single member.

- The quasi-contractual effect of s 14 CA 1985 should be examined. The report suggested that the terms of the company's constitution should be binding in relation to some outsider rights, i.e. rights contained in the constitution which affect directors and other officers in a management capacity.

- The present requirement that a private company register an objects clause should be abolished. The report also considered that in relation to dealings with third parties, the present law (s 35 CA 1985) should be clarified to ensure that a private or public company had unlimited capacity. The basis for this latter proposal was a fear that the problem surrounding *ultra vires* transactions continued to exist. However, with respect, it is submitted that such a fear is unwarranted in the context of corporate capacity. In truth, the inability of a third party to enforce a transaction with a company will not be a matter of lack of capacity but rather a question of whether the officer of the company involved in the transaction had the requisite authority to bind the company. Yet, it is to be noted that the report considered that the purpose of s 35A CA 1985 was to protect third parties when dealing with a director who was absent of **any** authority to enter into the transaction in question. With the utmost respect, it is submitted that the interpretation afforded to s 35A(1) is flawed. Section 35A(1) provides that, "In favour of a person dealing with the company in good faith, the power of the board of directors to bind the company, or authorise others to do so, shall be free of any limitation under the company's constitution. Section 35B then provides "A party to a transaction with a company is not bound to enquire as to whether it is permitted by the company's memorandum or as to any limitation on the powers of the board of directors to bind the company or authorise others to do so." In effect, the board may **authorise** an individual director to enter into any transaction which is outside the terms of the company's constitution. The crucial point is that an individual director in entering into a transaction must first have been authorised to do so by the board. As such, agency rules are still relevant to determine whether an individual director had the requisite authority (whether he had been authorised) to enter into a particular transaction.

CAPITAL MAINTENANCE (SEE CHAPTER 12)

In respect of reforming rules connected with capital maintenance, the report suggested the following reforms.

- The shares of private companies should no longer be obliged to have a par value. This reform could not apply to public companies in so far as it would be contrary to the EC Second Directive.
- A relaxation in the rules governing the reduction of share capital to the extent that a reduction would be permissible providing a company passed a special resolution to authorise the reduction and a solvency statement supported the decision. As such, it would no longer be necessary for the company to seek the approval of the court before instigating a reduction in share capital, although in the case of a public company, it would, in accordance with the EC Second Directive, still be possible for the company's creditors to apply to court to seek an annulment of the resolution.
- A significant removal if not the total removal of the rules which prohibit financial assistance by a private company for the acquisition of its own shares.

FUTURE REFORM – DIRECTORS DUTIES (SEE CHAPTER 17)

In September 1999, the Law Commission's published a report (Law Com 261) to advance its earlier (1998) consultatation document entitled "Company Directors: Regulating Conflicts of Interest and Formulating a Statement of Duties" (discussed in Chapter 17) Amongst other matters, the 1999 report paves the way for the introduction of a partial statutory codification of directors duties. In addition, it confirms and in some instances advances methods of reform (as discussed in the 1998 consultative document) in relation to Part X of the CA 1985.

The report considered that a full codification of directors' duties was undesirable in so far as the law governing directors' duties is dynamic and liable to change. Accordingly, the report concluded that any attempt to complete a full codification of duties would ignore the law's need to be flexible and to develop with changing commercial circumstances. In advancing a partial codification of directors' duties, the 1999 report (in Appendix A) gave its blessing to a draft statement of directors' duties, which the Commission believed to be settled, and standard duties. The said duties are:

(1) *Loyalty:* Acting in good faith for the benefit of the company;
(2) *Obedience:* Acting in accordance with the company's constitution and for a proper purpose;
(3) *No secret profits:* Refraining from using the company's property, information or opportunities for self-interest, unless the company consented to such use.
(4) *Conflict of interest:* For a director to account to the company for any benefit received as a consequence of a conflict of interest between himself and the company.
(5) *Independence:* For a director to refrain from agreeing to restrict his power to exercise an independent judgment, save in a situation where a director considers, in good faith, that it is in the interests of the company to do otherwise.
(6) *Care, skill and diligence:* To exercise the care, skill and diligence which would be exercised in the same circumstances by a reasonable person having the knowledge and experience that may be reasonably be expected of a person in the same position as the director; taking into account the knowledge and experience which the director has.
(7) *Employees:* To consider the interests of company employees.
(8) *Members:* To consider the interests of members and to act fairly as between members.

Although the partial codification of directors' duties may be welcomed, it is to be noted that the items 3 and 4 of the above list do not strictly speaking amount to duties but are instead constituents of a rule of equity (the conflict of interest rule). Although the consequences of a breach of duty and a breach of the equitable rule may give rise to the same penalty, it must be observed that a breach of the conflict of interest rule may not always give rise to a breach of duty to the company; indeed the breach may benefit the company, see eg, *Regal (Hastings) Ltd* v *Gulliver* (1942) [1967] 2 AC 134. Further, under Table A, Art 85, a breach of the conflict of interest rule may be exempted by disclosure to the board whereas a breach of duty cannot, in accordance with s.310 CA 1985, be so exempted by Art 85.

Part X of the CA 1985

In respect of Part X of the CA 1985, some of the major recommendations advanced by the Law Commission were as follows:

- The repeal of ss 311, 318(5) and (11), 323 and 327;
- A requirement that compensation paid to a director for loss of office should be fully disclosed in the company's annual accounts;
- A limitation on the interests, which a director is required to disclose to the board in accordance with s 317 CA 1985. The removal of criminal sanctions for a breach of s 317; to be replaced with civil penalties.
- The period of duration of a director's service contract requiring shareholder approval to be reduced from five to three years. Further, the introduction of statutory controls to regulate the practice of "rolling" contracts.
- Section 320 to be amended so as to permit a company to agree to a substantial property transaction with a director by contract, the validity of which would be conditional upon the company first obtaining shareholder approval.
- The extension of restrictions placed upon loans and similar transactions (governed by ss 330–337) to all companies.
- The introduction of a code of civil remedies to replace many of the criminal sanctions contained in Part X.

FUTURE REFORM – GENERAL MEETINGS AND SHAREHOLDER COMMUNICATION (SEE CHAPTER 18)

In October 1999, the DTI (the company law steering group) issued a consultation document entitled "Modern Law for a Competitive Economy – General Meetings and Shareholder Communication." The document advanced suggestions in respect of improving the efficiency and conduct of general meetings and the passing of resolutions. The need to reform this area of company law is most obvious in circumstances where the membership of a company is ultimately dominated by its board of directors and/or where the attendance at company meetings is absent of a fair and democratic representation. The document was primarily, although not exclusively, aimed at plc's.

In relation to the AGM's of plc's the document suggested two methods of reform. The first was to extend to plc's the right to dispense with holding AGM's, the second was to improve the current legislation in respect of its applicability to AGM's. It was recognised that the two methods of reform were not mutually exclusive.

In respect of the first proposal, it was suggested that the AGM could be dispensed with by a plc either by passing a special resolution or by a 90% majority vote of the entire membership holding voting shares. Where a plc decided to dispense with the holding of an AGM, the document recognised that it would be imperative to maintain the accountability of directors to shareholders. Accordingly where a plc resolved to abandon its AGM, it was proposed that procedures should be instigated to ensure that shareholders were adequately informed and kept up to date about the company's affairs. Further, it was suggested that a company should arrange a series of company meetings at different locations whereupon voting on matters discussed at the meetings could take place by post or electronically. In relation to matters, which were, in accordance with the companies legislation, currently required to be dealt with at an AGM, it was suggested that such matters could be adequately covered at EGM's.

The second proposal, in seeking to maintain but reform the current statutory regulation of AGM's, recommended that both a private company and a plc should be obliged to conduct specific business at an AGM. For example, companies should be obliged by law to lay before the membership, the annual accounts and the directors and auditors report. Further, at the AGM, auditors should be appointed and directors elected. In respect of the voting procedure at AGM's, the consultative document advised that because of the unrepresentative nature of the attendance at AGM's it may be logical to only allow poll votes as opposed to voting by a show of hands. An additional and quite radical, albeit interesting suggestion, was that of delayed voting to enable members to have more time to consider the way in which they would vote in respect of the debate advanced for and against motions put forward at AGM's. Although a worthwhile proposal, it should be observed as a matter of caution, that between the AGM and the date of the vote, interested parties would have the time to lobby for support, to the extent that members could be persuaded to vote in a given way for reasons which may, in some instances, be unconnected with the merits or otherwise of the motion.

In relation to shareholder resolutions placed at an AGM , the document favoured a reform of s 376 CA 1985, namely, save for limited exceptions, the company and not the shareholders responsible for advancing a motion at an AGM, should be responsible for the cost of circulating the proposed motion.

Further proposed reforms included, the rights of proxies to be permitted to speak at meetings of public as well as private companies and for proxies to be allowed to vote on a show of hands (if voting by a show of hands was to be a maintained practice). In addition, the document advanced the well trodden but nevertheless sensible suggestion that the extraordinary resolution be dropped as a separate category of resolution so that matters which were obliged to be dealt with by extraordinary resolution should instead be dealt with by a special resolution.

INDEX